LET THE LAND SPEAK

LET THE LAND SPEAK

A history of Australia:
How the land created our nation

Jackie French

HarperCollins*Publishers*

The information about the gathering and preparation of indigenous foods is for general information only. Indigenous plants and animals are also protected.

HarperCollins*Publishers*

First published in Australia in 2013
by HarperCollins*Publishers* Australia Pty Limited
ABN 36 009 913 517
harpercollins.com.au

HarperCollins*Publishers*
Level 13, 201 Elizabeth Street, Sydney NSW 2000, Australia
31 View Road, Glenfield, Auckland 0627, New Zealand
A 53, Sector 57, Noida, UP, India
77–85 Fulham Palace Road, London W6 8JB, United Kingdom
2 Bloor Street East, 20th floor, Toronto, Ontario M4W 1A8, Canada
10 East 53rd Street, New York NY 10022, USA

National Library of Australia Cataloguing-in-Publication entry:

French, Jackie, author.
  Let the land speak/Jackie French.
  978 0 7322 9675 9 (hardback)
  Includes bibliographical references and index.
  Land use–Australia–History
  Nature–Effect of human beings on–Australia–History.
  Human ecology–Australia–History.
  Australia–History.
327.9409

Cover design by HarperCollins Design Studio
Cover image by Leanne Walker/Getty Images
Typeset in Plantin by Kirby Jones
Printed and bound in Australia by Griffin Press
The papers used by HarperCollins in the manufacture of this book are a natural, recyclable product made from wood grown in sustainable plantation forests. The fibre source and manufacturing processes meet recognised international environmental standards, and carry certification.

5 4 3 2 1   13 14 15 16

To the past, present and future generations,
with gratitude, love and hope.

And to this valley,
which has given me the heart of my life and work.

Contents

The goat droppings that changed history

It began with a goat.

When James Cook and HM Bark *Endeavour* sailed from Plymouth in 1768 on the voyage that would first map eastern Australia (and led to the British settling a colony there twenty years later), the tiny ship, about twice the size of a suburban house, carried seventy-one crew, twelve marines, and eleven scientists and their servants. It also held seventeen sheep, a small mob of cattle for meat, four ducks, four or five dozen hens (which lived in the ship's boats) for eggs – no roosters, as hens can't hatch chicks in a ship's boat in wild seas – a boar to mate with a sow, her piglets, two greyhounds, and three cats to catch the rats that swarmed on every ship.[1]

It carried a goat, too.

The goat and sheep would help save the *Endeavour* when she was wrecked on the Great Barrier Reef, their dry dung spread on the inside of an old sail that was wrapped around the shattered hull. As the dung drew up water the sail clung to the ship, making an almost watertight seal. If it hadn't been for those goat and sheep droppings, no British colony would have been sent to New South Wales in 1788, or possibly ever, as that colony was sent only because of the enthusiastic but wildly inaccurate reports of one of the passengers on the *Endeavour*, wealthy amateur botanist Joseph Banks, who had provided most of the funds for the voyage.

I discovered the goat accidentally, hunting up English newspaper reports of the *Endeavour*'s return, and there she was, getting almost as much press as publicity-hungry Banks. But once I knew about the goat, and all the other animals crammed onto that small ship, I looked at the *Endeavour* letters and diaries – and a large chunk of Australia's history – in a new light.

The *Endeavour*, like other ships of its time, was a floating ark, with its cattle and breeding pigs, and hens that needed to be removed from the ship's boats before any expedition to explore the shore. In the days before refrigeration, ships had to carry live animals to feed the crew on their long journeys.

Even more importantly for Australian history, those small ships couldn't carry enough fodder to feed the animals. If you carried animals, you needed to go ashore to cut grass to feed them. Often. You needed fresh water, too, which can be difficult to find in unmapped territory, and especially hard in Australia, unless you know the land well. When you read the ship's log and diaries kept on the *Endeavour* during her visits to places like New Zealand or even bitterly cold Tierra del Fuego, a couple of phrases reappear over and over: 'cut grass' and 'filled water barrels'.

The goat, and her grass, made me realise that, like many other historians, I had misunderstood why Australia had been ignored by most of the world for so long. At school we were taught that it was because our land was dry, barren and useless; and because Australia had no gold or spices. The conventional story is that this continent was too far away to be of interest, an unknown land of unknown people, until James Cook surveyed the east coast. Australia has been portrayed as a Sleeping Beauty, waiting for the English hero to arrive and wake her up.

None of this is accurate. The land we now call Australia and its inhabitants had been known to the outside world for thousands of years. From at least two thousand years ago, and possibly even earlier, the continent and its many Indigenous cultures were only a couple of days' sailing south of the trade routes to the Spice Islands (Ambon and the Maluku islands of present-day Indonesia), the source of vast wealth for many trading, and later colonising, nations. Australia had and has native spices too, including some very similar to the ones being traded, like native pepper and native ginger. (They remain relatively unknown because the 'traditional' European species are now cheap and readily available.) Australian spices and valuable cedar trees were noted by the Dutch long before the *Endeavour* sailed up the east coast. Australia's northern soil and climate were also suitable for plantations of cinnamon, allspice, vanilla, pepper, sugarcane and coffee, the crops on which fortunes had been made for at least four thousand years. But both the existing spices and the potential crops remained unexploited by outsiders.

Why? Most of the north and west of the mainland and part of Tasmania had even been mapped long before James Cook and his crew reached our shores in 1770. Parts of the north were reasonably similar to nearby areas that had been colonised. Much of the west looked barren, but strategically useful places that were just as barren had been settled before, and the area around the Swan River in the west and most of Tasmania appeared green and fertile. A port on the southwest coast would have been a useful supply depot on the route to the major trading settlement of Batavia (now Jakarta).

However, Australia lacked grass: that lush, sweet grass that can be cut and dried to take on board and feed essential animals like Cook's goat. Australia's native 'grasslands' are made up of hundreds of ground covers, but many of them are toxic to sheep, goats and cattle[2]. In years to come the first European colony in Western Australia would struggle until the poisonous ones were identified, and their animals stopped dying. Most native Australian grasses grow in tufts, and nowhere near as lush as European grasses, or African ones like kikuyu. Without grass, Australia was relatively useless as a supply port.

But most of all, sailing ships need safe harbour from winds and storms. Australia has few great rivers like those of Europe and the Americas, that carved out harbours where they reached the sea and gave rich flood plains of grass to scythe and take on board. Even skilled navigators like James Cook either missed or was unable to enter the superb harbours that we do have, like Sydney Harbour and Moreton Bay.

And the Australian coast does have extreme winds: the 'roaring forties' that pummel Western Australia, the bitter southern ocean gales that Tasman warned other sailors to be wary of, the southerlies of the east coast that can be deadly even for today's well-engineered yachts in the Sydney to Hobart race.

Australia wasn't sitting at the end of the world, waiting for a hero like Cook to find her. The land itself, our geography, prevented earlier colonial expansion because these basic necessities – grass and safe harbour – could not be found. The goat, and all her implications, made me reassess other crucial areas of Australia's past, looking at the role the land itself has played in determining our history, and how that role has been underestimated. Once I began to look, there was a lot to find.

Australia's geographic position in large part determined who came here, from the founders of perhaps 60,000 years ago, to the desperate and the dreamers of the past two hundred years, and the boats that still arrive today. Indigenous cultures were shaped by the different areas they inhabited, but they would also change the land. 'Firestick farming' is a relatively well known concept now, even if its application is often misunderstood, but the even more profound reshaping of the landscape by Indigenous women is still vastly underestimated.

Australia's erratic weather patterns determined our first gold rushes.[3] Gold had been discovered many times before the 'rushes' of the late 1840s and 1850s, but gold panning needs water, and gold miners need food, and until the breaking of the 1840s drought there wasn't enough of either.

Australia would become one nation because of another series of droughts so severe that they revolutionised our politics, social life and economy. The men who fought at Gallipoli would be shaped by the land, as were the 'koala soldiers', the militia boys of World War 2 who helped slow down the seemingly unstoppable advance of the Japanese army heading this way for the Australian resources they desperately needed.

Five hundred years of misunderstandings

Australia's climate, soils, and varied ecologies have also been profoundly misunderstood, with disastrous consequences. Our first English colony at Sydney Cove was founded only because Joseph Banks misconstrued almost everything he saw at Botany Bay, from the rare green grass and fresh water of an unusually wet year to a 'safe harbour' that almost wrecked the First Fleet. Governor Hotham's misunderstanding of the vast spread of deep mine workings at Ballarat made him see wealth, instead of desperation, prompting him to impose a mining tax too high for miners to afford, which lead to the iconic struggle at Eureka.[4] Hotham's strategic military experience would also enable him to use the darkness of the diggings as a weapon, so that his troops could win against a far larger force. Underestimating that power of darkness, especially in terrain with deep unfenced pits, led to the often repeated myth that the Eureka stockade could never have triumphed.[5]

Our past misunderstandings of the land continue to shape the decisions we make today. This is a generous land, but the myth of a barren continent allows us to perpetuate the ideology that the bush must be transformed to have value: logged, turned into plantations, the rivers dammed, or the land carved into fenced paddocks and irrigated to be productive. The myth of 'endless land' and a narrow Eurocentric vision of what 'proper farms' were like would turn millions of hectares almost into desert.

Humans get attached to myths. Once we see the world – or history – in a certain way, it's difficult to budge the illusions. Hundreds of years ago European nations sent ships into the Pacific to find the land of gold they believed must be there, even though there was no evidence to support such a belief. As I write this, our government's economic policy is being shaped by a similar myth, which vastly overestimates the importance of mining to our economy. At the same time the development of those mining resources is still hampered by the lack of political insight to create the harbour, road and other infrastructure that our industries need.

The oversimplification that the whole of Australia was shaped by Indigenous 'firestick farming' has led to disastrous bushfire strategies. Our planners also fail to remember or understand our history of floods, storm surges and drought, and this failure means that flood, storm surges and sea-level rises, all easily predicted, will continue to cause tragedy, year after year. It is air-conditioned, centrally heated policy, far removed from the physical and social circumstances they write about. It is easy to forget or underestimate flood, fire and drought unless you have lived through their desperation.

From terra incognita to Eureka, Federation and the decisions governments must make today, the land's influence is often ignored or misunderstood. To understand the present, you need to understand the past. And to fully understand Australia's history, you need to look not just at how the land has shaped our past but how it will continue to shape our future.

This book is the story of the land's influence on iconic Australian events. It is as much memoir as history. It is difficult to realise the significance of 'cut grass' and 'found water' unless grass and water have been essentials in your life.

I grew up on the edge of suburban Brisbane, but our backs were always against the bush. The men of our street played cricket and fought bushfires together, and searched for and rescued a kidnapped child, a way of life that had served them well when they fought on faraway battlefields. My father-in-law fought at Gallipoli; my father's friends died at Kokoda. (My father's appendix burst during embarkation. He probably survived because of it. He felt the guilt all his life.) Those cricket matches and bushfires and weekends shooting pigs or rabbits were their training ground. To understand the battles, you need to understand the men who fought them. To understand those men, you need to know the land and how they lived with it. Perhaps to truly understand colonial and pre-colonial life, you need to have experienced life as they knew it.

In my twenties and early thirties I lived in a bush shed, with lamplight or darkness, much as women have lived here for tens of thousands of years. I still live in the same shed at the end of the Majors Creek gorge in the Araluen Valley in the Southern Tablelands of New South Wales, but the shed is now a house, and we have light when we want it, which is not as often as those who have never learned to love darkness, the thousand shades of dawn and twilight, or the purple shadows from the moon. It is a valley where the mullock heaps from the gold dreams of the 1850s have been turned into peach orchards, where the steepness and inaccessibility of the gorge country has created almost a world beyond time, so the quolls and rock wallabies and forests of neverbreak trees still survive.

For years I grew most of our food and other necessities, or gathered or hunted it in the bush around my house. It was a life without modern conveniences: learning to light a fire without matches; cooking on a fire; cutting stringybark to roof a lean-to; cutting tracks with brush hook and mattock; building a house from local stone; watching the honey drip from fresh honeycomb as my grandmother taught me; and knowing that if I miscalculated and served too many of the potatoes from the sacks in the shed, we'd have no potatoes to plant in spring. I still walk my land each morning, watching and noting its changes and seasons. I still grow and gather, although now from fulfilment, not poverty. At various times and places since I was sixteen years old, both white and Indigenous women have passed on traditions rarely glimpsed by male anthropologists, and possibly not fully understood unless you too live a life in which you need to use the lore passed on to you. Somewhere in the past few decades I realised I could predict what the next season would bring – for this valley, at least – with more accuracy than the weather bureau.

Much of my professional life has been spent studying the patterns of the land to create theories of pest and weed management, and tracing new paths through old documents to create patterns from the past that would eventually become historical fiction and non-fiction. Writing those books, and making a living from doing so, has allowed me the privilege of following historical obsessions, ferreting out source material or hiring others to do so, seeking firsthand accounts of the past and then turning them into stories.

The whispers from the land

History is stories. Some of them – not necessarily the most accurate or unbiased – get written down.

This is also a book of stories. My family were and are storytellers, with a passion for putting the tales passed on over generations into historical context, like my grandmother's tales of how desperation in the 1890s drought led to the atrocities of child labour that gave the women of the temperance and suffrage movements their passion to campaign for reform and Federation.

This book comes from six decades of listening to stories, and four decades of watching the land. The land is one of the great players of our past, and is still here to be studied, and its lessons applied to our history.

As I sit by the creek I can trace the clematis 'road', planted perhaps tens of thousands of years ago by Indigenous women to guide the girls to the stringybark harvest. As each vine dies, seedlings grow to take its place. Further up the ridges my husband and I traced the kilometres of water race dug and built by Chinese gold miners in the 1850s and 1860s, then used by their descendants to bring water to grow vegetables. The white irises just beyond our lower boundary are the only sign left of the Poverty Gully 'susso camp' of the 1930s, where hundreds camped in shanties made of corrugated iron and flattened kerosene tins. The grove of damson plums, each lichened trunk wider than I am, was the first of the orchards in this valley. Each piece of knowledge changes and deepens the understanding of the past.

When you know one area well you realise that there is no such thing as 'the bush'. Australia was once more than three hundred Indigenous nations[6], and this land is still far too ecologically diverse for any 'one size fits all' planning policy. Modern science's ability to understand the land and its history is giving us new insights or reinforcing old ones, but despite disasters and the even wilder swings of climate predicted, these voices of understanding become fewer as year after year research funding is slashed.

The past matters. The patterns of the past help predict when the gang-gangs will fly down from the mountains, when the boulders will crash down the gorge in the next flood, or when the wombats will scream in their mating chases. They also help predict stockmarket falls and political battles. These patterns are the foundation for the predictions in the final chapter. The boats will keep coming, as they have come for 60,000 years. So will drought, flood, fire, storm surge and covetous eyes on our resources.

To understand our history, you need to understand the land. Individuals, cultures, persistent ideologies (substantiated or not) and the innate nature of humanity are major forces too. But the land itself is underestimated.

The land will determine our future, too.

Understanding the land can be as simple as digging a thirty-centimetre hole in the soil to see if the ground you plan to live on is subject to flood, or fire. It can be as profound as realising how the age-old myth of 'endless land' still shapes the policies of our major political parties.

We need to listen to our land. If we fail, we will stumble into a future we can neither predict nor understand.

CHAPTER 1

The real First Fleet

A story from 60,000 years ago

They came by boat[1], a fleet of small canoes on a large grey ocean, the sky above them pulsing red as the volcano they had fled flared. The air was dark with ash, so black it was impossible to see more than a metre ahead.

They were frightened, not adventurers. They came because their former land had said, 'Leave, or your children die'. Three of them huddled in the first canoe, grim-faced but resolute: a man, naked except for the plaited belt around his waist that held his stone knife and spare fishhooks in place, and a tall woman with a child in her arms. The woman wore necklaces of shells and seeds. Jewellery can't save your life, but it weighs little. When your life has been ripped apart, a necklace declares your pride.

They navigated only by the position of the sun, a vague brightness in that blood-dark sky. Behind them lay devastation. Monster waves had swept across their camp in darkness after the volcano's first massive shudder. Now ash lay metres deep on the forest where they had once hunted and dug yams. When the tall woman found a canoe wedged up in a tree where the waves had left it, she had been seized with a certainty. They must leave now, before their children died.

Somewhere beyond the thin line of the horizon they might find refuge. The aunties had taught her to look for the land birds that flew from the southeast after each season of fruit. Each dry season she'd seen smoke from there, too. Birds and fire need land.

Now humans needed that land, too.

The woman had tried to convince the whole clan to leave. Some shook their heads; there are always those who think that when they wake up tomorrow the world will be like it was yesterday. But the young men had scavenged more canoes, plastering them with tree sap to mend the damage. The women filled dried sow bladders with water and filleted fish stranded by the tsunami into thin strips to dry in the sun for the voyage. The tall woman had pushed aside the ash to dig out yams; not to eat, but to plant when they reached safety. What if the new land had no yams, like some of the small sand islands? The sea gave fish and turtle, but people need yams and fruit. She touched her necklace made of last year's fruit seeds. She hoped they'd grow.

They launched the tiny fleet into the debris-laced sea at first light, carefully distributing their water gourds, stone axes and bundles of yams to keep the canoes steady. The men paddled southeast, towards the ash-dimmed sun and the unknown. The current pulled the canoe forward, a strange new current, forged perhaps by the tsunami. It seemed to be urging them along.

There was no moon that night, no avenue of stars in that strangely dark sky to point the way. At times they called out to each other, to keep the fleet together, to say to the darkness: we are still alive. When the grey smudge that was the sun rose through the ash they saw they had drifted off course. One of the canoes had vanished. They yelled again into the grey air. It might be day; there was no real light. But all they heard was the slapping of the waves. Had the lost canoe overturned or been attacked by crocodile or shark? There was no way to search for them now. The paddlers turned to face south now, the dim sun on their left.

The ash gradually cleared around them as they paddled south. The sunlight grew hotter. Their skin burnt under the coat of ash. The woman's daughter whimpered for water. The woman dipped her finger into one of the bladders and wet the child's lips. The water must be kept to keep the paddlers going. The woman herself stayed thirsty, her lips cracked from sun and salt.

She tried to peer through the brightness of sun and sea. Was there really land ahead? Perhaps she had seen clouds, not smoke. Perhaps the birds had chosen a strange seaward path for some reason of their own.

The real First Fleet | 13

If there was no land to the south then everyone in their fleet would die. It would take days to paddle back against the current, and to what? Death in the ash? If the new land had no fresh water then they would die too. Birds could fly over reefs that would shred a canoe. If the land in front of them was fringed with reefs, they might die in the wreck of the canoes.

If there was land at all.

She looked down at the sea. A piece of mangrove wood bobbed against the canoe. It might be a sign of land. It might also have been dragged from the land they'd left by the monster wave.

The child cried again. She held her to her breast. There was nothing to drink there either, but the child quietened, comforted.

Her husband slumped. He had paddled all yesterday, and last night too, keeping their canoe steady. His paddle drifted from his hand. The woman leant out of the canoe and grabbed it. The canoe lurched, swamping them with water. She bailed out what she could, swiftly, with cupped hands. The child copied her. The woman began to paddle. Men paddle faster, stronger, but women can endure longer than men. Women will keep going to save their children.

The woman kept on paddling.

The sky pulsed red, reflecting the eruption behind them. The woman navigated almost by instinct now, keeping at the same angle to the wind. The rest of the fleet followed her lead.

If she was going the wrong way then they would all die. Perhaps they would all die no matter what she did.

The child gave a cry. A smudge darkened the far horizon. It was a cloud, only a cloud. She looked again. Not clouds. Two small islands, and one so big it was impossible to see where the coast ended. She would have cried in triumph if she'd had the breath to waste.

The land grew closer, and closer still. The child's father forced his body up and took the paddle from the woman. She opened one of the water bladders, holding it to the child's lips and then to the man's before she drank herself. They needed water now to keep on going. If this new land didn't have fresh water, a bladder's worth of water wouldn't save their lives.

The grey smudge became blue, then green. She could see hills. Another small knife of terror dropped away. High ground meant water – probably. Trees meant forest, food.

She and her partner took it in turns to paddle now. Green became mangrove swamps. Mangrove swamps meant bats to hunt and roast, mangrove worms and mussels, and a sandy bottom that wouldn't rip the canoe apart.

The blue sea grew threads of surf. The fleet's men wielded the paddles, using the last of their strength to arrow the canoes across the waves. A surge of sea lifted the tall woman's canoe up. The spray stung her face as the canoe spun along the wave, closer and closer to a small white beach. The sea retreated, leaving the canoe on the sand.

Another wave might drag them back. The woman grabbed the child in one arm, balanced the bark-wrapped yams and seeds on her head and staggered ashore while her husband secured the canoe. One step, another and another. She looked down at the prints in the white sand. Human footprints, the first this land had known.

She managed a smile. Putting the child down, the woman touched her belly where a new life grew. She would become the mother of a continent of people.

The long route to Australia

Is this what happened 60,000 years or more ago? Perhaps. Northern Australia – or Sahul, the name now given to the continent that incorporated mainland Australia with Papua New Guinea as well as Tasmania and our outer islands – may have then provided refuge for small canoes from the north. Tens of thousands of years later the winds, cliffs and reefs of the west, south and east would keep the larger ships of travellers from further afield away.

Australia was probably first settled about 60,000 years ago at a time of geological upheaval in what is now Indonesia and Timor.[2] The first settlers may well have fled from the eruptions. I've seen a sky pulse red like that, with air too thick with ash to see, though that was from a bushfire, not a volcano. Ash means starvation unless food can be brought from somewhere else.

Humans walked out of Africa over 100,000 years ago.[3] During the following 40,000 years the ancestors of Australia's first settlers probably followed the coasts of Southeast Asia, with a long halt in what is now called Taiwan. They then paddled their canoes from island to island, reef to reef, via the Philippines, abandoning each landfall when food became scarce, or curiosity drew them on.[4]

The people on our 'first fleet' came from a long tradition of crossing seas in small craft.[5] Sixty thousand years ago the sea level was far lower than it is now, with much of the world's water frozen into ice sheets and glaciers. But even with lowered sea levels there were many areas where boats were necessary as it was too far to swim. The ancestors of Australia's first settlers had to cross at least sixty-five kilometres of treacherous sea beyond sight of land, with either the knowledge that they could navigate their way back again, or the bravado – or desperation – to keep going.

The men and women who took that bold step made the longest journey from humanity's original homeland in Africa.

Refugees or adventurers? (And the absent elephants)

Were the people in those canoes refugees? It's likely. Adventurers come by themselves, two or three young men together. The migration of enough humans to make a viable population suggests more than a few canoes blown off course.

Nor could the ancestors of our first nations have been washed here on floating logs. If humans could have floated here then so could monkeys and other apes, which would have flourished in the rainforests of northern Australasia. If humans and other animals could have walked or swum here so could elephants, which the Indonesian island of Flores had until about 10,000 years ago.

The place where that first foot came ashore is now probably under water. Was it a woman's foot? That's likely, too. If a man was paddling he'd let the women and children scramble out in the shallows before he hauled the heavy canoe up the beach.

Different Aboriginal nations have different arrival stories. The Gagudju people of the Alligator River area in the Northern Territory tell of their ancestress Imberombera, the Great Mother, who came from across the sea. Her womb was full of children and she carried woven bags on her head filled with yams and seeds and plants. The Gunwinggu people tell of their ancestress Waramurungundju, who also came over the seas in a canoe from the northwest. There is no one story (or suite of stories) that represents all Indigenous beliefs.

The DNA divergence

There were probably several refugee groups[6], over several years, 1000 to 3000 people, building up to a population of about 20,000 by 22,000 years ago, then crashing to less than half that as the Ice Age bit between 21,000–18,000 BC.

The genome of most humans shows a great deal of mixing in the past 60,000 years, not just with different groups of humans but with Neanderthals, Denisovans and probably other hominins still to be discovered. But the genome of Indigenous Australians illustrates the relative isolation of the Indigenous Australian gene pool from their arrival around 60,000 years ago until 1788.

DNA sequencing of a hundred-year-old sample of a West Australian Aboriginal man's hair shows he was directly descended from a migration out of Africa into Asia that took place about 70,000 years ago. The man's genome reveals that his ancestors separated from the ancestors of other human populations 64,000 to 75,000 years ago, when the ancestors of Asians and Europeans had not yet differentiated from each other and were still in Africa or the Middle East. His closest DNA match today is with people in the Papua New Guinea Highlands and the Aeta people of the Philippines.

This doesn't mean that Australia was totally genetically isolated. DNA patterns also suggest a link with the people presently on the Indian subcontinent dating from about 4000 years ago, which – coincidentally or not – is about the time the dingo arrived here, and various Indigenous languages changed along with tool-making methods.[7] This is also the time when vast trade routes were established through the Middle East and Asia as coastlines stabilised and climates changed, often growing dryer after the melting of the ice. It would not be surprising if trade routes down through Southeast Asia with links to Australia began during this period as well. As the Indigenous genome is studied in more depth, other links may be found. It's likely, though, that there was far less genetic mixing in Australia than in areas like mainland Europe and Asia.

Our eagerly breeding ancestors

In most of the world, through Europe, Asia, the Middle East, Africa and Polynesia, human populations moved both far and often. Genes were exchanged in marriage, rape, commercial transaction, or a bit of slap and tickle in the corn fields, wherever traders or invaders passed. Once horses were domesticated, about four thousand years ago, large amounts of goods could be transported thousands of kilometres. In the past ten years, satellite images have allowed the discovery of vast ancient trade routes across what are now deserts in the Middle East, going back perhaps five thousand years. The Silk Road connected ancient China to ancient Rome at least two thousand years ago, and probably for centuries or even thousands of years before that. Ships, too, would trade heavy goods, from tin to bales of wool.

But in Australia, although there were long trade routes right across Australia and up into Asia, trade was limited to what a person could easily carry, rather than the trade ships that sailed the Mediterranean three thousand years ago or the caravans of laden horses, camels, donkeys, alpacas, mules, oxen, reindeer or even hand-pulled sleds of much of the rest of the populated world. So the gene pool in Australia was predominantly made up of the descendants of those who survived and thrived in the extremes and changing climate of this land, with relatively few additions from traders or migrants.

A hard beach to land on

Why did so few come here over those tens of thousands of years? While Australia has few great harbours to shelter large sailing ships, it does have long beaches where it's easy to land small boats or canoes. This is, after all, a good part of the world to live in. People in small boats still regularly attempt to arrive here. Holiday-makers pay money to visit.

In every survey asking people for their idea of 'a nice place to live', no matter what the criteria, some part of Australia usually makes it into the top five, or at least the top ten. As we'll see in chapter 5, Australia's northern neighbours, as well as some across the world, knew that land was here, quite apart from the mythical terra Australis. Why did so many invaders compete for the damp forests of England and so few choose sunbaking and fishing in Australia?

One answer is that, in fact, for much of the 60,000 years Australia was inhabited, England (and a large part of the rest of frozen Europe and the United States) wasn't.[8] The first human colonies in what is now England either left or died out in the Ice Age. But England is only about thirty-four kilometres from mainland Europe, so close that in World War 1 people in the south of England could hear the sounds of war in France. As the world warmed about 15,000 years ago, the crossing from mainland Europe to England could have been done in a day in a small round leather boat, if the wind was coming from the right direction. England was a relatively easy place to both colonise and invade, and the highly diverse genome of those in the United Kingdom today reflects that.

In comparison, the sixty-five kilometres or more to Australia was a canoe trip into the unknown. It wasn't until sometime around the 1700s when the Macassan fishermen of what is now Indonesia had developed more efficient sails that the crossing became fast enough for them to sail to Australia safely, dive for trepang and then sail home.

The sea, the ferocious gale winds of the south and west, the teeth of coral reefs as well as distance all combined to keep Australia isolated for thousands of years.

Old soil versus new, deer versus wallaby

But even those who visited here from the nearest populations to the northwest might not have been tempted to colonise. The soils around the volcanoes to the northwest of Australia are fertile, easy land to farm and grow crops like rice or bananas. Volcanos may be deadly when they erupt, but there is a good reason why so many have farms or cities at their feet. To anyone used to rich volcanic soil, or bare fertile soils left by the retreating glaciers or the rich flood plains of Europe and North America, Australian soils look uninviting. The areas here with the richest soil were also likely to be heavily forested, not kept clear of trees by regularly flooding rivers or glaciers and vast herds of grazing animals that would eat tree seedlings as well as grass. Deer and goats can form herds of hundreds or even thousands; kangaroo mobs are usually limited to about thirty, and eat only grass. Australia's main 'young-tree eaters' are wallabies, who don't form mobs or create or maintain vast grasslands.

It's worth noting that even after the trepang fishermen made their voyages here from 1700 onwards, no large migration of people from the northwest followed. Local opposition may have been a deterrent, but the cultures to the north of us were extremely good at fighting for territory. This territory wasn't worth it.

The barrier of the reef

Australia also seems to have missed out on the great Polynesian colonisation.[9] By about 1300 Polynesian colonisation had spread from Hawaii to New Zealand, even to Easter Island, colonising previously unsettled islands in their massive double hulled canoes, with extraordinary navigational skill, and able to journey even against the prevailing winds and currents. They may even have traded with South America – a possible though controversial explanation for the presence of Auracana hens in South America long before Europeans could bring poultry.

Australia could have been settled in those migrations, too. But the Polynesian migrants would have most likely come from the northeast. Much of our northeastern coast is guarded by an extraordinary long and relatively unbroken series of coral reefs. Unless you are a sailor, the name chosen for our World Heritage reef may not mean much. But to anyone in a seagoing vessel, 'great barrier' means exactly that: razor rocks, often hidden under waves, that will sink ships and drown sailors who try to pass them.

Even the extraordinary Polynesian sea travellers would have found the Great Barrier Reef a major or even impossible obstacle. While it's possible that Polynesian travellers did arrive here, and stayed, they don't appear to have established their own separate nations, or gone back for more settlers, their journey becoming part of their culture's oral history. Nor did they arrive in large enough numbers to make a significant contribution to either genes or culture.

Gales guard the south

European travellers found a different barrier. They would come from the west, driven by 'trade winds', the extraordinarily strong and reliable winds that blow eastwards towards southwestern Australia, and could be used to sail across the Indian Ocean relatively quickly to reach the rich trading lands north of Australia. But the lack of grass, easily found fresh water or safe harbours did not tempt them to land here. And south of Australia are the Southern Ocean and the ice. There are excellent southern harbours in Australia, but there are also legendary gales. Nor has the south any equivalent of the Inuit people in the northern polar regions who might have migrated north to Australia.

So we are left with one major migration, as well as other smaller ones. People kept crossing the dangerous ocean to Australia, even if not in great numbers. Probably they always will, as long as there are humans and boats to sail in. My various ancestors, too, all came here by boat, of one sort or another, from many places, at many different times. All of them were fleeing persecution, or hardship, and dreaming of a better life, just as those refugees in the 'first fleet' may have been.

Life at the end of the world

Sixty thousand years ago, the north of this new land would have been similar enough to the one they had left for the new arrivals to survive reasonably well.

Fish, shellfish, fruit bats and even some of the plants would have been familiar, as would be the dangers of massive crocodiles. But there were also beasts that would have been both strange and terrifying, like the giant snake (*Wonambi naracoortensis*), nearly a metre in diameter and about five metres long, and an emu-like flightless creature (*Genyornis newtoni*) that stood two metres tall and was twice as heavy as a modern-day emu, as well as thylacines or marsupial lions.

Despite these dangers, it would have been a land of easy routes to travel along the coast with fish and shellfish, or through the lush land along the inland rivers. But when the first settlers arrived here, the Australian climate was already changing, becoming harsher, dryer, more erratic.[10] The megafauna – the giant kangaroo or wombat-like creatures, as well as many others – were already becoming extinct, and had been from about 350,000 years ago.

Australia was fast becoming a land that couldn't naturally support any animal that was larger than a western red kangaroo. Over the next 60,000 years the land would change dramatically. Isolation, desertification and a dramatically changing climate would force both the people and their cultures to adapt.

The rest of the world changed dramatically, too. In Europe, the Middle East, Polynesia and Asia over those 60,000 years, tribes migrated as glaciers grew and vanished, or as grasslands turned to desert. But elsewhere there was usually a choice: if the grass withered, the rivers dried up, or war like newcomers threatened you with spears, you could move elsewhere. About 16,000 years ago there were the vast Americas to migrate to, Hawai'i about 1700 years ago, or Aotearoa/New Zealand a thousand years ago, as well as the vast northern lands available as the glaciers of the last Ice Age melted about 15,000 years ago.

Once you got to Australia, it was difficult to leave. Those fierce westerly and southerly winds and the vast reef that kept out possible immigrants also kept those who lived in Australia here, apart from the few trade routes in the far north, where you needed skill, detailed local knowledge, and experience to make the journeys.

Australia is also, literally, the end of the liveable world. Once you reached Australia and found yourself facing new deserts, no matter how much further south you travelled there was no other liveable land to find.

Humans are good at adapting – we are all descended from those who adapted and survived. The new Australian cultures would be as diverse as the continent, but they would have one thing in common: in a land of wildly varying climatic extremes, where a drought could last for decades, their land use would be designed to survive the worst years rather than make a surplus from the best.

You adapted, or you died.

From fire to snow in forty minutes

All lands have their own climatic dangers. Parts of Australia, however, arguably face more frequent as well as less predictable extremes than much of the rest of world. In 1984, at the end of a four-year catastrophic drought, a newly arrived German exchange student fought a bushfire on his first day here, watched hail, rain and a dusting of snow extinguish it, then survived a flash flood when the ice melted in an hour as the temperature rose to thirty-six degrees Celsius. Then his companion was bitten by a snake. Six weeks later, a tornado hit.

CHAPTER 2

The Ice Age that made three hundred nations

The new arrivals changed Australia. Australia also changed them. The physical environment always helps shape the culture and bodies of those who live there,[1] although in those cultures that reject genocide it is currently politically incorrect to speak of racial differences, unless it's for health reasons, where people with ancestors from a certain area may have inherited recessive genes that may lead to the death of their children, to increased cholesterol and heart disease, or to the inability to process milk, alcohol or broad beans. In Australia, with relatively little DNA or cultural input from beyond our shores, the land itself probably had a far greater influence than on most other cultures of the world.

The first arrivals were likely to have been physically and culturally alike. They'd have used the same food-gathering techniques, probably the same tools, perhaps the same art. Even as clans migrated further away it would have been relatively easy to meet and trade, following the food-rich coastline or the rivers. Intermarriage and this easy access to each other may have meant that culturally they stayed similar for hundreds, even thousands of years.

The early spread of humans around Australia may have been relatively swift,[2] with the new arrivals following the coastlines and large river systems into the lakes and lush grazing of the inland. Back then the dry lakes of today were full of water and were rich in fish, shellfish, ducks and other wildlife.

By 30,000 years ago there were people in Arnhem Land, Cape York, the far south of Western Australia, southern New South Wales, Victoria and the south of Tasmania. By 20,000 years ago, Aboriginal people had settled over the whole of Australia.

But one of humanity's greatest challenges would change Indigenous societies, too, as well isolating them into many profoundly different cultures.

The Ice Age carves up a continent

From 25,000 to 15,000 years ago, glaciers covered parts of Tasmania as well as the Snowy Mountains in Victoria and New South Wales. As more water was locked up in the ice caps, the continent became drier. The archaeological records of places like Lake Mungo in southwestern New South Wales show how the lush lake country, with its frog hunts and fish feasts of 40,000 years ago, gave way to desert. The temperature dropped by about ten degrees.[3] (It is worth comparing this to the doom predicted if our climate changes by 2–4 degrees with global warming.) New cold, dry winds blew. In many areas rain simply stopped falling, for years at a time. The seasons, the floods, the droughts, would have been increasingly hard to predict. As climate changes, the weather can be more erratic, as well as different.

Survival was not easy. Possibly more than half the population died.[4]

Our ancestors were the ones who survived dramatic climate change, as well as years of long winters from vast volcanic events. *Homo sapiens* adapted; others did not. (This is also worth remembering if you feel despondent about global warming. Our ancestors were very good indeed at coping with dramatic climate change.)

The Ice Age separated Australia's Indigenous communities by glaciers and desert, as well as distance. Groups of survivors retreated to the southeast parts of Victoria and New South Wales, where rivers like the Murray still provided bounty; to southwest Western Australia and parts of the Pilbara, Kimberley, Kakadu and Arnhem Land in the north. Stories, tools and customs grew even more different, and distinct cultures began to evolve.

The two-centimetre water rise that brings devastation

By about 15,000 BC the world began to warm up. The Ice Age had brought disaster. The global warming brought disaster too. As ice melted, water flowed back into oceans. The seas rose and rich lands along the coast began to vanish. By about 12,000 years ago glaciers were melting all around the world. Sea levels rose at the rate of about a centimetre or two a year. This may not seem much, just as the sea-level rise of about 1.7 to 3.3 millimetres per annum over the past decade does not seem particularly dramatic either. And in many places, in most years, there may not even have been any visible changes. Then in one year there might be sudden and transforming disaster.

The 1978 flood in our valley brought water within two centimetres of washing over the rise that slopes down to the creek flats. Most Australian east-coast rivers and creeks that flood have this lip, made from layers of deposited debris from uncounted floods, protecting the land beyond it. If this flood had been two centimetres higher the water would have surged down across the valley proper, covering perhaps sixty square kilometres in froth and floodwater and rolling boulders, just as it did in the flood in 1852. A two-centimetre-a-year rise can bring disaster.

It is difficult to imagine the scope of chaos and tragedy that came with the melting of the Ice Age, from 15,000 to about five thousand years ago. In northern Australia, five kilometres of land inland from the coast could vanish in a year as protective coastal dunes were washed away. In the south, an entire kilometre of land inland from the Great Australian Bight might have disappeared in a single flood, a wall of salt froth crashing across the soil as the small rise that had held the sea back eroded in the storm.

By the time the sea level more or less stabilised, one seventh of what had been Australia, an area the size of present Western Australia, was under the sea. Peninsulas became islands, low-lying islands and reefs disappeared below the waves completely and people starved.

About 12,000 years ago Tasmania was cut off from the mainland, the rising waters creating Bass Strait and its islands. New Guinea was separated from Australia by rising seas about eight thousand years ago.

The mountains along the Queensland coast became the tropical reef islands we know today. The seas kept rising steadily until about seven thousand years ago, then rose slowly for about another two thousand years.

The megafauna vanish

By about 10,000 years ago, every creature taller than a human had vanished from the Australian landscape. The debate about how much humans contributed to their extinction by hunting or burning the landscape continues, with insufficient data so far to definitively decide on the relative contributions of humans and climate. But Australia is, and was, a diverse continent. The megafauna may have vanished for different reasons, or with different trigger points for extinction in different parts of the country. Assuming there must be a single answer perpetuates the myth that what holds true in one part of the country must necessarily work all over the continent.[5]

A changed land, a changed people

About five thousand years ago the seas finally stopped rising.[6] After so many thousands of years of periodic catastrophe there was now time to invent and create instead of struggling to survive. The tools that survive from that period have new designs: smaller, specialised awls to punch holes in cloth, adzes for shaping wooden objects, tools with handles to make them more efficient for heavy work. It is possible that a fresh wave of immigrants arriving from newly flooded lands to the north brought innovative tools and ideas, but the tools are distinctive enough to be native to Australia. Each area had its distinctive tool shapes and materials.

The first arrivals were probably physically and culturally alike. But 20,000 years of adapting to climate change and different climates combined with the barriers of new glaciers and deserts gradually turned the original Melanesian immigrants into around three hundred separate and distinct tribal nations, each with their own lore, art and stories. There were enormous cultural as well as language variations, as you'd expect with such vastly different environments.

Even today the myths persist that there is a single Indigenous culture of didgeridoos and bark humpies when there probably hasn't been a single Indigenous culture for 60,000 years.[7] By 1788, when the first European colonists arrived, the nations of Australia were as diverse as those of Europe or Asia. But then, as now, many or even most of the new arrivals saw only the similarities: spears instead of muskets, and the lack of palaces and uniformed armies of a physically acquisitive culture. The 'indigenous Australian' didgeridoo, for example, was only played in parts of the Kimberley and far northern Australia. Far from being a land of bark humpies, Indigenous Australians constructed a wide range of buildings, depending on what kind of shelter they needed.

The Arrente people of Central Australia, for example, needed only shelters made out of grass and saplings to keep off the sun and wind. The shelters look primitive to anyone expecting a slab hut, but in that climate a slab hut seals in the heat. The Arrente buildings are strongly woven, and angled to let in the breeze. In the south of Western Australia the Nyungar people's shelters were designed primarily to keep out the wind.

In colder, wetter climates, more solid or insulated structures were needed. The Ngunawal people, who occupied the area of present-day Canberra and the Australian Capital Territory; the Ngarigo, who lived on the tablelands to the south; and the Walgalu, of the high country with its frigid winters, built solid huts made of logs and branches, with roofs and walls made of big sheets of stringybark. Indigenous Tasmanians spent about a quarter of each year in small villages of dome-shaped huts, well thatched with bark, grass or turf to keep off the rain, and lined inside with warmly insulating bark, skins or feathers.

Pre-colonial Australia also had villages, such as the ones in the Lake Condah area in western Victoria[8], where the Gunditjmara people's settlements consisted of hundreds of huts. Each house had stone walls about a metre high, with a frame of branches and roof made of bark or rush. Every home's doorway faced the same way. The villages were supported by 'mobile agriculture' (see Chapter 4) and fish and eel farming. Archaeologist Heather Builth, who discovered the remains of hundreds of huts, estimated that the Gunditjmara eel farms, more than seventy-five square kilometres of artificial ponds, could have fed up to 10,000 people. 'Smoking trees' were used to smoke and preserve the eels for export to other parts of Australia.

Central Victoria also had several greenstone quarries. This hard volcanic rock could be flaked into chips and then ground to have a hard, sharp edge. These blades are as efficient as modern knives, and often stay sharp for longer.

The more isolated the culture, the proportionately larger the effect of the environment. Indigenous Tasmanians were perhaps the most isolated of all, cut off for more than 10,000 years from the mainland by a dangerously wild strait. The demands of the physical environment almost certainly influenced their physique, too. Indigenous Tasmanian women, for example, had exceptional swimming skills, diving for crabs, crayfish, mussels, oysters and abalone and spending up to fifteen minutes underwater, or swimming two cold kilometres to offshore islands for mutton birds or their eggs. Skills such as these may well have been part of natural selection – those who could swim best were more likely to survive or be chosen as wives. Tasmanian women built the huts; mined ochre and rock for tools; hunted possums for food and skins; carried the spears, game and babies as the family groups travelled around; wove baskets of rushes or grasses; made shell necklaces; and gathered most of the food. The Tasmanians ate little or no fish, preferring fat-rich foods like seal and abalone, and avoiding shellfish in the frequent times when they may host toxic bacteria.

The Indigenous nations of Australia were as diverse as the country they lived in, yet it's only been in the past decade or so that they have been referred to individually – as the Yuin, Gunditjmara, Noonuccal and so on – rather than simply as 'native' or Aboriginal. The work of artists like Timmy Payungka Tjapangati may fetch tens of thousands of dollars, but even today their art is still mostly referred to as 'Indigenous', not art from Papunya Tula, or Ngaanyatjarra. Newspaper reports still talk of someone being 'Indigenous' or 'Aboriginal', even in places like Alice Springs where it's relatively easy to identify which nation a person is from. (Yes, we do refer to 'Europeans', and it's a useful general term, but I suspect that a book like *French Women Don't*

Get Fat wouldn't have sold many copies if it had been named *European Women Don't Get Fat.*)

By 1788, when the first European colony arrived in New South Wales, the Indigenous cultures and way of life were as diverse as those in Europe, with arguably a higher standard of health, physique, medical knowledge and living than a peasant in England or Poland, or a crofter in Scotland. The European cities and large towns were squalid, where old age came in your twenties, if you survived that long. Periodic starvation was a fact of life in rural Europe. But in Europe, Asia and much of the rest of the world, you could save yourself and your family from starvation or squalor by taking your neighbour's resources, either by taxation, if you belonged to a hereditary or religious elite, or by conquering them with army or navy.

The Australian nations' language, tools, housing, food crops, art and other culture varied enormously. But their major differences from the European and Asian nations were markedly similar.

There were no armies, although there were warriors, and many stories of battles and raids for wives, or retaliation for broken laws. Yet there seems to be no history of all-out warfare between nations that was bitter enough to continue sporadically generation after generation, consuming enough resources to bring hardship or even death between battles. In much of the rest of the world especially desirable land was fought for, time after time. In Australia, areas of abundance, like the bunya nut groves of southern Queensland, or the waterlily harvests in the Araluen Valley where I am writing this, became the regular meeting places for many different clans to share the abundance, instead of fighting for it.

There was no royalty, no class of elite that ate while others starved. There were no accumulations of treasure, although beautiful items were valued. Apart from a tragic case of mental illness recorded by missionary Daisy Bates, there seems to be no cannibalism, despite the many archaeological finds in Europe, Asia, the Middle East and the Pacific of what look like ancient human bones other humans have feasted upon. The Indigenous Australian nations have no history of deep racial hatreds, like anti-Semitism and white supremacy, despite the major physical differences between various pre-colonial Australian nations, and no religious persecution, despite major differences in beliefs and a strong insistence within each nation that the law must be followed.

What was it about Australia, and its people, that made its cultures so different from so much of Europe, Asia, the Middle East, Africa and Polynesia?

CHAPTER 3

Cooperate or Die

Central Australia, 1990s

Fifty Indigenous teenagers sit in a small, hot library and silently stare at me. They've been brought here from outstations hundreds of kilometres away as part of an education project. We will create a story, I tell them. It will be fun. Who will suggest a character's name?

No one answers. They glance at each other, and then at me.

I'm worried. I've given this workshop to kids around Australia, and in other countries, too. There should be hands waving in the air or voices calling out, telling, suggesting.

All I can hear are the sounds of fifty-one people breathing.

At last someone says, hesitatingly, 'Yabba'.

The kids laugh. I assume that 'Yabba' is a local word, and wonder what it means. Later I find it was actually from 'Yabba dabba doo!', the cry of a character in the TV cartoon *The Flintstones*.

Okay, I say. Is the character Yabba going to be male or female? Human, animal, machine?

Again the silence, the quiet glancing around the room. For half a minute I think I'm boring them. But they don't look bored. They look ... polite.

They are, in fact, the most polite humans I have ever met. Over the next few hours we do create a story. It's set in a Hungry Jack's fast-food palace. (I had told them to choose a place where they'd love to be. I expected a waterhole, but they love Hungry Jack's.)

It's a good story, but each time, before anyone offers an answer, they check that no one else wants to speak first. They reassure themselves that I'm happy to keep going, that we are all working in a form of consensus I only vaguely understand. If I had yawned they may have politely left the room.

Don't get me wrong. These kids argue with each other, and probably annoy the hell out of their elders at times, too. But they also come from a culture based on consensus and cooperation.

In arid Australia, if you don't cooperate, you die. If you come up with a new idea that doesn't work, you die. If you live in a desert where droughts can be thousands of years long, where survival may depend on finding the right ant colony with its fat ant eggs at exactly the right time – and not too often, in case you wipe the ants out – you tend to be very, very good at reaching consensus. A rebel doesn't just risk their own life; they may kill the entire clan. You check, and recheck, then keep checking before you proceed at all.

These kids' culture certainly has rebels, and violence, too. But most of the mythic rebels in their oral history are punished by exile. Exile in that environment is often fatal. A culture of cooperation does not necessarily mean it's tolerant, or even non-violent. The harsher the landscape, the more necessary it is to work together, to cooperate,[1] and to be absolutely certain before you do something differently, because different can kill you. If you live in a land where misreading the chance of finding the only water in a hundred square kilometres might kill you and your family, you become extremely good at cooperating, not just with each other but with the land.

The land of few languages

The population of Indigenous Australians at the time of permanent European settlement has been estimated at between 318,000 and 1,000,000, roughly distributed much as Australia's present day population is, with most people living in southeastern Australia, and near the major rivers areas along the east coast and the Murray–Darling river system, as well as in southwest Western Australia.[2]

It was a land of about 300 nations and 250 languages, all but three of which came from one common proto-Australian language, Pama-Nyungan. (Most European languages are descended from one ancient language, Proto-Indo-European.) By comparison, nearby New Guinea, far smaller than Australia, has about 800 languages, not just dialects of the same language but ones so different that people on one mountain need a completely new language to understand their neighbours on another. In tiny medieval England, merchants needed to know 'Anglo Norman' French (a French dialect used in England) or Latin as well as the local language of Cornwall or Wales or wherever they were selling their wares; peasants from one village might find it difficult to understand someone from only twenty kilometres away. China still has about 292 'living languages' that are spoken even today, a small fraction of what it must have had several hundred years ago. So why were there so few languages for a country as vast as Australia, especially one so culturally diverse, where deserts and mountains made travel difficult?

Australia had relatively few languages for the same reason that it had no real indigenous 'cuisine'. There are many indigenous foods and cooking methods – and delicious ones – but no cultural equivalents of the French pot-au-feu, English cakes, Beijing duck, or the exquisite Thai foods that balance sweet, sour and crunchy. Australia can be a generous land – in most seasons, in relatively 'undeveloped' areas of bush where native tubers and fruits haven't been exterminated by sheep, cattle and feral animals, it only takes an hour or so a day to find enough food to survive and dry wood for a fire, as long as you know exactly what you are doing. But it is an erratic land. Droughts can last for years, or decades. Flood can cover square kilometres two or even three times in a single year. Fire, flood and drought are constant whispers on the wind.

This is a land where survival is an art[3], where you eat the food that is available, which often means focusing on one particular food – fish, or yams, mutton-bird eggs or bush tomatoes – rather than combining many ingredients into one dish. And this is also why there are few languages.

This is a land where in many areas you had to move from place to place, so you didn't exhaust the food supplies, and left enough seeds, yam roots, frogs or bandicoots for the populations to build up again – to be 'fat' populations, to use a concept from Australia's north. When desperation means you need to travel to find food, it helps to be able to communicate with your neighbouring nations. In a 'boom and bust' land, where a plenitude of bogong moths, bunya nuts, frogs or turtle eggs doesn't come every year – or even in a regular pattern – it makes sense for nations from hundreds of kilometres away to join in the feast, and you tend to learn your neighbours' customs, and their language.

How to get along

Mutual reliance on and cooperation with your near and far neighbours are good tools for surviving a country of extremes; different languages are a barrier to communication and cooperation. While the New Guinea nations battled, the Australian nations traded, sometimes for useful items like the tools of 'Darwin glass' from an ancient meteor, as sharp and long-lasting as any European implement that had been invented up until the new metal technologies of the 1960s, or for flint, or the large Cape York baler shells that contain a strong fish hook when you carved off the brittle bits of shell, which were prized as far south as the Great Australian Bight. The Gunditjmara's greenstone tools from central Victoria have been discovered more than three hundred kilometres from the mines where the stone was quarried, and were probably traded with people who had marriage ties or other social links with the miners.

But most trade was of ceremonial items like feathers, shells or various coloured ochres, such the red and white shades mined from the huge Wilgie Mia mines in central Western Australia. While the red and yellow ochres mined in the Murchison district in Western Australia were also prized for their purity of colour, the trade itself was more important than the item traded, a cementing of cooperation and exchange of knowledge.

Most, if not all, Indigenous cultures had and have complex and diverse kinship traditions and systems. Kinship ties (which may be different from the Western notion of kinship, and far more complex) govern your relationships, and potential marriage partners. The complex web of kinship meant that property crimes were rare. Most things could be borrowed, or taken, within the web of kinship. The relatively recent concepts of socialism and communism, giving physical security to those who needed it most, are pale ghosts compared to the strength of traditional kinship ties, benefits and duties.

But possibly the greatest bringing together of cultures and peoples was at the many regional festivals where clans from hundreds of kilometres around would celebrate and enjoy seasonally abundant foods. The Durrubul, Guwar, Njula, Quandamooka, Noonuccal, Kombumerri and Yugambeh people of southeast Queensland had their great cycad and bunya nut harvests and feasts. In summer, people came from as far away as the Bundaberg region or the Tweed River to feast on bunya nuts in the Bunya Mountains, while in winter huge groups met to hunt the sea mullet in Moreton Bay.

In summer the Ngunawal, Ngarigo, Walgalu and Yuin of the New South Wales south coast moved to different places to hunt, or to attend the rich bogong moth feasts at places like Jindabyne, Gudgenby or Omeo. Scouts travelled into the mountains and sent smoke signals when the moths arrived. About five hundred people from different nations travelled hundreds of kilometres to feast on the moths and to arrange marriages and conduct corroborees and initiation rites.

The Palawa clans of what is now Tasmania gathered together for elaborate kangaroo hunts – not just killing and eating them, but complex ceremonies that celebrated their ancestral past, with songs and fire-based management practices that provided the lush open grasslands that trigger kangaroo breeding. (Unlike most animals, kangaroos can stop their unborn foetuses developing until there is sufficient food for the young to feed on. If you want kangaroos to breed, you need to provide the mothers with enough lush grass to feed their joeys before they are born, not after.)

In the Araluen Valley of southeastern New South Wales where I live now, clans joined from as far as the Snowy Mountains and the far south coast to feast on duck and waterlilies, roasting the roots and stems and making cakes from the pollen and seeds. Young women were instructed; young men competed in sports and endurance feats. Indigenous Australia did have battles, but they tended not to be an entire nation against another. Ceremonial battles were more important than real ones.

A land without armies

Ceremonial trade and travelling hundreds of kilometres to join with other nations for feasts and games are excellent cultural adaptations to survive in a harshly variable land, where flood or fire might mean you needed to seek refuge far away. But these traditions leave you vulnerable if your continent is invaded by Europeans.

The English of 1788 were shorter, smellier, less robust, and mostly led far harsher lives than the Indigenous people whose land they claimed. But they had made an art form out of war, using much of their culture's resources to produce items like muskets, gunpowder and other weapons, as well as a class of people – soldiers – whose sole job was to fight its wars.

This too may have evolved as a response to the land the colonisers came from. In ancient Greece, for example, men tended to go to war in winter, when there was little agricultural work that could be done, and go back to tend their land in spring and summer. (There were of course many exceptions, like the fifth century BC siege of Athens by the Spartans, or the siege of Troy.) The early European winter, before the snow falls, is a good time to march – it keeps you warm, especially if there is a good autumn harvest behind you to keep you fed. If you look at the warfare patterns of Europe, even as recently as World War 1, you see wars occurring after a good harvest.

Cold winters don't necessarily create armies, nor do climatic extremes always create cultures of cooperation, but they may well be major factors in their development. England has its autumns of Keats's 'mists and mellow fruit fullness', but as Australian backyard vegetable and fruit growers know, in this country there is no 'off season': you can be harvesting different crops at any time of the year, and in a harsh climate – especially before dams and watering systems – you needed to keep harvesting all year to get enough to feed your family or to make a living.

This was a land of raids and battles. War was not an Australian art form. The Indigenous nations would fight the invaders but mostly as raids by small bands of men rather than a gathering of clans to push the invaders out. Van Diemen's Land bushranger Musquito, for example, a Dharug or Gai-Mariagal man from New South Wales, formed a gang along with another Aboriginal man named Black Jack and they led raids against white settlers and storekeepers from 1824 to 1832.

The Australian spears of early colonial times were fearsome weapons, but only when wielded by experts. A musket, on the other hand, is relatively easy to load, to fire, and to hit your target. An hour's practise is enough to learn the rudiments, as opposed to many years with spears. A skilled loader could load them again within a minute. (If you are not skilled, it can take an hour, and then you have to clean the thing.) Often two men worked together: one to fire, and one to load. But each time you cast a spear, you lose it, unless it can be retrieved.

The newcomers were far better equipped for long periods of warfare then the Indigenous nations, not just with weapons, but able to retreat to fortified positions, houses, small police stations built for just that purpose, or in the case of whalers and sealers – who may be guilty of much of the Australian genocides in the early 1800s – in their ships. Australian history is sadly rich in accounts of 'retaliation' raids by soldiers or vigilantes, attacking undefended camps of women, children and old men.

At Twofold Bay on the south coast of New South Wales, Yuin men continued to defy the sealers who came hunting their animals and kidnapping their women. But by the 1830s, disease and guns had killed so many that in one group of the Yuin (a clan of the Kundigal people) there were only seventy or eighty left out of a community of several hundred who had been living there ten years earlier.

The most successful resistance campaigns seemed to be in northern Australia, with leaders like Jandamarra of the Bunuba in the Northern Territory, who from 1894 to 1897 waged a guerrilla war against police and settlers in revenge for attacks on his people, or where the Tiwi islanders effectively routed the colony set up on Melville Island in 1824, and the Iwaidja people fought against the second northern colony, Fort Wellington, established in 1827 at Raffles Bay. (Scurvy, fevers, 'night blindness' from a lack of vitamin A, and starvation also helped – no one could work out how to grow vegetables in the tropical climate, much less harvest the abundant wild food around them.)

It may also be significant in their success that these northern cultures had faced threats from outsiders before, like the trepang fisherman from what is now Indonesia. Although the encounters with the trepang fisherman were often friendly, with some Indigenous men travelling to Macassar and back as part of their ship's crew, other confrontations were violent. The northern nations were also close enough to hear firsthand accounts from what are now Indonesia, Timor and Malaysia of what happened when you didn't fight off would-be colonists.

But there are far more accounts of help than conflict: of Indigenous people gathering stringybark to roof the newcomers' huts, helping harvest corn for a share of the cobs, warning of floods that would come in the next few weeks or months, and guiding settlers and explorers to good grazing land and waterholes. Cooperation and consensus and the expectation that others would follow legal and kinship duties had allowed Indigenous nations to survive 60,000 years of climate change and erratic seasons. Ironically it now helped in their dispossession.

The first recorded Indigenous blood spilled by an Englishman was in June 1770[4], when Captain James Cook shot and wounded a Guugu Yimithirr man while the *Endeavour* was being repaired after being wrecked on the Great Barrier Reef. The Guugu Yimithirr had shared fish with the newcomers. When the crew of the *Endeavour* had caught more turtles than they could use, a group of Guugu Yimithirr men asked if they could have some. Mr Banks refused; the Guugu Yimithirr took this as a declaration of enmity. They set alight the dry grass around the English camp, burning a piglet and the blacksmith's forge, then set fire to more grass where the *Endeavour*'s fishing nets and linen were drying. Cook ordered the men to fire a musket and small shot, then the captain shot one of the ringleaders. He didn't think he had badly wounded the man, but they never knew for sure.

Over the next two hundred years, muskets, black powder and shot, and the more sophisticated weapons that supplanted them, and a culture with a permanent fighting force whose sole job was to battle enemies as well as police to keep order, would win against spears and a culture of cooperation.

The Indigenous nations had survived ice age, desertification and erratic seasons not just by cooperating with each other but also with the land. Europeans would try to remake the land into their image of European fields and pastures. The mostly male European farmers and planners of the eighteenth, nineteenth and early twentieth centuries would dimly grasp a simplified form of Indigenous hunting and 'firestick farming', the periodic patchwork burning to clear scrubby regrowth and promote green grass that looked so easy to duplicate. But even in these attempts their misunderstanding of the land would have tragic consequences. The far more influential and complex land management techniques practised by Indigenous women would be perilously ignored.

CHAPTER 4

The women who made the land

Summer 2011

They came for lunch, six Djuuwin women ranging from young to elderly, driving up from further down the river and bringing baskets with them, ordinary baskets with bread and picnic plates as well as baskets of plaited lomandra leaves.[1]

We sat at the dining room table, and no one seemed to find anything incongruous in using modern serving spoons at the same time as a traditional stone knife. The small implement looked like any other stone till I took it in my hand and realised it was a perfect fit, that one side cut as well as any tool in my kitchen while the other rounded side could grind. This small tool with no handle may have looked primitive but in fact it was almost perfect, made for the smallness of a woman's hand.

They left the stone with me, along with one of the lomandra baskets and other gifts. I have been using it ever since; it doesn't get blunt like metal knives. Perhaps it will still be in use in one or two hundred years' time – unless it is thrown out by someone who looks at it and sees just a rock. At school and university I had been taught that 'hafted' tools with handles were superior, a sign of humanity's great technological leap forward. But this small tool was made to be cradled in the hand. It didn't need the extra leverage a handle would give it.

The women were from the Indigenous community 'down river'. One had read something I wrote about this valley many years ago and they wondered if I knew more than I had put into print. These women had never been here before, but they knew my land, could tell me where the fig trees and kurrajongs were, and why. They told me to watch for the clematis in spring, to see how it would form a highway to show the young girls where to go to gather the young inner stringybark that makes waterproof fishing line and string and many other woven products.

Five hundred or five thousand years ago, or even more, trees that gave food, medicine or other useful materials like sticky saps for bird traps or seeds for making torches were planted where they were needed, near places where ceremonies would be held, by camping sites, or as a signpost at the base of the ridge that this was the easiest way to get from the valley up to the tableland above. Everywhere we went that day, those women knew what we'd see before we came to it because their ancestors had planted the ancestors of those trees. I have walked this land and studied it for forty years, taken notes, written about the ecological successions, identified the plants and tracked wombats, pythons and brown snakes, but in many, even most ways, they knew it far better than I, from lore handed down in a continuous tradition for thousands of years.

The lower parts of the end of the Araluen Valley and the lower part of our property were profoundly changed by intermittent gold mining from the early 1850s until World War 2, when the dredges finally stopped churning up the river, although they never came up as far as where our house has been built. The creek flats have been turned over possibly many times looking for specks of gold. As you wander through what looks like untouched bush you'll find Chinese stone water races, mullock heaps, even the remnants of fireplaces or the vague outline of huts from long ago. The red gums that used to line the creek have been replaced by lines of casuarinas that once grew in only a few spots up a couple of gullies but spread as the creek was disturbed by humans and by floods, churning up the damaged land, sweeping away tents and grog shops, heaving soil and boulders and washing them down to the sea.

And yet, about 150 years later, these women knew what they would find here. Trees chopped down to feed the wood-fired dredges or for farmers' fence posts left seed behind in the soil. Those trees, bushes and climbers had been planted in the right place and so their offspring grew again, out of a devastated land, to take their place.

The land had shaped Australia's Indigenous nations, as it would shape the new settlers' lives and cultures too. But it was also shaped in its turn by hundreds of generations of women. Indigenous women made parts of Australia a linked series of farms that were so unlike traditional European farms that white settlers, and even anthropologists, few of whom were botanists or had lived a hunter–gatherer life themselves, either failed to recognise them or, until recently, underestimated their significance.

If you don't know what to look for in this valley, you might assume that the gotu kola that can help ease arthritis grows near the waterholes fortuitously – or the headache plants or best medicinal sap trees[2] – and never realise that the roots of the murrnong, or yam daisy (*Microseris lanceolata*), are fat because the best ones were selected to regrow by women. You won't know that the blady grass that cuts your fingers to the bone if grasped will give a rich harvest of oily seeds that can be ground into a paste and make delicious pancakes when fried on hot rocks by the fire. The tablelands above us are too cold and dry for a hundred kilometres for bunya nut or sandpaper and Port Jackson fig trees to grow, unless they were sheltered when young and watered. The bunyas and figs that grow in the gullies near areas of special significance to Indigenous women must have been deliberately planted, the seeds gathered at some gathering or festival and carried here – the nearest natural bunya nut plantings are too far away for birds to have carried the seed.

The women men don't see

Probably more than half, even nine-tenths, of the food in Indigenous diets was hunted, collected, caught or planted and then harvested by women. But looking at colonial paintings in art galleries, the classic Indigenous food-gathering theme is 'bloke with dead kangaroo and spear'.

Women turned areas near good water sources into living larders, with a range of foods that would be available not just at the various seasons of the year but also in years of extremes[3]: wattles that only give edible seeds in droughts, orchids that only flower and produce fat tubers for baking after wet years of flood. Some food sources like ant larvae were left for really bad drought years when there was little else available. Even in regions where there were permanent houses, large gatherings would rotate to different places so that food sources weren't overused. In other areas food would be harvested only in certain seasons or even every three, six or more years, so they wouldn't be exhausted.

Most cultures have their own traditional starch foods, from rice in Southeast Asia to south American maize and potatoes, north American wild rice, Africa's pearl and finger millet and fonio, Hawaiian taro … it would take a book in itself to list them all, from cassava, tapioca, millet and yams to the chestnut and hazelnut flours used in rocky areas of the Mediterranean where grains don't grow well.

Starchy food also played a major part in the Indigenous Australian diet, and varied across the country. In the outback grasslands, Australian millet (*Panicum decompositum*) was harvested from vast fields of five-hundred hectares or more, using much the same techniques that were used in Europe: slashing down the stems while the plants were still green, leaving them piled up to dry, then beating out the seed, leaving the straw behind and winnowing to get rid of the seed husks by throwing the husk-covered seeds in the air on a windy day, so the lighter husks were blown away, leaving a growing pile of seeds. These were then ground into flour using smaller grinder stones on larger flat ones, and then baked on hot rocks. In central Australia, spores of nardoo were collected, ground and baked as cakes. Portulaca was also spread out in heaps to dry, then shaken, leaving piles of tiny, oil-rich seeds behind.

In tropical areas, wild rice (*Oryza* species) were grown and harvested. In the coastal forested areas tubers were eaten more than breads or cakes from seeds, but tree seeds from various acacias, quandongs, kurrajongs, Moreton Bay chestnut, velvet bean (*Mucuna gigantea*) and many, many others were planted, harvested, treated to counter their toxicity by leaching them for days or weeks in water and other techniques, then made into breads or cakes.[4]

But even in forested areas there were many grass seeds that were planted, harvested and cooked, and well as seeds from ground covers like pigweed, the oily seeds of which can be made into a quick and delicious 'paper bread' by wiping the paste onto a hot rock by the fire.

A paper-like bread was also made from many sources of starch harvested from ferns, palm, burrawangs, cycads, and rock orchid stems, although once again you need to know how to do this safely.

Tubers and roots were also a major source of food, with the murrnong possibly the most important one in much of New South Wales and Victoria. Bracken root was baked in Tasmania. Only young and tender roots were harvested then placed on grass laid on hot stones by the fire, with another covering of grass so they steamed as they baked. In our valley, in the rare areas that have not been devastated by introduced animals, various crops of edible orchids carpet the ground from late winter to early summer. You need to know which are edible (and I am carefully not mentioning their names, as many are now endangered). But twenty minutes' digging could easily feed a dozen people. The tubers are starchy, often sweet, each with its own flavour. In areas where edible lilies and edible orchids were cultivated, they would be so thick that you could gather handfuls once you'd scraped back the soil.

Women also tended the water sources. The first job each day was to sweep away the accumulated animal droppings from the night before, keeping the water clean and drinkable. Use of water was women's lore, passed on to the children: yes, you can swim in this pool (only if you know where the crocodile is sleeping), but don't swim or wash in this hole as it is for drinking only. Clean this pool with coals from last night's fire: when the charcoal has settled at the bottom, it's safe to drink.

Why has the vital role women played in Indigenous agriculture and food gathering been relatively ignored, especially in comparison to the acknowledgement of firestick farming? Partly it is because any bloke with a box of matches can tell himself he understands firestick farming (he probably doesn't), but it's also because those who wrote history, colonial records or published diaries in the first hundred years of European colonisation here were mostly men, from a culture that undervalued women's contribution in their own homelands. It's telling that during the food shortages of the early Sydney Cove colony, only one officer, Lieutenant William Dawes, appears to have asked an Indigenous woman about local foods.

But the sheer complexity of knowing what to harvest, when and how – when getting it wrong could have deadly consequences – also meant much of the knowledge was lost relatively quickly.[5] Once local communities of women were forcibly taken from their own lands, they might not know how to recognise, harvest or prepare the new plants around them. The knowledge of a displaced people, where knowledge isn't written down but taught by example, is soon lost. Comparing our local bush foods with those of Arrente women in the 1990s, they told me that they were still trying to remember what their grandmothers had told them when they were children. Oral tradition had kept a vast and complex knowledge for tens of thousands of years, but it only needed two generations of women to stop passing it on, and much lore could be gone.

The potential deadliness of some foods when ill-prepared, such as Moreton Bay chestnuts, also meant that even when the knowledge of how to prepare them was passed on to colonial women, they were hesitant to use it. There was also a stigma of poverty attached to using 'bush' foods, an admission that you couldn't afford 'proper' food. We kids feasted on bunya nuts in southeast Queensland in the 1950s and 1960s, throwing the giant nut clusters into the fire and burning our fingers as we ate the roasted nut. But despite their abundance, I don't remember any adult even tasting one, although as they allowed us to eat them, they must have known they were safe to eat.

It's also difficult to appreciate the sheer depth of racism. The schools of my childhood actively discouraged or wouldn't admit Indigenous kids, because they were 'dirty' or 'spread diseases', or 'too stupid to learn and bad for discipline'. One of the girls I sat next to in class admitted once, in a whisper, that her mother wasn't Indian, as we had been told, but Indigenous. She moved seats soon after, and I think regretted telling me a secret that might have got her expelled if I'd spread the story. My grandmother, in particular, was paranoid that the slightly darker than northern European skin I'd inherited from her might make me appear Indigenous, especially in my childhood when my skin was suntanned.

At school and in church we were informed that the Indigenous races were, quite literally, subhuman. My year 7 class, in a school I will not name, as today it is a strong force against racism, even had an Indigenous skull on display, brought in by one of my fellow students. Our science teacher showed us how (in her words) 'the brain cavity was smaller than in other "intelligent" races'. My neurosurgeon grandfather informed me that skull size and shape had no bearing on intelligence. But even though I argued with my teachers about some aspects of history, this misapprehension was so deep and value-laden that I left it alone.

The lost lore of women

Indigenous women did pass on a lot of their lore to European women; several elderly white women passed some of that on to me, and others. In the nineteenth century, when more Indigenous cultures were intact and the people still allowed to live on the land they knew, white women too were rarely regarded as reliable authorities. And if Indigenous people generally were regarded as subhuman, an Indigenous woman was regarded as an even lower being. Women's knowledge, and interests, whatever the colour of their skin, was regarded as inherently trivial. Even in my youth it was almost impossible for a woman to become a university lecturer rather than a tutor or research assistant, or a scientist rather than a laboratory assistant. In the 1960s many Australians quite seriously believed that a women was incapable of learning to drive well, and that even if a female could pass the exams, their hysterical temperament made them unfit to be managers, doctors, politicians or barristers. White male anthropologists talked to Indigenous men, not Indigenous women. Even if they had, Indigenous women may not have talked about women's business to men.

The land with no ovens or cooking pots

Indigenous women's land management, food storage and cooking also left few easily recognised remnants. A fridge is still a fridge, decaying in a dump forty years after it chilled its last leftover pizza, but dried bogong moth cakes, underground caches of semi-dried bunya nuts or baskets of dried fish or eel last at most a few years. Grinding stones or the small women's knife/grinder that I use now don't look like tools unless you have been shown how they can be used.

Indigenous Australians used ovens. But unlike the easily recognised European bake houses, these were in-ground ovens, in use from Cape York to South Australia. A hole was dug, lined with rock, and then a fire was lit on the rocks. Once the rocks were red hot the ashes and coals were removed, a layer of leaves, seaweed or damp grass was added, and then the food: from meats to eggs, green vegetables, tubers, or cakes made from ground seeds or nuts, sometimes with added fat or fruits. At this stage water might be poured into the oven, to clear off the ashes and help steam the food. The food was wrapped in clay, or leaves, or barks, or seaweed to add flavour, or sometimes left in skin and feathers to protect the meat inside. It was then covered with more greenery and/ or soil, to bake for hours or overnight.

Ground ovens have several advantages over above-ground ovens. They are faster to make and don't need to be waterproof. The meat and other food in a ground oven is safe from flies and can be left for days, if necessary, without rotting, and may still even be warm. It is almost impossible to overcook food in a ground oven (not totally impossible: I've managed to burn a chicken and tubers), nor do you need to tend it while it cooks. The food stays juicy; the herb and wrappings add flavour; tubers soften, which is especially important if they are slightly fibrous, like young kurrajong root. A ground oven can be used for years, decades or centuries. But unless you know what it is, it just looks like a hole in the ground.

Large shells were used to roast or boil food, or food might be placed in rock pools and hot rocks added till the food was cooked. These techniques were fast and effective, but left no easily recognised traces, unless you know what to look for: small rock pools surrounded by an unusual richness of food plants, nearby grinding stones, or the slivers of rock nibbled by women's teeth into a fast cutting tool. Like the 'pots', these didn't have to be carried from place to place but could be made on the spot, as you needed them. These 'disposable' knives are one of the most common, but rarely recognised, remnants of the cooks of two hundred years ago.

Food was also steamed by placing it on woven mats of green vegetation on top of fire, or by wrapping meats and tubers in big balls of leaves, cress or moist seaweed, or in balls of clay, and baked by the fire. Once again these techniques used what was to hand but left no archaeological remnants. Nor did the baskets made of bulrush fibre that were used to cook tubers in central Victoria, left by the fire overnight to roast slowly, then eaten hot or cold.

Ancient Greek and Roman pottery amphoras are still being dug up from thousands of years ago. Indigenous drinks were made in containers of wood, shell, paperbark or leather: light to carry, quickly made, but decomposing quickly – excellent from the point of view of leaving no pollution behind, but of little use to an archaeologist a few hundred years later.

The flat rocks used to make cakes or breads are also difficult to recognise unless you look for them specifically. Rocks are often dusty, and that layer of dust helped seal foods and stopped them sticking to the rock, as did the natural oil in many of the seed and nut pastes. Fruit might be mixed with the starches extracted from a wide range of plants, then baked on the hot rocks, or starches made into a kind of porridge cake mixed from crushed kurrajong or other seeds, sweetened with honey. Waterlily, bulrushes and other plants gave large amounts of pollen which was also used as a basis for cakes and breads.

As well as being baked in ground ovens, or baked on a spit over coals, or softened and 'cooked' in acid fruit pulp, fish was also cooked on a platform of green branches propped up over the coals of a fire – much more delicious than baking, which can dry out the flesh, or frying, which can toughen it.

Smaller animals – the kind caught by women and children, like snakes, lizards and small birds, also needed no cooking implements beyond a small knife/scraper, though they did need skill. Snakes had to be stretched over a fire, and kept reasonably taut until the reflex movements after death stopped. They were then put on the ground, the belly sliced and the guts scooped out, and the head and neck cut off. Then cuts were made near each vertebrae, deep into the flesh. The snake could then be rolled up, a bit like a long coiled sausage, and cooked on hot, but not red hot, coals, turning several times so it cooked evenly. Goannas also needed their entrails removed, and their poison glands. An experienced cook could remove these through the goanna's mouth, so that ash or sand wouldn't adhere to the cut and make the meat gritty.

It was even easier to cook a flying fox, and as flying foxes mostly only eat foods that aren't toxic to humans, like blossom and fruit, their entrails needn't be removed. The fur was singed off over the fire as they were held by the wings, then the wing membranes cut out, then they were roasted in their skin at the edge of the fire.

Nor were there easily recognisable purpose-built Indigenous food storage areas, like cellars. In arid country many hundreds of kilos of grain and dried fruits would be parched – dried – and stored in caves, hollow trees, in baskets or bags made from skins or intestines or wooden containers. Nardoo flour was stored in woven bags, hung from trees. In wetter, forested areas bunya nuts were stored in giant pits and dried fruit in woven bags, loosely woven so the fruit could dry out if the ran wet it. Wooden and woven containers also held dried eggs or tubers that had been grated and then dried to powder or made into cakes. Fish, eels and whale meat were smoked and dried, hung from lines and stored in baskets hung from trees. European food-storage areas were defensible, in cellars or storerooms that could be locked or bolted. Indigenous emergency supplies needed only preservation, not defence.

Even the cooking tools that were carried from camp to camp and used by generations of women may be hard to recognise: the small handled knives and grinding tools that fit snugly into a woman's small hand, the fine-crafted hardwood digging sticks, with fire-hardened tips, up to two metres long. I used a digging stick instead of a spade in my vegetable garden for more than a decade – exactly what was needed for planting seedlings, or digging up a few carrots without bending down – until a guest tossed it into the fire, thinking it was kindling. It was perhaps the best gardening and farming tool I have ever used, but unrecognisable unless you had been shown what it was capable of.

The food we still don't see

When you are used to orchards of neat rows of trees, two or three native figs, some tussocks and a carpet of flowers near a waterhole don't look like farming. But if 'mobile agriculture' was hard to recognise, so were many, or even most of the foods harvested by Indigenous women. They still are.

'Bush tucker' has only been popularised in the past three decades. Even now, few Australians could name a dozen native fruits (there are hundreds, possibly thousands), and probably no native grains, tubers or spices. Despite being part of the gardening/plant loving community, I have only met a handful of non-Indigenous people who can look at a patch of relatively untouched bush and think 'Look at all the food'. Even those who can are usually expert in only a small part of Australia's varied ecologies. To be a botanical anthropologist you need to know not only botany and anthropology, but also be intimate with the area you are studying. The latter takes years or even decades to understand, even with good teachers, as the plants and productivity of the land can vary in seasons that may be years or decades long.

Many traditional foods are so foreign to modern and colonial Australian culture that their contribution and lore have been ignored, apart from a few like bogong moths, 'witchetty grubs' (a catch all name for many different larvae, as long as it's fat, white and wriggling) and ant 'honey'. As I write this, the sweet white sacks of condensed 'lerp honey' are ripe, each about the size of a sultana, the leaves falling to the ground so thickly that it takes about ten minutes to fill a cup. It's time to dig the wombat berry tubers, leaving enough for the vine to keep growing, and the orchid tubers (but I won't, as they are now protected), and a dozen other seasonal foods, like bee and termite larvae – a bit like the modern supermarket's 'on special, this week only'.

These can all be made into dishes that Westerners will enjoy – as long as you don't tell them what they are eating. It has taken more than two hundred years for kangaroo and emu meat to gain limited acceptance, despite their similarity to beef and chicken. I doubt there will ever be wombat berry tubers in the supermarket, and not just because the harvesting season is so short, and in dry years there should be no harvest at all. Our culture already has a wide variety of cultivated tubers, and a new offering would need to be not just good to eat, but have some major health or taste benefit to be worth attempting to market.

Few Australians even know that Australia has many species of native bee. Even fewer would be prepared to eat bee larvae, as well as bee honey. Possibly the one species that has really thrived since colonial settlement are possums, but although many suburbanites are happy to trap them and relocate them (which usually leads to a lingering death for fiercely territorial possums), even those who countenance their destruction wouldn't eat them.

Most of the deliberately cultivated living larder has also been destroyed by settlement. The murrnong was the staple food over most of eastern New South Wales and Victoria, a bright yellow flower that early explorers said carpeted the ground to the horizon. It's sweet, starchy and prolific – ten minutes' digging will feed a family for a day. Sheep and feral pigs and goats, in particular, will seek them out, though they can survive light stocking, especially if they are protected by fallen trees or on near-vertical banks. Tens of thousands of hectares of native millet and other grain-bearing species have been replaced by introduced grasses that provide more feed for cattle or sheep. Waterways have been dammed, contaminated and their water taken for irrigation, removing the vast harvests of native waterlily, bulrushes, water chestnuts, as well as the massive catches of giant fish like Murray cod, freshwater mussels and other plenitude from waterways.

But there is a more profound reason why the contribution of Indigenous women to the 'natural' landscape has been ignored: you need to know the land and its plants well to recognise it. Colonial settlers lived on meat, golden syrup and damper, suffering nutritional disease like Barcoo rot and scurvy in the midst of a vast richness of indigenous grains, tubers and fruits. An outsider here, looking at the mountain slope, just sees 'the bush'. Only someone who can recognise thousands of species will even see the patchwork of hundreds of interlocking niche ecologies. You can't understand the significance of kurrajong 'signposts' unless you can tell what a kurrajong coppice looks like among the eucalypt trees from several kilometres away.

Utilising a living larder is far more complex than learning how to plant apple or lemon trees, water and feed them, spray for pests, then pick and eat the fruit. If you want to learn the ecologically sustainable way to harvest kurrajong roots, native bee larvae or the other native foods and useful plants in this valley, you need to know not just thousands of species but also the different times and ways those species will fruit, flower and send out seedlings or root systems in years that can range from ten millimetres of rain in eleven months to 575 millimetres in a single day, both of which I have experienced here. Other years, decades and even centuries have been even more extreme.

Most visitors here look at the ground and see grass. In fact there are at least forty species of ground cover in every few square metres, and probably more I haven't identified or that are only noticeable in extremes of drought or wet, when some plants do well as others become dormant. You need years of studying the land to even begin to understand how Indigenous women manipulated it.

Huntin', shootin' and fishin'

But even the first colonials could recognise that Indigenous men contributed by hunting, even if the burning and hunting techniques were misunderstood. Europeans had come from a culture where hunting, shooting and fishing were admired, whether legally by a gentleman or on someone else's land by a skilled poacher.

Ask a kid what Indigenous people ate and they'll probably tell you kangaroos.

But in my area, as in many parts of Australia that have more wallabies than roos, kangaroo was a small, infrequent part of the diet, and wallaby even less so due to its tougher, gamier texture. Many of the clan would even have been unable to eat kangaroo meat because of its kinship associations.[6] (Others would have been unable to eat other foods, for similar reasons, but this is an area that is complex to explain, nor do I have the right to explain it.) Possum, which also provides superb soft, warm fur, is tastier, and relatively easy and fast to catch if you look for possum scratches on a tree and know where the possum is sleeping. But possums were caught and skinned by women and children.

Duck was another staple food here – early settlers claimed there were so many you could shut your eyes, shoot into the air, and six would fall down as your shot scattered. But duck catching, too, was women's work. Fish were another staple – like today, most Indigenous settlement follows the coast or inland river systems. In these days of overfishing, over irrigation and pollution, we often forget just how rich our waterways used to be in fish. Permanent stone fish traps, or temporary stringybark ones, catch large numbers of fish with little work. Fish flesh is also more easily flaked then dried or smoked as 'travel food' than kangaroo, which needs to be thinly sliced before it's dried or it will become flyblown or rot.

It is also surprisingly heavy to carry a dead kangaroo back several kilometres to camp. Once you've got it there you need to butcher it for fast cooking, or slice off bits as they cook while the kids are clamouring for dinner. Anecdotally, cooking the result of a roo hunt was a chore. As one woman told me, 'It's no good waiting all day for the men to bring the meat back – you get something else to feed the kids.'

Roo hunts were a bit like modern football games: a way for blokes to get together and show off their skill and fitness, then congratulate each other afterwards. Spearing food is dramatic, but it's also less efficient than many other ways of getting dinner. The kangaroo hunts were as much ceremonial as sport, often with men from several clans gathering to work out hunting strategy. Sometimes exceptional runners would take it in turns to run after the roos, with new runners waiting at points where they knew the roos would likely pass, keeping pace with them until the roos were exhausted. This needed not just knowledge of the roos' likely behaviour, but speed and stamina. At other times the spear holders would neither run nor walk. As other hunters drove the small mobs of roos into one larger mob, the spear holders would wait downwind so the animals didn't catch their scent, each waiting hunter standing on one leg to blind the roos to the characteristic 'two-legged' human stance, holding their faces side-on and eyes half-closed, looking sideways or upwards so their close-together predators' eyes were less noticeable. The roo hunts were more like the Olympic Games, but with a far deeper social and spiritual complexity, than a modern bloke in a ute, poking his firearm through the window and going 'bang'.

I have lost count of the number of farmers who have told me that 'shrubby regrowth' shows that the land needs to be burnt. In our area, at least, wallabies ate the young trees and shrubs, and so kept the land 'cleared', not fire. Shoot the wallabies and you get regrowth.

How a woman catches a duck

Indigenous women didn't just 'gather' food. They also hunted and fished, but without the drama of men's spear hunts. Turtles and echidnas follow certain routes at different times of the year. Snakes, bees, goannas, possums, water dragons, fat wonga pigeons, bettongs, bandicoots and ducks return to certain spots according to the time of day. In mid-summer, in the pools of our creek, for example, ducks fly back from the grassy areas where they've been grazing at about 4.30 p.m. in late spring, when the shadow begins to cover the valley. (This time is area and seasonally specific – different duck species and different ecosystem niches will mean different times for returning to water at different times of the year.)

Mrs Meredith[7] described women catching ducks of the Murray River in the 1840s by spreading a net over the water before the ducks returned for the night. The women gathered in strategic places to drive the ducks towards the net then threw pieces of bark over their heads to make the ducks land on what they thought was safe water, instead of flying away. Their legs became tangled in the net and the catch could be hauled in. But a single woman could catch a duck – or even two or three – by herself.

Slide into the water gently, so you don't disturb algae or waterweed – ducks will notice any disturbance. Sink under the water. Use a hollowed reed to breathe; you won't need to wait long. As the duck lands and begins to paddle above you, grab a leg, haul down, then swim up to the air. Breathe deeply and pull the duck's head sharply so the neck snaps. Carry your duck to shore. Bake it in hot ashes – the feathers will singe away and the guts shrink.

The myth that the land must burn

Firestick farming as undertaken by Indigenous men was and is equally misunderstood, and usually vastly overestimated in the area that was burnt, the severity of the burning, and its contribution to food supply.[8] It involved lighting small controlled fires to encourage new, young, nutritious grass tips for kangaroos (who don't like long shaggy grass) and bowerbirds, or so that flocks of cockatoo would come to dig up the grass roots, or goannas to feast on the flesh of rotting burnt animals. All these would in turn feed the tribes responsible for the fires. The second motivation was to burn back shrubby regrowth and make walking easier, or to trigger the blooming of ground orchids and other plants with roots that were good to eat or had medicinal or other uses. Small fires every few years made selected patches of land different: instead of the whole bush being green or dry, or all the wild plums fruiting at once, it could be managed to harvest different bits at different times.

This sounds simple. It isn't. There is no 'one size fits all' fire management strategy that works for the whole continent, or even for areas a few kilometres apart. Each area, and each year, had its own fire regime, with many variables taken into account. Yet forestry departments, National Parks and Wildlife and bushfire brigades are now encouraged to 'control burn', justified as a modern form of Indigenous firestick land management, with little or no specialised knowledge of which areas need to be burnt, when, and in what way.

Firestick farming is complex. Land wasn't burnt every year, nor was it burnt at the same time of the year. (Modern 'control burning' is almost invariably done in late winter and spring.) You had to know the right time to burn: in some regions or small patches that was every few years, in others only when so many blossoms set seed on the black wattle trees (*Acacia mearnsii*) and the gang-gang cockatoos arrived to eat them that you knew a hot, dry year was coming, and you had to burn more to stop big fires next year.

Many areas, like our 'neverbreak' (*Backhousia myrtifolia*) dry rainforest or the nearby plumwood (*Eucryphia moorei*) forests, and most forests that have – or once had – a fern understorey were never firestick farmed, and should never be if the forest is to survive. If those forest types are burnt then the trees and their associated shrubs and sub-shrubs and ground covers may be replaced by species that have evolved to cope with repeated fires and burn all too well, their seeds only ripening after a fire. But a fire-dependent ecosystem may need burning at least every decade so that seeds can germinate in the heat of the fire, or even more often after two or three wet years.

Few members of bushfire brigades, or even the officials who order the burns, could explain the differences between fire-sensitive, fire-resistant and fire-dependent ecosystems. There is a general flattening out of understanding, an over-simplification of the 'Australian bush recovers from fire' type that is trotted out after every bushfire, without any recognition that different species and ecosystems have completely different relationships with fire and wildfire.

So called 'controlled' burning has created fire-dependent forests. Ironically, large parts of Australia are now far more prone to bushfire, all in the name of trying to reduce it. Once you have created a fire-dependent landscape, it does need burning to reduce the fuel load. But even in these areas the wrong kind of burning increases the risk of uncontrolled bushfire, it doesn't decrease it. In fire-dependent areas, burning in the wrong way and at the wrong time can leave dead wood that will make a bushfire burn hotter, as well as encourage grass growth that may dry like tinder in summer.

'The bush' is not homogenous. Even in a small area of, say, fifty hectares there may be several forest types, with different burning regimes needed to maintain them. Most fire agencies try to control burn

Back-burning

'Back-burning' is different from 'control burning'. Back-burning is an extremely effective technique to stop an existing fire, as long as you know the terrain, and how the winds are likely to change while you back-burn.

Back-burning creates a firebreak in front of the fire, to lessen its fuel and improve access for fighting it. Fire burns faster up a hill. If a fire is coming down the slope, a small back-burning fire lit at the base of the hill will also create its own wind that may drive the fire back onto land it has already burnt. If a back-burn is done well, and the fire front isn't too extensive, it may even mean getting the fire under control reasonably swiftly.

Local bushfire brigades used to be very good indeed at using back-burning to save farmhouses or stop a fire entirely. Now the organisation and strategy of firefighting units is centralised, and on a regional basis, ticking off a certain number of hectares each year. In doing so they are making the bushfire danger far greater, creating larger areas that burn easily because the only plants that survive are the fire-dependent ones that burn hard, fast and often.

I have watched lightning strike a forest of mostly gully and ribbon gums and seen the fire spread, eating up the ground even as the rain fell. I have also seen lightning strikes in the local plumwood forest in a dry season, where the trees blackened but no fire spread in the fire-resistant system. But if this area had been sprayed with diesel to get a good burn (as frequently happens in a 'control burn') at the driest time of the year with a strong dry wind, the fire-resistant species would die, to be replaced with ones that thrive on frequent burning, and are much more likely to burn fast and hot.

Properly done – that is, a slow, cool burn – control burning does reduce the risk of bushfire in many areas, getting rid of dry grass and thatch and dangling bark. But if the fire is too hot it can kill shrubs or branches, leaving more dead wood to perhaps burn later in the summer in a bushfire. But control burning (well done or bad) will not make an area totally safe from bushfire. In the severe 2003 Deua fires near to

those who know the area are no longer in control of the way a fire is fought. The difficulty in getting permission from far-off bureaucrats to back-burn – a decision that needs to be made swiftly and by those on the ground – means that this technique is now used infrequently. Local volunteer firefighters from families who have fought fires in their area for generations, with the knowledge of how the wind will change or where the fire will spread passed on from generation to generation, may even be denied access to a fire area because it is been deemed too risky to fight the fire due to possible insurance liability. Volunteer firefighters along with the equipment bought by the local communities may now be ordered to fight fires far from their local area, leaving their own neighbourhood vulnerable. Meanwhile, the controllers in their air-conditioned offices wonder why experienced firefighters leave the bushfire brigades, and why younger locals don't join.

my home, a bushfire that started from lightning strikes raged through the same area three times in as many months. After the second fire it seemed that everything that could burn was gone, but then the wind changed, hot and dry and fast. Within hours the bushfire was burning back onto land that had already been burnt so severely that there were no trees or bush, just blackness. But the fire kept burning. This third time it burnt the soil itself, fusing it hard and black. In weather like that, no control burning will be effective.

As I write this in September 2012, more than a dozen blazes threaten New South Wales and Victoria. All of them are from control burns that gathered disastrous strength in gale-force winds that had been predicted at least ten days in advance. Each of these fires is the result of a refusal to consider easily available data like wind and temperature forecasts, and assess the high fuel load after our two summers of reasonable rainfall. Their severity is partly because these areas have been control burned so often that the only species left are those that can survive fire, and burn hard and hot. They are also a result of our culture's deeply held mindset that sees 'the bush' as homogenous, so simple that it only needs hours or days of study, instead of decades of observance matched with the inherited lore of tens of thousands of years.

Firestick farming is an attractive concept for every covert pyromaniac or public planner anxious for a big bang result for as little money, training and effort as possible. 'It's traditional,' they say, as they set alight yet another forest. It isn't – or not as it is mostly practised now.

The farms that no one noticed

Were the living larders created by Indigenous women agriculture? Yes, but not as we know it: intensive areas that are cropped either annually or even several times a year, leaving the soil bare in between, or planting orchards into otherwise bare soil. In most parts of Europe and the Americas regular drizzle means that bare soil soon becomes green growth. In Australia bare soil is an environmental hazard, where thunderstorms, wind, or months and even years without rain mean the topsoil washes or blows away. In northern Australia, the deadly bacterium *Buckholdereia pseudomallei* may also kill if the soil is disturbed.

(Our area appears to have a least one similar and potentially dangerous organism.) Possibly those who attempted New Guinea-type agriculture discovered that soil disturbance in the wrong place could kill.[9]

The living larders profoundly changed the land, but without radically disturbing the soil.[10] Some may have been created over hundreds of years. Others, from anecdotal evidence, may have been planted over one or two good seasons, when old watercourses dried up or river's courses changed. The most intensive farming was usually around good campsites, often sheltered water sources, but they could also be near areas of sacred significance, where the fruits, medicines or other crop might be needed. They might also be deliberately distant from camp sites, so that too much use wouldn't damage the plants or soil, and so future generations wouldn't be tempted to over-harvest. The 'larders' often only needed to be planted once, then, if they had been planted in exactly the right place, for hundreds of years new seedlings would take the place of the old trees or bushes.

Nor were the fruits and vegetables planted in the intensive way we use today, with possibly thousands of similar fruit trees grown together. I suspect the female 'farmers' deliberately created areas that would not tempt their descendants to take too much, stay too long or come too often, knowing that the land would not sustain them indefinitely. Sometimes an area would have many different fruits, tubers, seeds and so on that would all be harvested together over a period of weeks. In other places there would be fewer, to encourage a much shorter stay.

Indigenous women's farming was not primitive, nor a precursor to 'proper' farming. It was a sophisticated, deliberate choice of land use, and that choice was probably made many times over many thousand of years, as women heard about other forms of farming, and rejected them. Early agriculture in the form of domesticated bananas and other crops had begun in New Guinea even by the time that land was separated from northern Australia by rising waters about eight thousand years ago. Indigenous nations traded with those to the north and, as shown after European settlement, were eager to take up new technologies they considered useful, from metal axes to replacing dingos, which don't bark, with the new dogs that would warn of intruders. Their land-use techniques were diverse and adaptable.

But one technique they did not employ was carving up the land and using it over and over again each year. They moved on, letting the land recover till they returned. Even some of their ceremonial gatherings depended on the seasons and the resilience of the land. The bunya feasts, for example, varied according to the crop, as bunyas do not fruit reliably every year.

Most of Australia does not have deep topsoil. Fertile river flats and rich volcanic soil are relatively rare and, even where the soil is fertile, rainfall can be erratic, with droughts that can be decades or hundreds of years long, or violent storms dropping seven hundred millimetres in a few hours. Annual cropping creates bare soil that blows or washes away. It needs irrigation in dry times and as Australia is an old, dry continent, these can be frequent. Our soils are usually salty from millennia of winds from the sea, so every instance of irrigation builds up the salt level a little more.

The agriculture Indigenous women developed worked, but only for a population of probably less than a million across the continent. This population was limited to what the land could supply in the worst years.

Unlike many Polynesian cultures (and European ones too), Australian oral history doesn't have stories of mass starvation. Instead there are stories of dry years when some enterprising person or ancestor or land spirit (I am using a most inadequate English translation for a varied and complex concept here) discovers a new food source, like succulent ant larvae.

Modern Australian agriculture feeds millions of people, but at a cost. It is a cycle of boom and bust, where shortage in one area due to flood, fire or drought must be replenished from areas far away. It is dependent on fossil fuels, pesticides, herbicides and artificial fertilisers. On the other hand, it is not *necessarily* dependent on these. It is possible to develop intensive and sustainable agricultural systems, but to do so we need to go back to the underpinning philosophy of Indigenous farming – looking at each small piece of land, tree by tree and river bend by river bend, rather than trying to impose 'one size fits all' policies.

The ghosts remain

If you look at our valley even now – after large parts of it have been grazed by heavy footed introduced animals, burnt and otherwise mutilated – you may still see the edible landscape created by thousands of generations of women.

This was once the most generous of valleys with still pools of waterlilies, the stems chopped up as a vegetable, the seeds ground to a rich oily flour to bake cakes and a thin flaky bread a bit like Central American paper bread, spread and cooked quickly on hot stones. The waterholes were rich in ducks, fish, yabbies, freshwater mussels, the gullies planted with fruit and nut trees, berry bushes, edible grasses, the ridges with stands of stringybark, easily accessible, for weaving string and baskets, the 'roads' demarcated with white highways of wonga vine and clematis in late winter and spring, or the easiest ridge to follow marked with a kurrajong tree. Clans met yearly for ceremonies and games as well as feasting, but according to oral tradition and accounts written back in the 1850s the location would rotate so that no area was used more than once every four years here.

The 'old' valley died in the gold rushes. The river was dredged, the trees on the hills chopped down. Only sand and rock and mullock heaps were left, and hills that slumped and avalanched and eroded. But slowly, as the miners moved away, the land stabilised. It even became rich in species again, because so much of the land and its wet gullies were too steep to be cleared or mined. They provided species refuges. First of all bracken, native nettles, water mint and poa tussock grew on the piles of dirt and mullock heaps; then *Bursaria spinosa*, *Hymenanthera violacea*, emu bush and others; then black wattle, blackwood and Araluen gum (*Eucalyptus kartzoffiana*), which grows fast in disturbed soil; then gum trees or dry rainforest species, *Backhousia myrtifolia*, *Dicksonia* tree ferns, and thousands of other species. Finally the casuarina trees that grew on the disturbed creek edges are giving way to the red gums that once grew here.

When I first came here forty years ago, we camped on a small rise by the creek near a fireplace made of a small ring of stones. Years later, my husband, Bryan, decided to make the fireplace more substantial, digging down to properly bed larger rocks. He dug down to sand and charcoal, then more sand and more charcoal, layer after layer …

Suddenly that small rise made sense. It was, indeed, the perfect campsite. Every few decades or once a century, perhaps, the creek flats would flood and the fireplace would be covered in sand and silt. But someone would build a fireplace there again, till over thousands of years, perhaps, the site slowly became a rise.

I had always known that the area around the campsite, near where we now have our house, is richer in native food species than the surrounding areas; that the emu and kangaroo berries here are sweeter or more prolific than those five hundred metres away. But after that lunch with the women from down the river, I saw my own landscape in a different way: the tussocks of blady grass, the wombat berries and oval emu berries that taste sweet instead of cardboard-like; the clematis and stands of stringybark; the kurrajongs, Port Jackson and sandpaper figs; the native cherries, currants and grapes; the orchids; and the groundcover herbs that have so many medicinal uses but vanish with few even knowing they are gone once an area has been sown to introduced pasture.

I live in a land created by tens of thousands of years of women. I had studied it for forty years and still not understood.

How to spear a fish (for blokes)

A good hunter waits.

Stand still, above the pool or waves, your spear held a handspan above the water. Keep waiting.

A good hunter knows if the fish pass at dawn or dusk, if they hide in the warm shallows in winter or sink to the cooler water or currents in the heat. In the pools of our creek, for example, they will head to the small areas of sunlit water to feed at mid-afternoon.

As the fish passes, wait until its head is a handspan beyond the direction of your spear. Strike down. Lift up. You have your fish. It's taken an hour of concentration, and you have only one fish instead of the full net the women will have collected in a fraction of the time. But other men will respect your skill and, just possibly, a European artist will be inspired to paint the strong male body, the macho spears, the bloody fish.

How to catch fish (for women)

A good hunter waits.

Cut the lomandra leaves. Let them wilt a little, but don't let them dry out totally. Plait them, then after the plait is about as long as your hand, weave one of the threads into the start of the plait, so the plaiting slowly turns into a long basket. As you come to the end of each lomandra leaf, overlap it with another to keep the plait continuous.

To turn your basket into a fish trap, stake it into the waves with a stick at high tide, then wait for the tide to fall. Once a fish is in the trap it can't get out. It's no more dramatic than getting a fish out of the fridge (except this way the fish are fresh) and it's possibly the most energy-efficient way to catch fish in the world. You can use the same trap again and again, and then use it to carry the fish, or bush cherries, too.

Sit and gossip while you're waiting for fish to fill your trap, or gather whatever your great-great-grandmothers have planted around the campsite: grass and tussock seeds, berries, murrnong and orchid and young kurrajong roots, medicinal bracket fungi in case someone is ill or a woman is grieving for her dead baby, or the tiny-leafed plants that grow among the wallaby grass that will help stop the aches that come with age and stop old knees swelling so they can walk to the bogong feasts. Or collect the seeds that you chew sparingly, only two or three a day, for the illness that comes with old age, when your ankles swell and you feel breathless and your chest aches like it has been stabbed with a spear.

There's no hurry. The food is all around you, the land shaped for your needs, just as your great-great-grandmothers shaped the small stone tools that you'll use today to grind the seeds before you bake the paste on the hot rocks. If the young girls are going to gather the strands of inner stringybark tomorrow to turn into waterproof fishing line, make them sweets from dried wild cherries, geebungs, Billardiera and Port Jackson figs, mixed perhaps with cooked bracken root or blady grass-seed paste. Eat with laughter and many stories that are part adventure and part instruction about the land.

CHAPTER 5

Terra incognita: Dreams of gold, and a land without grass

Theoretically, Australia should have been colonised by invading Europeans long before 1788, like most of Southeast Asia, Asia, Africa and the Americas. Australia had sandalwood, cedar trees, native pepper and spice species similar to the ones that great trading empires were built on, and granite rocks that hinted at gold deposits. For over two thousand years, traders had been exporting spices like cinnamon and cassia from the East Indies (now Indonesia) using the power of the westerly winds to take boats to Africa and north to China, and from both to wealthy markets further off in Egypt, Rome and the Middle East. By the 1500s, far from Australia being 'out of the way' of the colonial powers, the strong winds meant trading ships headed for these spice treasures sailed far south and west near the west Australian coast before turning northwards up the coast to the Dutch East Indies, India and China. Western Australia was well sited to be a supply post on the way to fabulous wealth.

But western Australia had toxic shrubs[1], rock and sand instead of grasslands, where hay could be cut to feed the animals that supplied vital fresh food on sailings ships. Australia also lacked safe, obvious harbours for sailing ships and easily found fresh water. Add to this relentless winds that prevented ships from manoeuvring safely, high surf on long beaches (a delight for today's tourist brochures but a nightmare for mariners trying to get to shore in small boats), steep cliffs, and coral reefs with teeth on the northerly approaches, which was pretty much the direction that most of the rest of humanity lived.

Geography defeated colonialism.

Australia would be 'discovered' time after time, usually by accident, when the ships' captains were trying to head for somewhere else, either the Spice Islands or the treasure land that was variously named 'Beach' and 'Terra Australis Incognita', or the 'Great Unknown South Land', conjured from humanity's greed, myths and imagination.

Ironically, it was a series of profound misunderstandings of the region's geography that led to the first colonial settlement here[2]: James Cook's HM Bark *Endeavour* voyage to seek the 'land of gold' that so many stubbornly believed *had* to be somewhere east of Australia; Cook's decision not to take the safer north route back to Batavia but head up the east coast instead, despite the dangers of the Great Barrier Reef between the ship and a safe port; a wet year (for the Botany Bay area at least) when he was here which meant that grass grew and springs bubbled; and an eager but incompetent natural historian, Joseph Banks, with political clout and extreme overconfidence, who urged that a colony should be sent across the world to a dangerous harbour with sandy soil and only a small spring of fresh water – far too little water for a colony, even in the best of years.

Only another extraordinary coincidence would enable the first colonial expedition to survive.

The three great myths of Australian history

There were three immutable facts of primary school history until relatively recently, and they still survive in Australian consciousness: Captain Cook discovered Australia in 1770; Blaxland, Wentworth and Lawson were the first people to find a way across the Blue Mountains in 1813, thus unleashing centuries of sheep and settlers west of the Divide; and the early New South Wales colony starved.

None are true. Indigenous clans had been crossing the mountains for tens of thousands of years; William Wentworth may even have been told the approximate path to take by his Indigenous friends. The colony never starved. And Captain Cook (whose rank was really lieutenant, although he was captain of his ship) didn't discover Australia. He had a copy of a centuries-old map showing exactly where Australia was and how he could follow its coast to Batavia (Jakarta) after the *Endeavour* was badly damaged by Antarctic gales while hunting for a different, and mythical, land in the southern Pacific Ocean.

Australia's existence was known to traders and navigators in the northern hemisphere for hundreds or even thousands of years before Cook – it was a great big lump of land down south beyond the Spice Islands. Even the earliest world map we know of, made by Ptolemy of Alexandria in the second century, had a great southern continent. While some maps plonked land in the southern expanse of ocean to 'balance' all the land in the north, many gave a reasonable approximation of where Australia was relative to Indonesia, and even of the northern coastline.

The Indigenous nations of northern Australia traded prized 'Darwin glass' knives, as well as tools, feathers and exotic birds and animals through the Torres Strait islands and eventually north into Southeast Asia. There are anecdotal reports of a wallaby at a Beijing zoo in the 1600s, and of brightly feathered Australian birds. But none of the eager nations establishing colonies or annexing land or ports in Africa, the Americas, the Indian subcontinent, China, Southeast Asia and the Pacific seemed to want to establish a trading port here.

Why not? The most treasured trading lands in the world were only a few days' sail north of Australia: the Spice Islands (now part of Indonesia). Their rich crops of nutmeg, cloves, mace, pepper and cinnamon had been traded for thousands of years by Chinese, Javanese, Indian, Japanese, Cambodian and Siamese (Thai) merchants, followed by the Arab traders. Eventually the spices made their way to Europe to be sold at astronomical prices.

Look at the celebration foods of England and you see Southeast Asian spices: plum pudding, rich in cinnamon and mixed spice, a scrape of nutmeg on the custard, spiced fruit cake, gingerbread, spiced lardy cake. Europe learnt to treasure spices in the Crusades, from 1096 onwards, as European Christian kings tried to take Jerusalem and the Holy Land from the armies of their Islamic enemies (and also sometimes accidentally, and sometimes on purpose, from other Christians too). In the process they made themselves small, temporary Middle Eastern fiefdoms – and developed a love of spices. Spices made bland food fun.

Many also inhibited the rots that could turn stored food deadly. A small bag of pepper could be a knight's fee for a year of work.

Once you were in the general area of the Spice Islands, northern Australia would be hard to miss from the crow's nest on top of a mast, as would smoke on the horizon. Logically, it would be worth exploring south to see if this land had spices too.

It does: a true pepper *(Piper* spp.*)*, native ginger, lemon myrtle *(Backhousia citriodora)*, the pepper-like *Tasmannia* spp., and hundreds of others, all as richly fragrant as those from the Spice Islands. The Dutch and Portuguese found valuable sandalwood too. The monsoonal climate of northern Australia would also have made it suitable to grow plantations of spices to break the existing trading monopolies. Captain Jonathon Carnes would successfully break the European trading monopoly in 1798 when he traded directly with Sumatra to take his first cargo of pepper back to Salem in the United States. The monopolies for sugar, tea and pineapple would also be broken by establishing plantations in other lands. Northern Australia's soil and climate would have been – and still is – suitable for new plantations of spices, tea, coffee, sugar and other wealth-making crops of the era.

Australia also has gold. Admittedly, the local inhabitants hadn't turned the gold into easily stolen treasure troves, but some of those who came here would have recognised granite outcrops as being potentially gold-bearing. There were also vast amounts of iron ore, although the biggest deposits wouldn't be noticed until a small plane carrying the stubborn and far-sighted Lang Hancock accidentally landed on them in the 1960s.

Most temptingly of all, you'd think, the west of Australia was thinly populated, with often friendly inhabitants and no other colonial power in occupation – an excellent place to establish a supply port for the ships that had crossed the Indian Ocean on the strong trade winds and were then heading towards the rich trading lands north of Australia. From the fifteenth to the nineteenth centuries, a third of a ship's crew might die from scurvy because of lack of fresh food. Supply ports were vital.

But a supply port needs safe harbour for ships, and northern and western Australia didn't seem to have any that were sheltered enough for sailing ships to survive cyclones and tropical storms at anchor, nor any large rivers where sailing ships could shelter either.

Australia does have a few superb harbours, but they aren't obvious. This is an old country. Its few large rivers have carved out giant harbours but, like Sydney Harbour and Moreton Bay – both of which Cook sailed past without realising their true extent – many are hidden, protected by almost impassable reefs, islands or narrow openings. The small, high-prowed boats of the Indonesian trepang fisherman, who visited the northern coast from about the mid-seventeenth century, could pull their smaller, lighter craft out of the water onto the beaches. But the large European trading ships had to anchor well offshore in deep water, with the sailors coming to land in small rowboats, unless a pier had been built out into the sea to make loading and unloading easier. No harbour meant no exploration or trade.

Western Australia's best harbour, at what is now Albany, was too far south for most ships riding the westerly trade winds before they turned north to the Spice Islands.

And not only were there no obvious harbours but the long golden beaches of Western Australia with their strong surf and almost constant high westerly winds made it difficult to send ships' boats in to look for water – or, at least, to get back to their ship again easily through surf and against the wind. Few sailors could swim, so an upturned ship's boat in the surf was likely to be fatal. Much of the northern coast of Australia is edged with high cliffs, and the coast north of what is now Perth edged with sand dunes, impossible to see what the land beyond the sand is like. Further north are the rocky islands and the reefs that are now superb marine parks but, back then, meant danger.

Even those high winds that drove the ships towards the coast were a danger. Sailing ships are powered by the wind, but the interplay of sails and rudder means that experienced sailors don't need to go where the wind pushes them: for instance they can manoeuvre north with a westerly wind blowing or tack into a head wind, sailing east into a westerly. But if the wind is too strong – and the trade winds of the southwest can be strong enough to blow you over – you will run out of room to tack and jibe once you are too close to a lee shore. Experienced sailors knew not to get too close to Western Australia, or any lee shore, where the currents as well as the wind might drive you onto rocks or cliffs.

But there was an even more important factor in the delayed European colonisation than the lack of safe harbours: that lack of grass. The western coast that was surveyed by the Dutch and Portuguese was either desert or tussock or button grass – good for browsing wallabies, but not for grazing animals like cattle – or its ground covers were toxic to stock. Many of the early Western Australian colony's animals would die before the toxic plants were identified.

Australia may have been a superb staging point for ships to restock after they'd made the trek across the ocean from Europe and were heading up to Batavia. But without safe harbours, there was no way to do so. And without grass, there was no point.

If it weren't for the produce supplied by livestock kept on board, a ship's crew would have to survive on salted and dried rations or whatever fish they could catch. Sailors shanghaied while they were drunk (a common way to find a crew in most European ports) might eat salt beef or pork so salty it blistered their lips and ship's biscuit that crawled with weevils – they had little choice if they wanted to stay on the ship long enough to reach their home port again. But the captain, lieutenants, mates, ship's master and surgeon, all of whom were responsible for the ship and her crew, expected far better food. Their own stores provided dried fruit, puddings and port, but they needed fresh meat too, from pigs, sheep and small cattle, as well as milk from goats and eggs from hens.

And these animals needed feeding. Men can live on concentrates like salt beef and biscuit for about three months until they begin to die of scurvy. Herbivores need hay daily, a bulky food that easily becomes mouldy in damp sea air. Mouldy hay kills your stock.

You need grass.

Every time there was an opportunity, ships would anchor and the men row ashore, hunting first for fresh water for themselves as well as the animals, laboriously filling barrels then lugging them back in the rowboats to their ship. After that they cut grass, turning it in the sunlight to dry before raking it into large bundles called 'stooks' and carrying it, load after load, back to the animals.

If a ship stayed in one place long enough the animals might be taken ashore to eat the grass, although this too was hard work. It is easy enough to get a cow down a gangplank, but the mind boggles at transporting even a goat in a small rowing boat. But that is what you had to do to survive the months, or even years, at sea.

No harbours, no grass: Australia didn't seem to be able to provide even the basics. But there was another factor, too.

To European eyes, good land meant green vegetation divided into farms. Riches came from fertile farmland, or the jungle-like vegetation of Ceylon, the Philippines, Java and Malaysia. To them, sand and sparse vegetation meant desert, unproductive and useless. They had no experience of cultures that had adapted to the very different land of Western Australia.

Wealth also came from a population that could be either enslaved or at least harnessed to work cheaply. (To some extent it still does. Many of us possibly don't care to examine how our cheap clothes, telecentres or growing superannuation accounts may be based on employing people so desperate that they'll accept starvation wages.) The Indigenous nations' lack of full-time armies may have put them at a disadvantage when they needed to fight for their land. But their lack of obvious armies or groups of obedient workers supervised by an employer, overseer, priest or similar may also have helped them live relatively undisturbed by empires from over the seas for a surprisingly long time.

A thousand years of secrecy and vanished history

History is known by the records left to us. Australia has a long and complex history, but there are few written records before Governor Phillip's colony of convicts arrived in 1788.

Much of our history vanished with the oral traditions of the Indigenous nations. The coastal clans were the ones who would have seen and recorded contact with visitors from China, Southeast Asia and Europe. But these coastal clans were also most vulnerable to the whaling and sealer camps of the 1800s, where whole clans were wiped out – the men killed, the women kidnapped or, in some cases, going willingly as wives. It's worth noting though that Cook and many others were startled when the Indigenous people showed so little surprise at their ships. This lack of jumping up and down and yelling the equivalent of 'look at that' may have been a form of politeness. But it might also have been because this wasn't the first time the onlookers had seen sailing ships.

How much Australian history lies under the sea? Australia's coastline is liberally scattered with rocks, rips and reefs. It is also large and relatively unpopulated. Until the late nineteenth century ships had no way of sending distress calls; flares would only be seen by ships that were close at hand or people on the coast nearby. Roughly (and this is probably an underestimation) a third of ships would vanish before they were retired as unseaworthy. Even in the thoroughly explored Mediterranean, new shipwrecks from ancient Greek and Roman times are still being discovered. It is possible, even likely, that there are more early wrecks undiscovered about Australia's coast. It is also likely that other sailing ships in the past thousand years may have sighted the Australian coast but were wrecked or foundered elsewhere before the navigators could pass that knowledge on.

Between about 1400 and 1800 there was also an obsessive secrecy about trade routes. A map was not just useful – it might make your fortune, or your employer's. If the enemy did not know your route – perhaps through a reef, between islands or using favourable winds and currents – they couldn't follow you, either to attack or take your trade.

It wasn't just nations that kept their secrets. Navigators owned not only their skill but their store of maps, both those written and the even more secret ones they consigned to memory alone (though even memory might be plundered if the Inquisition wanted to know your routes). A good navigator could trade his knowledge for high wages but also for a share of profits. The best navigators could grow even wealthier than captains – assuming they survived. And if they did, it was the navigators' skills that took them there, and back.

This secrecy makes reconstructing explorations of the ocean difficult. We know that maps that show at least a blob of land in the right place for Australia exist. We don't know how many navigators knew of their existence at the time. The maps might even have been based on hearsay: the natives say there is a large land to the south. A map showing a land blob roughly where Australia happens to be doesn't mean that anyone actually came here. Alternatively, ship after ship may have come here and left no sign.

As I write this the discovery of Arab coins on the Wessel Islands, north of Australia, has aroused speculation that Arab traders, too, may have visited Australia. For hundreds of years – and possibly millennia – pepper, nutmeg, and cloves from the Indies and cinnamon from Sri Lanka had been taken to various centres like Malacca and Amboina. Arab traders were among those who took these to the Eastern Mediterranean, for further distribution. Did an enterprising Arab trader decide to head for the source of the wealth? (If a future archaeologist finds my hunks of French flint here in five hundred years' time, I wonder if they will speculate about the possibility of a Neolithic voyage from France to Australia, carrying enough flint to light their fires.)

So much is unknown. Even the maps are open to interpretation. While many ancient maps showed a Great South Land, it may have been added simply because the map makers assumed that the land in the north needed to be balanced by a southern land mass – especially when they showed a Terra Australis Incognita extending all the way to Antarctica.

Some early maps, like the one drawn by Henry VIII's map maker, Jean Rotz, in 1542, do show a reasonably realistic outline of the northern parts of Australia, like Cape York and parts of Arnhem Land, the areas that would have been most accessible to ships sailing around what is now Indonesia, the Philippines and Malaysia. French maps of 1540 and 1570 show a Java la Grande (Large Java) below the present Indonesia, and again there are some similarities between those and the northern coast. In all other details they are inaccurate. But it is possible that the knowledge of northern Australian geography didn't come from European explorers but from Southeast Asian and Chinese traders.

A continent in China's backyard

The history Australians learn at school is still strongly Eurocentric. Even today, an Australian school child is more likely to know of King Henry VIII and his six wives than any of the Chinese emperors. Yet for most of the past few thousand years China was a more powerful nation than England, and far closer to Australia. By the sixth century AD the Chinese knew of a land where men threw boomerangs and animals hopped on their hind legs. In the ninth century, Chinese fleets took control of the spice trade from the Arabs. Chinese maps of the thirteenth century show the land of Greater Java below Java – possibly the northern part of Australia.[3] According to Marco Polo (an often unreliable witness), thirteenth-century China had 3000-ton ships, with crews of several hundred men, sailing between China, Java and India. Thousand-ton ships are more likely, given the accounts in the next two centuries, but it's very possible that Chinese ships were indeed already trading as far south as Java.

By 1403 the new Emperor, Yung-lo, had an army of more than a million men, armed with guns. (Henry V's celebrated army at Agincourt in 1415 was only five thousand men with longbows and arrows, minuscule and primitive compared to the might of China.) Yung-lo's navy had more than a three thousand war ships, as well as two hundred and fifty 'treasure ships' each capable of carrying more than two thousand tons of cargo. Europe's biggest cargo fleet in Venice had only three hundred ships, the largest capable of carrying fifty tons of cargo.

China had traditionally conquered by land, not sea, but Yung-lo was an expansionist. He appointed his grand eunuch Zheng He commander-in-chief of the world's largest collection of fleets, to collect tribute from the barbarians and bring Confucian harmony to the earth, as well as to explore for minerals and collect new plants for medicine or foods. From about 1404–1433 Chinese fleets made seven voyages to Java, Myanmar, India, Sri Lanka, Arabia, Timor and east Africa. One of the fleets may have possibly reached South America (which would explain how Southeast Asian hens arrived there, though there are other equally likely explanations) and Antarctica. It's possible that one of the fleets reached Australia – surely they would have been curious about the large land to the South of Timor – but no definitive evidence has been put forward. After a series of natural disasters, Yung-lo's successors concentrated on projects like large granaries to help prevent starvation at home, rather than expansion abroad. Nearly all the records of the voyages were destroyed.

Probably the next to 'discover' Australia were the Portuguese. Once the Pope had divided the newly discovered world outside Europe into halves in 1494 – half for Spain and half for Portugal – the Portuguese quickly spread across 'their' half. The North navigation constant, the Pole Star, isn't visible in the southern hemisphere. By the late 1400s Portuguese navigators used the new tables that gave the sun's maximum altitude for every day or the year at every latitude, calculated by Professor Abraham Zacuto of Spain, translated into Hebrew, Latin, and then Portuguese. This allowed Portuguese navigators to venture south, not with confidence, but at least knowing where they were, even if they didn't know what they might hit next. Portugal was also relatively wealthy from the sugar trade using West African slave labour, and the gold captured in West Africa.

By the 1520s the Portuguese had discovered a route to the Spice Islands, sailing their ships past Timor and most likely even within sight of Australia. They would certainly have seen smoke, birds they knew had flown from land or even debris from storms. It is extremely likely that Portuguese navigators decided to see what lay to the south, and we can infer that they did by the small bits of almost accurate mapping that found its way onto the English and French maps, including references to a 'danger coast' that probably refers to the Great Barrier Reef. Any ship that struck that – literally or metaphorically – would have warned other ships that this land had teeth. But there's no definitive evidence that any Portuguese ship actually sailed here.

Our early maritime history is a wonderfully empty space for theorists. Did the Portuguese nobleman and explorer Cristóvão de Mendonça land here after 1521 when he searched for the Isles of Gold that lay beyond Sumatra? There are even theories that the mysterious Mahogany Ship that may – or may not – have sunk at some unspecified date off the coast of Victoria was Portuguese. But the wreck, if it ever existed, vanished. Did Portuguese Captain Gomes de Sequeira discover the 'Java le Grande' that appears in several maps of the early sixteenth century, and is Java le Grande really an inaccurate portrayal of north Australia, or any equally bad map of parts of Java or one of several other possible places? Did the Portuguese keep their explorations of Australia secret, in case it had spices or riches?

Most likely the Portuguese navigators did keep most of their maps secret so that others wouldn't find the best routes to Sumatra. (It would be several hundred years before shipping maps were regarded as public knowledge, not private information to be sold to the highest bidder.) And as for Australia – like travellers for the next few hundred years, if the Portuguese did see our coast, they probably decided that it was not worth bothering about.

The land of gold

But there was another large land in the far south that *was* deeply, gloriously enticing: terra incognita, the Great South Land of gold. The land mass known to be below Java (Australia) was obviously useless. But the Great South Land was a prize – or would be, if anyone could find it.

Each era has its own dreams. In the 1600s the dream was either of gold or the fountain of youth that would give eternal life – and possibly both at the same time. For centuries Europeans had been discovering new lands and riches: Newfoundland and its vast cod banks; South America and the treasures of gold; the Spice Islands, source of vast quantities of pepper and cinnamon; China and its silk; India and its cotton and other riches. Navigators and dreamers studied the old maps of the Pacific – somewhere, in all that vast blue, there had to be a land of gold. It was a glorious myth, too enticing to give up for lack of evidence, and it drew ships way beyond the normal trade routes.

The myth of the Great South Land was possibly begun by mistranslations of Venetian trader Marco Polo's *Book About the Variety of the World*, published after his successful trading trip to China, returning in 1295.[4] Whether or not Marco Polo did actually get to China, or only went part of the way and repeated travellers' tall stories, the book was an extraordinary success, translated from its original French into many languages. Marco Polo spoke of deserts, legends, palaces, but also fascinatingly about Kublai Khan and vast treasures of gold south of China.

This rich south land was not Australia – Marco Polo also said it was also rich in elephants. Australia has a conspicuous absence of elephants.

But little was known about the southern oceans. There was a southern blob of land added in maps since map maker Claudius Ptolemy (circa AD 80–165) created a picture of the world that would influence map-makers for the next 1400 years. There was also Polo's assertion that there was a land of gold south of China. Conclusion: somewhere down south there was a new land of gold to be found. And why not? Explorers had been discovering wealth for millennia, even if the wealth was slaves, rather than treasure. Today many assume that industrial growth can continue indefinitely. Back then, it must have seemed that there would always be new rich territory to discover.

One of the first explorers who set out deliberately to find this mythical unknown golden land was the Portuguese navigator Pedro Fernandez de Quiros, who in 1605 was sent by the king of Spain to find the Great South Land and claim it – and its gold – for Spain and the Church. Instead he found what was later called the New Hebrides (now the nation of Vanuatu) and named it Austrialia del Espiritu Santo. Unfortunately for de Quiros, the New Hebrideans didn't agree that they had suddenly become Spanish. He and his men were driven off, but his journey helped to fuel the rumour that the rich land of Terra Australis Incognita was down there – somewhere.

One of the ships in de Quiros's expedition passed through the strait that now bears the name of the ship's captain, Luis Vaez de Torres. Over a hundred years later Alexander Dalrymple, who also dreamed of finding the Great South Land and had studied ancient maps, gave Sir Joseph Banks copies of two maps that showed a strait between Australia and New Guinea. Banks showed the maps to James Cook.

That map's existence would change the history of the land we call Australia.

The Dutch bump into Australia (and don't think much of it)

Spain annexed Portugal in 1580, which more or less got rid of the great 'half to Spain and half to Portugal' divide. But Spain was too preoccupied with the vast – and real – treasures of the Americas to bother exploring unmapped lands in the south. At the same time, the Dutch lost the access they had had to Lisbon, the centre of the spice trade. The Dutch traders needed direct access to the valuable spices found just to the north of Australia.

In 1595 the first Dutch fleet to sail beyond Europe rounded the Cape of Good Hope, crossing the Indian Ocean from Madagascar to Java, and began to trade directly with Java and Bali. More fleets followed, trading with other islands as well. From this time until the Japanese conquered the area in 1942, and then the Indonesian National Revolution after the Japanese surrender at the end of World War 2, with eventual independence, much of what is present-day Indonesia became known to Europeans as the Dutch East Indies.

This time, at least some of the ships that explored the Spice Islands did map parts of Australia, and their maps still exist. The first voyage to Australia ever recorded, that of Dutch captain Willem Janszoon, sailed from Java and Timor on a voyage of exploration on the *Duyfken*. In 1605 to 1606 he entered the Gulf of Carpentaria, although he assumed he was charting the coast of New Guinea. In all, Janszoon charted three hundred kilometres of Australian coast.

In 1632 the Dutch ships *Pera* and *Arnhem* sailed from Ambon. Captains Carstensz and van Colster also charted the Gulf of Carpentaria, and also assumed it was part of New Guinea. This time they nailed a board up on a tree to claim the land for Holland, but they didn't think much of the new 'Dutch' territory. Carstensz declared that it had no fruit-bearing trees or anything that man could make use of, the most arid and barren region that could be found on the earth. Actually the area is rich in native fruits, but not any Carstensz would have been familiar with, like coconuts or bananas, or animals like pigs that the ships of the time loaded up as provisions from Southeast Asian ports.

The north of Australia had been seen – and most definitely rejected. Over in the west, the Dutch were finding and rejecting Western Australia, too.

Captured by the trade winds

It's no accident that Australia's first wind farm was sited at Albany. The day we went to look at it, the wind was so strong that four of us had to link arms just to walk against it, the spray from the sea five hundred metres away spitting in our faces. Every time I have been to Albany that wind has blown, hard, fast and reliable, and to truly understand what happens next in this story, you need to keep the overpowering wind of southwestern Australia in mind.

The direct route between Madagascar and Java often left ships becalmed in the tropics, without wind to fill the sails or water to drink. Every sailor had stories of coming upon ships empty of crew or manned only by skeletons, victims of the doldrums, the windless 'lands' of the ocean. Without wind a ship couldn't manoeuvre, and might drift onto the rocks or be unable to make its way over or around the vast freak waves the ocean winds created. Knowledge of the world's winds was as valuable as maps of land.

In 1611 a Dutch captain accidentally discovered that if he made a dogleg to a latitude of about forty degrees south he could use the strong west winds in the southeast ocean to push a ship due east for about three thousand kilometres before turning north to Java; these 'trade winds' are now called the roaring forties. It is entirely counterintuitive, but by going the long way round ships could get to Java faster, and with far greater certainty.

There was just one problem: Australia. Go too far east before you headed north and you crashed into it. The roaring forties are so strong that you might find yourself literally on Australia in the dark of the night, or without enough room to manoeuvre your ship away. And in those days before longitude could be accurately calculated, there was no precise way for shipmasters to work out how far east they had sailed.

Only five years after the new route was discovered, Dutch sailor Dirk Hartog *did* sail too far before he turned north, although he may not have been the first to find himself accidentally on the west coast. But we remember Hartog because he left proof that he had landed, hammering in a post at what is now Shark Bay in Western Australia and nailing an inscribed pewter plate to it that proclaimed his ship had landed there on 25 October 1616. Another Dutch explorer, Willem de Vlamingh, landed at the same spot in 1697, put up another plate and took the original back to the Netherlands, thus preserving the first written evidence of a European landing in Australia. It is also, presumably, the first formal European claim to the land. Hartog sailed his ship, the *Eendracht*, back to Java after naming the land Eendrachtsland for his ship. (As *eendracht* means concord, Australia should possibly be called Concordia, or even Consensus Island.)

But Hartog didn't find harbours, grass or even abundant fresh water. A settlement in the south of Western Australia would have been useful to supply Dutch ships, or even to construct a lighthouse to warn ship crews they were nearing land. But without a harbour – and grass – there was no way to do so. Southwestern Australia does have a stunning harbour at Albany, but, like Sydney Harbour, it has a narrow entrance and is easy to miss, especially as it doesn't have a river large enough to be noticeable from the sea to attract attention to it.

No harbour. No grass. No easy fresh water. A land that from the sea was sandhills, rocks, cliffs or desert. Not even bananas, coconuts and pigs. Why bother when the Dutch East Indies offered riches?

More Dutch captains accidentally sailed their ships to Eendrachtsland. In 1619 Frederik de Houtman landed on the islands off the West Australian coast and named them after himself; today they are still known as Houtman Abrolhos (Houtman Lookout). Captain van Hillegom arrived and left in May 1618, Lenaert Jacobszoon in the *Mauritius* in July 1618, and de Houtman, again, and Jakob Dedel in 1619. In 1622 the ship *Leeuwin*, skippered by an unknown Dutch captain, rounded the southwesterly cape that still bears its name. In 1627 François Thijssen and Pieter Nuyts followed the West Australian coast eastwards too and mapped it for about a thousand kilometres, after their ship, *t'Gulden Zeepaerdt*, was separated from the fleet. But neither of these ships landed: no safe harbours, no coconuts, no pastures of grass, no rivers of fresh water.

Yet that dream of a southern land of gold was still there. The south was *supposed* to have riches, like the gold of the Aztecs, the spices of what is now Indonesia, and the finely wrought jewelled treasures of the kingdoms of present-day India and Pakistan. By now most of Australia's western and north coast had been observed, and something more interesting than coconuts and pigs was conspicuously lacking: architecture and uniforms. In European minds, palaces and armies were strongly linked with the wealth of a land. Riches need defending. The Aztecs had their emperors, what are now India and Pakistan their sultans and palaces, Beijing its astonishing Forbidden City, Japan the armour-clad samurai with their superb weapons. Australia had parties of young men fishing with spears, or families picnicking on the beach waiting for the fish to swim into their fish traps. No armies or palaces must mean no gold.

There is no evidence that gold was prized by any of the Indigenous cultures of Australia, although in the 1850s Indigenous people would helpfully show gold hunters where they might find it. Why bother with gold? Gold has an extremely limited range of uses, unlike hard diamonds. Most isn't even used for jewellery but locked up as reserves. The value the modern world places on gold is arbitrary – we could have hit upon rare green ochre instead.

But unlike green ochre, gold gleams even in shadow, or dimly lit medieval palaces. Its value is still almost entirely symbolic: gold crowns, gold wedding rings, pots of gold at the end of the rainbow, gold medals. Even now, when electric light makes cheaper metals look good, gold is still valued as a safe investment when the stock market crashes, even though an empty factory is more useful than a bar of gold.

Europe dreamed of gold. Spain had found treasure troves of gold in South America, therefore another gold land *must* be somewhere south in the Pacific. Besides, when Marco Polo wrote of his trip to China back in the thirteenth century, he described the southern kingdom of Locach where gold was so plentiful that no one who hadn't seen it would believe it. Myths are often more powerful than reality, and the speculations about a golden land were enough to send whole expeditions in small ships across vast oceans.

That land of gold obviously wasn't Australia, or Eendrachtsland, so it must be somewhere else. Dutch mapmakers now put an accurate west coast of Australia on their maps, but they still included the mythical unknown south land, Terra Australis Incognita, far to the east.

The hunt continued. And then Abel Tasman found the land of giants.

The land of giants

In 1642 Anthony van Diemen, colonial governor of the Dutch East Indies, sent Captain Abel Tasman of the Dutch East India Company, with the talented pilot, hydrographer and surveyor Frans Jacobszoon Visscher, on two ships to search for Terra Australis, the unknown south land, and all the provinces of 'Beach' (possibly a mistranslation of reference to 'Locach' in Marco Polo's work).[5] Tasman was also supposed to find a southern passage from the East Indies to the Pacific, so the Dutch could attack the Spanish settlements in South America.

Hopefully this new land would be as rich in spices as the Spice Islands but healthier for the colonisers and traders. Dutch-held Batavia was known as the white man's graveyard: colonists died from malaria, typhus, cholera and other tropical diseases. The malaria was home grown, but cholera, dysentery and typhus were the consequences of the polluted water, stinking cesspools and other poor management by the Dutch East India Company. The spice trade was so rich that many were still prepared to risk their lives, but it would be convenient if a new colonial acquisition could be in a southern, cooler and less dangerously polluted country.

Once Tasman found Terra Australis he was to negotiate a treaty with its king to secure all rights for Holland and the Dutch East India Company. Tasman was ordered to keep well south of barren Eendrachtsland (the continent of Australia) and to head east into the Pacific.

Tasman sailed far enough south to catch the most reliable of the trade winds, the consistently strong winds of the Southern Ocean. These would not only make his voyage swifter but also, he assumed, keep him far south of Eendrachtsland.

The ships were small, the waves gigantic. If Tasman had been able to keep on his intended course he'd have landed at New Zealand without ever sighting southern Australia. He might even have missed New Zealand altogether and sailed long enough to dispel hope that a new land of gold lurked in the South Pacific.

But the dense fog, continuous drizzle and vicious winds of the Southern Ocean forced him further north than he intended. The fog continued, so dense that they dared not raise much sail for danger of running into the other boat in their party, or being wrecked on any land that lurked in the whiteness. Where were they?

On 4 November 1642 the ships' captains conferred, trying to work out where the wind and currents had taken them. Over the side they could see the type of seaweed that was usually found on rocks, and then a seal.

Land must be nearby.

They furled the sails, trying to sail as slowly and cautiously as they could under a grey sky, through fog, and then fog with hail and snow. But the relentless wind still drove them westwards, far too fast for safety. Any moment the ships might hit reefs or rocky islands. All they could do was keep up the lookouts and hope. The fog and snow continued. The men, noted Tasman briefly, were cold. They headed north again, trying to find respite from the wind.

Day after day they sailed north, rock weed still floating about the ship. At last now the fog lifted; the wind was a breeze, not a gale. Tasman could once again see the sun and stars, and calculate (not quite accurately) where they were. But they had no way of knowing what dangers lay between them and safety.

At last, on the afternoon of 24 November, they saw high green mountains, perhaps fifteen kilometres away. But how dangerous was the coast? It would be dark by the time they reached it. Again the ships' captains conferred. They would head south, away from land, into what they hoped was safety, unless there were reefs or islands. They'd approach the unknown coast in daylight. They let down the sounding line and found the sea was two hundred metres deep, a sandy bottom covered in shells. They let down the line once more and found black pebbles, but still enough depth for safety.

When day dawned they were becalmed and had to wait till noon for a wind. Tasman made a note warning future sailors who came this way to run before the wind in a storm – the land appeared abruptly. The weed indicated that there might be small islands that could wreck a ship.

At last the breeze rose. The ships headed north towards the land, taking soundings as they went. Tasman named the bit of land he could see Van Diemen's Land after Batavia's colonial governor. Then the haze came down again. Tasman sailed on cautiously, as slowly as possible. The fog deepened and the rain was hard and cold, the day too dark to see. They kept sailing with most sails furled, peering out to try to map the coast. But there were no harbours, not even inlets that might offer safety.

On 29 November Tasman found what might be a safe passage to the shore. At 5 p.m. they attempted to sail into it, but the harsh north wind forced them away again and again. By now they were desperate. They needed fresh water, firewood, stores, and grass for the ships' pigs and goats. But there was no harbour to be found, just a straight coast backed by forbidding mountains.

On 1 December their luck changed. An hour after sunset, in the dim light of dusk and with accommodating winds, they managed to find a fine harbour with a sandy bottom and a safe forty-metre depth, within rowing distance of the shore. The captains and the crew gave thanks to God for their deliverance 'with grateful hearts'.[6]

Early the next morning they rowed the ship's boat around a sandy point, drew her up on the shore and looked around. The land was high, but level; the trees tall and straight, not cultivated, but 'growing naturally by the will of God'. There was a wild plant, not unlike edible samphire, and a freshwater stream, but so shallow that only a small bowl could scoop it out.

But there was something else that terrified them. The trees had notches about one and a half metres apart, cut as though they were handholds to allow men to climb up them. Some looked to be no more than four days' old. Under the trees were the tracks and spoor of tigers. Far off among the trees they could hear sounds that seemed human, music and perhaps a gong.

This was a land of giants – and tigers too.

They left, swiftly. Large amounts of smoke from various points convinced them that it was not safe to linger.

But one task still had to be completed: they must fix a plate on a tree to formally claim this land of giants for the Dutch. They tried to row the boat ashore again, but the surf and wind prevented them. Finally, heroically, the ship's carpenter swam to shore, through the breakers, pushing the pole and flag in front of him. The flag was flown and the plate fixed to a tree at what is now North Bay on the southeast coast of Tasmania. Tasman made a note of the tree to which the plate was fixed: this 'new' land, and its giants and tigers, was officially Dutch. The carpenter dived into the waves again and finally made it safely to the rowboat.

Tasman finds the Land of Gold

The two ships of the fleet sailed on, mapping the land but not landing. They saw smoke, but no boats, and assumed the giants had none. They tried to keep sailing north, but the strong wind forced them east – far further east than Tasman realised.

On 5 January they sighted the 'giants' they'd been expecting to see walking along the shore, armed with sticks or clubs. At last, on 19 December 1642, there it was, the land of rich gardens they'd expected, with orchards of fruit that smelled delicious and tall but definitely not giant warriors of brown and yellow skin wearing what seemed to be mats, their hair dawn back in the Japanese manner. The warriors weren't wearing gold-plated armour, but there could still be no doubt: Tasman had found the massive Great South Land.

Except, of course, he hadn't. Tasman had landed on the South Island of Aotearoa, or what is now New Zealand. But Tasman believed that he had reached a vast continent that stretched all the way to Staten Land, east of Cape Horn: the Land of Gold at last.

How could such a competent man get so much of what he saw so wrong?

Imagine you are at sea in the lurid and blinding whiteness of the fog. The wind hurls you forward, even with furled sails, or leaves you becalmed, so that none of your skill can manoeuvre your ship to safety. Without the stars or even the sun to guide you, you have no accurate way of telling how far you have come apart from lengths of knotted ropes, almost impossible to use in rough seas. Day after day the ships of your fleet are pushed who knows where, unable to hear anything beyond their two ships except the howl of wind, the clatter of hail or the eerie silence of the snow, knowing only that land, rocks or reef were nearby. Your stores are low, as is the supply of fresh water and firewood. And then the crew saw tiger tracks and scats, almost certainly that of Tasmanian tigers – savage enough to eat an ailing lamb, but not to attack grown men. But you would not have known that. Then those axe marks in the tree at North Bay hacked by giants – or foot and hand holds to collect sweet sugarwood sap, almost a body length apart, instead of more close together as footholds alone might be. (Or, if Tasman really did see giants, then there is a corner of Tasmanian history that no one else has come across.)

The crew were scared: scared to the point of hysteria and delusion. They had been scared for weeks, and terror is contagious. They expected giants, and that is what they saw. Tasman expected a Great South Land, and assumed he had found the tip of it.

Tasman mapped more of what he thought was his 'new' continent, then sailed back to Batavia via Tonga and Fiji, around the north of New Guinea. His journey had been a magnificent failure. He had brought his two tiny ships through some of the world's most treacherous seas and along unknown and dangerous coasts, but he had found nothing that his Dutch masters valued.

He *had*, however, proved that what was now known as 'New Holland' wasn't connected to Antarctica, as some maps had shown it to be, and that it was physically possible, although dangerous, to sail south of New Holland to get from the Indian to the Pacific Ocean. From now on, most new maps would refer to Australia as New Holland, recognising the Dutch claim to the land.

Tasman had also stirred up the dreams of gold. Just as Tasman had been so sure that there were giants lurking in the forests beyond the fog that had engulfed his ship that he did indeed see giants, the dream of 'Beach' and its gold needed no real evidence to keep spreading through the centuries. The new land that Tasman had touched on – even if he saw no evidence of gold there – might be the tip of a land of treasure. Terra Australis and its fortunes had to be out there somewhere in the vast blue of the southern hemisphere's oceans.

Van Diemen hurriedly ordered a new expedition to secure the mythical Terra Australis for the Dutch before anyone else could settle there. In 1644, Tasman set out on his second voyage to map his Great South Land, among other instructions. Not surprisingly he was unsuccessful, as the land he was searching for didn't exist, and the land he had found – New Zealand – didn't stretch most of the way to Cape Horn. Setting off from Batavia, he travelled along the south coast of New Guinea into Torres Strait, which he assumed was only a bay and impassable, then returned along the coast to map most of northwestern Australia. His orders had been to explore the east coast too, and find out if New Holland was one great land or two. Instead he found reefs and rough weather. The east coast remained unmapped. Like James Cook more than a century later, Tasman regarded his voyages as failures.

The Dutch, pragmatically, stopped looking for the land of gold that wasn't there. They already had a prosperous empire to run, after all.

But Tasman's mistaken belief that he had found the tip of the Great South Land would be instrumental in sending yet another explorer out to survey Tasman's 'new' land again – James Cook, who would then decide to disobey his orders and sail on to New Holland/Australia to map the east coast that would be chosen for England's next supply fort in the Pacific, colonised by convicts.

And voyagers still crashed upon the coast of western Australia now and then on their way north to Batavia.

The publicity-hungry pirate

William Dampier would not have described himself as a pirate. He was an English privateer, someone who had permission from the king or queen to plunder other ships and give a proportion of their loot to the Crown. This made piratical murder, theft, pillage and rape on the high seas entirely respectable.

Dampier's naval career wasn't illustrious, but it is well known – he kept detailed memoirs and used them to publish a sensational book about his exploits. He and the rest of the pirate crew of the *Cygnet* were on their way to raid the Dutch East Indies when they beached the ship near what is now King Sound, Western Australia, to repair it. Pirate ships didn't have easy access to shipyards so had to maintain their ships in out-of-the-way places – and a beach in the west of New Holland was about as remote as it got.

After a hair-raising trip involving being marooned by the captain of the *Cygnet* on the Nicobar Islands, a capsizing canoe, storms and other adventures, Dampier arrived back in England with only his journals and two tattooed slaves he'd purchased, who may or may not have been the prince and princess of the southern lands he claimed them to be. Dampier published his journals as *A New Voyage Round the World*,[7] and exhibited his royal slaves both as publicity for his book and to make a living.

Dampier's account of Australia is possibly the most damning of any European who had visited here. He claimed that the inhabitants were the most miserable people on the earth, who kept their eyes half-closed to keep the flies out. They had no houses, tools or religion, nor any roots or grains to eat or weapons except for 'wooden swords'. The soil was dry and sandy with no trees that bore fruit or berries, few fish but many manatees and turtles. The inhabitants weren't even any use as servants. The sailors had given some of the men old ragged clothes, hoping they'd carry the water barrels for them, but the new 'servants' just grinned. They took the clothes off while the sailors lugged the water barrels back to the ship.

Almost all of Dampier's assumptions were wrong. The people he saw did have tools, weapons and religion – and far better-quality food and an easier lifestyle than most people in Britain at the time. But his book became a bestseller in 1697, and his descriptions of a barren land populated by miserably poor and wretched people effectively deterred any deliberate exploration or settlement of Western Australia for many years.

His description of the unwilling servants also illustrates another reason why there seem to have been no expeditions into Australia's interior. To make a fortune from growing spices back then you needed cheap or even slave labour. An expedition usually needed 'natives' to carry supplies for vast distances; Dampier's would-be servants wouldn't even carry water to their ship.

But Dampier, too, and the British Admiralty, believed that the Great South Land of gold still waited for them, and that Tasman really had touched the edge of what must be a large, rich continent. Dampier was given command of an ageing English navy ship, the leaking, rotting *Roebuck*, so he could chart the east coast of New Holland.

Dampier headed back to New Holland via the route taken by Dutch sailors to the Spice Islands, then sailed along the west coast from what he called Shark Bay, where he shot a local man while looking for fresh water before heading further north. His opinion of New Holland didn't improve.

By the time Dampier reached New Britain, his ship was leaking so badly he had to turn back towards England before even reaching Australia's east coast. The *Roebuck* sank off Ascension Island in the Atlantic on the way back. Dampier was court-martialled and found guilty of cruelty, having had his lieutenant jailed in Brazil on the voyage. He was dismissed from the navy, his pay withheld for the voyage, and he was refused permission to ever captain a navy ship again. He published another book, the damning *Voyage to New Holland*, and went back to a pirate career. The English privateers concentrated on robbing the Spanish ships that carried silver from Mexico to the Philippines, well away from the routes to Australia.

Tasman's misinterpretations of the land he'd seen would eventually bring James Cook to Australia, and then a colony. Dampier's scathing assumptions were possibly the reason why it took the English almost another hundred years to send an explorer like Cook to investigate further.

Better land, but no safe harbour found

Visitors continued to bump into the west coast from time to time. In 1696 the Dutch captain Willem de Vlamingh went to look for any survivors of the *Ridderschap van Holland*, which hadn't been seen since it left Cape Town in 1694 and had probably been shipwrecked on the Abrolhos Islands off the West Australian coast. De Vlamingh gave the most favourable account so far on the land in the southwest. He found giant hopping rats (quokkas) on the island he named Rottnest (rat's nest), now a popular island resort near Perth, and fragrant timber from sandalwood trees. He also explored up the Swan River, delighting in white cockatoos, blue and green parrots and two strange black swans, thus proving the predictions of those northern hemisphere naturalists who had stated that all swans must be black in the south, the opposite of swans in the north. This country was more fertile than the land to the north. The river provided fresh water and rudimentary shelter for a ship, but there were still no gold, spices, pigs, coconuts or bananas to stock the ships, nor was the Swan River a safe enough harbour to base a supply port there. Coconuts and bananas could be planted, pigs could be left to breed (as Cook would later do, thereby launching a feral pest in north Queensland). But the Swan River couldn't easily be turned into a safe harbour.

De Vlamingh sailed up the coast and found the plate left at Dirk Hartog Island eighty years before, taking it and nailing up another in its place to show that this land still belonged to the Dutch. (When De Vlamingh brought it back to Batavia, the governor sent it on to Holland to prove the Dutch had claimed the land, along with a watercolour painting showing where it had been found, a bit like taking a photo today.) Finally the ship sailed away with a volley of shot to celebrate leaving what even he called 'the wretched south land'.

A return voyage for the plate

In 1801 French explorer Louis de Freycinet found de Vlamingh's engraved plate on Dirk Hartog Island but was ordered to return it by his captain after making a copy of the inscription. He returned in 1818 to recover it and take it to France, where it was eventually delivered to the Académie française via a shipwreck on the Falkland Islands. After the liberation of Paris in World War 2 the plate was discovered on a bottom shelf among other dusty old plates, and presented to Australia as a gesture of goodwill in 1947. It is now in the Maritime Museum in Fremantle.

Abandoned for riches elsewhere

The world's far south was still a place of mystery, possible home to the unexplored land of gold (which Tasman may have landed on) or even another great continent further east. It was even the site as the imaginary world of Lilliput, in Jonathan Swift's 1726 novel *Gulliver's Travels*.

But there were riches elsewhere. The English were carving out empires from the existing principalities of India and Pakistan. The Dutch had their spices in the East Indies. The Spanish were busy in South America. The French had their territories in North America, and the Chinese ruled their own empire.

Two more East India Company vessels were shipwrecked off the west coast of Australia in 1712 and 1727, and two more Dutch expeditions followed in 1705 and 1756. By 1700 most of the western, northern and large parts of the south of the continent had been mapped. Most maps had New Guinea as part of Australia as it had been tens of thousands of years earlier when the seas were lower during the previous Ice Age.

Only the east coast was unknown territory for Europeans. The most obvious place to approach it was from the north, but the Great Barrier Reef acted as exactly that – a barrier to further exploration. And why bother? Why think that the east was any better than the deserts, scrub, or the land of tigers and giants already mapped?

The trepang trade

From about 1720 Indonesian fisherman sailed their praus to northern Australia each year to spear or net trepang. They boiled them, removed their guts and boiled them again in big pots with mangrove bark to give them a better colour and flavour. After that the trepang were dried in a smokehouse and taken back to the mostly Chinese merchants in Macassar, who exported them to China where they were used in soup or valued as an aphrodisiac.

The trepang fisherman set up big camps along the coast, usually in places that could be defended from attack, like promontories or small islands. They never ventured further inland as the land was strongly defended by the local people. The trepang fishermen, too, may have been deterred from travelling further east by the hidden teeth of the Great Barrier Reef.

A good place to avoid

New Holland, all too well known to be both dangerous and useless, was a place to be avoided while hunting for Terra Australis. In 1764 the English sent an expedition to the unmapped South Atlantic Ocean, and another to the South Pacific in 1766. Day after day they searched the horizon for Terra Australis until at last they seemed to have found it – a long grey landmass to the south. Unfortunately their 'Land of Gold' turned out to be a band of cloud. But there were rumours – which grew to a certainty in later years, as rumours do – that someone on the ship had glimpsed land, but the wind had not allowed them to pursue it. Once more the loneliness and terrors of the vast ocean – and the dream of gold – bred illusion.

The French also hunted for the fabled south land. In his 1768 search, Louis-Antoine de Bougainville saw and avoided the Great Barrier Reef. In 1772 Louis François de Saint Allouarn sighted Cape Leeuwin, sailed north to Dirk Hartog Island and claimed the west coast of Australia for France, and Marc-Joseph Marion du Fresne landed on the south coast of Tasmania. Du Fresne's expedition didn't bother to follow the Australian coast north but instead sailed on to New Zealand, once again seeking the land of gold. And didn't find it.

Australia had now been 'discovered' many times. But without safe harbours, harvestable grass, easily acquired slave labour or an existing empire that had collected gold that could be looted, it had no value to Europeans even as a staging port for their valued trading partners. And it was so obviously not the land of gold that Marco Polo had promised.

But there was still a large blank of blue on maps of the world where Terra Australis might be lurking. Despite the many expeditions, most of the Pacific was still largely unknown, partly because the ships were small and the Pacific Ocean is large, but also because there'd been no systematic survey.

A pedantic ex-grocery clerk from the north of England would change that.

CHAPTER 6

The goat, the grocer's assistant and the mistake that led to a nation

Australia was colonised by mistake. If 1770 hadn't been an unusually wet season for Botany Bay in New South Wales, providing the grass and fresh water needed to keep the *Endeavour*'s crew alive as well as giving a misleading impression of lushness, Australia would not have been colonised by the British in 1788.

Instead we might – possibly – have been colonised by the French (although they had many chances to do so, and didn't). We would more likely have been haphazardly invaded by the whalers and sealers of the early 1800s as they harvested the newly discovered rich whaling grounds of the Southern Ocean, with farms and merchant settlements around the coast to supply them.

The First Fleet was sent to found the Port Jackson colony (now Sydney) because of the complete misreading of the land by a slapdash but enthusiastic rich amateur botanist, Sir Joseph Banks, and because of the longing to map new land of a calm, meticulous captain, who would disobey his orders and risk his crew, his ship and his life to sail up the uncharted east coast of Australia.

In the rank and riches-dominated Britain of the 1700s, James Cook should never have been given captaincy of a ship much less placed in charge of an expedition. Born in Yorkshire, the son of a Scottish farm labourer, Cook began work as a grocer's assistant before at eighteen becoming an apprentice merchant seaman on a collier, a ship used for hauling coal along the English coast. He worked his way up from apprentice to seaman, and from seaman to mate. In 1755 he was offered the captaincy of a collier, but Cook refused.

Instead he enlisted in the Royal Navy as an able seaman – the bottom rank of the navy ladder – although he did not remain in that lowly position long.

Cook timed his career move perfectly. The English fleet was building up for war and there weren't enough trained seamen, so Cook was promoted quickly. By 1757 he was master on a warship – a non-commissioned position, and as high as any man who wasn't born a gentleman could hope to rise.

Cook would never be a gentleman, but he was a brilliant, meticulous surveyor, forging his reputation during General Wolfe's campaigns against the French in Canada. Cook was selected to survey the coast of Newfoundland when peace was declared in 1763.

Cook spent the next four summers surveying Newfoundland, and each winter in London with his wife, Elizabeth, preparing his charts. These were accurate and comprehensive – surveying classics. He also, as a private citizen, observed an eclipse of the sun and wrote a paper on how the observation of the eclipse could be used to measure the longitude of Newfoundland accurately. It was well received by the Royal Society.

Cook also had the Comptroller of the Navy as a patron. Sir Hugh Palliser gave Cook command of an unusual expedition to the Pacific: a joint venture of the Royal Navy and the Royal Society, a club of wealthy and, mostly, well-born scientists.

It was an age of naval empires, with the British, French, Spanish and Dutch vying for supremacy. And the dream of a Great South Land of gold was still very much alive.

An excuse to sail south

The well-connected Scottish scientist and hydrographer Alexander Dalrymple had translated Spanish documents captured in 1652 in the Philippines which showed Torres' discovery of a Strait between New Guinea and New Holland.[1] Dalrymple – a brilliant but mostly an armchair explorer – was convinced that the vast Great South Land (not New Holland) existed. He persuaded the British Admiralty that a top-secret expedition was urgently needed to find and claim the Great South Land before any other nation did. If the other nations knew that a British expedition to the south had been mounted they might follow, even mapping and claiming the land before the English could.

The expedition needed an excuse to voyage to the south. The Admiralty chose the forthcoming transit of Venus as their cover story. The best chance of observing this phenomenon required a voyage to the Pacific to measure how long it took the planet Venus to cross the face of the sun. It was an excellent excuse. The measurements would let scientists work out how far earth, Venus and the sun were from each other, and navigators could use this information to calculate where a ship was on the surface of the earth using the stars, otherwise known as celestial navigation. In 1769 it would be possible to see the transit of Venus really well from Tahiti. There wouldn't be another chance to measure this until Venus crossed the face of the sun again in 1874, more than one hundred years later.

Top secret southern survey

James Cook's other orders, to search for Terra Australis Incognita, the mythical Great South Land, were kept sealed and secret, not to be opened or disclosed until they were at Tahiti.[2] He was to sail to a latitude of forty degrees south, to where the 'continent, or Land of great extent, may be found'. If Cook didn't find the Great South Land he was to head back and map the land Tasman had touched on, now called New Zealand. By now Staten Land had been mapped, so Tasman's theory that New Zealand reached almost to the Cape of Good Hope had been disproved. But New Zealand might still be the tip of a vast continent. Cook was to continue mapping; he had just enough provisions to get back to a port and resupply for the return to England. He was to claim New Zealand for Britain: 'You are also with the Consent of the Natives to take possession of Convenient Situations in the country in the name of the King of Great Britain; or, if you find the Country uninhabited take Possession for His Majesty by setting up Proper Marks and Inscriptions, as first discoverers and possessors.'

There was no mention of going to New Holland. Why bother?

We have grown so used to the expanse of blue Pacific Ocean on our maps that it is difficult to comprehend the certainty with which so many authorities believed that the Great South Land *had* to be there. The scientific consensus was that another large land mass must be there to balance northern Europe, otherwise the spherical earth couldn't maintain its equilibrium.

It was true that no mariner had discovered it yet, and there had been many, many journeys south. But European ships kept to the known northern routes across the Pacific, using the trade winds to get there. Very few had gone south or, if they had, had not returned.

A most unusual expedition

A non-commissioned officer like Cook could not be made captain of a ship, but Palliser argued that his protégé should be. To the conservative ranks of the Admiralty this was heresy – a labourer's son could not be an officer! Finally they compromised, giving Cook command of the ship but with the rank of first lieutenant.

Cook immediately rejected the Admiralty's assumption that a navy frigate would be used for the voyage. Navy frigates needed deep water. If Cook were to go close enough to shore to map the land accurately he needed a shallow-bottomed ship.

He asked for a collier, the ships he was most used to sailing. The *Earl of Pembroke*, a Whitby cat – a sturdy, broad-beamed, flat-bottomed, three-masted collier built in Whitby – was selected: not quite four years old, 106 feet (just over thirty-two metres) long and twenty-nine feet (nearly nine metres) wide. It only needed four metres of water to stay afloat even when fully laden, and the flat bottom meant that if it did go aground it could be beached and refloated. The ship cost £2800 and was then refitted, with another outside skin of thin planking lined with tarred felt, a third deck put in the massive hold to accommodate the extra crew and marines, as well as extra cabins, store rooms, a powder store and a great cabin that Cook would end up sharing with the gentlemen naturalists.

Renamed HM Bark *Endeavour*, the rebadged ship had no figurehead, no smart paint. But it was superbly fitted out for the expedition to the unknown: twelve swivel guns and ten carriage guns; tons of coal for cooking; barrels of tar and pitch and planking for repair of the ship when no port was near; carpentry tools; spare canvas for the sail makers; 1200 gallons of beer, 1600 gallons of spirits, 4000 rounds of salt beef, 6000 rounds of salt pork, 160 pounds of mustard seeds, twenty tons of ship's biscuit and flour, and 107 bushels of dried peas.

They also loaded the breeding animals necessary for such a long voyage: seventeen sheep and a small mob of cattle for meat, four ducks, four or five dozen hens housed in the ship's boats, a boar, a sow and her piglets as well as the hay and dried peas to feed them, plus three cats to catch the rats. And, of course, the single famous milk goat.

There was also more controversial food: 7860 pounds of fermented cabbage, 80 pounds per man, to test the new theory that fresh vegetables might keep away scurvy.

Scurvy killed more sailors than shipwreck. Your gums became inflamed; your teeth loosened. Finally your body swelled, and you died in agony and delirium. The great Polynesian sailors took bananas and coconuts on their voyages, as well as dried yams and other dried fruits, dried fish or dried fruits mixed with flour and fat. Their long voyages might leave them thin and starving, but their food was nutritious. European ship's biscuit provided kilojoules but not much else. The salt beef and pork combined with inadequate fresh water in the long months at sea left men's lips blistered and bleeding, but it was eat them or starve. Cook's voyage would possibly be the first European expedition during which no man would die of scurvy.

Cook was given one other important cargo: Joseph Banks, and his party of assistants.

Joseph Banks was twenty-five years old, handsome, rich and a gentleman, with an income of £6000 a year. He was also arrogant, slapdash and absurdly self-centred. He didn't finish his university degree, would jilt the fiancée who waited for him for three years and, when due to Banks's own stupidity one of his servants died on the voyage, would lament the death only because the man 'was of some use to me'.

But Banks, a member of the Royal Society, was also fascinated with plants and animals. He had already been on one scientific expedition to Newfoundland and knew what life aboard ship was like. And he was enthusiastic. This voyage would be an opportunity to collect and name new species or, rather, species not so far catalogued by Europeans. A young man as rich and well-connected as Banks usually got what he wanted, especially as he put up a considerable amount of the money required for the scientific side of the expedition – £10,000, according to the expedition's naturalist, Dr Solander, a Swede who had studied under the famous botanist Linnaeus (Professor Carl von Linné).

In a stroke of extraordinary luck – though neither man would possibly admit it – Banks was paired with the scrupulous man of integrity James Cook. Each time Banks would endanger the expedition, Cook would counter him. Without Cook, the expedition would have been lost. Without Banks, it possibly would never have happened at all.

Banks insisted on the trappings of a gentleman as well as a scientist. Cook was forced to find room on the small ship for Banks's scientific library, equipment and five assistants – Swedish naturalist Solander, secretary and draughtsman Sporing, and botanical artists Buchan and Parkinson as well as an astronomer, Charles Greer. While the assistants would collect species that were new to Europeans, a painting of the living plant was more valuable than dried specimens. Even today, botanical artists are highly valued because they can draw parts of a plant that a camera can't see or pick up, and put bark, buds, flowers, seed capsules, new and old leaves in the one drawing or painting.

Banks himself would do some collecting – his work could later be easily identified as he used the 'snatch and stuff in it a bag' method instead of carefully selecting and cutting buds, seeds or juvenile leaves, then drying them and pressing them, as his assistants would do.

Banks also brought four servants, two of them fashionably black, his greyhounds (the mythical Great South Land must be rich in game as well as gold) and his personal musician, to play for him while he ate. One might be heading into the unknown, but one still dined like a gentleman. He would also have brought his own stores of superior food and alcohol, not listed in the ship's inventory.

The crew desert

The expedition was as planned as a meticulous man like Cook could make it. Yet there was no denying that its captain had never commanded a ship before, nor had he ever faced the seas of the Southern Ocean. This mattered: a ship's survival might depend on its captain having enough experience of the area to know where and when the wind might come from, wave conditions and much else. Cook's career had been mostly hugging coastlines.

This expedition would also only have a single ship, unlike Tasman's. If the *Endeavour* sank, there would be no rescue. Eighteen men deserted before the ship even sailed from Plymouth, about a third of the crew. Although the orders to search for the Great South Land were still under seal, the crew must have guessed from the very size of the stores that this was no relatively easy jaunt to Tahiti and back. Other men were hired, but there were not enough volunteers to man the ship. The rest of the crew were impressed – kidnapped, either from the docks or while drunk in nearby pubs. Slavery might have been outlawed in England, but the Admiralty still had the power to take any able-bodied man and force him to crew their ships.

It was not an auspicious beginning.

The *Endeavour* and its willing as well as unwilling crew prepared to sail on 19 August 1768 with ninety-five people on board.[3] But the wind was from the wrong direction, and a ship like the *Endeavour* could only manoeuvre with the right wind. Banks and Solander went back to wait in comfort on shore while Cook and his crew remained on board. Day after day, and no wind filled the sails. It must have seemed an appalling omen for the voyage.

At last on Thursday, 25 August the wind veered to the northeast. Cook hoisted a signal flag to tell Banks and Solander to come on board. Banks was hungover from the night before and he still hadn't told his new fiancée that he was about to leave on what would be a three-year jaunt around the world.

They climbed aboard and sailors ran to set the topsails. The ship's timbers creaked as the ship began to move. Up at the wheel two sailors waited until the ship had picked up enough speed to allow them to steer, though not yet into the unknown.

The voyage south was a well-followed route. The *Endeavour* rolled like a pregnant duck even in relatively calm weather and Banks was seasick for the first few days. At Rio de Janeiro, the Portuguese viceroy decided that the *Endeavour* was a smuggler's ship, the story of an expedition to measure Venus's shadow crossing the sun an obvious fabrication. How could a planet pass through the sun? The *Endeavour* was certainly no British naval vessel – yet it was armed. Eventually the viceroy allowed Cook to purchase fresh food, but when a dozen sailors went ashore to load the supplies they were flung into jail along with the English merchant who was supplying them. No explanation was given, though it is possible that the viceroy had learnt that Banks and Solander had disobeyed orders and sneaked ashore.

Cook protested vehemently and at last the men were released, but worse was to come when the harbour fort fired upon them on the way out – the viceroy had not informed them that the *Endeavour* was free to leave. A sailor fell overboard and drowned before he could be rescued. And then the winds failed. They lay becalmed, with five thousand kilometres of ocean between them and Cape Horn, the gate to the Pacific. At last the wind rose. It kept on kept rising. The gales sped them on, but the sea grew steadily rougher. The sky loomed grey, and darker every day.

Cook kept strict order on his ship, apart from Banks and his party, who refused to admit his authority. The sailors refused to eat their pickled cabbage. Cook decided on a stratagem – it would be served to the officers and gentlemen, but not to the sailors. Cook smugly reported in his log that within a week the sailors were eating so much sauerkraut that he was forced to ration them to a day's allowance.

The *Endeavour* stopped at Tierra del Fuego, off the tip of the South Americas, to fill the barrels with fresh water and to cut grass and let it dry into hay to feed the animals. Tierra del Fuego was cold, even in January, midsummer.

Banks was bored. Against Cook's advice he raised an expedition of twelve men to go ashore and look for specimens, despite the clouds heavy with snow. The blizzard caught them without provisions. In the morning two of Banks's servants were dead, his greyhound just alive. The survivors stumbled back to the ship the next morning.

At each port Banks's arrogance had caused disaster. He even shot an albatross – sailors were superstitious and it was a well-known sailors' superstition that if you shot an albatross the expedition was doomed.

The *Endeavour* sailed out into the Pacific, heading west into the cold giant waves of the south of the Pacific instead of the usual route to the northwards. Even before the orders were opened and announced to the crew at Tahiti, Cook was already hunting for the Great South Land.

The cold was extraordinary. It grew worse. Five of the crew were lost to cold and waves as they rounded the Horn. Day after day the ship plunged across the waves in seas where possibly no boat had ever been. Slowly the grey sky turned blue, the dark sea shifted to aquamarine. Another member of the crew committed suicide, vanishing overboard after being disciplined. Many times the lookout called out that land was on the horizon, but each time as they sailed towards it the 'land' turned into a bank of cloud.

There was no land. Worse, there were no new currents. As Cook was to write in his log: 'this must be a great sign that we have been near no land of any extent because near land are generally found currents; it is well known that on the north side of the Continent in the North Sea we meet with currents above 100 Leagues from Land.'

Banks, too, accepted that there was no Great South Land in this part of the Pacific Ocean. He was to write of the armchair scientists back home that 'they have generally supposed that every foot of sea which they had believed no ship to have passed over was land'.

The *Endeavour* kept searching. It had now been three months since they had sighted land. Even Banks, well-fed on his private stores of food, found his gums bleeding with the early signs of scurvy. He took an extra ration of lemon juice mixed with brandy and found himself improving. But there was too little to give out to the crew, although their sauerkraut and malt wort kept them alive and functioning.

It is difficult to imagine the monotony of a three-month voyage with nothing but sea, sky and apprehension on a tiny ship. The officers and gentlemen at least had private cabins, books and their scientific observations to distract them. But the fear of the unknown must have been worse than the boredom.

Land was dangerous, but the sea could be worse. No one had mapped this ocean, marked doldrums where no wind blew or rocks that might smash the ship at night when no effective lookout could be kept. Day after day they waited for disaster, but at least Tahiti must be near – they were on the right course. Cook had never navigated in the southern hemisphere, away from the familiar northern stars he knew. Tahiti is only about thirty kilometres long in a vast ocean. Its position had only been mapped a year before Cook set out. With no accurate timepieces to correctly work out latitude, and long before GPS satellites, Tahiti might not even be where it was supposed to be.

It was. And Cook's meticulous observations, using hourglasses and knotted rope to measure the ship's speed, and sextant and almanac to measure its position by the sun and stars, had been precise. Most of the crew had even survived.

The *Endeavour* hadn't found the Great South Land yet, but they had found a large area of sea where they could now prove it wasn't. And for now, they were safe.

The hunt resumes

They waited from 13 April 1769 until the transit on 3 June. It was not a hardship. As Cook wrote, the women of Tahiti were liberal with their favours. He was more concerned to find that a third of his crew had syphilis or gonorrhoea, and had possibly passed it on to the Tahitian women, from whom the diseases might spread across the Pacific.

The intense sunlight and Venus's atmosphere made a strange dusky shade about the planet, which meant that the transit couldn't be observed accurately, though they were able to make some calculations. At last Cook opened the sealed orders. If the crew muttered at yet another journey into the unknown, it isn't recorded. Perhaps, by then, they had learned to admire, even revere, this meticulous disciplinarian who led them. Perhaps, too, the paradise of Tahiti led them to hope there'd be more of the same to come.

The *Endeavour* sailed south, to hunt for the Great South Land in the vast unknown of the Pacific Ocean. Banks was convinced that it must be there, somewhere. Cook was sceptical. Day after day they sailed with no sign of land. A comet flared across the sky with an astonishing forty-two degrees of tail – yet another sign of calamity for the sailors, as well as for the Polynesian navigator and translator named Tupaia who Banks had persuaded Cook to take on board.

By the time they reached forty degrees south, the most southerly limit of the Admiralty's instructions, there was still no land, no land birds, no sign of seaweed, nor any possible indication that there was land in the vicinity. The air seemed to freeze around them and their livestock began to die of cold and lack of fresh feed. The sky grew grey and the waves towered so high that Cook ordered the sails furled.

There could be no habitable land further south.

Cook now turned west, hoping to find the Great South Land towards New Zealand, though it was difficult sailing against the current and into the prevailing wind, but they continued west all through September. One day a seal swam by. For the first time they saw tangles of seaweed, and hauled aboard a barnacle-crusted log. The water grew paler. Land had to be near. They had now been away from England for more than a year.

And then, in early October 1769, land was sighted. For three hours they were convinced they were sailing towards the Great South Land. Slowly, one by one, those on board accepted the truth. It was another bank of cloud.

But they still had the seaweed, the change in waves and currents that promised that the Great South Land must be near. Cook offered a keg of rum to the first person to see land.

On 6 October at 1.30 p.m., 'Young Nick' (Nicholas Young, amongst the youngest of the crew) yelled, 'Land, ho!' from the masthead. The crew clustered on deck. Others shouted that they could see land as well – even though it was in the opposite direction from the mountain top Young Nick claimed to have seen. They sailed towards it until at last even those on deck, not up on the mast, could just see a group of islands – land, not clouds. They stared as the sun sank ahead of them.

The *Endeavour* sailed due west that night. As dawn lit the sky, the land was only about forty kilometres away. Banks would write: '[A]ll hands seem to agree that this is certainly the continent we are in search of.' They had found the Great South Land at last.

But Cook looked at the shape of the coast. He deduced that this land that Europeans now called New Zealand was not the edge of a great continent, as Tasman had hoped, but an island. Cook was right.

At least Cook could now map and claim this land for Britain, as he had been instructed to do. They sailed on. Banks still hoped that, as Tasman had thought, this might be the tip of a much larger continent. He even cited a rumour that the Dutch had sent other ships to Tasman's discovery, and they had been able to follow the land southward to a latitude of sixty-four degrees, making this a continent, not an island. However by March 1770 Cook had mapped the coast meticulously, outlining harbours, winds and currents for all the ships that would follow them, and even Banks had to admit to 'the total demolition of our aerial fabrication called a continent'.

This land was fertile, well watered, with excellent harbours. The inhabitants were at times friendly, though also fierce defenders of their country; at the Bay of Islands the crew needed to fire the cannons to save their boats from an attack by war canoes. Cook had the Union Jack hoisted on the island of Motuhora off the northern coast and took possession of the land 'in the name of and for the use of His Majesty King George the Third'. Cook and Banks even speculated about establishing a colony there.

But it was not the Great South Land.

Cook wanted to head back across the Pacific at more northern latitudes to prove once and for all whether a Great South Land still lurked in the Pacific. But winter was approaching, and the *Endeavour* had been badly damaged in New Zealand storms. The fresh food and grass they'd gathered in New Zealand would only allow them another six months' voyaging at two-thirds of the usual rations for each man, assuming they didn't find another source of fresh food.

The quickest way to Dutch Batavia, the nearest port where the ship could be repaired, would be to take the southern route that Tasman had already charted beneath Van Diemen's Land and New Holland then north to Batavia. But could the tattered sails and damaged masts of the *Endeavour* survive the gales of the Southern Ocean that Tasman warned of?

The most sensible option was to follow Tasman's route north, so they could stop at Fiji, Tonga and the other Pacific Islands for fresh water, pigs, coconuts, bananas and other provisions, then go around the north of New Guinea, as Tasman had, and approach Batavia that way.

Then there was option three: to sail up the east coast of New Holland and use the strait discovered by Torres to get to Batavia – if the strait existed. Tasman had said it didn't, Dalrymple said it did. But Dalrymple has also been sure the Great South Land existed, and his only evidence for that vital strait was one old forgotten map. Cook must also have known about the 'dangerous waters' the Portuguese maps warned of.

But it was his only chance to map land no other European had surveyed. If he headed back to England by a known route now, he'd just be yet another captain who didn't discover the Great South Land. If Cook could prove that Torres's strait existed he'd have found a new and possibly faster way to get from Batavia to the Pacific.

Cook was a cautious, careful man, deeply protective of his crew, especially the younger ones who were traditionally bastardised, insisting that each man ate as healthily as possible and that their quarters were scrubbed twice a week. Other captains had found New Holland to have little grass or fresh water, except Tasman's Van Diemen's Land, a place of giants, tigers and ferocious winds that could batter a ship against the cliffs. Cook would be risking his ship, his crew and his life – and all his new maps of the Pacific, Southern Ocean and New Zealand – just to map uncharted shores.

Against all orders, and expectations, and common sense, Cook and the *Endeavour* sailed to Australia.

His decision would wreck his ship.

Towards the unknown

The *Endeavour* left the northern tip of New Zealand's south island from near the point they named Cape Farewell at the beginning of April 1770 and sailed across unknown seas to the uncharted coast of New Holland. Cook wanted to land on the south coast of Tasmania, so he could start his maps where Tasman's had stopped. But gales from the south forced the *Endeavour* north. Three weeks after they left New Zealand, birds and waves indicated land ahead.

At 1 a.m. on 19 April, Cook ordered the crew to 'drop line' and see how deep the water was below them – approaching unknown land in the darkness was risky, as there might be shallows and reefs. At 5 a.m. he ordered the top sail reefed so that the ship travelled more slowly and cautiously during the darkness, when waves and wind might drive them onto unseen rocks.

Then, with the first light on the morning of 19 April 1770, Lieutenant Zachary Hickes, Cook's second-in-command, 'saw ye land making high', as he recorded in his *Journal of a Voyage in the Endeavour*. The land was about thirty kilometres away. Below them was a fine sandy bottom, with no rocks or reefs. There was no sign of land to the south of them, though according to Tasman's calculations land should have been in sight, so Cook was unable to tell if Van Diemen's Land joined the land he now saw, if they were two islands, two continents, or one continent and one island. The land that they *could* see went off to the west and north, which made Cook believe that this was the most southerly point.

Cook named the place he first glimpsed Point Hicks after his lieutenant, who died of tuberculosis on the return voyage to England. (Point Hicks and its lighthouse are now in Croajingolong National Park, on the northeast coast of present-day Victoria.) It was a green and hilly country covered in trees, with large stretches of sand along the coast. Smoke rose above the treetops, a sign that this part of New Holland was probably inhabited, as Tasman had said Van Diemen's Land was.

The ship sailed north, looking for a safe place to anchor and send the ship's boats ashore with barrels to get fresh water, as well as to cut

The wrong point

The position and date Cook gave for the expedition's first Australian land sighting were wrong. This led to years of arguing about where the first European sighting of land on the east coast was.

In 1852 a surveyor named George Smythe mapped the area and named the point Cape Everard. But in 1970 the premier of Victoria, Henry Bolte, renamed it Point Hicks in honour of the Cook expedition.

grass and gather firewood to replace the coal for cooking that was now almost used up. But the strong southerly winds didn't allow the ship to manoeuvre into the bay that Cook named Batemans, or into Jervis Bay either.

Sting Ray Harbour

At last on the morning of 29 April they found a reasonably sheltered bay. The strong southerly dropped enough for them to sail inside. If a storm blew up they might be dashed on the rocks but now, in fine weather, it seemed safe enough.

There was no river or even a creek to be seen. But there were grass and good trees. There were also the Kameygal people, dark-skinned and naked, with their huts, women, children, men with white powder on their faces, spears and four canoes. If there were people, there must be fresh water. Below the ship the stingrays flapped slowly in the waves. Cook named the place Sting Ray Harbour, but when they departed he would rename it Botany Bay, in honour of Banks's and Solander's botanical discoveries.

The *Endeavour* dropped anchor. The crew gazed eagerly at the people on the shore, but the Kameygal people didn't gaze eagerly back. They didn't seemed surprised or even interested in the large canoe that had appeared in their harbour. More Kameygal women and children came out from the trees. The fishermen hauled their canoes out of the water. An old woman began to cook dinner.

The people on the *Endeavour* dined too, though probably not nearly as well as the Kameygal. After dinner, Cook ordered the ship's boat to be launched (removing the hens and scrubbing out the chook manure first, as they had to do on every visit ashore). As the crew rowed towards the shore the locals vanished, except for two men, one middle-aged and the other about nineteen. The Kameygal might not have been fascinated by the newcomers, but they were wary. The two men waved their spears and spear throwers and yelled, obviously telling the newcomers to go away.

They were only two warriors facing a party of forty sailors. Cook admired their courage. He asked Tupaia the Tahitian to try to talk to them. Tupaia yelled a few words across the waves at the men; the warriors yelled back. But even though Tupaia had been able to understand Maori, he wasn't able to understand anything of the language here.

The sailors threw nails and beads to the two men to try to appease them. The Kameygal warriors failed to be impressed. At last Cook fired a musket between them. The youngest warrior dropped his spears in shock at the noise, smoke and smell, then picked his spears up again. The other threw a stone at the boat.

Finally Cook ordered a musket filled with small shot – small pieces of metal that would scatter when the musket was fired but not do any great harm – to be fired, and the shot hit the leg of the older man. The English had not even set foot on New Holland before local blood was spilled.

The wounded man ran to one of the huts to fetch his shield. The two men threw their spears at the landing party. They were superb throws at that distance. The spears landing in the boat among the sailors but didn't hit anyone. Cook ordered a third musket with small shot to be fired. The men threw one more spear and ran towards the trees. Cook wanted to chase and capture them but for once Banks was the cautious one, warning that their spears might be poisoned.

And then they landed.

A superficial survey

The shore party explored. The Kameygal had vanished. Cook judged their huts were rough, but the spears superb. Cook ordered the spears to be confiscated so that they couldn't be used against them. At last they found a little fresh water in a hole in the sand.

They landed again the next day. Cook, Banks, Dr Solander and seven others explored the country, while others of the crew cut grass and slowly filled the barrels with water. The grasslands were lush and green; the timber looked good. Above them flocks of bright birds flickered through the trees. It was beautiful.

For a botanist and zoologist like Banks, it was also paradise. He shoved handfuls of specimens roughly into bags while his assistants worked methodically, collecting and sketching. He noted a fascinating 'quadruped' as big as a rabbit, which his greyhounds almost caught – perhaps a small wombat, or more likely a pademelon or bandicoot, as the soil of Botany Bay is probably too sandy to support wombat holes.

They had no more contact with the local people. As Cook put it in his log: ' [A]fter our first contest at landing they would never come near enough to parley; nor did they touch a single article of all that we had left at their huts.'He did not think much of them. '[T]hey did not appear to be numerous, or live in societies, but like other animals were scattered about along the coast and in the woods.'[4] Cook came from a culture where status was measured in possessions: great houses, uniforms, the ermine cloak of a member of the House of Lords. What he found here was both an environment and a culture he didn't understand. Even Dampier hadn't referred to his 'servants' as animals.

Every day they were ashore Cook had the ship's colours displayed, a display any onlookers who happened to understand British naval protocol would recognise. The ship's name, with the date and the year, was inscribed on one of the trees near the freshwater pool. This effectively – for Cook and other Europeans – declared that Cook had claimed the land for Britain, although he would make a more formal proclamation when he believed they were leaving the land.

These days it seems a ridiculous custom – few 'claiming' plates or trees would ever be found again. But it was the ceremony that mattered, and the description in the captain's log that it had been performed, backed up by maps to show that you had been there. Like the other captains who had claimed parts of New Holland, Van Diemen's Land, and Eendrachtsland for their various kings, Cook saw nothing odd about acquiring a continent merely by stepping onto it and carving a name and date onto a tree.

It is hard, these days, to understand the philosophy behind it. It wasn't just a matter of discrimination against those who didn't build palaces; the Europeans also assumed they had a right to exert dominion over India, China and the Malay states, all with their own kingdoms, empires, courts, literature and culture. In part, by then, it was about dark skins. Centuries of slavery had at last resulted in discrimination purely on the grounds of skin colour. In Roman times, a dark skin was merely a physical characteristic. Shakespeare could make dark-skinned Othello a romantic a hero for English audiences. Discrimination on the grounds of skin colour was a slow process, but by Cook's time it was well in place.

But mostly it was a subconscious assertion that might is right. British law only protected other British people. These were still the days when British privateers could take whatever they could grab. A British naval officer could become rich with 'prize money' from enemy ships captured in war. British armies routinely raped and looted even the European places they conquered. Cook may not have explicitly thought: we can take this place, therefore it is ours. Instead he shared the mindset that the ability to defeat other cultures was a product of a superior society. No amount of sophisticated culture would outweigh cannon and muskets.

Cook entirely misunderstood the sophisticated culture that was to be found here, one that was wrought from relationships with the land and other people, not focused on material objects. It takes seconds to observe a palace or an army of men, but it would take more than two centuries for even a rudimentary appreciation of Indigenous cultures to develop. Cook's survey was less than two weeks.

Cook and Banks also misunderstood the land around them. The lush green grass and the height of the trees tricked them into thinking the land was fertile, that this was its normal state. It wasn't. The *Endeavour* may have visited just after a rare La Niña or wet year, very roughly and unreliably occurring every seven years. It's also possible that it was a dry year, but the southerly gales that had carried them so far north had also brought recent rain. Whatever the cause, it is obvious from Cook and

Banks's descriptions that they saw a bay that had received far more rain than 'Sting Ray Harbour' usually gets.

Nor was the soil fertile. Rather, Cook and Banks were probably seeing a brief flush of growth spurred by the accumulated detritus – animal droppings, decomposed leaves, and so on – of the last dry period. Ground covers shrivel in dry years, but within weeks of rain after a dry period the lushness is extraordinary. Sometimes it may last for months, or even years; rarely it may last for decades, but usually it is gone the following year.

Banks decided that the sparse trees were so far apart that the whole area could be cultivated without having to cut own a single tree, with sandy soil that produced excellent grass and in other areas tall trees growing on a rich back soil that should grow any kind of grain.

But the tall trees were not a sign of deep, fertile soil. Neither Banks nor his assistants appear to have dug down to see how far the topsoil extended. In fact, the eucalyptus trees of 'Sting Ray Harbour' grew tall and thin-topped to minimise their exposure to sunlight. Tall eucalypts can have taproots that can penetrate deep down to the subsoil where there is moisture. The tallness of the trees was not a sign of good soil but the opposite. Instead, they should have looked at the width of the trunk and branches – a far more reliable sign of fertility in Australia.

They didn't. The land spoke to them, but they didn't understand its language.

How a glimpse became a colony

Nearly twenty years later, when the British government was looking for a site to base troops and ships to counter the French presence in the Pacific, the now knighted Sir Joseph Banks, even more eminent than when he'd left on the *Endeavour*, partly because of his book about the voyage, would recommend that Botany Bay was the best place for a colony.

Why?

Yes, he had reason to think the land was fertile, and the timber good. But the *Endeavour*'s crew had only found minimal fresh water –

enough to replenish the ship's stores with some effort, but not enough for a colony to drink, much less for irrigation. And the harbour was too shallow too provide safety for a ship, much less a naval fleet.

Was Botany Bay so much more inviting in memory than it had been in reality? It was, after all, the site of his most successful collecting adventures. Why didn't Banks recommend the colony be sited in New Zealand, with its lush countryside, many rivers, deep fjords, fields of flax for sails and cloth, gigantic timber trees, and pigs and crops that could be bought from the Maori to feed a colony?

One possible answer is that the Maori had shown themselves both numerous and ready to defend their land. Britain in the 1780s wanted to establish a colony, not fight for one. Banks and Cook had assumed that Australia had relatively few inhabitants and that their weapons would be no match for muskets. In the late 1790s British traders, missionaries and British and American whalers did begin small settlements in New Zealand and eventually had to battle for the land, but those early invaders needed none of the expense and elaborate preparations that were necessary for the colony at Botany Bay.

Banks was not one to hide his light. It's probable that Banks chose Botany Bay because, as its 'discoverer', the colony would immortalise his name.

The colony would survive, but from luck, not good judgement. Banks really had found a generous land, even if he totally misinterpreted it.

North to disaster

The *Endeavour* sailed north from Botany Bay, bound for the Torres Strait that they hoped was there, and not another figment of a sailor's miscalculation or imagination. If it wasn't, then they would need to go all the way around New Guinea to reach Batavia, with little chance to stop for grass or water. They might not make it.

By midday they were in the ocean off what we now call Sydney Heads, but the wind was too strong for them to enter the narrow gap between the headlands. Cook noted that it seemed a safe anchorage and called it Port Jackson after Sir George Jackson, lord commissioner and judge advocate of the British naval fleet.

The ship continued slowly up the coast against the southern current. Cook kept the ship well offshore, away from the pounding surf. They passed Moreton Bay, again missing one of the largest Australian harbours, then on 23 May anchored at Bustard Bay, north of present-day Bundaberg, named after the scrub turkeys they shot and ate. Their next landing was a place further north that Cook referred to as Thirsty Sound, so called because there was no fresh water to be found.

It wasn't until I read Cook's log for the fourth time that I realised that I had been indoctrinated to think of him solely as a hero. James Cook was certainly heroic, but the voyage that resulted in the English settlement was foolhardy and unnecessary. It was a stroke of luck that they found land that their government could find useful. It was a miracle that any of them survived, especially at this point.

The *Endeavour* was now between the mainland and the Great Barrier Reef. Tasman's expedition had two ships: if one were wrecked, the survivors could be transferred to the other, or at least be assured that they still had a ship to bring help. The *Endeavour* was not just alone but way off her intended course. If she were wrecked now, the ship, crew and all the dearly won charts and knowledge would be lost with her.

They desperately needed fresh water for the crew and animals.

The journey up what is now the Queensland coast was tortuously slow, but it was too risky to go faster, hoping to find safe harbour and fresh water and grass. Cook ordered the ship's boat to row ahead of the *Endeavour*, checking the depth of water and looking for rocks and coral below. At times they had to wait while the smaller boat hunted out a channel between the banks of coral lurking below the green water. Nights were the most dangerous. The only safe way to stop was to drop anchor, and even then the ship might still drift onto rocks. Instead they sailed as slowly as possible, hoping that the lookout and 'soundings' to check the depth of water would keep them safe. Speed was deadly, but if they didn't find water soon they'd be dead anyway.

North of the place Cook christened Magnetical Island, so named because the compass swung wildly as they passed it, Banks, Solander and Hicks went ashore to look for green coconuts that might supply juice. The palm trees they'd seen turned out to be cabbage palms. There was no water.

On 10 June Cook named and landed at Green Island – no fresh water there either. The ship's company must have felt like the ancient mariner in Coleridge's poem: 'Water, water, every where, Nor any drop to drink'.

Cook sailed on, even in the darkness. He was risking shipwreck, but if they didn't find water they were doomed.

Shipwreck came first.

The goat and sheep droppings save the ship

Sunday, 11 June was a fine, clear night with a good breeze. Cook ordered the ship to sail further offshore. They were now in the latitude where the maps of earlier explorers had noted islands. They could see shoals under the water. The danger of running aground in darkness was extreme.

But the water grew deeper and deeper, from fourteen to twenty-one fathoms (twenty-five to thirty-seven metres). Everyone relaxed. The officers were eating supper when suddenly twelve, ten then eight fathoms were called out, all within a few minutes.

Cook ordered everyone to their stations to anchor the ship. Then suddenly the water grew deeper. Cook decided the danger was over. At ten o'clock the water was still a comfortable twenty-one fathoms. The gentlemen went to bed in 'tranquillity'.

At 11 p.m. the ship hit the reef. The *Endeavour* stuck fast, motionless except for the battering of the waves about her. They were three and a half hours' sail from shore. Few of the crew could swim. Less than half could fit in the ship's boats. But the crew must have known that if the ship sank the officers and Banks would load the boats with stores instead of people, to give them food and water to get to Batavia. The crew's only chance would be to mutiny – to seize the boats and save themselves.

The deck shuddered so hard that it was almost impossible stand upright. The darkness prevented them seeing how badly they had been holed, but wreckage floated all about the ship including its false keel, the reinforcing that had been attached to the true keel to protect it. Had the keel itself been wrenched away? If it had, the ship was useless, impossible to steer even if it didn't sink.

Amazingly, no one panicked. No mutineers tried to launch the boats. Cook's two years of discipline held good. The rowboats were put to sea to investigate the damage. The men peered through the darkness at a great hole gaping in the ship's side, growing larger all the time. As the tide fell the ship would sink even further down onto the reef that snagged it.

Cook ordered everything possible thrown overboard to lighten the ship – the six great guns on deck, iron and stone ballast, casks, hoop staves, oil jars, decayed stores … Each man knew the situation was desperate – so desperate, Cook wrote years later, that the men even stopped swearing. Death seemed too near.

All night they felt the ship grind as she sank down on the coral below them. She couldn't hold together long; they could only pray that she didn't break up in darkness. In daylight there might be a chance to grab floating wreckage and a faint chance of making it to shore before dying of thirst, sharks or sunstroke. The wind dropped leaving a dead calm about them, which was one blessing – if the wind had stayed strong the waves would have battered the ship to planks and bodies.

Daylight came. Miraculously, the ship was still in one piece. Was there a chance that the ship might float off the reef at high tide, and even keep floating long enough to get closer to shore for repairs? They could see land in the distance, about forty kilometres away.

The crew threw off another fifty tons of cargo and waited for high tide. The water rose about them. Would she lift, giving them a small chance to repair her and get to shore?

But the ship stayed stuck on the reef, the water gushing in through the hole, growing deeper and deeper around them. The two pumps were only just enough to keep her from flooding. No one slept. Each man took their turn pumping, working till exhausted, then flinging themselves down on any available surface above the water to rest until they took their turn again. By 2 p.m. the ship was listing badly. More water gushed through the hole.

The next high tide was due at midnight. Could the ship last till then? She did. Slowly as the tide rose the *Endeavour* righted herself, and it became clear that the coral was blocking the great hole in the ship's hull. Once the ship floated off it the hold would fill with water. Their frantic pumping had bought them only a few hours – they were waiting for death. Cook knew that as soon as the ship began to sink his authority would vanish. Men would kill for a chance at the boats and life.

The ship lifted higher and higher still. The men kept pumping, clinging desperately to the hope that they could keep pumping out enough water to keep the ship afloat. By now they had been pumping for twenty-four hours without a break. Exhausted men collapsed into the rising water, dragged out by their friends. Suddenly, at twenty minutes past ten, the ship floated off the reef. But no matter how hard the desperate men pumped, the water was winning.

A young midshipman named Jonathon Monkhouse came to Cook with a preposterous suggestion, one he claimed he'd seen on board a merchant ship. They'd sew oakum (fibres picked from old rope) and wool into one of the sails, then spread the sail with dry sheep and goat dung. They'd guide the sail under the ship with chains and the suction of the water into the dry dung would seal the sail around the hole.

Could manure really save the ship? It was impossible. It was also their only chance. Cook gave permission.

It worked.

The solution showed desperation and ingenuity, but it also indicates something more. That tiny ship had a lot of sheep and goat manure, enough to plug a massive hole in the ship. At a minimum there must have been two or three barrels full. (Pig and fresh cattle dung is wetter, even when they are fed on dry rations, so less likely to have been used.)

Cook was rigorous about keeping the ship clean. It was scrubbed twice a week, the decks several times a day, though presumably not since the emergency began. But in that time enough manure had been deposited – and dried in the sun. To the image of a deck full of desperate men we also need to add sheep, pigs and the goat, squealing their terror. But they weren't even mentioned in Cook's log or any of the diaries kept on board. Like many other matters of everyday life in the past, their presence would be taken for granted.

The goat and sheep had saved the ship. But the fact they provided enough manure to do so shows just how important live animals were, and how vital the grass, water and frequent trips ashore to find them.

Australia had been ignored for centuries because of its relative lack of grass, fresh water, and harbours. Within twenty years the British government would see the grass and fresh water reported by Banks as a way to supply their navy and merchant ships at a time of increasing strategic tensions. Grass and fresh water – and the lack of it – have influenced a large part of Australian history, from first settlement to the planning policies of today. But the wreck of the *Endeavour* is one of the few clues to their importance in the centuries of sailing ships.

More miracles for the *Endeavour*

It took five long, desperate days and nights to get the *Endeavour* with her sail and manure-covered hull to the shore, pumping all the way. Two more miracles saved them. After weeks with no fresh water they had been wrecked near what is now the Endeavour River, where Cooktown is today. It was both a secure harbour and a safe place to beach the ship to try to repair it and a place where good grass and the fresh water they desperately needed could be found. When they finally inspected their ship they saw the second miracle: the largest hole was still plugged by a giant piece of coral. If it had fallen out the ship would have sunk.

The ship's carpenters began work on the keel and new false keel while the smiths were making bolts and nails in a forge on the shore. The animals were unloaded and put to pasture. The grass was thick and plentiful, as was the game. Cook sent a party out to shoot pigeons for the sick. They saw a swift animal the size of a greyhound and the colour of a mouse – possibly a wallaby, although if it were, then it's strange no one mentioned that it hopped on its hind legs – as well as many 'Indian houses'.

Finally, on 10 July, they saw some of the Guugu Yimithirr, four men spearing fish from a canoe. This time, for a while, there was a polite exchange, instead of shots and spear-throwing. Cook's men offered clothes, nails, food, beads and paper. One of the Guugu Yimithirr presented them with a large fish.

The repairs went well. The land provided both water and fresh food, with plenty of stingrays, turtles and roast 'kangaroo' – the first Australian word to enter the English language, although what they ate was probably wallaby, not kangaroo. But then on 19 July a party of the 'natives' came aboard to ask if they could have some of the turtles that the *Endeavour*'s crew had caught. Mr Banks curtly refused.

The Guugu Yimithirr men paddled back to shore. One grabbed a burning bit of wood from the fire and two warriors lit the tall grass all around the ship's camp. Luckily the gunpowder supply had only just been taken back on board – if it had exploded most of the crew and the stores would have been destroyed. A piglet was scorched to death.

More grass was set alight where the *Endeavour*'s fishing nets and linen were drying. Cook ordered the men to fire a musket and small shot, then Cook himself shot one of the ringleaders. Cook didn't think he had badly wounded the man but they never knew for sure.

The Guugu Yimithirr retreated. Later an old man came up, carrying a lance without a point. Cook believed this was a sign of peace. The Guugu Yimithirr left their spears against a tree, and the *Endeavour*'s crew returned the spears of theirs that they had taken.

There were no more battles. But the Guugu Yimithirr refused to go aboard the *Endeavour* again. The peaceful contact had become the second skirmish in what would become a long, slow war.

Two hundred years later, we can see how the two groups misunderstood each other. The Guugu Yimithirr shared their food. They would have believed the English acted like enemies when they refused to share the turtles. Fire was a traditional weapon against enemies. Cook admitted in his diary that the ship had more turtles than they needed – the British simply objected to the Guugu Yimithirr taking 'their' property. And those on the *Endeavour* believed that all that they could take was theirs.

It took seven weeks to repair the ship. The crew stocked it with fish, stingray, turtle, shellfish, shark and greens like the wild 'kale'.

Bad weather kept them at Endeavour River for another two weeks after the repairs were complete, leaving them time to contemplate what was to come. The passage to the north was full of rocks, reefs and shoals and islands. Could they find their way through without disaster? The master suggested they should go back the way they'd come. If they went on they might be trapped, unable to turn round, or wrecked again.

Cook refused. If they turned back they'd have to beat into the strong wind from the south. Even with the new stocks from the Endeavour River they had only three months' food. If they went back through the territory where they had been unable to find food, water or safe harbour, they would starve or die of thirst. Cook could only hope there would be a way ahead through the reef.

He ordered the ship to head out to sea, away from the coast and the reef. This would mean he could do no more mapping, but at least they might survive. It didn't work. The wind drove the ship back onto the reef then dropped, leaving them stranded among the waves that could dash them against the rocks and coral.

At least the sea inside the reef was calm. They sailed back, inside the reef, then north. Slowly they wound their way through the rocks and islands. Was Torres Strait really there? Or would they have to try to take their roughly repaired ship all the way around New Guinea to get to Batavia? Finally, on Tuesday, 21 August, they were at the most northerly part of the continent. Cook named it York Cape.

Now they could sail westward. Torres Strait did exist, after all. Cook had also proved that New Holland was separate from New Guinea. He had mapped a new coast, and proved that a valuable strait and shortcut between the Indian and Pacific oceans existed. They were now within a few days' sail of Batavia and what they assumed was safety. It was time to claim the rest of the land he'd mapped for the king. Cook wrote later: 'I now once More hoisted English Colours, and in the Name of His Majesty King George the Third took possession of the whole Eastern coast from the above Lat. down to this place by the Name of New South Wales, together with all the Bays, Harbours, Rivers, and Islands.'

Once again, the ceremony mattered most to those who performed it. Cook must have known that his maps claimed the land he called New South Wales more firmly for Britain than flying the flag had done. Any ship that sailed this way would have to use English maps – and, in doing so, admit the English claim.

A mapmaker had won a country.

Death and triumph

The shipyards of Batavia repaired the *Endeavour*, but the crew weren't safe yet. Also known as the 'the white man's graveyard', Batavia was a Dutch creation of fetid swamps and polluted water, rife with diseases like typhoid and dysentery.

In the end, disease from Batavia's squalid water would kill a third of the *Endeavour*'s crew. They had survived the soaring waves of the Southern Ocean, the gales of New Zealand and the teeth of the Great Barrier Reef. They could not survive the man-made filth of Batavia. Jonathon Monkhouse, the boy who had saved the ship, was one of those who died on the voyage home, the polluted water the *Endeavour* had taken on board continuing to kill so many of the crew that it might have become a ghost ship, with too few crew to sail her. But the ship, Cook, Banks and the goat made it home.

The goat, in particular, was a heroine. She died the year after the voyage, in April 1772, only two days after parliament had voted to give her a state pension. A poem in Latin by the celebrated Dr Samuel Johnson and inscribed on her silver collar was her epitaph:

Perpetua ambita bis terra praemia lactis
Haec habet altrici capra secunda Jovis.

Or:

In fame scarce second to the nurse of Jove,
This goat, who twice the world had traversed round,
Deserving both her master's care and love,
Ease and perpetual pasture now has found.[5]

Terra nullius

Nearly two hundred years later, the legal basis for Cook's claim – terra nullius, or an uninhabited country – would be challenged in the Australian courts. In the controversial 1971 Gove land rights case, Justice Blackburn ruled that there was no such thing as native title in Australian law. In 1992, Torres Strait Islander Eddie Mabo fought for and won recognition of his people's traditional right to their island, the High Court of Australia issuing a judgment that was a direct overturning of terra nullius.

But the concept – and the legality of the British acquisition of the land – is still controversial. Did terra nullius really mean 'uninhabited', or 'not subject to civilised rule'? The Indigenous nations of the time

Cook's log and Banks's diary were combined and published. In it Cook gave a promising account of Australia:

> ... this Eastern side is not the barren and miserable country that Dampier and others have described the western side to be ... In this Extensive Country it can never be doubted but what most sorts of Grain, Fruit, roots, etc., of every kind would flourish here were they once brought hither, planted and Cultivated by the hands of Industry; and here are Provender for more Cattle, at all seasons of the Year, than can ever be brought into the Country.

Cook was finally made captain, and his second voyage (1772–75) was possibly an even greater achievement than his first, finally disposing of the myth of the Great South Land. He crossed and recrossed the Antarctic Circle and the Pacific in long methodical sweeps from Antarctica on one side to Polynesia on the other using New Zealand as his base, coming within sight of the great banks of ice that edge the most southerly continent. This voyage brought him far more personal fame, as Joseph Banks had been given most of the public recognition for the discoveries of the first voyage.

Cook was persuaded to take what would be his final voyage in 1777. This was as secret an expedition as his first: supposedly to go to Tahiti, but were arguably as civilised as British society, with its hangings, child labour, poverty, social inequities, female repression and abduction of sailors. Britain at the time was not a democracy. Few men could vote, and no women, and their Parliament was restricted in its powers. The Indigenous people lived lives of more comfort, health, security and leisure than most Britons.

They did not, however, have muskets – their cultures were more generous than confrontational. In the end, the muskets would rule. Perhaps this is the most honest summary: the British fought for the land against a people who often didn't realise their land was being taken – or even that that anyone could 'own' land in the European fashion – until it was too late. The British won.

then to head north to Alaska to find a passage in the northwest linking the Pacific and Atlantic oceans. (In these days of engines it is hard to appreciate how reliant ships were on the wind and currents, forcing them to take long routes that we would now wonder at.) Cook landed at Australia once more, at Van Diemen's Land, to rest the crew after the gales of the Southern Ocean and to restock with firewood, fresh water and grass for the stock. He left three pigs behind so that they would breed up and feed any other crews that might need stores. Luckily the pigs either died or were eaten before they could become feral: Tasmania was spared – for the moment – a feral pig problem. But the pigs Cook had left behind at Endeavour River are still breeding and devastating the land.

Cook did not find a northwest passage. When he met his end at Hawai'i in 1779 he was already exhausted and ill from too much journeying. Once again misunderstanding the local culture, he was clubbed to death in the surf as he tried to lead his crew to take hostage the king of Hawai'i, Kalani'ōpu'u, after the theft of a rowboat. Cook's body slid under the bloodstained water and then was dragged away by the Hawaiians.[6] The British officers demanded that his body be given back for burial. Only a slice of his thigh was returned, and then other parts wrapped in a feathered cape, recognisable only by the scar on the captain's hands.

Cook would go discovering no more.

The public was fascinated by Cook's voyage, Banks's discoveries and the goat. But no one seemed to think it worthwhile to go back to New South Wales. It might be possible to grow grains and fruits on the east coast of New South Wales, but why should anyone bother taking them across the world on a voyage that would take about nine months? The west coast could have been useful to the Dutch as a supply port, but the east was too far away. Charts to a worthless land were worth nothing.

In 1772, just two years after Cook's 'discovery', on yet another failed voyage to find the non-existent Terra Australis, Louis François de Saint Allouarn claimed the west coast of Australia, this time for the French. But neither France nor Britain really cared.

CHAPTER 7

The colony that didn't starve

Sydney Harbour, 1963

We clamber across the rocks just after dawn. The world is empty apart from us, two ten-year-old girls, and a fisherman further down the beach, his dog nosing at a dead seagull. We snack as we go, bashing oyster shells with rocks and eating the briny flesh, nibbling shreds of seaweeds, sucking the nectar from flowers dotted in the crevices. In the cool light before adults wake up and the world of rules begins, it is a place of plenty.

At school we have been learning that the first colony starved here, near the cove once called Tumbalong, 'the place where food is found'. (These days it's Darling Harbour. Food is still found in abundance, though now you have to hand over money for ice-cream, sushi and nasi goreng, unless you are a seagull foraging in the garbage bins.)

That early starvation has been described over and over again in school history books, novels and television dramatisations. But the two of us wonder how could the first colony have starved when here, almost two hundred years later, the harbour is still rich in sweet, salty oysters and tough winkles? The old men with thin fags and grey stubble fishing from the rocks or casting into the waves along the beach almost invariably have a bag of fish, and sometimes – if we look admiringly enough – they give us a couple to 'take back to cook for your breakfast, love'.

We were lucky not to catch salmonella, or at least get heavy metal poisoning – the 1960s harbour was a soup of industrial and household pollution. But I still remember the tiny bushes that decades later I'd learn bore edible fruits, the ground covers that gave edible seed for 'breads' to be cooked on hot rocks, and the fat-leafed plant we now call warrigal greens that can spread to a three-metre patch even in a drought and give enough veg to feed a clan.

It was a world of food. How could a colony have starved in a 'living larder', tended and planted over many generations to provide food no matter what extremes of weather? And if the colony didn't starve, why has the myth persisted?

The base in the south

Australia's first colony began only because of a complete misunderstanding of the site it was being sent to.

Australia had been known, and rejected, by the various colonial powers for centuries. But now it was in the right place at the right time – and so was its newly discovered fresh water, grass and presumed safe harbour of Botany Bay.

Britain had been at war with France and Holland, and further war seemed likely. The British urgently needed a new base in the south to supply their ships for both war and trade, in case they were no longer able to restock their ships at the Dutch-controlled Cape of Good Hope in Africa, or Dutch-controlled Batavia.

The problem was where to put it. Gambia? Too hot and barren. Das Voltas Bay in South West Africa, now Namibia? The scouting party said it was rocky, hot and without fresh water. But Sir Joseph Banks – who had seen the place that Cook named Botany Bay for a few days more than a decade before – said that it was the perfect spot for a colony, with plenty of grass, fertile soil, fresh water, a good sheltered harbour, and strong, straight timber not just for houses but for ships' masts.

Botany Bay had none of these. Admittedly, Banks probably saw it at its most lush, with greenery and a few springs of fresh water. But even a wet year can't make a poor harbour stormproof, nor make twisted trees into good straight timber or turn the springs Banks saw into a stream big enough to irrigate crops. Botany Bay was also too far away for a scouting party to go and check on conditions. James Cook might have given a much more sober assessment of Botany Bay, particularly its dangerous winds and treacherous sandbanks. But Cook was dead, and what Banks lacked in skill, knowledge and humility he made up for in enthusiasm and political influence. The First Fleet would sail an eight-month voyage on the word of well-connected but incompetent amateur botanist.

Supplying a new land

To give Banks his due, he did help ensure that the colony would be well supplied, personally drawing up lists of seeds, fruit trees and tools. Only parts of those lists survive, but they still show evidence of intelligent planning. Banks may have misjudged the vegetation, but he had noticed that the weather was hot and planned the fruit and vegetable lists accordingly.

The varieties of vegetable seeds, for example, were specified. Green savoy cabbage as well as york cabbage; one for fast cropping, the other for storage. Long orange carrot was probably a recent introduction from the Netherlands, where the vegetable growers had been breeding improved varieties; most carrots before this were white or pale yellow. 'Prickly cucumber' may have been apple cucumber, a heat-hardy variety grown in both South Africa and India at that time. 'Speckled kidney beans' may be the hardy 'Freckles' variety, good both fresh and dried, and excellent survivors in hot, dry climates. They might also have been runner beans, as these have a speckled seed and are extremely hardy. Banks may have chosen either variety because they did well in the hot, dry conditions of Cape Town and so, presumably, would flourish in New South Wales.

Among the seeds listed to be carried by one of the First Fleet ships, the *Sirius*, was 'white beet', useful both as sugar beet and for animal forage. Dwarf marrow peas would have been good both fresh and dried to make the staple pease pudding, boiled in its cloth with a little ham or bacon. Banks listed both 'cabbage lettuce', a sturdy hearting variety, and cos, named for the Mediterranean island and, again, a heat-hardy variety. There was 'white broccoli' as well as cauliflower, and twenty-six bushels of 'Best onion seed' – enough to sow onion seed for several years to feed the entire colony. Potatoes, rhubarb seed, hemp, flax and tobacco seed were recommended, and presumably much more besides in the lists that have vanished over the years.

There was also wheat, barley, buckwheat and oats, and pasture seeds: many hundreds of bushels with an extremely wide range. The *Sirius* alone carried 274 bushels of vegetable seeds, and well as plants of artichoke, horseradish, grapes, figs, strawberries, and many others, stored in wooden barrels, canvas bags, sacks and casks.

The cargo was divided between the First Fleet ships, so if one sank nothing irreplaceable would be lost. If the amounts of seed were similar to the *Sirius*'s twenty-six bushels of onion seeds, they were carrying enough to ensure that crops could be sown for several years, even if they failed to produce new seeds. Most vegetable seed is viable for at least five years, and sometimes decades, if stored properly, although an eight month sea voyage in small ships 'stored properly' makes that a big 'if'.

Banks also chose fruit trees that would suit both hot and cold climates, with an emphasis on the ones known to do well in Rio de Janeiro, where more fruit trees were taken on board. There were bananas, coffee and cocoa plants, which presumably failed, or more likely died in the chill of the Southern Ocean during the voyage, as there's no record of them fruiting. While bananas and even coffee may fruit as far south as Sydney, no one who knew anything about cocoa plants would have recommended them for a climate so far from the equator. Banks recommended shaddocks, as well – a good choice, heat-hardy giant citrus fruits like overgrown grapefruit. The expedition's Lieutenant David Collins also mentions 'Indigo, Coffee, Ginger, Castor Nut, Oranges, Lemons, & Limes, Firs & Oaks'. At least one of the varieties of 'lemon' was probably citronelle, or what's now known as 'bush lemon': thorny, drought resistant, but used extensively in the early colony as a prickly hedge to keep stock out of orchards or vegetable plots. Some trees were seedlings; most probably grated; others taken as cuttings.[1]

It would be difficult to convince free settlers to head across the world to an unknown land, therefore the colonists would be convicts. The tale in my school history books was that England needed a place to house the convicts they could no longer send to newly independent America.

But it would have been cheaper to keep prisoners in English jails, or even the old ships on the Thames, than send them across the world with enough equipment to build a colony. It was only much later, when the colony was self supporting, and convicts were housed and fed by the landowners they were assigned to, that shipping criminals here became a relatively cheap option.

The school history books – and our wish to romanticise our ancestors – also say that most had been guilty of petty crimes like stealing a loaf of bread, or a handkerchief; that these were poor innocents, jailed for poverty and desperation. They weren't; most had already been convicted before. Their crimes look minor because the magistrates and judges were sometimes compassionate men. A theft of goods worth more than a guinea meant death by hanging, so if the magistrates believed there was a chance of rehabilitation they would convict for stealing only a part of what had been stolen, or young men and boys were sent to the navy away from the English slums, smog-ridden, filthy and crowded, ruled by the leaders of criminal gangs and filled with an underclass of wretches who rarely lived to twenty. Children were often born with foetal alcohol syndrome, physically and mentally impaired, the babies fed gin instead of milk to keep them quiet – and gin was cheaper. It was cheaper than bread, too, and eased both physical and mental pain.

The first convict colonists were chosen with care, except towards the end when a bit of a grab bag was added to make up numbers. They were young, as healthy as the horrendous prison system allowed, weren't guilty of any major crime, and if possible had useful skills. This was their chance for redemption, and when they served their sentences the males would even be offered free land.

This selection is important. Many of Australia's first settlers were lazy, ignorant, and prejudiced, but they had also been chosen as those most likely to succeed. (It is also possible that the 'laziness' of the first few years was a symptom of widespread depression in new and frightening circumstances, with little hope of return to the life they'd known, rather than a true dislike of hard work.)

Of the 1487 people on the First Fleet, 759 were convicts, thirteen were convicts' children and 252 were marines (soldiers sent to sea) and their wives and children. There were also 210 Royal Navy seamen and 233 merchant seamen, but when the ships had unloaded their human and other cargo they would sail away, and these seamen with them, leaving the colony with only the two small ships *Sirius* and *Supply*.

Nearly all the convicts were thieves – pickpockets, sheep stealers, poachers – with seven swindlers and four forgers.[2] Most were young but had been starved in filthy, disease-racked prisons and hulks, and lice-ridden and ragged. Almost half the men were farm labourers, and had some farming experience. There was only one gardener and one fisherman, five cobblers or shoemakers, six carpenters, five weavers (including a silk weaver), two bricklayers, a jeweller, a baker and a scattering of other trades. Most of the women had been servants, so could presumably sew and knew the rudiments of cooking. There were also oyster sellers and cloak, hat and glove makers, who would know how to do fine sewing.

Polynesian brides for the colony?

Of the approximately 759 convicts, about 586 were male, plus the male marines and sailors. There were only about 217 women in the whole fleet, about 192 of whom were convicts. (This number also included the wives of non-commissioned officers, but as record keeping wasn't good, various sources give slightly different numbers.) This was at least better than the original plan, in which there would have been only seventy women. A young officer suggested hopefully that Polynesian women would be eager to marry English men. The British government informed the fleet's captain (and later colony governor), Arthur Phillip, that he might ship five hundred Polynesian women back to the colony.

If the plan had worked and shiploads of Polynesians had been brought to Australia, our rugby teams might be more successful and our rate of melanoma lower. But the dream of eager Polynesian lovers was as unfounded as Banks's illusions of a harbour of good trees and grass. The young colony would have more pressing duties for its ships than fetching five hundred dark-eyed women, nor would the women have been likely to come willingly, though admittedly that didn't stop blackbirders later in Australia's history from capturing Melanesian slaves to work in the canefields of Queensland. Many Australian men would suffer lifetimes of loneliness until the male–female ratio more or less evened up in the 1870s and 1880s.

Stripping and scrubbing

The prisoners' wrists and ankles were chained before they were sent in open carts from their various prisons to the port of Plymouth, then rowed in small boats out to the waiting ships. On board they were unchained and their filthy rags stripped off before they were washed in two big tubs of water – not so much to get them clean but to get rid of the fleas and lice that might carry diseases. Once a disease caught hold on a ship it might spread to everyone – sometimes ships were found floating and empty, everyone on board dead of plague or typhus, or with too few healthy crew members to sail to shore.

The convicts were given coarse off-white shirts and trousers; the convict arrows came decades later. Their chains were put back on and they climbed down the ladder to below deck.

Captain Phillip had argued long and hard with the authorities about providing proper food, tools and clothing for the convicts. A crooked contractor, Duncan Campbell, had stolen half the food supplies, and ignorant Royal Navy bureaucrats had tried to give the fleet only enough food to get to the Bahamas, no cloth for new clothes and only six scythes for an entire colony.

Phillip got his way, but it is worth remembering how hard he had to work to get adequate supplies. He and the officers would have every reason to make their needs known, in the most vivid terms possible, in letters sent back to the authorities in the future. Even with all his arguing, most of the stores were years old even before they were loaded onto the ships: rancid butter, weevilly flour, maggoty dried peas and hard ship's biscuit. The food for common sailors was usually the cheapest possible (officers and passengers brought their own stores), and frequently spoiled, but due to Campbell's conniving, the fleet's stores may have been even worse than most.

Finally the ships set sail in May 1787. It was the largest expedition in European history: eleven ships carrying 1487 people travelling 15,063 miles. (Earlier Chinese fleets were larger, and may have journeyed longer.) HMS *Sirius* and *Supply* were Royal Navy ships, with naval men and officers. The *Alexander, Charlotte, Friendship, Scarborough, Prince of Wales* and *Lady Penrhyn* were merchant ships chartered by the British government to transport the convicts, as were the three store ships, *Borrowdale, Golden Grove* and *Fishburn*. The largest was only thirty-six metres long.

The only light down below came from the hatch, and the ships stank. The toilet bucket was generally emptied once a day, though in rough weather they weren't emptied at all. Instead buckets would have floated back and forth in the water between the two rows of bunks, where three convicts shared each bed, along with the faeces, vomit and dead rats. But Phillip provided fresh food wherever possible and, except in storms or when the ships were in port, the shackled convicts were allowed up on deck for part of each day.

Free settlers

It wasn't until 1791 on the Second Fleet that a single free settler arrived, James Smith or Smyth, but was found 'too advanced in years' to work. Eleven free settlers would arrive in 1793.

Farewell to old England forever

All on board knew they had about a thirty per cent chance of shipwreck on the way – one in three English ships of the time was lost on each long voyage. And about thirty per cent of sailors might die on a bad voyage, though the convicts would rate their chances at far less. Few, if any, could swim, and the ship's pinnaces (small wooden boats that could be sailed or rowed in the event of an emergency, or used to row to shore) could not carry more than a couple of dozen people away from a wreck.

The convicts had been sentenced to either seven or fourteen years, though some had already served several years of their sentence. In five years or less they might be free. But they would face another nine-month voyage, with all its dangers, to get back again. The men might sign aboard as crew; the only hope for the women was to find a man who might provide for them.

They would have feared the ocean, its storms and, even worse, its doldrums, where no wind blew and ships rotted, becalmed, till all on board died of thirst. Most of all, they would have feared the land ahead. The ignorant might have imagined dragons or cannibals. The better-informed would have been as worried, for they might understand just how little Banks had really experienced of the land he had so confidently selected for them.

We don't know what the marines, Captain Phillip and officers ate on the voyage – while they would have eaten some of the official stores, or claimed that amount of stores to sell later (the food ration was part of their wages, and so theirs to dispose of as they wished), they are more likely to have dined on traditional traveller's fare for the time: 'portable soup' (soup bones and vegetables boiled down to a tough jelly before being wrapped in greased paper), dried fruit, port, well-boiled plum puddings, portable lemonade (sugar with dried lemon zest), tough digestive biscuits, possibly long-baked ginger biscuits too, well-smoked hams, wax-wrapped whole cheeses – all tried and traditional foods for gentlemen to take while travelling. They probably also ate fresh meat, eggs and possibly milk from privately owned animals taken on board. As only the official stock was listed, we don't know exactly what animals were on the ships when they sailed from England, but it's likely that the officers followed common practice and did bring some stock.

Convicts were fed twice a day. At sea the rations for each adult man for a week were seven pounds of salt beef (or four pounds of salt pork) stewed with three pints of dried peas, plus one pound of flour (which equated to about two hunks of bread a day, but due to Campbell's thieving they often had weevilly rice instead) and six ounces of salty, rancid butter. Women received two-thirds of this.[3]

At Tenerife, Rio de Janeiro and Cape Town, Phillip ordered the convicts to eat all the fresh fruit they could – and be lashed if they refused to eat – as well as fresh meat and vegetables to help keep scurvy at bay during the next leg of the voyage. At Rio, Phillip bought a hundred sacks of tapioca so that the women convicts might use the tough bags to make clothes for themselves – many were in rags or nearly naked. They also loaded orange trees, guava trees, and prickly pear.

At the Cape of Good Hope, nine head of cattle and seven horses were led on board, as well as chickens, pigs, sheep – at least five hundred animals – and also plants and more seeds. These were selected by the 'King's botanist' there, Mr Mason (or Masson), according to the account written by David Collins.[4] Sir Joseph Banks had hoped that Mason would join the colony. He didn't, but did make sure they were provided with sugarcane sets, grapevines and quince, orange, lime, lemon, apple, pear and many other fruit trees. As well as the official plants and animals, many of the officers and marines bought more animals, trees and seeds for themselves. All were crammed in below.

The next part of the voyage was the most dangerous – the great rearing waves of the Southern Ocean where Cape Agulhas marked the place where the Atlantic and Indian oceans met. Sheep would have bleated; convicts clung to each other or their beds. The waves of the Cape were the ship destroyers unless you were lucky to meet them on the few days they were calm.

The First Fleet was not lucky. Day after day the tiny ships climbed each great wave, then tumbled down between the swells only to face another monster, white-tipped with spray. The storms continued on even when they were past what was supposed to be the worst. Lightning and wind split the *Golden Grove*'s topsail and blew the *Prince of Wales*'s mainyard away. But at last the relentless westerly winds were blowing them towards Australia, taking about a month off the expected nine-month voyage. Miraculously, only twenty-three convicts had died during the voyage, fewer than might have died in the squalor and starvation of British prisons or workhouses.

Finally, on 19 January 1788, the lookout on the *Supply* saw land for the first time since leaving the Cape.[5] The next morning the ships were all anchored in Botany Bay, looking at the land that Banks had promised them.

Across the world to a sandy waste

It didn't look good. Exposed and sandy, with scattered tussocks and twisted trees. No river or even a creek. And on the shore were natives – not the meek inhabitants promised by Banks but warriors with two-metre spears tipped with long, sharp bone. According to the chief surgeon of the expedition, Surgeon John White:

> Although the spot fixed on for the town was the most eligible that could be chosen, yet I think it would never have answered, the ground around it being sandy, poor, and swampy, and but very indifferently supplied with water. The fine meadows talked of in Captain Cook's voyage I could never see, though I took some pains to find them out; nor have I ever heard of a person that has seen any parts resembling them.[6]

If the land looked dismal to the marines and sailors, the newcomers must have looked even worse to the Kameygal people (a clan of the Dharug language group) gathered on the shore. They had seen big ships before – and been shot at by the sailors – but Cook's men had recuperated in New Zealand, with fresh food and time ashore. These intruders would have been pale from too long with no fresh food.

The watchers grew wary. A mob assembled on the beach yelling, 'Warra warra' – 'Go away!' One man threw his spear, though not right at the newcomers. Then a second man aimed his at the marines. A marine fired a blank from his musket. The Kameygal ran, startled by the noise.

If Australia wants heroes from the First Fleet, we have Captain (later Governor) Phillip. Not only had he secured the supplies that would enable the colony to survive, he had also brought his people safely across the world. He stepped out of the ship's boat and walked alone towards the angry Kameygal, holding out some bread. His confidence and deep integrity must have shown. The Kameygal returned. They even showed the newcomers where to find fresh water – a seeping spring, not the ample water supply promised by Banks.

A land to starve and die in

But the colony had far greater problems than the fact that there were a lot more Aboriginal people than Banks had said. The sheltered harbour they expected could only be reached if the ships passed over a sandbar where they risked running aground. There was no turning back now for far-off England.

For hundreds of years, Australia had been ignored because of its lack of good harbours. The nearest known good harbour was far to the north, at Endeavour River, near present-day Cooktown, but to get there they'd have to navigate the deadly reef that had wrecked the *Endeavour* and nearly cost Cook and his crew their lives.

Cook had already charted this coast minutely and found no harbour, just the small opening between the cliffs he'd named Port Jackson but hadn't been able to investigate because of the strong southerly. With few other options, Phillip sent a boat of officers north to investigate. It must have seemed a hopeless task, to go where the great mapper and navigator had already found no safe mooring. Large harbours aren't usually well hidden, nor are large rivers of fresh water. The colony desperately needed both to survive.

It must have seemed a miracle when they found them: a vast harbour, big enough to house Britain's entire navy, with deep water close enough to the shore to make transferring humans, stock and supplies relatively easy. The narrow entrance could be defended against invading French or Dutch ships. Port Jackson had fresh water, good soil, and tall, straight cabbage trees that looked (deceptively) as if they'd make superb timber. After a small collision as the ships manoeuvred their way out of Botany Bay, the fleet anchored at Port Jackson and began to unload.

We can only imagine what the watching Cadigal saw: the big, white-topped ships, the small, pale men wearing what must have seemed hot and heavy skins. It is easier to reconstruct what the newcomers gazed at: the beauty of the harbour, long inlets of blue water, green bush flowing down onto black rocks and golden sandstone; curls of smoke from the fires on the shore; small, low-slung canoes where women fished and children dived into the waves or shrieked as they saw the strange ships. The trees grew thick and strong, and the creek they'd name the Tank Stream flowed rippling down to the water alongside beaches of white-gold sand (most now vanished under port facilities) and great golden-brown fissured cliffs (now hidden behind the hotels of the Rocks and the Toaster at the Quay). According to Surgeon White's diary entry for

26 January: 'Port Jackson I believe to be, without exception, the finest and most extensive harbour in the universe, and at the same time the most secure, being safe from all the winds that blow …'[7]

They had left Banks's sandy desert of Botany Bay behind. This was a paradise.

A food Eden

In 1787, the year before the British First Fleet arrived, the Dharug people ate extremely well. It only took an hour or two each day to gather enough food and starvation was an almost impossible concept: every metre or so would bring new things to eat. A Dharug woman would eat as she walked, plucking berries or fern tips, the children sucking the nectar from banksias, wattle, melaleucas and grevilleas, or collecting them to soak in water to make the sweet drink called *bool*. Even a child could pull baby bettongs out of their nests in the tussocks, make a bandicoot trap from long grass, catch a snake-necked turtle, pull a sleepy possum from its hole high up in a gum tree, or grab a snake sleepy from winter cold and snap its neck quickly.

The food was partly cultivated, with fruit and fibre trees and shrubs planted near the best campsites, and partly carefully harvested. The clan moved on before the food source was exhausted. There were also seasonal eel gatherings at Parramatta, whale feasts or grass-seed harvests. Fish were plentiful the year round if you knew which ones to catch according to their season. The Dharug women netted fish or threw lines overboard from their small bark canoes that sat low in the water, with tiny fires on board to cook the fish for their children. Back on shore, long lines were strung up to smoke excess fish as travelling food. Freshwater mussels in the creeks and oysters on the rocky foreshore were there for the taking. The Dharug women even 'called' whales to the shore, dancing on the squeaking sand to make a high-pitched whale-like cry. A whale feast lasted for days or weeks. Sometimes the entrails were thrown out into the harbour as a reward for the fish-eating orca whales that had herded the other whale species towards the hunters. The Dharug lit hunting fires, but also dug ground traps and covered them with branches to catch wallabies, kangaroos and emus. Woven reed, lomandra or sticky fig sap traps caught birds and smaller animals like bandicoots. Fruit bats and possums – both excellent eating – were captured while they slept during the day. The women smeared themselves with mud to disguise the scent of human, then lit smoky fires of bark, or banksia cones. As the fruit bats fell to the ground, confused by the smoke, they were grabbed and despatched.

Compared with a modern supermarket, there was an extraordinary abundance of different foods, so many that it would take several volumes to describe them all: yam daisies grew in the grasslands, the best and biggest plants left to set seed to keep improving the quality of the species, and three kinds of lilly pilly (*Syzygium*, *Eugenia* and *Acmena* spp.), sandpaper fig (*Ficus coronata*), Port Jackson fig and native raspberry *(Rubus parvifolius)* flourished in the wet gullies. There were native cherry (*Exocarpos cupressiformis*), native grape (*Cissus* spp.), native currant, native orange, native mulberry, kangaroo apple *(Solanum spp.)* and geebungs (*Persoonia* spp.), apple berry *(Billardiera scandens)*, wombat berry *(Eustrephus latifolius)* and sweet morinda *(Morinda jasminoides)*. Don't be put off by the bitter or tasteless varieties of those you may come across today: those around camp sites and useful waterholes had been carefully selected to be larger, sweeter, and more flavourful. The massive flower stems of the giant flame lily (*Doryanthes excelsa*) were roasted until tender. The core of starch was extracted from various palms, tree ferns and cycads, using a range of techniques to make them edible, including coating the hands in 'latex' from fig tree sap so that any toxins wouldn't be absorbed through the skin.

There were grains and roots in abundance, too. Pigface (*Carpobrotus glaucescens*), with its tiny nutritious seeds and sour fleshy leaves, grew on the dunes; bulrush *(Typha domingensis)*, with its thick pollen for making small cakes, grew in the swamps and also had thick starchy white roots to bake. Rock lily (*Dendrobium speciosum*) stems could be eaten raw, or baked on hot coats. Burrawang (*Macrozamia communis*) seeds were leached in running water to remove the toxins then ground for flour, as were lomandra seeds. The sweet small roots of ground orchids were baked, as were kurrajong roots. An extraordinary number of species of blossom were soaked for their sweet nectar, which was sometimes fermented. Some are extremely rich in vitamin C, others with other vitamin and minerals.

But the harbour was a food paradise only if you knew what was good and what could kill you. The fruits, roots and grains were unfamiliar to the newcomers, though the intrepid experimenter Surgeon White would try as many new plants as he could find, both for food and medicine. But even as the first settlers came ashore they must have seen what they knew was food: oysters and winkles on the rocks, possibly mussels in the mud, the tracks of crabs in the sand, the scent of cooking fish from the Dharug women's canoes. The flocks of birds winging through the trees alone would speak of food to any gentleman who had shot for sport, or farm labourer who'd done a bit of poaching. Even to a newcomer, this was a land of food.[8]

The colony of bitter bread

The ships unloaded the able-bodied men, five women to act as cooks, and the animals. This last was urgent, as the stores of hay and other food had run out, and the animals dying of starvation. Axes bit into the trees to clear enough land to erect the tents and the canvas governor's house. Once Phillip stepped ashore he became the colony's governor, as well as captain of the fleet. The blacksmith's forge was set up, fireplaces were built of stones and the first vegetable garden was hastily planted. On 6 February the women were rowed ashore, and there was a wild party that night – wild in both senses of the phrase, as a storm blew in from the south. Lightning struck a pig and some sheep; the colony was drenched.

At first the convicts were shackled, but it is difficult to cut down trees or dig gardens in chains. They were soon freed, with the more responsible convicts as overseers. Australia was, in effect, a prison without bars. The convicts were free to do everything except go home.

Governor Phillip had expected the marines, under Major Robert Ross, to oversee work parties, act as magistrates and generally help keep order in the colony. But Major Ross made it extremely clear that the very suggestion was an insult. His marines were there only to guard against an attack by the French, or the Indigenous inhabitants. Apart from that, they would keep to their traditional activities: parades and getting drunk at regimental dinners, as well as a bit of huntin', fishin' and shootin', a gentleman's hobbies of the time. The marines were also assigned male convicts to dig their vegetable gardens, and female convicts to wash their clothes, cook their food and presumably, in a large number of cases, share their beds.

After eight months at sea, many of the women had already established relationships with sailors or marines. The first huts were therefore raised by their lovers, built mostly of the cabbage tree palm that grew tall and straight and was relatively easily felled and hammered, with the palm leaves used for roofing. (Both the wood and palm leaves would start to rot within a year.) The massive central hunk of greenery at the top of each palm could also be boiled to make the 'hearts of palm' well known to any English sailor who had eaten supplies from the Pacific. Parties of women were despatched to gather oyster shells to burn to make lime so that stone and lime mortar chimneys could be made, or even stone cottages. Presumably the oysters were eaten first, as all the colonists would have been familiar with the city cries of the oyster sellers, a cheap and popular English street food at the time.

Meanwhile, the first seedlings were shrivelling in the newly dug gardens. Australia's first European-style vegetable garden was dug, fenced and planted on 29 January 1788, supervised by keen gardener Lieutenant Philip Gidley King. It was small, with beans, peas and 'small salad' plants. The first orchard appears to have been planted next to the portable canvas house erected by the now Governor Phillip, with the trees bought at Rio de Janeiro and the Cape of Good Hope, including grapes, apples, figs, oranges and pears. On 11 February, a more extensive garden was dug and planted on what was named Garden Island, hopefully safely away from potential thieves as well as wandering sheep that might prefer cabbages to native grass.

Unfortunately the clear areas of good soil Banks had described weren't to be seen. Land needed to be cleared to plant anything, and Australian hardwood eucalyptus trees are much tougher to chop than European softwoods. The first colonists soon began to focus on clearing the cabbage trees – easy chopping, but the wood would soon rot.

One notable omission from the many descriptions of planting the gardens is the adding of manure or fertiliser. This was probably because there was none to be had. Back in England every farm had dunghills.

Crop rotation was common: land would be cropped for two years, and then left 'fallow' for animals to eat the weeds and manure the ground in the third year. Pigs were kept in sties, fed scraps, and produced large amounts of dung for vegetable gardens.

But there were no dunghills yet in Australia, and for the next hundred years most stock would be allowed to roam, kept (more or less) in check by shepherds. The land seemed endless, and building hardwood or stone fences hard work. The hedges that could be used to keep stock enclosed in England took at least five years to grow to a useful size. Using human waste was regarded as a 'heathenish' practice – until the 1970s, most human waste would be consigned to creeks, rivers and the sea wherever possible. James Ruse would work out how to compost native grasses mixed with dung to feed the crops in the next three years, but in 1788 there was no fertiliser to be had.

January and February in Sydney are not a good time to plant, especially if you don't have a hose handy. The 'salad stuff' did well, as did the pumpkins, maize, turnips and potatoes, but other crops withered, and the beans and peas didn't set much of a crop. But this didn't seem to worry anyone (although violent fluctuations of the weather were a shock: from 109 degrees F in the morning to the cold of a southerly wind in the afternoon; from dry weeks to violent thunderstorms). The colony had enough basic food supplies for two years, and expected a supply ship to follow within a few months. They had plenty of seed, enough for the next three or four years. An immediate planting had been worth trying, even if it came to nothing. The diarists and letter writers of the time assumed that when the seeds were planted at the proper time the crops would flourish in the warmth.

Even though the land at the newly named Sydney Cove wasn't – and isn't – as fertile as the river flats of the Hawkesbury River or Parramatta, enriched by tens of thousands of years of flood silt, the natural soil of Sydney Cove is good enough to grow a decent vegetable garden, even without fertilisers and hoses. Back in the 1960s, when my grandmother lived on a long sloping block of land above Quakers Hat Bay in Sydney's north, she had a small area of what had been untouched bush cleared and terraced by her gardener. Without any fertilising, watering or much weeding, the plants in that new ground grew extremely well. (Magically well, for a small girl entranced at seeing shrivelled seeds and what looked like dead sticks turn into garden.)

European forest soils are often deep and rich, made up on thousands of years of autumn leaves. Once the trees are cleared you can grow many years of crops without adding fertiliser, though doing so will give you a far larger and more reliable harvest. The soil around Sydney Cove is naturally thin, but it can support a few years of annual crops like vegetables or wheat before fertilising is vital. Even through that first late summer and winter of 1788 the fruit trees and vines grew abundantly, and so did autumn plantings of potatoes and maize. Fish and game were plentiful.

Rations were distributed once or twice a week, to be cooked by each convict in their own pannikin around communal fires. There were two styles of cooking them: boiling the crumbling dried peas, flour, cheese, rancid and heavily salted butter (already several years old without refrigeration), and salt pork or beef in one great mess; or boiling up everything except the salt pork or beef, and roasting that over the fire. By our standards – and those of the Dharug, who refused to eat anything but freshly caught meat, fish, or fresh vegetables or bread – the food was disgusting. But that boiled mess wasn't so far removed from one of the most common country dishes of England, pease pudding: dried peas, sometimes with flour added, flavoured with salt meat, boiled in a cloth or any bit of rag. But it was still a long way from palatable fresh food. Governor Phillip wrote that while the 'natives' politely took bread or meat if it was offered to them, they usually threw it away as soon as they left. If offered fresh fish, on the other hand, they ate it.

Bread was made with sour, weevil-infested wheat flour – wonderfully familiar bread, even if it had to be baked in the ashes rather than a bread oven, which the colony still lacked, and was heavy from lack of yeast. Dried yeast had not yet been invented, and if the colony had bread – and beer-making yeast it was likely to have become contaminated with wild yeasts, so that the bread was heavy and bitter. I suspect, however, that the colony wouldn't get decent yeasts for several years. There is no mention of the convicts making beer, but many complaints that the colony was virtually alcohol-free.

Convicts started work at dawn, but by early afternoon they were free to tend their own gardens on the land each man had been assigned. Phillip's dream colony was a facsimile of an English village: small cottages where each family grew all their own vegetables and helped in the harvest or 'gleaned' the leftover wheat after the main harvest was brought in. With hens and a pig to eat the scraps, most European villagers grew more than ninety per cent of their family's food, using the dung from the pigs and hens as fertiliser, and wood ash to add potash and keep the soil neutral. (Not that most would have known that was what wood ash did, just that a gentle dusting helped the crops and prevented black spot on their broad beans.) The European poor of the 1780s lived mostly on potatoes, onions, and cabbage, but here they were given free seed for fresh peas, carrots, brussels sprouts and other vegetables. With fish and game for the taking, the colony should soon be if not self-supporting then at least producing sufficient food.

There were the native foods to try, too. With recklessness beyond the call of duty, Surgeon White and Governor Phillip tested and tasted everything that seemed edible, both to ease the scurvy from a lack of fresh fruit and vegetables during the voyage and to supplement the supplies.[9] They seem to have relied on the 'it looks like an apple therefore we can eat it' technique, possibly one of the most unreliable ways to find edible food known.

Humans have modified their favourite foods over hundreds of years or even millennia, creating red-blushed pears, uniformly red apples, and so on. In Australia, brightly coloured fruit is more likely to be poisonous. Green veg are safer: if they aren't bitter they may be reasonably safe to eat, although native greens like warrigal spinach are even higher in oxalic acid than English spinach, and should be blanched in water before being eaten in large amounts. As the English method of cooking greens at the time was to boil them in large amounts of water for twenty to thirty minutes until resembling a grey sludge, the colonists were probably reasonably safe from the long-term effects of oxalic acid.

White, Phillip and the other food scouts did, it seems, have the knowledge and sense to avoid unknown seeds, or perhaps, at that stage, they felt they had enough flour for their needs. But more than once they suffered severe stomach trouble and diarrhoea from their experiments.

Within a few months they had come up with a goodly list of native edibles. Lieutenant Collins wrote of cabbage trees:

> The Cabbage is at the Top, enclosed in a Fibrous Network, and about this, large Fan-like leaves spring out ... Of Fruit Trees we have found a small Fig, and Berries of unknown species, One bears a Nut, which after some preparation, the Natives Eat, but one of the Convicts has been poisoned by it, in its crude State. As to the Shrubs and Plants and Herbs of this Country 'Tis beyond the Power of Botanists to number up their Tribes. Among the useful we have discovered, Balm, Parsley, Samphire, Sorrel, & a kind of Spinnage, but, all indifferent in kind a Shrub bearing a Fruit like a Sloe, and here is a Fruit which tastes exactly like the Currant when green, but these Fruits are scarce.[10]

This spinach is presumably warrigal greens, which quickly grows into two-metre clumps and one patch will feed several families. The fruits could be any of several hundred that grew in the area.

Captain William Dawes, one of the few officers of the First Fleet to have volunteered for the new colony and a keen linguist, described the new foods: 'Wigi are berry-like fruits including the tyibung [geebung or *Persoonia*], burrawang tukuba [probably the native cherry], marrinmara, magar, bomula, mirriburu and twiwaragang.' He also listed 'flowers bearing honey in sufficient quantity to render them notorious' – such as watangal [a banksia], ngurumaradyi, wiyigalung, koamea, warata [waratah], kamarang, burudun and mirrigaylang'.[11] Surgeon White also described native raspberries – 'but they had not that pleasant tartness peculiar to those in Europe' – and making soup from various wild birds.[12]

The fresh meat, fish, fruits and vegetables should have been a welcome change from rations. But convicts and officers preferred the familiar food from home.

That first winter of 1788 was a hard one. There hadn't been time to build huts for everyone. But there were supplies for at least two more years, as well as the local food. However, many of the convicts refused to eat the fresh local greens and fruits, and still suffered from scurvy after the voyage.

The wheat, maize and vegetables had been planted too late to get an autumn harvest, which made the more experienced gardeners nervous. They were used to an English autumn that Keats would soon describe as one of mists and mellow fruitfulness. Australian southern gardeners now know that peas planted in late summer will give a good crop in spring and early summer, as will broad beans and potatoes. But in that first year no one in the colony knew what should be planted when, or how long or extreme the seasons would be. They didn't even know whether to expect regular rain, like the storms at home, or the kind of seasonal tropical monsoon of ports like Batavia. The future harvests of their whole colony were based on a few days of observation, twenty years before.

They watched the bean flowers open and not set. Much of the wheat and barley seed didn't even germinate – it had either been too old when it was supplied or damaged by saltwater and humidity during the voyage. Fish, once plentiful, seemed to have vanished. (They hadn't – the colony simply didn't know where or how to catch them in winter.) Two bulls and four cows wandered or were deliberately herded away, and all but one of the sheep died or vanished. The convicts either didn't work or skimped on the job unless closely watched. Trees were felled but the roots not grubbed from the soil, earth was not dug well for planting, tussock and grass roots were left so they grew again and crowded out the vegetables. They lost or broke the tools to avoid work.

Other shortages also became obvious now, like the fact that there were no blankets or sheets for the hospital. The hospital itself filled with dysentery and scurvy patients again, despite the abundance of fresh greens and fruit. Phillip had threatened the lash to force the convicts to eat the more succulent fruit at Cape Town but now there was no one to supervise the convicts' diet – or rather, the marines could have, but wouldn't. One man died of starvation not because he had no food, but because he was hiding his food to sell and buy his passage back to England.

Phillip sent the *Sirius* back to the Cape of Good Hope for more supplies, and a pound of flour was deducted from each person's weekly rations to help the stores last until fresh ones arrived. This was not Phillip's dream colony.

Depression after elation

After the euphoria of surviving the voyage and the miracle of finding a perfect harbour, depression set in with the cold weather. The diarists and letters of that first winter reveal more from what they don't say than what they do. There are no more accounts of 'a grand day's sport' as they shoot ducks, no rhapsodies about the beauty of the harbour. But equally there are no descriptions of blistered hands from cutting timber or grubbing out tree roots. The marines were soldiers of the king, not manual labourers.

Fights broke out among the marines, even murders. Lieutenant-Governor Major Ross – bitter at being a subordinate officer to the governor, angry that he had been forced to leave his wife behind (he had, however, brought his young son with him, giving him an officer's rank, pay and rations) – fomented even more trouble, writing bitter letters to be taken back to England when the First Fleet ships returned from their supply mission.

This wretched country would never support a settlement, stated Ross. It would be cheaper to feed convicts on turtle soup and venison back in London than send them to Port Jackson. He remained adamant that no marine under his command would demean himself by manual work, or even supervise it. Ross seems to have deliberately painted the blackest possible picture of the colony at a time when it still had plenty of supplies, his purpose perhaps to have Phillip or even the whole colony recalled.

But there is another possible interpretation of Ross's ranting and much of the convicts' 'laziness' as well – shock and depression.

One of the major symptoms of depression is lethargy, an inability to work, a feeling that there is no point to anything. Sydney Cove was a town of mud and squalor, on the very edge of the known world with a vast unknown void at their backs. The little they knew of the rest of the country was even worse than Port Jackson – sandy soil, no harbours or fresh water. It might have been hard that first winter to see any future, either for the colony or themselves. Depression, like hysteria, can be contagious, especially in a small, closed and totally isolated community. Sydney Town was all these.

Things improved both physically and mentally with the colony's first spring. Far better farming land was found upriver at Rose Hill (later Parramatta): good rich loam. Fruit trees didn't just spring to life but grew at an astonishing rate. The vegetable gardens that had been well tended, like the one at the hospital and those of the officers, gave wonderful crops, especially of potatoes, cabbage and corn. It seemed that the land could be lavish, and food grown all through the year, unlike during England's brief growing season. The colony's hens had produced chicks that were giving eggs now too, and there were more oysters and wild spinach than anyone could gather. Phillip said the crops of maize were as good as any in the world.

But the convicts and marines refused to eat maize flour – they wanted wheat flour, the flour they had known all their lives. This is not the act of people who are genuinely hungry, but it could be a symptom of desperation and displacement. They wanted to be home, they craved the familiar. Most would never see home again. So they had tantrums about the bread.

Spring brings plenty again

By September of the colony's first year Captain Phillip wrote to Banks in England: 'Vegetables of all kinds are in plenty in my garden and I believe very few want them but from their own neglect.'[13] Strawberries, pumpkins and melons did particularly well.

Captain Watkin Tench was a marine and one of the few who seemed genuinely fascinated by the new land, his vivid journal later becoming a bestselling book about his colonial adventures. He also recognised that, given manure, the soil of the colony would grow vegetables all year round unlike England, where crops freeze and rot in frozen winter soil.[14] The early gardens gave their owners massive potatoes, giant cabbages, radishes, turnips, beans, peas, tomatoes, endive, melons, cucumbers, pumpkins, strawberries, rhubarb, spinach and more. Fruit trees grew so quickly that the settlers were stunned: by the colony's second summer, apples, oranges, figs, grapes, pomegranates and possibly others were bearing fruit, although there would only have been a few on each tree. Lieutenant Collins refers to his gardening efforts as a hobby. This, too, is telling: the food situation can scarcely have been worrying if he refers to growing vegetables as 'an amusement'.

There was meat from kangaroos, parrots, wallabies and emus, even though game was getting scarcer due to the increased population in the area, and powder for the muskets was in short supply too. The colony ate crows, ducks, swans and probably wild eggs as well.

In fact, the colonists were eating better than most of them ever had before and were healthier, too. Surgeon White saw a steadily improving state of health, with improved fertility and lower death rates, very little scurvy (presumably still an issue for those who refused native fruits and wouldn't eat vegetables) and no sign of deficiency diseases like pellagra.[15]

The officers and Phillip ate far better than the convicts. They were given a third more in rations and still had their own stores of far fresher food that they had bought at Cape Town, and fresh meat they'd either shot themselves or had their convict shooters bring in. White's book is dotted with references to the new meats, from swan to duck and emu. White refers to both roasts and broths, so some of the women may have been good cooks, especially as so many had been servants. In June 1788, to celebrate the king's birthday, the officers had eaten pork, mutton, duck, fowl and drank Madeira and porter.

The officers also had convicts assigned to them to build their huts, and dig and tend their gardens. The cabbage tree huts would soon rot; their roofs would leak, and their chimneys crumble. But for now, with an abundance of food and alcohol from home, as well as the new fruits and game animals, they were comfortable.

Crooks not cooks

The male convicts probably were in the worst position, as far as food went. They were still in ragged tents, too, crowded into an area of about two square kilometres, surrounded by unknown bush. The food in English prisons was gruel, a thin slop that was both cheap and could be eaten by people whose teeth were crumbling or who had none, like many convicts. While servant women would have been taught to cook, the London poor, as a whole, didn't cook at all. Fuel was prohibitively expensive, and they didn't have pans to cook with or access to kitchens.

Instead the London poor ate the eighteenth-century version of takeaway from food vendors who cooked on small coke fires, either on the pavement or in barrels: gruel made from stewed potatoes, turnips or even swedes in the north, thickened with flour and with only enough meat to add flavour. If you had a little more money you might buy bread to sop in your gruel; a few more pence bought you a roast potato, which was a luxury that warmed your fingers as well as your belly when you ate it. Other vendors sold oysters, winkles, jellied eel, mussels and roast chestnuts.

The convicts of the First Fleet all had a pannikin to cook with, and knives, as well as a spade, shovel, felling axe, three hoes and a hatchet each. But this would have been the first experience of having to cook for most of the men. Most of the convict women had been assigned to the officers, or had made their own arrangements with the remaining sailors. Worse, there was no safe place to store your weekly rations in this colony of thieves. They had to be hidden. One convict made up his entire week's ration into eighteen cakes that he ate at one sitting – and died vomiting and stinking the next day. These were people who had lived hand to mouth. The habit of gorging on ration day, leaving nothing for the rest of the week, eventually led to Phillip ordering that the rations be given out twice a week, and then daily.

Huddling on the edge of an unknown land

This was not just a new land. For those used to city streets it was a terrifying openness, especially after eight months of darkness and confinement at sea. Even those who had known the countryside would find this land strange: the trees were the wrong colour and shape, the sky a hard clear blue, the storms like a hammer of God descending with lightning that seemed to wrench the earth apart. Even the stars were wrong.

As a child I wondered about the terrace house huddles of 'old Sydney'. Collins's drawings of Sydney in 1791 show the small houses uncomfortably close together, despite the fact that land and space were things the colonists had in plenty. But it was a strange land, unknown –

no wonder they clung together, huts crammed close to their neighbours. It wasn't just that this was how houses had been back in London and villages. The proximity meant you could hear your neighbour snore or yell at his pig, you could smell his dungheap and wood smoke, and hear the mutter of voices on either side, almost drowning out the eerie sounds of this new land, the harsh buzz of cicadas, the chortling of kookaburras, the shrieks and arguments of possums in the night.

Even the stench of sewage may have been comforting, because it was familiar. Already the formerly pristine Tank Stream was muddied. Once the Dharug women had swept its banks free of animal droppings each day. Maintaining fresh water was one of the great duties for those who cared for the land, with lore and ritual to keep it safe. But no lore, or law, protected the water now.

Isolation

In November the last of the convict transports sailed back to England. The colony now only had two small ships – the *Supply* and the *Sirius* – to send for more stores, or take passengers to the smaller colony that had also been established at Norfolk Island in March.

This too would have added to the malaise of the colony. Those two small ships might take a few dozen passengers each to England, India or Batavia. But if the French attacked there was no way now to send all the colonists to safety. And the French knew of the colony – coincidentally, French ships had been at Botany Bay at the same time as the First Fleet. The French ships had in fact been wrecked on their journey home, but the colonists did not know this. A more real threat was from the Dharug. Four convicts had already been killed in isolated incidents, and others were wounded when they attacked Dharug women or refused to share their catches of fish, an enormous affront in a culture where food was always shared.

There is one glaring omission in all that had been done to found a colony: there had been no formal meetings with the native people, no bartering for the right to use the land, despite explicit orders from England that formal negotiations should be made. Even more extraordinarily, no one seems to have tried to find out from the locals more about their land. Were there any major rivers nearby? And what, exactly, was safe to eat? A short exchange with the locals might have saved Phillip and Surgeon White some extremely uncomfortable days and nights as their bodies tried to purge toxic fruits.

Phillip's method of fostering good relations seems bizarre. In December the marines had captured an Indigenous man so that he might be an ambassador to his people to communicate the colony's good intentions.

His name was (partly) Arabanoo; as a respected Cammeraygal elder he almost certainly had a far more complex name, but it seems that the colonials caught a few of the syllables and latched onto them, so he has remained Arabanoo to history. Captain John Hunter wrote, 'The terror this poor wretch suffered can better be conceived than expressed; he believed he was to be immediately murdered.'

He was forcibly bathed, to see if any of his colour would wash off, had his hair cut and his beard shaved off and was forcibly clothed. An iron handcuff was put about his wrist with a rope attached. It tells a lot about both Dharug culture and Arabanoo, as an individual, that he accepted the bathing and the clothing, thinking they were gifts. Initially, according to Watkin Tench, who had been responsible for scrubbing him, he called his manacle an ornament and seemed pleased with it until 'his delight changed to rage and hatred when he discovered its use'. Here was a man who expected strangers to act well towards him, as most of the Dharug had acted towards the intruders, allowing them to build huts, pollute their water, spear their game and take their fish. He didn't even recognise the chains of his prison.

That first day, Arabanoo was given bread and meat and alcohol – he spat out the grog – and locked up for the night. He was kept locked up for three months. He ate enormously, but almost solely of fresh food – eight large fish for breakfast, about four kilos' worth, and perhaps three kangaroo rats and a kilo of fish at midday. He would always offer children the best of his food if they appeared while he was eating.[16]

He was unfailingly courteous, friendly – and desperately lonely. Phillip led him down to the harbour, like a dog on the lead, to talk to his countrymen. They seemed to ask why he didn't escape. Arabanoo pointed to his shackle. After that it seems that the Dharug wouldn't talk to him. Were they contemptuous of a warrior taken prisoner by such scrawny white men? Or did Arabanoo discourage them, perhaps thinking that they might be taken prisoner too? There were no witnesses who understood either the man or his culture to write accounts of what did happen, only officers who seem to have regarded Arabanoo with amused and affectionate contempt as a childlike primitive; the pleasure he took in the company of children seeming to reinforce this. And the violence between the Dharug and the convicts continued.

The spring and summer of 1788–1789 had brought more good vegetable crops and catches of fish, but there was no sign of the expected supply ship. Six marines were hanged for stealing food from the government stores, and the colony had its rations cut by a third. But this did not mean hunger, simply a greater reliance on home-grown or foraged food.

Autumn brought good harvests of potatoes, cabbages and maize, but not wheat. Maize is hardier, and stores better, too – you can twist the tops of each maize stem downwards and let the cobs dry in their husks on the plant, harvesting them as you need them, or toss the cobs into a rat-proof shed. Much of Mesoamerican cuisine is based on maize, from burritos to posole; maize had already been taken up by southern Italian farmers and turned into polenta dishes; and in the USA there were hundreds of variations of grits and cornbread. But at Sydney Cove the colonists wanted real bread: bread made from wheat flour. And the store of wheat flour was running out.

Bread mattered. In these carbohydrate-conscious days most of us eat two to four thin slices of bread a day at most, and usually far less. The convicts would have been used to eating a whole loaf per day, or even two if it could be obtained, with cheese or butter from the stores, or the drippings from their ration of salt beef or pork held over the fire so that fat ran onto their bread, or dipped into their gruel.

A meal was unthinkable without bread. Bread *was* food. Just as in Japan the traditional greeting of 'Have you eaten?' translates as 'Have you had rice today?', 'bread' stood for all food. This extreme identification of bread with food explains part of the myth of colonial starvation. From the spring of 1789, when the flour ration was changed to maize rather than wheat, until the colony finally had good silos in which to store its wheat and flour in about 1820, a lack of bread was synonymous with extreme deprivation, even if there were plenty of other carbohydrates like potatoes or maize.

'Real' food was wheat bread with meat, butter and cheese; not fish, not corn bread. Vegetables were side dishes, garnishes. Back in Europe, the starving French crowds were crying for bread (and their queen was infamously telling them to eat brioche instead). Bread was life.

If the colonists had been truly hungry they'd have eaten their maize, either as cornbread damper or cooked up in their gruel. It wasn't hunger that nibbled at the colony now, but depression.

And then depression became nightmare.

The plague around them

From April 1879, all around the harbour the Dharug began to die, bodies lining the shores and floating in the harbour. The little fishing canoes with the laughing children vanished. Those who didn't die, fled.

Surgeon White diagnosed smallpox, one of the most contagious of diseases. The colony cared for the ill Dharug, but only a boy and a girl, Nanberry and Baroong, survived the illness, and were adopted into the colony. The colony must have spent that autumn and all winter waiting for the smallpox to strike them too.

It didn't, and two hundred years later I wonder if it wasn't indeed a severe variant of cowpox. The symptoms would fit, and it would explain why no colonists – not even the children who had played with Arabanoo, who also died in the plague – were infected. Cowpox is spread by physical contact with cows, but also by rats. Europeans have a high resistance, but the populations of Australia did not. The only colonist who died or even grew ill was a Native American sailor.

But the colonists were not to know that. Even if they had, it might have been of little comfort. A smallpox plague that had mysteriously left the colony untouched might as eerily strike them all.

And still the expected supply ship didn't appear.

By August 1789 the colony was in a strange, almost paranoid, mental state. Collins writes as though the land itself was trying to destroy them:

As every circumstance became of importance that might in its tendency forward or retard the day whereon the colony was to be pronounced independent of the mother-country for provisions, it was soon observed with concern, that hitherto by far a greater proportion of males than females had been produced by the animals we had brought for the purpose of breeding. This, in any other situation, might not have been so nicely remarked; but here, where a country was to be stocked, a litter of twelve pigs whereof three only were females became a subject of conversation and inquiry. Out of seven kids which had been produced in the last month, one only was a female; and many similar instances had before occurred, but no particular notice was attracted until their frequency rendered them remarkable. This circumstance excited an anxious care in every one for the preservation of such females as might be produced; and at the moment now spoken of no person entertained an idea of slaughtering one of that sort; indeed males were so abundant that fortunately there was no occasion.[17]

And yet the crops were doing well. Collins wrote again in September 1789: 'At Rose Hill, where the corn promised well, an Emu had been killed, which stood seven feet high, was a female, and when opened was found to contain exactly fifty eggs.'[18]

Storing food, however, was another matter. Potatoes can be stored over winter in the ground in Sydney, or on racks. Maize can be dried and stored in its husk. Wheat is more difficult to store – and the colony still demanded its wheat bread. Collins wrote in October 1789: 'Our enemies the rats, who worked unseen, and attacked us where we were most vulnerable … Eight casks of flour were at one time found wholly destroyed … they rioted upon the Indian corn which was growing, and did considerable mischief.'[19]

The rats may have been bush rats, but there had also been time for ship rats to have come ashore with the stores and bred to plague numbers. The convicts were still gorging on their rations as soon as they were handed out. Collins again, in November 1789:

It was soon observed, that of the provisions issued at this ration on the Saturday the major part of the convicts had none left on the Tuesday night; it was therefore ordered, that the provisions should be served in future on the Saturdays and Wednesdays. By these means, the days which would otherwise pass in hunger, or in thieving from the few who were more provident, would be divided, and the people themselves be more able to perform the labour which was required from them. Overseers and married men were not included in this order.[20]

There was still food in plenty. The gardens and farms had produced crops and also, presumably, viable seed to keep planting indefinitely. But they had now been here for almost two years, with no sign of a supply ship or any contact from England.

Terror and depression, not starvation

The rations were reduced again. But there is no indication yet that this reduction would cause physical hardship – doubtless there was plenty of non-rationed food. As Collins wrote, it was a precautionary move:

> The ration … was … reduced to two thirds of every species, spirits excepted, which continued as usual. This measure was calculated to guard against accidents; and the necessity of it was obvious to everyone, from the great uncertainty as to the time when a supply might arrive from England, and from the losses which had been and still were occasioned by rats in the provision store.[21]

Their farms were producing now. The fish catch was good. The wheat crop was moderate, the oat crop poor, but the barley and 'Indian corn' good. And yet … still no sign of a sail from England.

By March 1790 it was obvious that the colonists would have to be more self-reliant. Many of the convicts had neither built themselves a hut nor dug a garden. Governor Phillip distributed the dwellings and gardens among those who had none. No more hens or pigs were to be eaten.

The governor also decided on the ultimate nanny state: the rations would be distributed daily. The official working hours were also reduced, so that convicts could work their own gardens. But there is no hint at this stage that the working hours had been reduced because the workers were starving. Instead it was a desperate measure to get the idle to work, to become self-supporting, to finally get their soft hands dirty and blistered. For the first time, the marines were also expected to get out there and work, supervising the convicts on fishing parties, using private boats owned by the officers.

And still there was no ship from England.

On 19 March 1790, the *Sirius* was wrecked unloading supplies on Norfolk Island. Now the tiny *Supply* was the only ship left and Phillip sent it to Batavia to buy more food. It would take six months to get there and back. The colony was now totally isolated and had no way to send supplies to their colony at Norfolk Island either.

Food was continually guarded against theft. Convict William Lane was sentenced to two thousand lashes for stealing biscuit, Thomas Halford the same for stealing three pounds of potatoes and William Parr got five hundred lashes for stealing a pumpkin. A fisherman was given a hundred lashes for keeping some of the catch. A rumour went around the camp that the marines were going to sail off in the *Supply*, leaving the convicts to starve alone.

That too indicates the mental state of the colony: suspicion, isolation, desperation. It is even possible that the rumour was true. While Phillip would have had too much integrity to abandon his post, the same could not be said for many of the officers. This was, after all, the same era when the officers of His Majesty's Ship *Bounty* mutinied against their captain, stole the ship, picked up Polynesian women and sailed off to Pitcairn Island. It is not beyond belief that the officers at Sydney Cove might have mutinied and sailed the ship from a colony they believed doomed, or insupportable, if things grew worse.

The two previous winters before had seen a sharp reduction in the amount of fish caught. Now, in autumn, it looked like this would happen again. Lieutenant Collins, March 1790:

On the 7th, about four hundred weight of fish being brought up,
it was issued agreeable to the order; and could the like quantity
have been brought in daily, some saving might have been made at
the store, which would have repaid the labour that was employed
to obtain it. But the quantity taken during this month, after the
7th, was not often much more than equal to supplying the people
employed in the boats with one pound of fish per man, which was
allowed them in addition to their ration.[22]

Nor was much advantage obtained by employing people to shoot for
the public: at the end of the month only three small kangaroos had been
brought in. The convicts who were employed in this service, three in
number, were considered as good marksmen, and were allowed a ration
of flour instead of their salt provisions, the better to enable them to
sustain the labour and fatigue of traversing the woods of this country.

And yet the colony still had large reserves of food – the private stores
held by the governor and the officers. We have no way of knowing how
much flour and other goods the officers had (it is telling that none of
those who kept diaries ever complain about being hungry themselves),
but we do know how much the governor had in his private store, even
after more than a year. Collins, April 1790:

The Governor, from a motive that did him immortal honour, in
this season of general distress, gave up three hundred weight of
flour which was his Excellency's private property, declaring that
he wished not to see anything more at his table than the ration
which was received in common from the public store, without any
distinction of persons; and to this resolution he rigidly adhered,
wishing that if a convict complained, he might see that want was
not unfelt even at Government House.[23]

That 'immortal honour' does tend to imply that other officers, too, still
had large reserves of stores.

This period from May to June 1790 is the only time food was really
short in the colony, when men risked their lives to steal it and workers

like the convict shooters needed larger rations to enable them to do their jobs. But even then the food intake was adequate by modern standards.

Starvation on 10,000 kilojoules per day

Eight weeks is about the time most of us stick to a diet, and for those eight weeks in 1790 the rations had more kilojoules than a nutritionist might advise a dieter to eat today, especially as the rations could so easily be supplemented by oysters, wild spinach, vegetables and whatever fish and fruits had been harvested the day before.

According to Collins:

> On the 20th of the month, the following was the ration issued from the public store to each man for seven days, or to seven people for one day: flour, 2½ pounds, rice, 2 pounds, pork, 2 pounds. The peas were all expended. Was this a ration for a labouring man? The two pounds of pork, when boiled, from the length of time it had been in store shrunk away to nothing; and when divided among seven people for their day's sustenance, barely afforded three or four morsels to each.[24]

By modern standards, this might still mean an adequate allowance of energy. A man needs about 10,000 kilojoules per day to maintain his weight. That two and a half pounds of flour had about 20,000 kilojoules, about 10,000 kilojoules in the pork and 12,000 in the rice, a total of 42,000 kilojoules weekly, or 6000 a day. Those rations were supplemented with fish, vegetables, including energy-rich potatoes and maize, and as many shellfish as they wanted to gather. One oyster is 250 kilojoules, and it's hard to stop at one. Sixteen oysters a day, which would take five minutes to harvest from the rocks, would give an extra 4000 kilojoules.

But were they eating their vegetables, oysters, winkles and mussels?

There was plenty of food for the hungry – if they chose to supplement their diet with what was around them. Those too depressed or traumatised to seek out food or grow it would indeed have been hungry in those eight weeks. But they certainly would not have starved, nor is there evidence they did.

Instead there is the evidence of what *didn't* happen. There are no records of scurvy. If the population of Sydney Cove had been eating only the official rations they would have had a major deficiency in vitamin C. The absence of scurvy means that they were, indeed, eating the produce of the land.

What those two months were filled with was genuine terror at the *idea* of starvation. It was a displacement activity: you focus on one fear rather than admit to the other, deeper ones. Medical supplies were almost gone, tools broken, blankets few, clothes in tatters, the marines barefoot, their huts made of cabbage tree beginning to slump and rot were grim. But they must have wondered if they had been forgotten, if a small colony could survive with no ships, isolated from the world.

In a letter back home the Reverend Johnstone spoke in bitter desolation. 'Tis now about two years and three months since we first arrived at this distant country. All this while we have been, as it were, buried alive.'[25]

The colony was also facing winter. Our winter garden, in a climate colder than Sydney's, produces more than enough food to sustain a family all through the cool weather. But the colonists would not yet have grown used to the security of winter vegetables. Winter is not a growing season in northern Europe. They expected the supply of fish to decrease again, and the hens may have stopped laying. (Today's hens are bred to lay year round; the colony's birds would have been more seasonal layers programmed to lay a large number in spring, but few or none in the colder, darker days of June and July.)

Sydney Cove was a village of mud and tatters, on the edge of a mostly unknown continent. From Cook's first landing, the British had established their foothold with firearms. But that required gunpowder and it too was in short supply, nor does it keep forever, especially if not kept in dry conditions. While poachers in England knew how to catch animals without firearms, there is no reference to the colonists laying snares or digging traps at that stage, until colonial boys were taught by their young Indigenous companions how to trap bandicoots in the tussocks. Instead the colony seems to have relied on the gentleman's method of shooting game, which needed gunpowder. They did not have enough domestic stock yet to provide meat, nor the skills to hunt it once the gunpowder was gone. The colony lacked four great staples of 1790s European life: wheat bread, salted meat, a safe store of food to see them through winter, and the feeling of being part of the world of men.

Tench gave the most vivid description of the despairing colony:

> Our impatience of news from Europe strongly marked the commencement of the year. We had now been two years in the country, and thirty-two months from England, in which long period no supplies, except what had been procured at the Cape of Good Hope by the 'Sirius', had reached us. From intelligence of our friends and connections we had been entirely cut off, no communication whatever having passed with our native country since the 13th of May 1787, the day of our departure from Portsmouth. Famine besides was approaching with gigantic strides, and gloom and dejection overspread every countenance. Men abandoned themselves to the most desponding reflections, and adopted the most extravagant conjectures.[26]

'Famine besides was approaching': it was not already there. The colony had children – from later accounts, often with little or no care from their parents, left to wander and even sleep in the streets. It would have been easy to steal a child's ration, yet there is no account of malnourished children.

Nor do starved women easily become pregnant, then carry their children to term and have them survive. About forty-six babies and children arrived in 1788. There were 161 women of child-bearing age in the colony who gave birth to eighty-three babies, when prolonged breast feeding was a reasonably effective contraceptive – a woman feeding her child rarely got pregnant until the child was eating a large amount of solid food instead of mostly breastmilk. Twenty-five babies or children had died – a large number for today, but not when about 50 per cent of babies born in London didn't survive, especially given the hardship the mothers and babies had experienced in their long voyage from England. The lack of contagious childhood disease may have helped this high survival rate (for the time). But equally, the high birth rate and child survival rate indicates that they were reasonably well fed.

Nor are there accounts of deaths from starvation, pellagra or scurvy during this time. Only one man died from lack of food: he'd had his pannikin stolen and was forced to give up most of his rations to barter the use of others' cooking gear. (Potatoes, maize, warrigal greens and other available foods needed to be cooked. The only easily available kilojoule-dense food he might have eaten raw was oysters, and he'd have needed carbohydrates to survive on.) In fact the colony was, at last, seriously trying to become self-sufficient, boiling its own salt, and spinning fishing line in a way taught to them by the Dharug people.

Collins's words tell of a food-fixated colony. But they also imply that the colony was indeed producing a lot of food:

> The Governor's garden had been the object of frequent depredation; scarcely a night passed that it was not robbed, notwithstanding that many received vegetables from it by his Excellency's order. Two convicts had been taken up, who confessed that within the space of a month they had robbed it seven or eight times, and that they had killed a hog belonging to an officer.[27]

It is a good garden that can keep producing enough for thieves to raid it many times.

Ignorance among plenty

One of the most striking aspects of the colony's extreme uncertainty about the source of their food is that although the governor and some officers like Tench, Dawes and Surgeon White had questioned Arabanoo and the colony's next prisoner/ambassador, Bennelong, about language and terrain, they don't seem to have asked them, 'What can we eat and how can we find it?' The two adopted children, Nanberry and Baroong, could also have been questioned about indigenous foods. And perhaps the colonists did ask questions but got no answers apart from the names of certain foods the colonists had already found were edible. We only know what the men put in their diaries, books and letters, and a lack of information might not have seemed worth putting down. Or perhaps they just didn't like the answers. The colonists would have been used to English orchard trees and bushes that gave their harvest over a few weeks. Many of the native fruits of the area have a longer season, but without that 'all at once' abundance. Other foodstuffs, like murrnong roots and native grains may just have seemed not worth the gathering. To those used to harvesting fields of wheat once a year and reaping enough to last until the next harvest, the Indigenous way of harvesting food as needed and storing little was so unfamiliar that the abundance of the land around them was unrecognisable.

Both Arabanoo and Bennelong may have refused to answer questions about native fruits and vegetables. Arabanoo was a respected elder and, while gentle and tolerant, did expect the colonists to allow him the dignity of his position. Bennelong was a Wangal warrior, with possibly less respect in his community than Arabanoo and all the more insistence on being accorded respect. Warriors did not gather berries, dig for roots except for medicine or ceremonies, or at that stage fish with nets in the harbour. (Although Indigenous men would soon take to fishing with nets once they discovered the colonists' eagerness for fish, and their relatively poor fishing skills.)

Possibly, even probably, Bennelong and Arabanoo would have laughed or refused to show they understood when asked about finding vegetable foods. Men fished with spears – women and children did everything else.

It seemed that the only person in the colony who had bothered to ask Indigenous women about food was surveyor and engineer William Dawes. Fifteen-year-old Dharug girl Patyegarang shared Dawes's hut and taught him her language. It's likely that as well as teaching him the words for various foods she also showed him which ones to eat. But Dawes was a bit of a renegade and unpopular with almost everyone in the colony: a scientist, he was genuinely fascinated with the study of Indigenous culture, and wanted to become a colonial farmer. Dawes had already quarrelled with Phillip after buying flour from a convict: Philip said that trade in rations was illegal; Dawes maintained that the flour was 'earned', and so could be traded. Later in 1790, when Dharug man Pemulwuy speared one of the official 'shooters', John MacIntyre, in retaliation for his attacks on the Dharug people, Dawes refused to join the expedition to hunt Pemulwuy. Dawes said publicly that he thought MacIntyre was at fault. Finally the Reverend Johnstone persuaded Dawes to join the (unsuccessful) manhunt. But when they returned Dawes expressed his regret at taking part, nor would he apologise. Phillip would later order Dawes sent back to England in 1791, despite his great wish to stay in the colony.

William Dawes and Patyegarang presumably ate extremely well, with a combination of English vegetables and indigenous game, fruits and other foods. But from all accounts no one asked for Patyegarang's help in feeding the colony. One whale lured to shore would have fed them for weeks, but then, gentlemen did not eat whale meat. (It would take a major propaganda campaign – and hunger – in World War 2 to get the British public to eat whale.) Nor did officers live so openly with 'natives' when there were white women available. (Patyegarang's age might bother us now, but by the standards of both her culture and Dawes's, she was an adult.)

A man of compassion

After unwillingly leaving New South Wales, William Dawes became governor of a colony at Sierra Leone, not altogether successfully. A strong and active opponent of the slave trade, his last years were spent founding schools for slave children in Antigua and as correspondent for the Missionary Society. He died in relative poverty in Antigua in 1836, but with great apparent fulfilment, leaving behind his second wife, Grace, his clergyman son and his daughter. His fascinating study of indigenous foods and language, however, would be mostly ignored for nearly two centuries.

The Dharug could also have supplied meat, and fish. (Dharug men would soon become the colony's major source of fish.) But at the time of greatest shortages the Dharug population had been drastically thinned by the mystery plague of April 1798, and by the survivors leaving the area. Nor did the colony have much to trade with; they badly needed more tools like axes and knives themselves. Ironically, the Dharug may have helped feed the colony with fish and game if they'd been asked, expecting nothing more than similar help in the future if they needed it, or if the colony had a surplus of things the Dharug might want, like cobs of maize.

No one seems to have thought to ask.

Sails on the horizon

So throughout May 1790, the colony waited: for attack, for starvation for those who would or could only eat rations, or for a ship, whichever came first. The lookout at South Head watched for sails on the horizon – essential, as any supply ship would head to Botany Bay, where the colony was supposed to have been located. A ship from England might miss the new colony entirely, sailing away without realising that they had moved up the coast. A flagpole was erected so that the lookout could signal as soon as a sail was seen, and everyone in the colony now continually glanced towards it, waiting for the first flicker of a flag.

Finally, on 3 June 1790 the flag flapped in the wind. *Lady Juliana* glided through the Heads.

The *Lady Juliana* was no store ship – she carried about 220 women convicts. They had not been carefully selected as the ones on the First Fleet were. Many were too old and feeble to do much work, but others were young and healthy, and all had been fed and given regular sunlight on deck on the voyage. But she brought even more important news. The colony had not been forgotten. A supply ship, the *Guardian*, had been sent soon after the First Fleet, but had been wrecked on an iceberg off the Cape of Good Hope. The *Lady Juliana* brought some of the supplies that had been saved from the wreck.

She also brought the news that a Second Fleet would arrive any day – she had outsailed the others. They would bring another thousand convicts. The Second Fleet also had a supply ship bringing extra food. Immediately the rations were restored to the full amount, even though there were extra mouths to feed. Once again the drum beat out for the convicts to start work every morning and afternoon.

At last the longed-for ships arrived between 20 and 28 June 1790, the convict transports *Scarborough*, *Neptune* and *Surprize*, and the store ship *Justinian*. But these ships brought death, not life.

The waiting officers had seen war, death and hardship, but they had never seen a sight like this. The convicts had to be carried up to the deck, most too weak to even stagger, their eyes blinded by the sunlight, their skin festering. Others died on the deck as they were brought into the sunlight or as they were rowed to shore or crawled onto land on their hands and knees, unable to rise. The stench was unbelievable.

Two hundred and sixty-seven people had died on the way out, twenty-six per cent of the total. The convicts were so starved that many chose to remain chained to a dead and rotting companion in order to get the dead man's food rations. On the *Neptune* the convicts had been deliberately starved to death – the ship's master, Donald Traill, a sadist and possibly insane, had been paid per passenger, and the more who died meant more stores for him to sell. Convicts on the *Scarborough* had been given their allocated rations but been kept below decks because of an early attempted mutiny. The months of darkness left them temporarily crippled and blinded.

Even as the ships came through the Heads more people died. Their bodies were thrown over the side, so for weeks the corpses washed up on the beaches. Of the surviving 759 convicts, 488 were ill from dysentery, scurvy and fever. The colony's Reverend Johnstone would later write of indescribable misery, the convicts wretched, naked, dirty and covered in lice, many unable to stand or even move their hands or feet. He also wrote of the compassion and generosity of the former thieves of Sydney Town, trying to help the dying.

Yes, there is starvation in our colonial history, but it was a result of human greed, and at sea, not on land. The contractors had stolen most of the food that the convicts should have received. As soon as the ships anchored they opened their stores to sell the stolen rations at the highest prices those in the desperate colony were able to pay. It was morally repugnant – but no legal crime had been committed, not even theft, because the supplies had been their own. Despite public outcry when the story was told in England and a public enquiry, no charges were laid (and the same contractors were given the right to supply the Third Fleet). Phillip was powerless and the goods were soon sold.

In October the *Supply* finally returned from Batavia with the ship *Waaksamheyd*, bringing further stores. There would still be many times when the colony was forced to buy food for convict rations from overseas, and when they were short of wheat flour, mostly because of lack of storage facilities, and foods like butter or cheese. But the fear of starvation was over.

By now, too, the ex-burglar James Ruse had shown that the colony could grow wheat. Ruse had been granted one clear acre and more bushland at Rose Hill (now Parramatta) in 1789. By 1790 he had a harvest of one and a half acres of wheat, and half an acre of maize was producing excellent crops. Ruse used as much manure as possible but also made his own compost – farm and garden waste piled up until it rotted into rich soil, as well as turning over the grass when he dug so it too rotted into the soil. He also dug well and deeply, even though he had no horse or plough, and added wood ash, high in potash. In these days of small backyards this may seem a large amount for one man to achieve, but for several years my vegetable patch was about two acres, tended by myself, without a plough. It produced not just enough food for myself and my young son but also a surplus to sell. A neighbour in her late seventies cultivated a similar area, also selling the surplus.

Ruse would soon be granted thirty acres. It's likely that now the trauma of jail, transportation and relocation had worn off, many if not most of the convicts did in fact create Phillip's dream: build their own small house, plant their gardens, milk their goat, and have many children. But this assumption is based only on the family records of those who have traced their ancestors back to First Fleet arrivals. It's biased towards convicts who were successful enough to marry and have children who survived. As the descendent of three convicts (one was later pardoned when the real criminal confessed, but preferred to stay in Australia), I admit my bias here. All three went on to have prosperous and fulfilled lives, and I am grateful to the magistrates who commuted their sentences to transportation.

The colony's real hunger had lasted, at most, eight weeks. It had resulted in no cases of starvation, or even malnutrition, pellagra or scurvy (and Surgeon White was experienced enough to diagnose any of these).[28] It was the threat of starvation that was most terrifying, born of a real fear of abandonment and having to live forever on what the land could produce, instead of the safe, familiar supplies from England.

This is not to say that the next few years were easy. Even if the colony did not starve, its early years were nightmarish, the living conditions squalid, the rations foul. Nearly five hundred people died in the winter of 1792 – not from starvation at the colony but because of the hell ships of the Second Fleet. Bodies were buried in haste, and so shallowly that dingos and goannas dug up the corpses. The colony stank of death.

In May 1792 the weekly rations had to be reduced once more: a pound and a half of flour, two pounds of maize and four pounds of pork per person per week, with women and children receiving less. But by now the colony's gardens were providing well. The officers of the New South Wales Corps had also seen how the Second and Third Fleet captains had made a fortune selling stores. They formed a syndicate to hire a ship to bring stores for their own use and for sale. This too would ensure that the colony was well fed; it was also the basis for the vast fortunes many of the New South Wales Corps would make, both by granting themselves a monopoly to sell food and alcohol, as well as illegally granting themselves – and their descendants – vast areas of land.

From now on supply ships arrived more regularly. Despite periods of flood and drought, the colony's fertility stunned the new settlers. The colony was becoming a land of small farms and rich acres. At Rose Hill/Parramatta each house along the village's only street had its own luxuriant vegetable garden, enough to feed a household. The huts and tents of Sydney Town became a town: small, neat houses with good gardens in some areas, with flourishing crops of maize, beans, peas, cabbages, lettuces, melons, turnips and green vegetables, just as Phillip had dreamed, with slums, prostitutes, shanty pubs and half-naked children begging in the street down by 'The Rocks' at the harbour. The Dharug men turned fishermen and sold their catch to the colony; presumably the colonial fishermen eventually got the bright idea to follow the Dharug and find where the fish were biting. Until the late twentieth century, anyone casting a line into Sydney Harbour from rocks, beach or ferry wharf could expect to catch dinner.

The first free settlers arrived on the *Bellona* in January 1793. They didn't have to pay for the voyage – all free settlers were allowed free passage till 1818, and given complimentary land, tools, convict labour and provisions for them and their convicts for a year. These voluntary settlers joined the growing number of convicts who had served their sentences and been given twenty-five-acre (ten-hectare) farms.

From now on the colony's main food problem would be the sudden irregular arrival of more convicts to feed (often weak and starving from the harsh treatment on board ship and needing rations from the government stores) combined with Hawkesbury floods and the lack of silos to store the crops.

By 1820 Sydney was a town of plentiful, cheap food with Saturday markets where people could buy everything from eggs to artichokes. In New South Wales, the poor did not have to live on gruel and hot potatoes as they did in London, and even the poorest person could afford to eat meat and butter every day. Fruits like oranges, lemons, guavas, pineapples, peaches, apricots and grapes that only the rich ate in Britain were so plentiful they could be fed to pigs and hens. Chooks and milk goats roamed the streets and had to be fenced out of gardens and orchards. Butter was expensive (more colonists had goats than cows, and goat's milk isn't suitable to make into butter as the cream doesn't separate) as was cheese, though the cheese from Bathurst was said to be especially good. Eggs were expensive to buy, but most households had their own hens. Sugarcane was grown around Port Macquarie, as well as imported from Mauritius and Java. Visiting the Sydney fruit and vegetable markets around Christmas 1820, you would find oranges, lemons, citrons, grapes, peaches, nectarines, apricots, rhubarb, figs, olives, loquats, granadillas, early apples, plums, cherries, mulberries, raspberries, strawberries, pomegranates, rockmelons, watermelons, preserved peaches, quinces, pears, peach cider, potatoes, cabbages, broccoli, asparagus, lettuces, onions and beans. (In Sydney, Christmas is too early for corn and pumpkins, two of the main foods in the colony.) In 1820 – as it had been for tens of thousands of years – Sydney Cove was a land of plenty.

The seductive starvation myth

So how has the myth of the starving colony taken such a firm grip on our history?

Partly, I suspect, it's because starving convicts make good drama, whether in novels, plays or TV shows. Fiction is accessible to more people than the primary sources that actually describe conditions at the time. It's joined other myths that make our nation's past more romantic: innocent men and women convicted for nothing more than stealing a loaf of bread to feed their children; convicts shipped across the world just to get rid of them; a disastrously planned First Fleet that landed without enough food or tools. Once myths have taken root, they are hard to dislodge.

The myth of the starving colony was also deliberately begun by Major Ross in his first letters back to England. But those were sent at the end of 1788, when the colony still had sufficient stores for two years, plenty of fish and game, and the diarists were writing optimistic accounts of their gardens. Major Ross was a troublemaker, resentful and obdurate. Whether he deliberately lied or not, his account can't be relied upon.

There are also the firsthand accounts of the time of real shortages, written by other officers like Watkin Tench. These speak of the *fear* of starvation in that short period in 1790, not of starvation itself. Tench describes the parade ground looking 'as if' the numbers had been thinned by starvation and the almost paranoid diligence with which the stores were guarded. But no marine did starve. This describes the colony's state of mind, not the state of their stomachs or health. The colony's terror that they *might* starve has been interpreted as actual starvation.

This is illustrated by one of surgeon John White's letters to a friend that was published in England. In it he describes how 'Hope is no more ... all the grain of every kind which we have been able to raise in two years and three months would not support us two weeks ... the people ... who have not had one ounce of fresh animal food since first in the country.'

Surgeon White was a man of deep integrity. But 'not one ounce of fresh animal food', when he had described eating so many of the native species? (White would not have counted fish, eels, mussels and oysters as animal food.) His letter grossly exaggerates the grain supply – the wheat had failed, but there was plenty of maize and potatoes. But when he said 'hope is no more' he was probably despairingly accurate.

There is also another aspect to the picture painted by those early writers. The diaries and letters that survive from those years are primarily written by the marines. The reduction in rations affected them deeply, but not because they went hungry.

During the voyage and until the stores were severely depleted, the marines received as much as two-thirds more food than the convicts. Part of the marines' wages until the Crimean War, more than half a century in the future, were a daily allowance of bread, meat and alcohol. The amounts were set out as a condition of service and were more than one man would be expected to eat. They could be used to feed dependents or sold for profit. Each marine was responsible for cooking – or selling – his own rations.

When Governor Phillip insisted that all in the colony receive the same rations, he effectively drastically cut the marines' wages, insulting their dignity and their military tradition. While non-commissioned officers could bring their wives with them, the other officers and enlisted men might not see wives or families for many years. Nor were there decent prospects in the colony for earning more money to make up for it. War in those days was an opportunity to earn 'prize money' if you won, and be granted land as a reward for service or an education for your children. But the orders from England were clear: officers were not to be granted land. A convict or ex-convict got land, but not the men who felt themselves to be the convicts' superiors.

This edict would be ignored as soon as Governor Phillip was recalled to London, but in those first three years it caused a deep resentment. Consciously or unconsciously, these men were not unbiased witnesses.

A more able officer than Major Ross might have negotiated higher wages for his men, in lieu of the lost rations. A more well-intentioned, less cantankerous officer would also have allowed his men to oversee the convicts, instead of most of them doing little except form their parades and wait around to defend the colony from attack.

But the main reason the myth has persisted, or even grown more dramatic in the past fifty years, is the vastly different experience of the land then and now. It is easy for anyone standing at the edge of Sydney

Harbour today to assume that without supermarkets – or supply ships – you would starve. The kangaroos, wallabies, bettongs, bandicoots and other game have gone, leaving only the possums, which have done well in suburban gardens. The sea around much of Sydney is a dead zone, with few fish or other creatures, and the rocks of the harbour are bare.

But mostly the myth has persisted, and grown, because our society is increasingly dislocated from the growing or harvesting of the food we eat. Few people today have wandered the Australian bush or seaside, gathering more than enough food to survive on as they walk. Much of the bush accessible to city bushwalkers has been dramatically simplified, and its food potential reduced, due to overgrazing by European animals, stock like cattle, sheep and horses, or feral rabbit, deer and goats, as well as repeated bushfires – not the firestick farming of the Dharug, but hot, out of control flames as well as repeated 'control burning' with little understanding of what, or how much, needs to be burnt. The bush that most Australians see now is no longer a living larder.

Nor are we a peasant society anymore, used to growing our own food. Many gardeners grow vegetables, but they assume they need to buy fertilisers and watering systems to do so. (You don't.) Foods like pasta, rice and chicken are so cheap that it's a rare gardening cook who feeds their family purely on homegrown produce. Yet it's not only possible to do so, it was actually a common experience two hundred years ago, and there are those in Australia who still manage it.

Tumbalong, or Darling Harbour, is indeed a place of food. But the tumult of ice-cream parlours, sushi bars and pasta palaces blinds us to the abundance there once was, when the women cooked the fish in their canoes and with every step you took the land offered you food: fresh, healthy, but also social. Plaiting fish traps with the other women in the shade of a tree while the kids gathered freshwater mussels – the laughter as well as the indigenous food has vanished from that generous land below the concrete of Darling Harbour.

The first colonists failed to recognise the living larder around them. Over the next two hundred years European settlers would destroy much of the bounty of the land, and think they were doing good as they extinguished it.

CHAPTER 8

The second, third and fourth Australians

The United States might proclaim, 'Give me your tired, your poor, your huddled masses yearning to breathe free'. It has usually been more difficult to get to Australia.

The first Australians survived a sea voyage with the desperation and courage needed to sail beyond sight of land. Their descendants were those able to survive an ice age, subsequent catastrophic flooding and increasing desertification, as well forging cultures that enabled them to thrive in Australia's climatic extremes. The land had shaped the people and their cultures.

Most of the 'second' Australians were convicts. Apart from a few like those on the *Lady Juliana*, they had been relatively carefully selected to come here. That selection process is important: they might have been criminals, but they had been judged worthy of a second chance. Australia was never a 'dumping ground' for prisoners; it was cheaper to keep them starved in the filth of the Thames hulks, the rotting ships that were too old to be seaworthy, than send them here. Most were young, as fit as their time in jail and at sea permitted, and hadn't been convicted of crimes like murder or rape. Despite the horror of the Second Fleet and on other notorious ships, on average less than two per cent of convicts died on the voyage here. That seems a high number today but not compared to the mortality rate for sailors of the time.

Roughly 163,000 convicts were sent to Australia from 1788 till transportation ended in the 1860s. (This is a very rough figure – accurate records weren't always kept and many of the records that were no longer exist.) Eight out of ten had been convicted of theft, and estimates vary from one in five to one in a hundred convicted of political crime, from being in a trade union to violent rebellion against the English in Wales or Ireland, or burning down the houses of English landowners or poaching or stealing from them. The convicts' average age was about twenty-six. About two-thirds had been convicted in England and so were probably English; about one-third were convicted in Ireland, with relatively few from Wales and Scotland.[1]

According to the official census of the colony of New South Wales, in 1820 there were 17,271 adults, of whom 9451 were convicts, 5768 were ex-convicts or those with their 'ticket-of-leave', effectively freeing them before they had served their sentence, and 2802 were free settlers, or those who had convict parents but were freeborn. In Van Diemen's Land there were 5448 adults, of whom 2588 were convicts, 961 were ex-convicts and 899 born free. The census did not count Indigenous Australians, nor was it accurate – like many Colonial figures, the numbers don't add up. And it was impossible to count those beyond the colony's official boundaries, living in the many whaling and sealer camps around the coast.[2]

There are no reliable figures about how many convicts survived their terms of seven or fourteen years, or how many stayed in Australia once they had served their time. Even when they had served out their sentence many weren't allowed to return to Britain. An ex-convict also had to have a certificate of freedom or an absolute pardon – anyone who didn't possess either of those and was found in Britain would have their pardon revoked. Any convict or ex-convict who was embarking to return to Britain also had to advertise his or her intention in the *Sydney Gazette*. The official (and incomplete and contradictory) data suggests only two to three per cent of convicts went back.

On the other hand, it was easy enough for any able-bodied man or boy to sign up as ship's crew, even if they had no sailing experience. So many sailors died at sea, or jumped ship, that ship's captains always needed able-bodied men – or even a man with a peg leg and a hook instead of a hand, who could cook on a tiny coal fire in a heaving ocean. Back in the days before passports, an ex-convict could get ashore in

Britain without detection as long as they didn't go back to their home village or street, where an informer might tell the authorities they were there. (In the late 1700s and early 1800s informers were paid for each criminal they helped apprehend.)

By 1800 Australia's seas were dominated by American sealing and whaling ships. A convict who had been assigned to a farm, rather than shackled in a road gang, would still have been able to illegally join one of these ships and make a new, free life in the United States.

It's also possible that even by 1820, and certainly by the 1841 census, ex-convicts were carefully hiding their pasts and claiming to be free settlers.[3] It was easy enough to do in a land of large distances, few documents or need for any, and shifting populations. At least three of my own ancestors would recreate a more respectable family background in the 1830s and 1850s, carefully confusing not just where they were born but other identifying details in case their real history could come to light. (One even claimed to be the son of the Archbishop of Canterbury, a tale accepted not just by the neighbours but by his descendants until a family researcher a few decades ago discovered quite a different past for him.)

Many convicts – like those who had been shackled in government labour building roads, or had spent years in isolation as shepherds – may have been too mentally and physically damaged to even try to leave, or lead normal lives. In those days before easy legal divorce the New South Wales government allowed convicts who had left their partners back in Britain to remarry in Australia, as long as they had been separated for seven years, but many could never hope for family life. Of the 148,000 convicts sent to eastern Australia, only about 25,000 were female. From 1790 to 1850 there were also two male free settlers for every female.

There are no reliable statistics to tell us how many convict thieves went back to their old profession. Australia was certainly rich in burglars, pickpockets, and the new 'bushrangers', especially during the gold rush, when fortunes were transported with little security. Other men would became 'Orangatangs' – ragged, mentally unstable men with untrimmed beards, like 'Cranky Jack' in Steele Rudd's stories of the late 1890s. But probably a majority genuinely did make good, just as the magistrates who had sent them here hoped.

'Made good', of course, came in a variety of guises. Some, like my ancestors, became wealthy landowners, factory owners or army officers, carefully hiding their convict antecedents. For others, a cottage and small holding – and all the meat they could eat as well as the chance of a grant of free land, and even convicts assigned to them to work it – was paradise compared to what they had come from back in Britain.

It is tempting to think that those who 'made good' were stronger, smarter or simply more stubborn and adaptable than those who returned, died, or became so mentally unstable that they died without adding their genes to the population. This evolutionary 'weeding out' of the less capable happens everywhere. But in the Australia of the first half of the 1800s there were both more opportunities (free or cheap land and labour) as well as dangers (isolation, lack of experience of the land's dangers and few family support networks), so it's reasonable to assume that the land continued to influence those who survived to breed – and whose children survived – to a greater extent than in more established societies.

Male and macho?

Australia wouldn't get a fairly even male-female ratio till about 1900.[4] Did this early gross imbalance change our society? South Australia was the first place in the modern world to give women the vote; federal Australia was the second. Were women valued more in a society with relatively few of them?

But until the late 1960s Australia also had a grog-swilling, male-only culture that wouldn't even allow women into a public bar – except for the barmaid – very different from the British pubs where women would join in for a quiet half-pint of ale. Even though the first professional shearers in Australia were women (from what is now Germany), even up till 1970 if a woman even entered a shearing shed all work would stop, with the cry 'ducks on the pond' until she left.

It would take a much longer book than this to evaluate the effects of the scarcity of women for the first 110 years of European settlement had, but it is unlikely that there would be no effect at all.

Currency lads and sterling lasses

The 'third' Australians were their children, born in Australia and referred to as 'currency lads and lasses' as opposed to immigrants from Britain, who were known as 'sterlings'. The currency kids were mostly illiterate but, compared to their immediate ancestors, extremely well fed.

Others came, the fourth Australians. Some were poor, refugees from religious or political persecution, or those who were left starving when the potato crops rotted in the fields. Some were younger sons who wanted an estate in those times of primogeniture when the older son inherited almost everything, leaving younger sons and all daughters to shift for themselves, coming to Australia to buy land and establish their own prosperity. Black sheep (the dissolute and disreputable offspring of respectable families) and the shiftless, like Charles Dickens' two younger sons, were sent out to the colonies in an attempt to make them independent of their fathers' support. (One of Dickens' sons became a politician, the other made a living by giving readings of his father's work.) An Australian estate was also sometimes a gift in return for distinguished military service, especially after the Battle of Waterloo in 1815 and the Crimean War of 1853–56.

They came for many reasons, but all had one thing in common. They chose far-off Australia.

Still the longest voyage

That choice is important. Back in the 1800s there was a wide choice of destination for poor and scapegrace alike. Of the 27 million people in Britain in 1841, 120,000 emigrated. Forty-four per cent went to the United States; only 28,000 came to Australia, and this was in the year of the greatest immigration until the gold rushes. The United States were still welcoming the 'huddled masses', and it was faster – and cheaper – to go to the States or Canada from European ports than Australia. If you were a starving Irish peasant you had a far better chance of getting to New York before you died of hunger than Sydney or even Perth. A bag of potatoes might even last the journey, if you couldn't afford a fare that also gave you meals.

Even when better sails and then steamships brought the voyage down to about six months by 1830 and three months by 1860, Australia was still at the other end of the world. Why not go to India, where fortunes in trade might be made, or South Africa, Rhodesia and other African colonies, where, as in the United States, Canada and Australia, land taken from the inhabitants was given or sold cheaply to the colonisers.

Rich passengers might travel in reasonable comfort, with separate cabins, their own servants, stores like dried fruit, 'portable soup', plum puddings, a terrier to keep rats from their cabin, or even their own personal cow (with her fodder) to give milk. But they still had to face the dangers of rounding the Cape and the storms of the Southern Ocean. Those unable to afford their own cabin lived in divided holds, where men slept on pallets or mouldy hay on one side, and women on the other, eating a hot gruel of oatmeal or ship's biscuit twice a day if it was calm enough to light the fire in the galley, or cold ship's biscuit if it wasn't. A better ship would offer bunks or hammocks, with salt meat and dried pease stew and bread and cheese, and ship's doctors to ensure that no one who was ill came aboard, inspecting hair and bodies for fleas or lice that might carry disease. There was no way to tell who might be infected and not yet showing symptoms. The cramped conditions meant that cholera, whooping cough, typhoid, typhus or tuberculosis often swept through the passengers and then through Australian ports, until quarantine stations were introduced by Governor Darling. Why risk a longer, more dangerous voyage to come here?

Economic refugees

Yet despite distance, cost and privation, free settlers came in increasing numbers. Poverty drove most of them – Britain in the 1820s and 1830s was a time of desperation, with bread and fuel expensive, and farm and factory wages so low that a family still needed to grow or gather most of its food. Many arrivals had been oppressed by England's domination of Ireland, Scotland and Wales. In Wales and Scotland, absentee English landlords had been granted much of the land. Roman Catholics in Ireland were prevented from owning land, and weren't allowed to even own a horse worth more than five pounds till 1829; they couldn't go to school, or vote. It was even illegal to meet and discuss Catholic suffrage.

Scotland was in upheaval from what would be known as the 'Highland Clearances'. By 1800 the tribal chiefs in Scotland had lost most of their powers to the English – and also the close ties that bound them to their people. The chiefs cleared their glens and hills of men and women so that they could lease the land more profitably to English farmers to run sheep on. Men, women and children were forced from their homes that were then torched so that they couldn't return. Whole villages vanished and rural Scotland lost most of its people.

The evicted might harvest seaweed, knee-deep in near freezing water, dragging it to pile on the beach to be sold to make jellies; they might gather winkles, huddling for shelter in rough huts on the shore.[5] Mostly they ended up starving in Glasgow slums but, if they were young and healthy and 'of good character', they might be chosen by one of the main charitable committees that raised funds to send them to Canada, the States – or Australia.

And this was why so many did come here, and not to the nearer United States or Canada. Charities, often with Australian connections, paid their fares or even paid them a bonus as well as their fare, especially if they were farm labourers (men) or domestic servants (women). Only about a third of free settlers between 1815 and 1850 paid their own fare.[6] Possibly, too, the warmth of Australia was especially tempting to those who had seen their loved ones lose limbs to frostbite as they gathered seaweed to burn to make kelp ash for glassmaking, or who had come from highland crofts, snowbound for four months of the year, with only a few hours of daylight in mid-winter.

The men of Sollas, a town on North Uist, one of the Western Isles of Scotland, were told that as Australia didn't have enough women any man had to have a wife before the Perth Migration Committee would allow them to go. Bachelors roamed the island for weeks trying to find a woman willing to marry them – and to go to the end of the world with them. But it is said that each man found one, even if they were not matched in age or temperament, such was the desperation to leave.

They were the lucky ones. Highland chiefs – or English gentry who had been given their lands and title – would also do as Colonel Gordon of Cluny did on the island of Barra in August 1851, calling his 1500 tenants to a meeting where his men overpowered them, tied them up, and put them on a ship for America, the cheapest option to get rid of men who might rebel against his rule.

Life in Ireland would grow even more desperate when the potatoes the poor depended upon for survival rotted from the 'blight' during the 1840s. A poor Irish family would eat little else, only half-cooking them as raw potatoes took longer to digest, staving off the pain of hunger. Between 1845 and 1850 more than a million Irish out of a population of about eight million starved to death while other food was still being exported. Another million would emigrate. The starvation and poverty was also a product of the large estates granted to English landlords, disposing the original tenants, as well as once prosperous farms being divided into small and smaller farms with each generation of sons given a share.

The poorest went to England, to tramp the lanes looking for work helping with the harvest, sleeping under hedges, dying of hunger in hay barns. Those who were homeless either because they had been evicted by landlords or were orphans were sometimes able to get shelter of a kind at their local workhouse. But in the 1840s it was cheaper for the workhouse governors to send orphan girls between fourteen and eighteen years of age to Australia than to feed them in the workhouse. In 1850, more than 4175 girls from Ennistymon in Ireland alone were sent out to serve in Australian houses.

But others migrated here by choice, men like my ancestor Peter Ffrench, younger son of a prosperous farming family, who could hope for a large, cheap estate in Australia instead of a few cold acres in Ireland. Irish army officers of the 1840s could sell their 'officer' commissions for about a thousand pounds, enough to buy two thousand acres of farmland in New South Wales, and even more in Tasmania.

Australia offered hope – if you had the courage to spend months at sea, rather than the days or weeks to get to England, Canada or the United States. It is also possible that just as immigrants after World War 2 chose Australia principally because it was the furthest they could travel from the horrors they had seen, the earlier immigrants also wanted a symbolic as well as a literal distance between their new lives and their old ones.

Nor did the newcomers have to be so very respectable to get their fares paid, and even a bonus, from the charities. Most societies merely asked for a reference from a clergyman, magistrate or employer, easy to forge or cajole. The *Layton*, for example, left London on 15 August 1833 and arrived in Port Jackson on 17 December, bringing 232 women of supposedly good character to be brides for lonely Australian men. Their fares had been paid and each given five pounds bounty. It turned out that many of the women were London whores, who shocked other female passengers by their behaviour with the sailors. They may not have been respectable but they were certainly enterprising, and probably excellent businesswomen.

My great-great-great-grandmother, Anne Lamb, was on that ship; a cook, not a prostitute. But when the family needed money in the 1860s she remembered the stories she'd heard of the balls held by the more expensive courtesans of London. A gentleman would pay a fee to attend them, and another fee to dance and otherwise disport himself with the lady of his choice. Great-great-great-grandma Anne did not ask her daughters to provide her guests with anything but extremely good food and drink (my source here is my great-grandmother), but she did organise balls at her new inn with the same efficiency as her old companions on the *Layton*.

A helping hand for the worthy

Australia's first assisted immigrants arrived in Sydney on 15 November 1831, fifty young girls from the Foundling Hospital orphanage at Cork in Ireland, brought out by Dr John Dunmore Lang, a Presbyterian minister. Lang dreamed of purifying the corrupt stock of New South Wales by bringing out worthwhile women or girls, for this was an age when children as young as eight pulled coal carts in Welsh mines (children were cheaper than ponies, and more easily replaced). A ten-year-old girl could be a cook's assistant, washing up and peeling vegetables. A ten-year-old boy might shine shoes as 'boot boy', too, but Australia needed girls, not boys.

In October 1835 New South Wales Governor Bourke offered free passage for selected immigrants to try to overcome the shortage of labour in the colony. Wealthy settlers were also offered a bounty in exchange for bringing out their own workers.

But most immigrants were probably assisted by smaller charitable organisations of which there were many amidst the poverty of the 1830s. A local church group might sponsor several local young men or couples. Two more of my ancestors, a Church of England minister and his wife, were found starving, their cupboard bare of food, despite the tithes (a tenth of parishioners' incomes) paid to the Church; a poor parish had little to tithe. Their family donated enough money for their fare, with a little left over to establish themselves respectably in Sydney, which they did with alacrity.

The girls of God's police

Other schemes became famous, the best known probably that of Caroline Chisholm. After Chisholm and her husband arrived in New South Wales in 1838, she began her work taking in many of the poor Irish women, single and illiterate, who arrived on the bounty ships with nowhere to go except the streets. Chisholm trained them as servants: any woman in the colony who could cook, clean and sew had an assured job as a servant, although with such an imbalance of men and women, few would remain servants for long. Convincing Governor Gipps to open the disused army barracks as a place of refuge for women, she established a network to get single women into service, often accompanying them on carts and bullock wagons throughout the colony to find employers.

By the 1840s Chisholm decided that respectable women would revolutionise the dissolute ways of the colony, especially drunkenness, and the rape and prostitution of Indigenous women. Good women were 'God's police' and would do more to civilise rough and drunken Australian society than any number of clergy or schoolmasters.

She set up the Family Colonization Society in London and moved back there with her husband to supervise it, despatching thousands of families to Australia, as well as offering them money through her Family Colonization Loan Society. Families would be lent money to come to Australia and would repay the loans once they were settled. Chisholm organised ships that would take her charity cases at reasonable rates and under respectable conditions and placed them in hostels and jobs once they arrived. By 1846 hundreds of men were writing each year to Chisholm, thanking her for providing them with wives.

It is easy to scoff at the image of ladies with pursed lips and parasols acting as God's police. But Chisholm had a point – the lack of women in the colony meant that for many men there was no chance of companionship, a family life or a settled home. A freed convict might dream of owning a pub, but a family of his own might be impossible.

The women brought more than morals and offspring. The diaries and letters of the time tell of men building their huts, bringing their flocks of sheep or cattle. But it was their wives who ordered fruit trees or planted them from seed; who ordered rose bushes or at least a few geraniums; who set up hen yards for eggs and demanded a paddock for a milk cow and who made the butter and the cheese. In the 1800s men built empires, or made a living. Women made homes.

'Respectable' and 'enterprising' were also the criteria for the settlers to the new colonies in the west and south. Western Australia was begun not as a convict prison but by British administrators like Stirling, who founded the colony in 1829 and was funded by independent investors who brought out their families and the men they employed to work their land, as well as farmers and labourers brought out by the British investor Thomas Peel in return for grants of land.

Respectable South Australia

South Australia, too, was founded by the respectable, although the man who first proposed it, Edward Gibbon Wakefield, wrote his influential *Letter from Sydney* when he was in prison for kidnapping a fifteen-year-old heiress, hoping that she'd be forced to marry him to save herself from the disgrace. Published in the English newspaper *The Spectator* in 1829, the *Letter from Sydney* had a lot of influence, even if Wakefield had even less actual experience of Australia and its farming potential than Sir Joseph Banks.

Wakefield urged that land in this colony should be sold at a high price so that only wealthy people could buy it – and by wealthy Wakefield meant respectable. The money from land sales would pay for the emigration of labourers to work the farms. There would be an equal number of men and women, and thrifty labourers might in time earn enough to buy their own farms.

Within a year Wakefield had inspired enough supporters to form the National Colonisation Society to encourage emigration to Australia. Land in New South Wales and the other colonies was to be sold and part of the money used to subsidise people's fares to Australia. Wakefield's plan inspired George Fife Angas, a rich ship owner and banker who was also a 'dissenter', a religious radical. Dissenters weren't allowed to go to university or be buried in churchyards, but they still had to pay a tenth of their income to the Church of England. Angas dreamed of a colony where labourers had hope for a future, where immigrants would be carefully selected, where there'd be no convicts and all the crime a convict class might bring – and where no one would have to pay a tithe to the Church of England.

For five years English idealists formed committees, wrote pamphlets and worked towards a South Australian colony. A South Australian Association was formed, with the respectable Member of Parliament Colonel Robert Torrens as chairman. Finally in 1834 the British government passed an Act that established the British province of South Australia by removing about 800,000 square kilometres from New South Wales. The new settlers were carefully selected by Angas's company and the government's Board of Commissioners.

Angas also paid for German Lutheran refugees to come to the colony after they had been forced out of Silesia when King Frederick William tried to set up a state religion. By January 1839 four boatloads with 537 German migrants had arrived and leased land from the company, led by their pastor, Augustus Kavel. They began building a village they called Klemzig, after their native town in Prussia, on the Torrens River.

Wakefield and Angas's South Australian plans to establish a colony of prosperous, respectable farmers failed in many respects, but the town of Adelaide still has the nickname the City of Churches. (My father was on a troop train the day World War 2 ended. He danced in Sydney's streets. In Melbourne he was part of a two-up game. In Adelaide he went to church.)

Cooksland: A suitable destination for criminals and the virtuous

Brisbane – or rather Moreton Bay – began its existence as a penal colony when, in September 1824, Governor Brisbane sent fourteen soldiers and thirty convicts under Lieutenant Henry Miller to set up the settlement. But reports of fertile land and high rainfall soon attracted immigrants. It was also seen as a suitable destination for the virtuous. In 1845 the Reverend Dunmore Lang convinced a boatload of settlers to sail for Moreton Bay by promising they'd get land grants in return for paying for their passage. They didn't, but one way or another Lang enticed about a thousand sturdy Presbyterian Scottish settlers to the Queensland colony.

On 30 March 1849 another 250 Scottish immigrants arrived as part of Reverend Lang's 'Cooksland' scheme to start cotton farming in the area and stop Australia becoming an Irish Roman Catholic colony. Unfortunately, Lang had not got around to either getting permission from the British or colonial authorities nor getting land grants. The settlers camped temporarily in the valley they named Fortitude after the ship that had brought them to Australia. (Lang's ghost may have haunted 'The Valley' a century later, when it was a byword for carousing and brothels.)

By the 1840s the respectable white residents of Australia – or those who had made a reasonable pretence of being so – outnumbered convicts and ex-convicts. By 1841 in New South Wales there were 131,000 settlers of which 27,000 were convicts still serving their sentences and about 20,000 were ex-convicts.[7]

Australia's very distance from Europe and northern Asia continued to create a selection process for the settlers. To come here required a degree of fortitude that could accept not just the terrors of the voyage (the longer the voyage, the greater the danger of shipwreck, storms and disease) but also the knowledge that following their emigration they were unlikely to ever see their home again. Letters would take more than a year to exchange. Those tempted by the Australian gold rush could more easily have gone to the Californian goldfields. Even post-World War I and 2 there were easier, closer destinations, and official Australia has never been particularly welcoming to newcomers.

So has the fortitude and enterprise of colonial to post-World War 2 settlers affected Australian society? The popular image is that those who had the endurance and stamina to stay here and raise families created a proud nation of independent, resilient men and women: our clichéd sun-bronzed Anzacs, the settler wives who gave birth under the dray, then turned the handle on the chaff cutter with one hand while they held the baby in the other. While there were many who fitted the cliché above exactly (I still have the chaff cutter that Mrs Griggs used with one hand while she fed her babies in the early twentieth century) there are also stories of the lazy, the stupid, and the feckless, as well as the extremely unremarkable.

But you can tell a lot about a nation from the clichés it clings to. It doesn't mean that the cliché is true, but it does mean that there is likely to be a whisper of reality. We are not, and never have been, a nation of strong, selfless heroes and heroines. But our distance from the rest of the world – until the last decades of cheap air travel – did dictate and select those who came here. Even now it takes courage and imagination to leave your land. As you get older much of your joy comes from sharing memories. When you leave your community, you leave the daily sharing of those memories, too. ('Why did you come?' I asked my elderly Greek landlady, forty years ago. 'For the children,' she answered. 'Always, always for the children.')

Distance helped select our ancestors. But that same distance – and the inevitable deep, unknowing ignorance of the land that they were coming to – would annihilate much of the Australian soil, ecosystems and 'living larders', too.

CHAPTER 9

The lost tigers and the sheep that ate Australia

They toiled and they fought through the shame of it -
Through wilderness, flood, and drought;
They worked, in the struggles of early days,
Their sons' salvation out.
The white girl-wife in the hut alone,
The men on the boundless run,
The miseries suffered, unvoiced, unknown -
And that's how the land was won.

Henry Lawson, 'How the Land was Won'[1]

A young man stands on the deck of the ship that has carried him from Galway to Port Jackson. It is 1839. His wife, Charlotte, is at his side, twelve years older than him and with a jaw that denotes a far stronger character than her mild-looking husband.

My ancestor Peter Ffrench, like most free immigrants to Australia in the 1820s, 1830s and 1840s, was the offspring of a farmer. He had grown up among cultivated Irish acres, stone fences, fields of potatoes and maize, fat cows and white sheep on green grass. It had been a mostly treeless land: few survived winds and the need for firewood. Peter knew his land well. But not this land.

Peter Ffrench had come here to farm. His older brother would inherit the family property in Ireland, but here in Australia land was, if no longer free, very cheap indeed. A young man of industry – especially

A woman's tool. I was taught that handles were the great 'stone age' revolution, but this small multi-purpose tool needs no handle, perfectly fitting my hand. It cuts, scrapes, grinds, and doesn't get blunt. Yet like so much of the lore of Indigenous women, it could be invisible to outsiders as 'just a rock'. Photos: Bryan Sullivan

Food or toxin? These berries grow side by side in the bush at our place. Those on the left are good to eat; those on the right could make you seriously ill, though similar berries that grow on a twining vine are edible but bland. Native Australian foods were so unfamiliar, so diverse, and so potentially deadly that they were mostly ignored by the new settlers, even when starving or suffering deficiency illnesses like scurvy or Barcoo rot. Photos: Bryan Sullivan

This stringybark bag was given to me forty-four years ago. It wasn't new then, and it's survived flood, life in a damp shed, and much use since. Correctly made, stringybark twine is strong enough to hold a climber, and can be used to make fishing line, fish traps, baskets, doormats and much else. It can also be beautiful.

Photo: Bryan Sullivan

Macadamias: perhaps Australia's best-known native nut. Modern commercial macadamias are *Macadamia integrifolia* varieties bred in Hawaii from Australian seed. Pictured is *M. tetraphylla*, a rough-shelled wild species. The number of wild macadamia species surviving in gullies and bush along the Australian east coast is still unknown. *M. tetraphylla* produces a few nuts at a time all through the year, rather than one crop; is drought-tolerant and cold-resistant to -6° C; and the shells are too tough even for the cockatoos to open. Photos: Bryan Sullivan

The fig tree by the pool. The next Port Jackson fig territory is hundreds of kilometres away. Like the local bunya varieties chosen for larger, sweeter nuts, various fig species were planted in the small pockets where they would survive, and around the living areas, ceremonial sites, harvest areas and other places where they were needed. Like the 'clematis road', the 'kurrajong highways' and the 'mobile farms', if these figs were planted in the right places, new plants would grow as the old ones died. Photos: Bryan Sullivan

A rock pool below our house – a paradise of food, if you know where to look – and know what not to eat. Photos: Bryan Sullivan

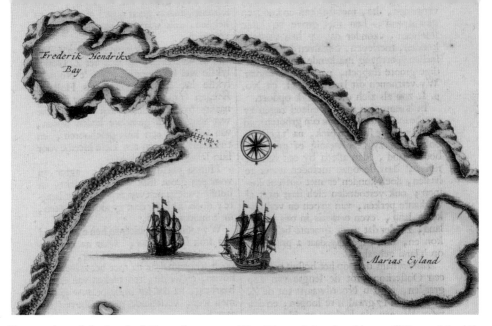

Tasman charted the Land of Giants (later named Van Diemen's Land and later still Tasmania) while hunting for the mythical Land of Gold so many Europeans were convinced had to be in the Pacific, well away from the disappointing land mass of Australia, with its lack of safe harbours and grass for food for the animals kept on board – and the dangerous winds that nearly wrecked Tasman's ships.

Frederik Hendrikx Bay Marias Eyland/F. Ottens fec. direxit. Pub. 1726. State Library of New South Wales, Z/M2 881.38/1726/1

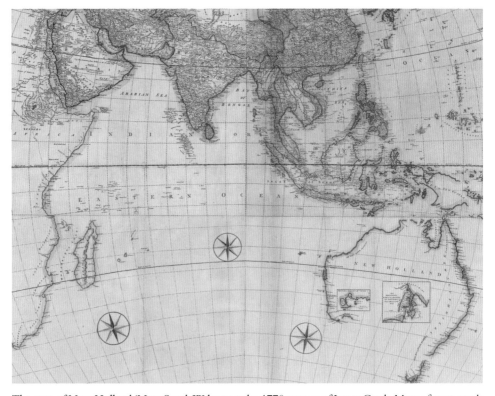

The map of New Holland/New South Wales post the 1770 voyage of James Cook. Most of west, south and north Australia – or New Holland, Concordia, or Van Diemen's Land – had already been mapped by Europeans before Cook charted the east coast. Jean Baptiste Bourguignon d'Anville, c. 1794. John Oxley Library, State Library of Queensland Neg: 262496

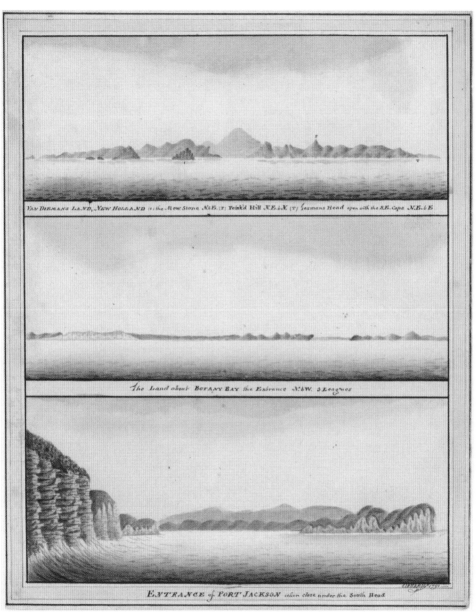

Van Diemans Land, New Holland (1) the New Stone N.E. (T) Peak'd Hill N.E.1N. (T) Tasmans Head open with the S.E. Cape N.E.6E.

The Land about Botany Bay the Entrance N.bW. 3 Leagues

ENTRANCE of PORT JACKSON when close under the South Head

European sailing ships needed the shelter of safe harbours. Australia has few of the big river systems that might create those harbours, and those we do have could be easily missed, as James Cook missed the potential of Sydney Harbour, passing the narrow gap between the headlands of 'Port Jackson' as the *Endeavour* was pushed northwards by a sharp southerly wind.

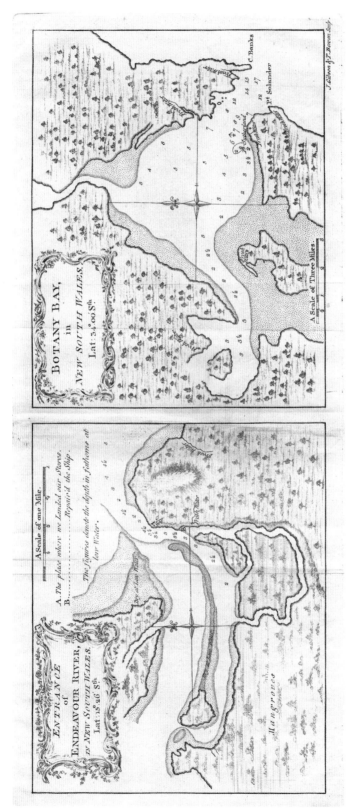

Entrance of Endeavour River, and Botany Bay, in New South Wales, c. 1773. John Oxley Library, State Library of Queensland Neg. 397436. Entrance of Endeavour River, and Botany Bay, in New South Wales, c. 1773. John Oxley Library, State Library of Queensland Neg. 397436

Cook had found only one relatively safe harbour along the coast of New Holland. By extraordinary fortune there was another, at what they named the Endeavour River, near enough for the ship to sail into when she was wrecked on the Great Barrier Reef, the 'dangerous waters' marked on the old maps that Cook knew he was leading his ship into.

Against all orders, and even commonsense, James Cook sailed the *Endeavour* up the east coast of New Holland. The decision wrecked the ship. Only luck and the ingenuity of a young man, Jonathon Monkhouse, saved it. William Byrne, *A View of Endeavour River*, 1773, National Library of Australia, an9184938

Australia owes its British settlement to goat droppings. When the *Endeavour* was wrecked on the Great Barrier Reef, dry goat and sheep droppings saved the ship. This is an Arapawa descendent of the Old English goats Cook took on his first and second voyages to Australia. The presence of so many animals aboard ships like the *Endeavour* – all needing grass – also partly explains why Australia was ignored by European colonial nations for so many centuries.

Photo: Dr Karen Nicholl & the Rare Breeds Conservation Society of NZ

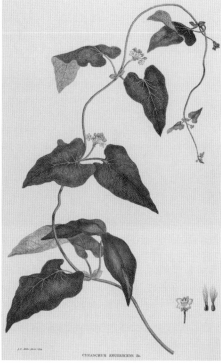

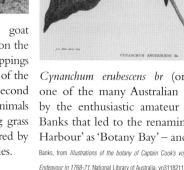

Cynanchum erubescens br (or *pedunculatum*), one of the many Australian plants collected by the enthusiastic amateur botanist Joseph Banks that led to the renaming of 'Sting Ray Harbour' as 'Botany Bay' – and a colony. Sir Joseph Banks, from *Illustrations of the botany of Captain Cook's voyage round the world in H.M.S. Endeavour in 1768-71*, National Library of Australia, vn3118211

Two views of Sydney Cove, eastern (top) and western (centre), with a map (opposite) showing the extent of the colony c. 1798. The new colony was laid out to fit Governor Phillip's ideal of large gardens and small farms, like those of England. But the colony would soon become drunk on the concept of 'endless land' – a myth that still underlies many of today's planning and political decisions.

Illustrations from *An account of the English colony in New South Wales* by David Collins, State Library of New South Wales.

One of the few native plants that the colonists did know and use was what we now know as warrigal greens. A plant can grow thirty centimetres a day, and feed an entire family with all the greens they need. To eat, blanch the leaves to remove some of the oxalic acid before cooking as for spinach. Photo: Peter Abell

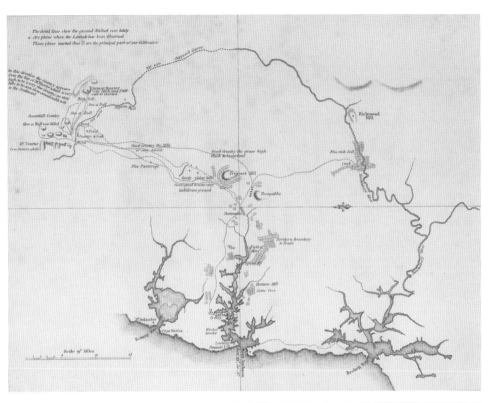

Jackie among the maize, 1975. Anyone who doubts that the early colonists could have survived on garden vegetables alone has probably never lived off their own vegie patch. Even during the hungriest period, the colonists demanded wheat bread, even though maize was far more suited to the area.

Inset: colonial maize. Unlike modern sweet corn (and wheat), old-fashioned maize varieties are drought-hardy and easily stored for long periods. Colonial maize can simply be left to dry on the plant in its husk, then tossed in a shed, husk and all, until needed, then ground to flour. These cobs are about fifteen years old and show the different colours that used to be common. Inset Photo: Bryan Sullivan

Sheep – and that 'endless land' – could make you rich. But the sheep would also turn parts of Australia to desert, and drastically simplify the Indigenous 'living larders' almost beyond recognition.

Men rounding up sheep, Shelbourne, c. 1895. Photographer: J.P. Lind Studio. Source: Museum of Victoria

The 'squatters' moved rapidly beyond the official colony's boundaries, using local material like 'wattle and daub' to wall their homes, and sheets of stringybark for roofing, and living on 'pumpkin and bear' (koala) and kangaroo until their sheep bred them wealth. Tom Walker and family outside their wattle and daub home, c. 1880. Photographer unknown. Source: Museum of Victoria

Indigenous women's farming rarely disturbed the soil, but their agriculture only supported a small population. Crops like wheat would feed far more, but by the 1960s six tonnes of topsoil could be lost for every tonne of wheat. Men and bullock team clearing land, Mollongghip, c. 1900. Photographer unknown. Source: Museum of Victoria

Gold was a dream, as it had been for the ships' owners of the fifteenth to eighteenth centuries, hunting for the mythical Land of Gold. But miners were more likely to starve, succumb to scurvy, or die in floods or mine collapse than get rich.

David Tulloch (print after), Thomas Ham, (lithographer, publisher). *Golden Point, Ballarat 1851.* 1852. Colour lithograph, National Gallery of Australia, Canberra. Purchased 2000

Imagine the darkness of the diggings: true darkness, with no torches, few fires, and deadly mine pits every few metres. Darkness won the battle of Eureka. To understand Eureka you need to understand the darkness, too.

John Skinner Prout, *Night Scene at the Diggings*, c. 1852, National Library of Australia, an4446213

If the rebels at Eureka had won, might we be a state or territory of the United States now, with no Gallipoli or Anzacs in our history?

The Eureka Stockade, 3 December 1854, engraved by Patterson, Shaggs & Co., painted by Thaddeus Welch and Izett Watson, State Library of New South Wales, a1528649

The drought from 1877 to 1903 caused squalor and desperation for the 'cocky farmers' and the slum dwellers of Sydney alike. Henry Lawson lived with both, and wrote about it. That drought would turn a collection of states into one nation.

The rabbit plagues made the drought far worse, not just because they ate grasses and other vegetation, but because their stinking corpses piled up by dry dams and creeks. But at least anyone with traps or a firearm could live on 'bunny', and the iconic hats made from their skins kept off the sun.

The Women's Christian Temperance Union of South Australia – the Mothers of Federation. Henry Parkes, constitutional lawyer, is known as 'the Father of Federation', but our nation is equally the child of the stalwart efforts of the Women's Temperance Unions, fighting for a new parliament that might make new laws giving women the vote, and ending the horrors of child labour.

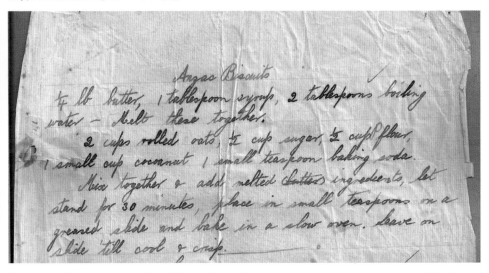

The Anzac biscuit recipe of Mrs Thelma Edwards, my grandmother, handwritten possibly by my great-grandmother Emily Sheldon in about 1916 – a tough biscuit for a tough land. The troops were issued bully beef and soldiers' biscuits, too hard to eat unless soaked in the usually filthy water of the trenches, especially for the roughly 70 per cent of men with poor teeth. A good, slow-baked Anzac biscuit survived the long journey from Australia to the battlefields, and the men who ate their oats, sugar, flour, butter and coconut were possibly slightly more likely to survive because of them.

Young men playing on an Aussie beach. The Anzac troops of Gallipoli were lauded in the British newspapers and parliament as being the bravest of the Empire. They were not, however, described as 'the best soldiers'. But a tradition of neighbourhood sport and fighting bushfires together may have added to their mateship traditions. Blakeley family collection, c. 1900–1917, Pictures Collection, State Library of Victoria

Amateur cricket match c. 1900. Wherever there was a bat, a ball, and a few square yards, Australians of all classes played cricket, usually in a more egalitarian spirit than back in England.

Floodwaters in northern South Australia, about 1914. One sure prediction is that if a piece of land has flooded once, it will almost certainly flood again. Photographer unknown, State Library of South Australia, PRG 280/1/13/176

Queensland floods, January 2011. Old-style Queenslander houses were designed for floods to pass under them. But over time the 'under the house' areas were enclosed, and more cleared land meant that water moved faster. Land known to be flood-prone was built on regardless ... then the floods came again. Shutterstock.com

Some bush types need fire to regenerate, but misunderstood 'prescribed burning' in other areas has instead encouraged fire-loving species and made the land more vulnerable to burning again.

Photographer unknown, Pictures Collection, State Library of Victoria H2002.199/1476

Always be suspicious of the word 'impossible'. It is possible to build a house that will survive bushfire. It is also possible to learn enough about our land to control them.

Totajla/Shutterstock.com

backed by a wife with a determined chin – might end up with a large estate.

He did. Peter Ffrench went first to work on the farms of the pardoned Irish rebels who lived at 'Irish Corner', now Reidsdale in the Southern Tablelands of New South Wales. Peter's father, John, had fought and won against the English at Vinegar Hill. (The family history does not relate how many Ffrenches fought against the English and lost.)

The Irish Corner squatters had been rebels in their youth, and transported for their rebellion. Now, in Australia, with part of their sentences served and a pardon for the rest, they left politics alone and became prosperous farmers, respectable apart from brewing poteen, the illegal homemade whisky that Irish Corner was famous for.

When gold was discovered in the area Peter didn't join the digging. (I am tempted to speculate that Charlotte of the firm jaw dissuaded him.) Instead he became a bullocky, selling supplies at vastly inflated prices to the often starving diggers – or rather to those who made enough to buy food. Before long he became wealthy enough to buy many thousands of acres and developed a nearby property he called Glenelly after the district he grew up in. (It was broken up by the successive inheritances of generation after generation of large families. My cousin three times removed now owns the last portion of it in family hands.)

Peter knew what a proper farm should be like. He recreated his hunk of Australian landscape and within two decades it looked much like the Glenelly of Ireland, at least in a wet year. The trees were ringbarked and burnt or cut down. The understorey of thorn bush (*Bursaria spinosa* and *Hymenanthera violacea*), hop bush (*Dodonea* spp.), wild cherry (*Exocarpos cupressiformis*) and tens or even hundreds of other species of natives were burnt, too. His sheep and cattle, tended by ex-convict shepherds and his tribe of sons, soon exterminated the native ground covers, orchids, dichondra, murrnong and hundreds of other plants, as well as the native grasses.

I first saw the land near the old homestead in 1983. It looked like Ireland: grey rain from a grey sky. The erosion gully ran swift with clear water, disguising the clay bank that would have glared pale and bright in dry weather. The mist hung over green rye grass and clover. The cattle were fat and wet, looking at us with that resentful gaze of domesticated animals who know you have come from a dry ute and have coats to keep off the rain. The only trees on the property were old pines, half rotted and perhaps even dating as far back as Charlotte Ffrench. There was no gum tree to be seen, except on the far-off hills.

Peter Ffrench and his descendants had done a good job of recreating his Glenelly, but they stole the land's health and productivity to do it. They thought they were heroes, not villains, taming the wilderness and bringing forth grain and fruit and civilisation where there was none.

The truth was that civilisation was already here, nor was the land a wilderness but a carefully created sustainable living larder. Don't underestimate the courage, determination and endurance of these early settlers and their families. But their inability to see the land as it was, and determination to recreate it into British parkland, would lead to the 1840s and 1890s depressions, and add to the misery of the 1930s Great Depression and the recessions of the 1990s and the later global financial crisis. They also turned a generous landscape – one where every two or three steps would give you something to eat – into a simplified semidesert.

Almost every form of standard Australian agriculture is an example of a profound misunderstanding of the land[2], from ploughing and land clearing to adding superphosphate or growing orchards in neat rows. These were compounded by stocking with animals unsuited to the soil, water resources and native vegetation, from domestic stock like sheep, goats, pigs, deer and cattle to wild rabbits, cats, starlings, blackbirds, pigeons and cane toads. These were all introduced because of a rigid mindset: this is the way a farm should be, with rabbits nibbling at the hedges, sheep eating rain-fat grass on pastures grown with almost daily showers, and all on young soils washed down by recent rivers. There was no understanding of the burden of salt carried by this ancient land where millennia of winds from the sea have raised natural salt levels, so that clearing and irrigation could create a desert in less than a hundred years.

First they cleared the land, making it vulnerable to erosion in dry years, or in the violent storms Australia is subject to, leaving only an English park-like scatter of trees. This made the few remaining trees easy targets for pests like Christmas beetle, who recognise their food by its silhouette, an attack intensified by the removal of plants like thorn bush that support the blossom-feeding wasp that predates Christmas beetles.

Farmers like Peter Ffrench shot eagles and goshawks, fearing that they'd attack their lambs. Actually, both only attack feeble newborn lambs as they prefer smaller prey. But the loss of the predator birds led to plagues of the species they had kept in check, like white cockatoos. In Van Diemen's Land, the Tasmanian tiger was hunted to extinction because the farmers believed it was a sheep eater, not a scavenger.

Swampland was drained, or compacted by the feet of sheep and cattle, more heavy-footed than kangaroos, driving away colonies of cranes and ibis. One mob of ibis can eat two and a half tonnes of grasshoppers or plague locusts a week, but if you spray for grasshoppers you are killing the food supply of the animals that would control them. Now plagues of locusts can destroy tens of thousands of square kilometres of crop and pasture a year.

They meant well, those men like Peter Ffrench, the women like Charlotte who endured isolation and childbirth away from family networks or even the village midwife to carve what they thought of as civilisation from wilderness. They were farmers, from generations of farmers, who had grown up with the lore of the land – but not this old, worn down land, with slow rivers that cycled between flood and drying up completely.

It takes time to learn to see the land. To begin with the early settlers often saw what their land wasn't – it wasn't cleared, it wasn't grassed – instead of what actually was there. How did they get it so wrong?

Various historians have implied that the new farmers in New South Wales had little knowledge of farming, but even in the early colony – and in the First Fleet – this isn't true. The most common convict profession (apart from thief) was 'farm labourer'[3], and even those who just put down 'labourer' as their profession could well have grown up in the country. Probably most had a great deal of farming expertise, even if they hadn't put 'farmer' on their immigration sheet. Looking at my own family tree (a diverse sample from seven countries and at least six denominations), every ancestor who arrived here had a farming background, even one who was a thief – he had been convicted of stealing a dray and bags of seed. The one who was a clergyman lived in farming communities and came from a farming background.

The Ffrenches had worked their land for hundreds of years, and prosperously. They knew how to tend the land so that it would feed generations to come. Peter Ffrench arrived with reasonable capital; Charlotte had a head for business. Peter could have chosen a life in Sydney or Melbourne, with luxuries like next-door neighbours and a pub down the road. But he must have loved farming, known how to coax crop after crop from the land.

But not this land.

A land fit for sheep to live in

The devastation began with the two dreams the immigrants brought with them, from as early as the First Fleet in 1788. The first centred on a mob of sheep, wobbly and starving from months at sea (only ewes are recorded, but presumably someone had thought to bring rams, as there were soon lambs). The wobbly sheep were part of the dream of neat green fields, small farms in villages and almost self-sufficient farmers.

There used to be an old English saying, from Romney Marsh, I think: 'Stock ten sheep to the acre until you can stock ten sheep to the acre.' It means that the sheep will clean up woody weeds and keep the turf short until only the turf remained, thus creating perfect sheep country. Instead of fertilising the land you fed the sheep hay until their dung had fed the soil.

This works in small neat English fields, where it rains regularly and often and the turf is thick and tough and able to cope with sheep' hooves, and the area is evenly grazed. It doesn't work in the bigger paddocks (whether fenced or kept by shepherds) of Australia. Instead the sheep camp by waterholes, concentrating their dung there, polluting the water and compacting the ground. Sheep 'follow the leader' to water, creating paths that will erode into gullies.

England was once marsh and forest, not fields of sheep or 'England's green and pleasant land', as Blake wrote. Sheep changed England, too.

But England with its regular rainfall is perfectly suited to small fields of sheep, marked out by fences or hedges. In winter, stock might even be brought indoors, letting the land rest. A good snow, farmers said, fed the land, helping break down animal dung and washing it into the soil. But sheep (like feral goats, pigs and deer) can turn the wrong land into desert, especially where much of the land – as it is in Australia – has a relatively thin covering of topsoil.

European and North American rivers and ancient glaciers dropped vast amounts of deep rich soil over wide areas, leaving the fertile cropland that still exists today. Deciduous trees also drop their leaves every year, so nutrients are recycled annually.

Australia has relatively few big rivers and flood plains, and those it has do not behave like the rivers of Europe and North America. They are slow moving for the most part, with a tiny gradient and enormous catchments. When the rain doesn't fall they dry up and stop flowing, reduced to a few deep pools and, once they dry up, what water remains flows beneath the surface. When the rain does return they collect water from thousands of square kilometres of country and the rivers run, opaque and soil-laden, until they top their banks and spread for kilometres across the almost flat country; it can take months for the water to recede and travel once again between the now remodelled riverbanks.

Soils in bushland are mostly regenerated by the slow dropping of eucalypt leaves and bark, the annual fall of insects like Christmas beetles that feed on those gum leaves, and the dung of grazing animals – all minute in comparison to European soils' yearly autumn leaf replenishing. Europe's climatic extremes also help create new soil, as freezing breaks rocks down. Australia's extreme weather events – floods, fires, cyclones, tornadoes, hail like cricket balls – wash soil away, especially if it has been disturbed. And Europe has many more native annuals than Australia, the bare soil of a European winter warming in spring allowing them to germinate. Soft annual plants recyle their nutrients much more quickly than tough perennials – last year's growth is this year's soil. Of the roughly four hundred species I have identified on our place (a minute fraction of what is here) only one, the paper daisy

(*Xerochrysum* sp.), is an annual, and it blooms mostly on road verges. Our land needs perennial ground covers and deep-rooted trees like river redgums (*E. tereticornis*) to hold the land and trap sediment.

Sheep nibble closer to the ground than roos, wombats and wallabies. Within years or decades they had killed the native pastures – not just the native grasses, but the hundreds or even thousands of ground covers present in native pasture.

Australian ground covers have evolved with our dramatic fluctuations in weather, decades of drought then years of rain.[4] A few species take over while others lie dormant, either as rootstock or as seed in the dried droppings of kangaroos and other wildlife.

Wombat teeth grow throughout their lives. They need tough tussocks, rich in silica, to grind their teeth down. When they eat the tussock seeds they spread them in their dung. Poa tussocks survive here when grass species have vanished after two or even three years of drought. But sheep kill poa tussocks if they are stocked too heavily, or are desperate in a drought. Sheep don't, however, eat the similar-looking, sharp-bladed introduced weed called serrated tussock, or the other introduced weeds either, which is why they are 'weeds', unpalatable or poisonous to stock and taking over land bare from drought, flood or storm.

The hard, cloven feet of sheep are harder on the soil than the feet of roos and wombats. When Australian soil becomes compacted, water runs off it instead of soaking into the subsoil. Compacted soil means that creeks flood after rain, carrying away topsoil, but relatively little moisture is left deep in the soil to keep the creeks flowing till the next rain.

Sheep (and cattle and wheat) led to a loss of topsoil – up to six tonnes a year according to a CSIRO study in the 1980s – as a result of devastation by pests, weeds, salination, erosion gullies and dust storms. But bare soil not only blows or washes away, it is also vulnerable to weeds, especially the new ones brought by colonial settlers. In the 1980s I watched two sites recover after devastation from a tornado, one in eucalypt forest in the Araluen Valley and another in the nearby Monga rainforest. Both were at least a kilometre from introduced weeds and quickly recovered, with fast-growing native grasses, emu berry, native nettles and other soil 'stablisers', then fast-growing canopy trees. But overgrazed paddocks fill instead with Paterson's curse, thistles, serrated tussock, broom and other weeds.

Sheep and cattle also need water. Colonial Australians would show enormous ingenuity transporting water to areas of grass, using windmills to pump from springs and creeks to stock troughs and paddock dams. Up until the 1970s, when petrol pumps and poly pipe changed irrigation, most paddocks had their windmill, an iconic but now almost vanished part of the Australian farmscape. But those dams and stock troughs meant that more land could be damaged by stock.

We drained water tables, too, and are still doing so. Back at school we were taught that this was a virtue: we Australians were making the desert come alive, drilling deep wells into the artesian basin and other aquifers. But Australia's soils are also older than Europe's or North America's, with salt blown in from the ocean over millennia. Add regular irrigation with slightly salty water and the salt builds up until it becomes too salty to grow even grass. Clear too many trees and the salty watertable below the ground rises again, turning what was once living larder into vast, salinated desert.

All this from a dream of green fields dotted with snowy sheep.

I can imagine putting this to my ancestor: 'Peter, you are going to destroy the land, not make it a paradise.' I imagine him answering, 'But a man must feed his family.'

There are alternatives[5] to going back to the living larders of pre-1788 Australia, feeding at most a population of a million: micro-managing even sheep, with electric fencing and other techniques, so that the land can regenerate, with windbreaks of trees and shrubs and mixed pastures of perennial and annual species of grasses and legumes; farming kangaroos and emus, or using stock like alpacas, which may be gentler on the soil; researching and using native pastures; and, most importantly, looking at the land, assessing both damage and possibilities and continuously monitoring soil, weeds and pests. But that wouldn't happen for nearly two hundred years.

Sheep may not even have been a disaster if Australia had been parcelled into small farms, where farmers were forced to work out ways to manage it sustainably, or die. Instead, for over a hundred years, colonial settlers had free, or very nearly free, land.

When ground cover isn't grass

Most Australian paddocks are sown with introduced grass: usually one to three species, including a legume like sub-clover, whose bacteria fix nitrogen from the air. Native pastures are enormously diverse in comparison. Our paddocks at Araluen, for example, contain the plants listed below and many others not yet identified. These paddocks were lightly grazed for decades and haven't been sown with introduced grasses, yet even this was enough to destroy the murrnong (yam daisies) and the many ground orchids that still exist in the small forest glades beyond the paddocks.

Rough spear grass (*Austrostipa scabra*), Three-awned spear grass (*Aristida vagans*), Vanilla lily (*Arthropodium* spp./*milleflorum*), Yellow buttons, common everlasting (*Chrysocephalum apiculatum*), Yellow buttons, clustered everlasting (*Chrysocephalum semipapposum*), Barbed-wire grass (*Cymbopogon refractus*), Blue flax lily (*Dianella longifolia*), Kangaroo grass (*Themeda australis*), Weeping grass (*Microlaena stipoides*), Paddock lovegrass (*Eragrostis leptostachya*), Forest hedgehog grass (*Echinopogon ovatus*), Kidney weed (*Dichondra repens*), Slender tick trefoil (*Desmodium varians*), Stinking pennywort (*Hydrocotyle laxiflora*), Small St John's wort (*Hypericum gramineum*), Twining glycine (*Glycine clandestina*), Poison rock fern (*Cheilanthes sieberi*), Soursop (*Oxalis radicosa*), Native raspberry (*Rubus parvifolius*), Soursop (*Oxalis perennans*), Native geranium (*Geranium solanderi* var. *solanderi*), Ajuga (*Ajuga australis*), Poa tussock (*Poa labillardierei* var. *labillardierei*), Native sorrel (*Rumex brownii*), Clustered wallaby grass (*Rytidosperma racemosum* var. *racemosum*), Wild sorghum (*Sorghum leiocladum*), Short-haired plume grass (*Dichelachne micrantha*), Creeping cudweed (*Euchiton gymnocephalus*), Variable glycine (*Glycine tabacina*), Narrow rock fern (*Cheilanthes sieberi*), Hairy speedwell (*Veronica calycina*), Native bluebell (*Wahlenbergia gracilis* or *stricta* subsp. *stricta*).

The cheap land disaster

Free or extremely cheap endless land for anyone who wanted it was our second agricultural mistake. Put together sheep and 'free land' and you had an ecological disaster. When land is free and seems to be in unlimited quantities, you don't need to tend it as you would two or even a thousand acres back in the United Kingdom. Land there usually needed to be fenced (though in the Welsh hills, parts of the Scottish Highlands and some other areas this wasn't the case – mobs of sheep passed on knowledge of 'their' territory to their descendents). It might need draining and labourers to chip away at the weeds in winter, the 'off season' when you used the labour you needed for sowing and harvesting in spring, summer and autumn to do maintenance jobs. But this new continent didn't have winter, at least not by British standards. In most parts of Australia crops and feed grew all year round.

When you have what you think of as infinite land – land you can either just take, 'squat' on, or buy or rent for a pittance compared to what you might expect to make from it – then you can afford to move on to new land, or extend your acreage as feed grew scarce on the land you already had. 'Free' land meant that instead of closely managing one acre to get fifteen bushels of wheat from it, or raise fifteen sheep, you could use fifteen acres to grow one bushel per acre or raise fifteen sheep. You could even have a thousand acres – which would make you wealthy in England but be a recipe for bare subsistence in much of Australia – or measure your property in square miles, with one sheep or beast for every ten acres. Land could make you wealthy both in England in Australia: in Australia you just needed more of it.

The costs for farming 10,000 Australian acres were lower than farming ten English acres. Even in the 1980s many large Australian properties did not even have fences along their boundaries much less fenced paddocks, except around the homestead. Sheep would be rounded up once a year for shearing, or two or three times a year for dagging (removing the dirty wool that could attract fly strike) or, later, dipping in pesticide.

Cattle needed even less work than sheep. In vast areas of marginal country, all a farmer had to do was round up the young 'poddies' every year and brand them before the neighbours could duff them, replace a 'scrub bull' every four or five years with a good one, and drive the ones you wanted to sell to a market town, hundreds or even thousands of miles away. And if you were curious about how many head of cattle you were actually running you could give them a 'bang tail muster', where every animal you put through the yards had its tail switch cut off and thrown in a pile to be counted later.

Modern Australia is still slightly drunk with the infinite land concept, so easy to believe in as you fly over forested mountains and paddock after paddock. That myth, which began in 1788, still haunts us: there's always more where that came from. If we make a mess here we can move on.

How did it begin?

The infinite land myth

The myth began on 26 January 1788 as the First Fleeters gazed at what they saw as a vast and still mostly unmapped continent. The officers at least knew that large parts of the west coast were dry, but Tasman has noted giant trees in the south, and Cook had restocked the *Endeavour* in the good grasslands of the north. It was a reasonable assumption that much or even most of New Holland's interior was grassland or forest, with inland lakes and rivers. That had, after all, been the case with the 'new' continent of North America – the central areas were superb farmlands, needing at least a century of immigrants to carve it up into homesteads (and to completely displace the traditional owners).

And this continent was free for the taking. Yes, the Indigenous owners did battle, but they could be overcome by overwhelming numbers and muskets.

Large parcels of land didn't even have to be taken legally, that is, according to the laws of England, and much of it wasn't. Australia has a long tradition of those in power taking land then using political or financial pressure to get the laws changed to legitimise stolen wealth. Even in the first decade of the colony officers of the New South Wales Corps like John Macarthur took advantage of the temporary absence of a governor after Phillip left to change the regulations, gaining themselves the vast estates of land on which their fortunes would be built. Now and then the English government or its representatives would try to put limits on further settlement, sometimes with apparent guilt at the dispossession of the Indigenous owners but, more often, because the massive areas and huge distances made their colonies too unwieldy and expensive to govern.

These days the word 'squatter' has romantic overtones, the now fashionable 'squatter's chair' a symbol of colonial luxury. Back then a squatter was just that: one who took their stock to an area no other person of European descent had claimed and said, 'This is mine.' They simply took, and often made fortunes doing so.

Squatters didn't even pay the small fees the government required. By the 1820s, for £500 you would be granted one square mile of land (640 acres, or 259 hectares) by the government. There was a limit of two thousand acres on land grants (later raised to 2560 acres). The £500 didn't have to be cash – it could be in sheep. Over the next seven years a grantee had to spend a quarter of the value of the land on improvements to get legal title to it. You also had to pay a 'quit rent' of five per cent of the value of the land, but never more than five shillings an acre, so for 2650 acres you paid £33 per year.

Even that easy ride to becoming a landholder was not enough to satisfy the hunger for land. 'Squatters' paid nothing to the government, and their occupation of land was impossible to police. By 1822 Governor Brisbane was forced to introduce a 'ticket of occupation' system, so that farmers could legally occupy their land before it was surveyed and could also keep other people off it. Legal landowners would have to employ one convict at their own expense for every hundred acres, and sons wouldn't automatically be granted more land unless their father's land was being worked productively.

In 1824 Governor Brisbane declared that no one family could be granted more than five thousand acres and no one person more than four thousand acres. The squatters took no notice, occupying as much land as their flocks needed.

In 1829 Governor Darling proclaimed the 'Limits of Location': only settlers within the nineteen surveyed counties would have police protection and laws administered by magistrates. Again, all attempts to limit the land grab failed. Sometimes squatters found new grazing lands even before the explorers as they took their flocks ever outwards in search of good grazing. Surveyors like Thomas Mitchell were often surprised to find a farm and a welcoming dinner when they thought they were in new country. There were 'overlanders' too, the men, and sometimes women, especially Aboriginal women, who took the great herds of sheep or cattle from one part of Australia to another, often finding both new routes with more water or land with good grazing that could be acquired by themselves, their families, or the information about it sold on to others who would grab it.

The land grab was not just because the land was there. After all, it had been there – and known by potential colonisers – for several centuries at least. But for the first time the vast landscape could be made to earn money from the new breeds of merino and merino cross sheep, and the new markets for their wool and meat.

In those days of slow sailing ships and no refrigeration, Australia was too far from international markets for large meat animals like cattle to be profitable. But there were now three other factors: free convict labour to manage vast mobs of sheep, a large and growing market for selling foodstuffs, especially fresh or salted meat, to whalers and sealers, mostly from North America, and the tough merino sheep bred by Elizabeth Macarthur while her husband, John (one of the New South Wales 'Rum' Corps), was in England facing legal charges for participating in a duel, or was back in Australia but mentally incompetent, needing to be physically restrained. Macarthur earned the name 'father of the sheep industry', and that first tough little herd of merinos was his brilliant idea, but it was his wife, and then his children, who mostly ran the properties, and kept breeding even tougher sheep who could survive not just the heat but had the stamina to walk miles each day, browsing among scattered tussocks for enough to eat, than get back to water by dusk without dying.

Those long-nosed sheep not only produced good quality and fine wool for the established woollen mills of England, they also fed the crews of whaling and sealing ships. That now almost forgotten industry was the foundation of much of Australia's early wealth, and the reason why it was profitable to grab so much land, so fast.

The wealth from whaling

It's 1959 and I'm standing with Dad on the beach south of what is now Surfers Paradise, but back then was just sand dunes. I'm wearing my red and white flowered 'cossie'; Dad is in his swimming trunks and Panama hat as he points out the great humps of passing whales.

In 1959 there were still whaling stations around Australia – and there were still whales, though nowhere near the vast numbers of a 150 years before. By the mid-1960s, when my father and I again stood on the same beach, there were no whales to be seen and growing worldwide agitation to stop the whaling industry.

These days, when volunteers try to rescue stranded whales and a healthy hunk of the tourism industry relies on whale watching, few probably realise just how massive the whaling industry was, especially in the early years of colonisation.

Sealing and whaling, primarily for oil but also for seal fur, was our first really profitable industry. Even though the whale oil fortunes went back to the lands the whalers came from (mostly the United States as well as France and England), the whalers needed to buy food supplies, blankets, new sails, repairs, candles, clothes and barrels as well as imported supplies like lamps, leading to the growth of a middle class of merchants. By the 1820s whalers operated all along the eastern and southern coasts, while sealers operated in Bass Strait and the south coast of New South Wales, with much of the seal oil going to China. Their crews were American, French and British too, but there were also escaped convicts, Maori, Aboriginal and Tahitian men, either volunteers or shanghaied while drunk or simply hauled on board. Once at sea there wasn't much you could do to get home.

The whalers set up camps on coasts or islands, coming ashore with guns and clubs and even packs of dogs, hunting game to eat while they boiled the blubber for oil, kidnapping Aboriginal women, killing the men, spreading disease, all beyond the reach of the colonial authorities or their own government. Not that the colonial government tried to control them – they had too few resources to even try, and the industry was too valuable to antagonise whalers who might get their supplies from New Zealand instead.

Sheep, both for meat and wool, were also too valuable to the colonies to put any realistic limit on the squatters either. In the 1820s and 1830s the price of wool was high in England and the price of meat was high in the colony. The power and wealth of the squatters grew. They had almost, or totally, free land, and free labour – the convict shepherds who lived in bark huts on damper and mutton – plus a ready and eager market for both fine wool and meat. Banks gleefully gave loans to any bloke with a belt for his trousers to buy the sheep necessary for him to take the short journey to land ownership and riches.

By 1837 Governor Bourke gave into the inevitable: squatters could have as much land as they could use and pay a pound an acre for their homestead plot, with a levy on the number of sheep they had – calculated, of course, by the squatter himself. It was a land without fences, mostly without law, and seemingly boundless opportunity.

But – there is usually a 'but' when you talk of a short road to riches – the myth of 'infinite land' was about to lead the colony to disaster.

Australia's boom goes bust: Part one

Australia's first major economic depression in the 1840s is often put down to the English recession and the subsequent steep drop in the price of wool and wheat, combined with financial ineptitude. Those contributed to the disaster, but its major cause was drought and graziers' deep misunderstanding of the land they had acquired.

In 1839 the lush years swung back to dry, the grass withering in the east as well as South Australia. Creeks dried up, sheep died. And 1840 was as dry. Australian squatters should have been able to ignore the lower demand and, hence, prices for wheat and wool. Their land properties cost them almost nothing to run, labour was free, and a property beyond the settlement boundaries was too far away for a Sydney bank to foreclose on, especially now when the land itself had no resale value.

The farmers should have been invincible, able to sit out the lower prices for a decade or more. Yes, much of their stock would die, but the tougher ones would survive to breed when the rain returned. Even in the late twentieth century an advocated strategy for drought-affected farmers was to 'let the weak ones die'; that way you ended up with a drought- and heat-resistant strain of stock. Some older farmers still practise that form of management, not often explicitly or publicly, though with easier transportation there are now more attractive and viable options.

Drought can be a disaster both for farmland and for farmers, unless the land is very carefully managed. Stock tend to congregate by waterholes, under trees or by gates where they'll be fed. Their hooves compact the land, their droppings sour the ground and, when rain finally comes, the earth is too hard for the moisture to penetrate, the last of the grass wearing away. Weeds, plants unpalatable to stock, survive once the grass has been eaten, and then flower and seed and spread so that even when a good year comes the paddocks may be filled with weeds, not grass. Eradicating the weeds takes either money or labour when the farm finances have already been eroded by drought. One disaster leads to another.

But back then sheep could wander from waterhole, to waterhole, with just a shepherd or two to keep them in one big mob – as long as you knew where the next good water might be. There were far more trees for shade in the 1840s, unlike the paddocks of the 1870s onwards, with a token tree per paddock, or even none.

The low prices of the 1840s should have meant an interregnum where fewer great fortunes were made, but it should not have been the disaster that it was. Without the drought and poor land management, the young Australian economy could have waited out the drop in wool and wheat prices and the hesitancy of speculators in land.

The major problem was the drying up of what the newcomers had regarded as permanent waterholes. The colony had known drought before, but those who were fresh to the colony would not have known how dramatically lush, well-watered country here can become bare and waterless in a matter of months. Whole lakes, like Lake George in New South Wales or Lake Eyre in South Australia, can stay dry for decades. What look like substantial rivers can become dry beds.

Many parts of the United Kingdom don't get more rain than much of Australia, it just comes more regularly, and as a gentle seep rather than hard torrents puddling at the soil. The United Kingdom's lower temperatures also mean less evaporation. A district's soil moisture index is usually a better guide to how much can be grown rather than an area's annual rainfall. Now the creeks and waterholes the squatters had thought would always be there were vanishing. Without the network of streams it became impossible to move the stock long distances to better pasture and water, or even to drive them to Sydney or Adelaide to sell.

A further problem was the eating habits of sheep. Kangaroos, wallabies and wombats don't pull grass out by the roots, or graze as close to the ground as sheep. This means that when there is a small amount of rain – the showers of a millimetre or less that are the most common precipitation in east coast droughts – the native perennial pasture grows just enough to provide a small amount of feed. Many native pasture species are drought resistant, with deep roots and oil-rich narrow leaves that resist moisture loss in the heat and dry.

Wallabies, wombats, possums and koalas have adapted to browse more unpalatable foods when their preferred foods are scarce. Kangaroos and emus can travel hundreds of kilometres with far less expenditure of energy than short-legged sheep, especially if the latter are burdened with heavy fleeces. Sheep stay pretty much near water and turn drought land into desert in the process.

Sheep also don't survive well if they are not shorn annually. The wool grows over their eyes and they become 'wool-blind'. Ewes with heavy wool can become 'cast' when they are pregnant, unable to get up from the ground and dying within twenty-four hours. Sheep have to be tended even when they don't provide an income. Sheep do excellently in Australia in good seasons; in bad seasons you need to be a kangaroo to survive. The pasture also needs kangaroos to survive.

Kangaroo droppings contain grass seeds, and dried roo droppings last for ten or even twenty years, and perhaps much longer. When it rains the seeds can germinate again, along with the microflora that the soil needs to let the roots most efficiently take up nitrogen and phosphorus. Australian pasture and kangaroos have co-evolved for hundreds of thousands of years, if you count the ancestors of modern-day roos. In the hands of the inexperienced, sheep can destroy the land.

By the 1840s the vast harvest from previously untouched whaling and sealing grounds also dropped sharply – too many animals had been killed in too short a time for the populations to stabilise. And the market for whale oil for lighting and whalebone for corsetry was drying up as gaslights became widespread in cities and underwear fashions changed. Whaling and sealing were mobile industries that could move elsewhere. When they did, the colony's most valuable meat market also vanished.

In Western Australia the new colony begun by John Stirling was in trouble, too. Like Sir Joseph Banks, Stirling had totally misread the land. The land around Perth was too sandy for most European crops, and many of the native pasture plants were toxic to sheep and cattle. Ships found it hard to navigate the Swan River, and the harbour at Fremantle didn't give enough protection from storms to their ships. The nearest good harbour was at Albany about four hundred kilometres away. There were good reasons why the Portuguese and Dutch had not colonised Western Australia or even explored it for possible mineral wealth or spices. No grass then, and no grass now.

The 1840 depression was bad. Banks failed, including the Bank of Australia. The value of land sales dropped from about £324,000 in 1840 to about £9000 in 1841. Instead of sitting back while convicts built them a homestead, squatters were reduced to boiling their sheep for their fat (tallow) to make soap or poor quality candles. It was a filthy, stinking job – literally. The stench of carcasses spread for miles, as there was nothing to be done with the unwanted meat except let it rot. Even the crows and goannas were too few to feast on it. But at least tallow could be exported.

Squatters walked off their runs – one was sold for a pound of tobacco and two gallons of rum. Robert Dulhunty's run named Dubbo on the Macquarie River in the central west of New South Wales was offered to anyone who bought a thousand of his sheep. By 1842 six hundred people (from a free – and white – population of about 100,000 in Australia at that time) had been declared bankrupt. Wages had been halved.

Land sales and rents were a large part of colonial government revenue. In desperation the colonial governments responded by making the land grab even easier. By 1844 New South Wales squatters could stay on the land they'd taken without paying for it for five years. After that they could farm twenty square miles for £40 a year. The generosity was copied in other colonies. In 1846 the *Australian Lands Act* was passed – finally the squatters could get long leases on the land they occupied but hadn't bought.

A lesson in Land Use 101

The more successful squatters may have had Indigenous help – I say 'may' as there is no way to quantify how often this occurred. There are accounts of plenty of Indigenous maids and stockmen and of Indigenous guides showing 'explorers' to good grazing country or water supplies. Much of the best land was 'discovered' with Indigenous guidance, as were tracks like those across the Blue Mountains (explorer William Charles Wentworth spent much of his childhood with Indigenous companions).

In Chapter 14 I explore the times Indigenous people warned colonials of floods, but there were many more intimate friendships, too: the men who took Indigenous wives or mistresses, or the lonely white women who grew close to the local dark women. White settlers

Sometime in the 1990s, Alice Springs

A very old woman has come to the library to meet her granddaughter. Somehow we begin to talk about European explorers. 'And those three buggers,' she said. 'The ones with camels.'

'Burke and Wills?' I ask.

'There was another, too.' She shakes her head. 'Auntie told me we tried to tell them to turn back. We threw stones at them. Wrong time of year to go into country like that. Go there, they die. The young men, they threw spears at them to try to get them to stop. They all died,' she said.

'I think one lived,' I said.

'Not for long, I reckon,' she said. 'Just wouldn't listen.'

didn't boast about these relationships. They didn't say, 'I built my homestead and home paddocks here because an old woman with black skin told me that the waterhole never grew dry.' It's not written. Perhaps, somewhere, it is still remembered. Or perhaps it never happened to that degree. But the Indigenous people I have known have been generous with their knowledge of the land, sharing willingly, freely. I suspect it is a piece of lost history, a thousand friendships and conversations that marked our land but whose details we may never know.

The golden days of rain and hungry mouths

The economic future of the colony would be saved by the gift of the land that every history book recognises: gold. The gold rushes that began in 1851 meant mouths to feed, and (if they were lucky) the money to spend on it. Miners flocked to Australia.

And it rained. With no rain there'd have been no gold rush (see Chapter 10). With so many miners to feed and the rain-lush decade of the 1850s, both small and large farms became profitable again.

By 1865 Australia produced the world's finest wool. The demand for mutton to feed miners had meant that it was also profitable to cull your sheep, selling those that produced less fine wool and keeping only the best. Despite the romance of gold, half of Australia's export earnings even in the 1850s came from wool.

With green grass, improving wool breeds and assured markets, the political and financial power of the squatters grew. At the same time land was opened up to selectors, small farmers who 'selected' 160 acres of land, often from the land the squatters had regarded as their own. Many squatters retaliated by selecting land in the names of their children or even servants, who were then forced to sell it back to them by ties of family feeling, self-interest or outright intimidation.

There had always been small farms – market gardens and orchards, with a few sheep or cows, dairies, even some wheat – near the towns and cities. Now smaller farms spread outwards, once again misunderstanding the land and trying to impose a European model of land use: big estates balanced by small mixed farms.

It was an impossible dream. Most small grazing properties would be sold to make larger, more viable properties, or even abandoned. The small farms that survived were those that grew vegetables or fruit or ran dairy cows, often producing butter and cheese to make the small holding viable. The introduction of fast sailing ships (clippers) and refrigeration in addition to the opening of the Suez Canal in 1869 also made it possible for meat, butter and cheese from the new cheese factories, tallow for making soap and candles and hides, and even fresh fruit to be sent 'home' to England.

Chinese goldminers often stayed and began market gardens, too. Many were indentured, owing years of income to businessmen back in southern China. Australia offered racial prejudice but also a greater degree of freedom, and the chance to make not just a good living but a fortune, as Sydney's Quong Tart and Braidwood's Nom Chong family would do, even transcending the deep and often violent British hatreds to become beloved members of the community. Chinese market gardeners knew how to grow vegetables in arid country, building 'water races' or channels that ran for kilometres from creeks or swamps. By 1880 there were Chinese market gardens on the edges of all the major towns. Without them, large-scale settlement where children didn't die of scurvy or Barcoo rot would have been impossible.

In north Queensland the first big banana farms were started by the Chinese, who travelled there for gold and stayed to farm along the Barron, Johnstone and Tully rivers, and later around Cairns and Innisfail. In those days every banana crop was planted onto newly cleared land; bananas are a hungry crop, and fresh land would be more fertile. But until the past two decades or so bananas in Australia were also inbred, each banana plant a division of the same ancestor and extremely vulnerable to fast-spreading diseases. Growing them on fresh land was a way to cut down this risk – and a lot of 'old banana land' was available for other farmers.

From 1850 to 1878 it appeared that the land would again be ever-generous: wool, mutton, gold and more mutton to feed the miners and the employees in the growing industries. It is in this period that many

Australian icons were born, from rags to riches tales of finding a massive nugget, to the lonely drover's wife struggling to care for her children and keep a small holding going in her husband's absence.

Death by dust and sheep: Part two

By 1865 sheep (and to a lesser extent cattle) roamed over all but the driest or most tropical parts of Australia. And then came the next drought, compounded again by the lack of understanding of the land and climate.

The 1877 to 1903 drought was tough for both large and small farmers; by the end of the drought Australia had only half the number of sheep that had grazed its grasslands in 1870. But, unlike the 1840s drought, most of the large property owners were able to ride this drought out with off-farm investments and low costs.

Closer settlement meant there was odd-job or seasonal work or shearing for men from the selections. The poems and stories of those times talk of poverty, despair and hardship, but they also tell of a culture where, by and large, the wife and family were expected to stay on the land and keep the farm going.

When the dust storms of 1900 hit there was already a growing realisation that wide-scale clearing might be bad for the land. Clearing still continued (as it does in some parts of Australia even today) but at least by then there was a growing dialogue about what the land needed, as well as agronomists and farmers who actually looked at the land rather than superimposing a European vision on it, or assuming that they could acquire more land to make up for the productivity lost on the land they already had.

Land was slowly being fenced, especially with the new barbed wire. Superphosphate was spread on land from which the phosphorus had already been exported as wool or wheat. New pasture grasses were tried, with combinations that included subterranean clover, which has bacteria associated with its roots that fixes nitrogen – one of the three great elements needed for soil fertility – from the air.

For the first 150 years of white settlement, Australia still lived 'on the sheep's back', a reference to the major part wool later played in our export economy, then on mutton and its by-products, tallow and wool and drippings. Until the 1920s much of Australian life was based on sheep, from the food we ate, to the clothes we wore, to the shapes of our towns and cities, with long straight central roads you could drive a mob of sheep down. Even our long Christmas school holidays mark the time when children needed to be available to help bring in the first and second cuts of hay that would be used to feed the flocks.

The decline of the 'true merino'

Sheep – especially their wool – remained Australia's major export until the 1960s, gradually being overtaken by industrial products, then mining. Many of the great squatter families (popularly known as 'true merinos') could still trace their family back to members of the 'Second Fleet', who had often gained their land through illegal grants and corruption, or to ancestors who had simply squatted and used political pressure (derived from their wealth, and the early franchise that gave the vote only to male landowners) to have the land that they'd taken made legally theirs. Many or even most of those families remained rich but not necessarily from wool, or from wool alone.

Wealth was diversified over the generations, allowing many to ride out droughts, replenishing their fortunes in good seasons or when the price of wool was inflated by war. (War is extremely good for woolgrowers, or it used to be before uniforms began to be made from synthetics. Many of the hideous burn injuries combatants experience now could be reduced if their uniforms had been made of flame-retardant wool.) But, increasingly, grazing families would face the 'long paddocks' in dry times, leaving their farm for years to take their stock along roads in search of ungrazed feed, or along established stock routes with water at regular intervals. By the 1960s drought, those who relied solely on farm income were often hard-pressed indeed, or simply walked off the land, unable to sell it. Mansions or large comfortable houses rotted, unwanted and untenanted.

By the 1970s drought, and even more so in the 1990s drought, a canny farmer had a wife with an off-farm income – often teaching, accountancy, pharmacy, working on the council or at the Rural Lands office in town, which was enough to survive on in bad times and helped to pay the mortgage or put the kids through school in good years. Mostly.

But by the 1990s farming – and farmers – had changed. (Never call farmers conservative. Show most of them that a better way works and they'll take it.) Few farmers these days just 'do what granddad did'. They study both their land and farming economics and ecology.

And the sheep continue

Mutton production is more profitable than ever. Wool has given way to synthetics and other fibres, but fat lambs – or even elderly merinos – are valued as meat in the emerging markets of Asia, Southeast Asia and the Middle East. Some sheep are transported live, so they can be killed according to religious law, or cryovacked, even more efficient than freezing or refrigeration. Fat lamb is one of the most profitable products today – possibly *the* most profitable.

Merino sheep grow fabulous wool but do not make good eating. Sheep bred for meat have much harsher wool. Using merinos for meat or using crossbred wool in clothes undermined both the popularity of woollen garments and the quality of lamb for eating.

Meat breeds like dorper are now increasingly popular, which are more or less without wool and whose meat isn't toughened with stress hormones from shearing, so their body effort can go to meat not wool production. Soft, fine merino wool is still prized but it is now for the more expensive end of the market. (Most cheapish wool garments are made of recycled wool, not 'pure new wool'. Recycling wool is a good thing, but compared to new wool it is harsh and scratchy. Other cheaper and thicker woollen garments are made from coarser wool from crossbred sheep.)

A sheep's life can be a hard one: scavenging in the dust for grass, roughly shoved by shearers, mulesed, drenched, cut by rough shearing, trucked to abattoirs. But in smaller flocks, and with proper management, the life of a sheep bred to give fine wool can be a good one. If stocking rates are kept to responsible levels with a good range of both introduced and native pastures, it can even be an ecologically sustainable enterprise.

Well-run farms can make money, but only if you don't have a crippling burden of interest to pay and the seasons are kind – or at least not all of the seasons are bad, or climate change doesn't relatively suddenly change your land's tolerances. Perhaps the best way to weather bad years is still to have that off-farm income, whether from a spouse, or by working yourself on contract for others, fencing, road building, digging dams; or by to selling all but your best stock and working elsewhere for the duration.

Increasingly these days, rural land is owned by retirees or urban 'tree changers' who can afford high prices for land and don't depend entirely on its income. This isn't necessarily a bad thing for the land. In fact, if they know what they are doing (some do, some don't), not having to push your land to increase production and run yet another hundred head of stock to pay the interest bills can be very good indeed, especially if there is capital to plant belts of trees and fix erosion gullies. But it can be bad for the social framework of the district. Weekend hobby farmers rarely join bushfire brigades, bring a plate to the Christmas party, send their kids to the local school, or otherwise become part of the fabric of the area.

Few farms these days support two or even three generations, as they did fifty years ago. For a while, back in the eighties, it looked like all the family farms in my area would be slowly broken up for hobby farms. This was as much due to the rise in lifestyle expectations as it is a comment on our rural economy – the days of kids being happy with plates full of meat and vegies and new shoes once a year have vanished with the rise of the iPod and holiday 'escapes' once a year generation. But new industries have grown: alpaca farming, with a second income from alpaca fleece products; cheese-, beer- and cider-making; farm tourism, from holiday cottages to B&Bs. And now it looks as though much of our land might sustain farming even longer than the Ffrenches farmed their acres back in Ireland, with managers eager to listen to their land.

And sheep – once again – is a favourite food on our tables. Tender dorper lamb, or lamb tagines with Moorish spices, Dorset lamb for a beautiful Sunday roast, Wiltshire Horns for lean but tender and tasty meat from all parts of the carcass, or fat-tailed lamb on a spit for Australians whose ancestors came from the Middle East, not England. The sheep farmers still survive, even if both their recipes and their vision of the land have changed.

CHAPTER 10

How we almost won Eureka

In 1850 a giant of a man sailed from Australia to the Californian goldfields. As Edward Hargraves gazed at the granite outcrops and veins of quartz, so like those in Australia, he had a vision: a gold rush for Australia, as spectacular as California's. He sailed back to New South Wales and informed the inspector-general of police that he was going to discover gold.

The inspector-general was not enthusiastic. 'A wild and unprofitable undertaking,' he said.

But Hargraves was sure gold was waiting for him. According to the stories he told later, he didn't even visit his family in Gosford to say he was home. On 5 February 1851 he galloped across the Blue Mountains and down onto the Bathurst plains, on a great brute of a horse that bucked and stumbled the whole way. And there was the gold, shining in a creek, just as he had dreamed, a greater goldfield than any in California.[1]

That, at least, was the romantic tale Hargraves told to the press. The reality was somewhat different. Hargraves was a drifter, a charismatic dreamer, not a worker. He had bought a farm, a pub and a store with his wife's dowry then deserted her, leaving her to work the store. He was lured to California by the dream of easy money. But mining was hard work. Hargraves already knew there was gold back in Australia, near Bathurst in New South Wales – over the past few decades there had been several accounts in Australian newspapers, and probably even more gossip in various pubs. The problem was that the colonial governments didn't want a gold rush – and legally, the government owned the gold.

Hargraves hatched a plan to pressure the colonial government to pay him a reward for finding gold in Australia.

Finding that gold wouldn't be difficult – it had been 'discovered' many, many times before.

The gold discovery myth

It's difficult *not* to find gold in granite country in Australia, once you know where to look for tiny grains among the gravel in creek beds, or shining in seams of the rock. There's a lot of granite in Australia. There are tiny flecks of gold in the creek on our property, and even more in other creeks nearby. According to the old-timers here, the local gold rush started when an elderly widow cut open the gizzard of a turkey (turkeys need grit to help digest their food) and saw flecks of gold. 'Gold! Gold!' she yelled, and her son hurried to peg out their claim. Every decade or so another company 'discovers' gold again, and floats the idea of a gold mine.

Gold exists in many parts of Australia, but not in large enough amounts to make much money. Few Australian goldmines make a profit: gold is valuable, but the costs of finding it can be greater than the proceeds from the gold. This was as true in the 1840s as it is today.

The first gold discovery by a European settler may have been in 1823 when surveyor James McBrien found gold in the Fish River east of Bathurst. In 1841 Anglican clergyman and geologist the Reverend William Branwhite Clarke, principal at the King's School, Parramatta, found gold near Hartley in the Blue Mountains, and more in Bathurst and Liverpool in the next few years. But he claimed that when he told Governor Gipps about his finds he was told to 'Put it away, Mr Clarke, or we shall all have our throats cut'.[2]

The colonial governments made most of their money selling the vast amounts of unoccupied land. But now, with the collapse of the wheat and wool prices in England and the 1840s drought, the governments were struggling financially too. Colonial administrators had sent out surveyors to find useful mineral deposits, like coal. There were no orders to hunt for gold. Gold, in fact, had been noted but the colonial authorities had decided not to follow it up. Gold might bring chaos.

The Indigenous people, too, knew where gold was, of course. But what use are bits of soft yellow metal? They'd later point it out when asked. The Bendigo gold rush, for instance, would be started when members of the native police showed Sergeant McClelland large amounts of surface gold. The Eureka claim, too, was found when miner Paul Gooch sent a 'blackfellow' out to look for a strayed horse and he returned with a nugget of gold as well, then Gooch sent a party to find out if there was more.

The Reverend Clarke did keep silent about his gold finds until after Hargraves had made his 'discovery'. But despite Clarke's discretion, the rumours of gold abounded, so why wasn't there an Australian gold rush before 1851? The reason was simple: all minerals like gold belonged to the Crown, in this case the New South Wales government. There was no point prospecting if miners weren't allowed to keep or sell it. Nor did the colonial governments want a gold rush – they were already overstretched trying to govern the expanding colonies. They assumed, correctly, that the dream of gold would also bring a need for police and troopers to protect those on the diggings and attract far more prospectors than the colony could easily house, feed or transport.

Hargraves didn't look for gold, he looked for someone who knew where it was. He soon found him – John Lister, the son of the innkeeper where he was staying at Guyong, near Bathurst. Lister and his friends, brothers William and James Tom, led Hargraves to Lewis Ponds Creek. Between them they panned about £13 worth of gold.

Hargraves tried to claim a reward from the colonial secretary, but the government still didn't want to disrupt the economy with a horde of frantic, dreaming miners. Hargraves' genius was in manipulating the public to demand the right to follow their dreams of riches. In February 1851 he announced to the press that he had discovered a vast goldfield, and publicly demanded a government reward.

The dream of gold seduced first thousands, then tens of thousands, far too many for the colonial authorities to stop. As the colonial authorities had feared, clerks dropped pens, shepherds let their flocks wander around wool-blind; sailors jumped ship. They all went to look for gold. Once they starting looking, they found it. With so many following their dreams of riches, the colonial authorities were powerless to stop them. But they could at least make money from the miners. That gold in the ground still belonged to the Crown (gold and other minerals deposits still belong to the government). The colonial governments began to issue licences, in effect selling the right to search for the gold.

Hargraves kept up a public campaign till he got his reward. (He failed to mention John Lister or the Tom brothers, nor did he share the reward with them.) Within four months more than a thousand prospectors had raced to what would become the Ophir goldfields near Orange.

In fact, Ophir had relatively little gold. Hargraves would later be attacked by furious diggers returning to Sydney, broke and starving. But Hargraves' dream was contagious.

A scientist hero

If there is a visionary giant in this story it's the Reverend William Branwhite Clarke, not Hargraves. Clarke would be called the father of Australian geology, as well as pioneering meteorological observation and rigorous scientistic procedures in the colonies.[3]

Rain brings a gold rush

But the Australian gold rushes were created as much by the weather in Europe and Australia as they were by Hargraves' contagious daydreams. Europe in the 1840s was a time of starvation; cold, damp summers that turned the wheat and rye harvests to rusts, blights and mildew. There were tens of thousands who were desperate enough to sail across the world to look for gold.

But if Australia hadn't had a series of wet seasons too, there could have been no gold rush. Australia was in a drought-fuelled depression in the early 1840s. But in the late 1840s, and even more in the 1850s, it rained. And rained. And rained. Gold mining back then (and to an extent even now) requires large amounts of water to sift out the gold from crushed rock or sand or gravel. If the drought had continued, gold mining wouldn't have been possible. The Araluen Valley where I live now, for example, was one of the largest Australian goldfields in the 1850s, with perhaps 40,000 gold miners in about twenty square kilometres of valley, using the water from the Araluen River and what were once the valley's lagoons, shaded by red gums, filled with ducks and waterlilies. Races carried water tens of kilometres from high up in the gorge down to otherwise dry parts of the valley. But the river dries up in drought years, apart from the deep pools fed by seepage through the rock, and did so even before increased settlement took more and more water for households and irrigation. If the 1850s had been a drought, there'd have been no Araluen gold rush until the wet years came again.

Gold prospectors also need food. Back before easy irrigation with poly pipe, crops needed rain. Grass for sheep needed rain, too. A cold, wet Europe and China, and warm, wet Australia gave us our gold rushes. Gold-hungry 'diggers' arrived from Europe, China, America and New Zealand, but most came from the United Kingdom. In 1852 alone, 370,000 immigrants arrived in Australia. The area we now know as Victoria had 77,000 people in 1851 and 540,000 people in 1853, mostly men. (There is enormous variation in the population estimates of the time, but all agree that the increase was major.)

Australia's first 'gold rush' had involved sea captains seeking the mythical land of gold. None found it. Only a few would find wealth in this gold rush, too. For most, the riches would remain a seductive myth, luring them from comfort, jobs and families to risk their lives in the hope of finding that useless mineral that gleamed even in shadow. Most gold-panners and miners lived in squalid, starving poverty. There were indeed fortunes to be made but, apart from the relative few who found nuggets or workable seams of gold, the fortunes were made by those who grew or sold food, grog, sex, woollen blankets, rabbit-skin hats and other supplies to the newcomers.

Gold was panned to begin with, washed out of creeks and from the sandbanks along rivers. As the alluvial gold (the fine gold deposited in the sand and gravel of creeks and rivers) ran out, miners dug for it, at first in the sand and gravel where past floods or glaciers might have dropped it (gold is heavier than sand and collects in pockets where water slows down). Others who weren't lucky enough to stake their patch of gold-rich gravel claimed land further away from the creeks, where ancient deposits might have been left by long gone streams, digging like wombats deep into the earth.

Gold was a dream. The reality of the goldfields was poverty, starvation, brutally hard physical work, crippling accidents and disease. A digger had little more chance of making it rich than someone today does of winning the lottery.

Those who reached a goldfield first had the best chance of making money; in February 1852, maybe five miners in a hundred became wealthy, forty-five made enough to live on and fifty starved. But by December, as the easily panned gold was claimed, perhaps ninety per cent of diggers were unable to pan enough even to eat. Most miners lived on flour and water, made into watery stews with a little meat if they had money or firewood, or into damper or sinkers – lumps of dough wrapped around green branches and cooked over the flames – if they couldn't afford meat. The scenario was repeated at goldfield after goldfield: wealth for a lucky few followed by poverty for many.

It was this poverty and desperation that led to the battle that would be Eureka.

The muddy track to Eureka

Most history books describe the Eureka Stockade as a scuffle, a protest about gold licences that was over in ten minutes. Yet two weeks before the Eureka Stockade, 10,000 men knelt in the dust and swore to make Australia independent of England. How could 10,000 men lose a battle in ten minutes, when every day more armed men arrived at Ballarat, including the mounted Californian Rangers?

Eureka, according to popular myth, was doomed to fail. Ten thousand men, many with military experience, doomed to fail? In fact, the Eureka Stockade nearly became the trigger for a rebellion that might have secured Australian independence from Great Britain. But to understand the Eureka Stockade – and why the rebellion almost succeeded – you need to understand the terrain.

In 1854 the Eureka gold claim was just one of thousands on the Ballarat goldfields in Victoria.[4] Ten years before, the land had been a paradise: a river, and lagoons of ducks, swans and waterlilies. Now the lagoons were called the 'Gravel Pits' and they were a scene from hell. The water was still there, but brown and bubbling now, forced into hundreds of small channels and pools. Down in the filth of gravel and water, men huddled over barrels, buckets or tin dishes, scooping, lifting, shovelling up the gravel, sifting, swirling, examining. All around the pools was a vast warren of tents so close they almost touched each other.

'The noise would deafen you in an hour. Flies clustered around the faces; not bush flies but fat black ones from well-fed maggots that bred amongst the filth. Nasty, sneaky, cheeky little things of flies got into my eyes,' wrote Raffaello Carboni, an ex-Jesuit scholar turned failed Italian revolutionary and democrat, who hunted for gold, survived the stockade, then wrote about his experiences. 'I could see no more, no ways. Mud water one shilling a bucket! Got the dysentery; very bad.'

Yet over the whole place lay a feeling of excitement, as though the breeze itself whispered the words, 'Gold … gold … gold …'

And only the lucky had claims at the Gravel Pits. Squalid as they were, at least they did contain gold. The land sloped down to them, but beyond that slope the land was flat. Once it had been covered with tall trees, a richness of koalas, possums, wallabies and bandicoots. Now every feature of the landscape had been erased except the dirt itself.

The Ballarat goldfields stank, human waste dropped down abandoned mine shafts. Those desperate enough to reopen old claims dug through faeces, hoping for a gleam of gold. Tents crowded into strangely neat streets, bits of cloth drooping between two poles, though one or two were fancier, with many poles and even flaps for windows. Tents began white and within days they were the colour of mud, the colour of the miners themselves. Most had rough stools out front or fireplaces, and wet trousers hanging heavy on washing lines strung between the trees. By 1854 some had tiny gardens with what looked like leafy vegetables growing in neat patches, or even flowers protected by low rocky walls if their wives and children had accompanied them. There were few fires: nearly all the trees had been use for pit props, and it was a day's walk or more to gather firewood. A rough township had formed, shanties with bark walls and roof, and even more solid hotels and stores.

If you had the money, Ballarat could sell you all you needed (except the antibiotics to cure it when you got it), from a two-minute 'knee trembler' to a pink lace bonnet or a gander at the dancing girls, paid two pounds ten a week for simply kicking up their legs, more if they held their skirts up for longer. There were few women miners (although some were disguised as men), but respectable women made good money taking in washing for those whose claims gave them the luxury of clean clothes, or selling stew, home-brewed beer or hooch, or lemonade. There was even a lending library, and a theatre.

At dusk the diggings exploded as miners shot their weapons to check if their powder was dry – or that, at any rate, was the excuse for the daily ritual of machismo.

A land of sails and wombat holes

Beyond the tents were massive mounds of dirt, as though a mob of kids had been making forts or giant wombats digging holes, each with a ragged sail above it to direct air down underground, otherwise the miners died of carbon dioxide poisoning. These were the horror pits of Eureka.

The shafts in the Gravel Pits were dangerous – gravel is not a stable substance to dig through. But at least there was a reasonable chance of finding gold amongst the gravel. The muddy gold shafts beyond the Gravel Pits were as dangerous, but few miners even made enough to pay their licence fees.

When Governor Hotham visited Ballarat in 1854, the depth of an average shaft was 120 to 160 feet and took six months to a year to dig. Hotham assumed that the diggers must be men of capital to be able to afford to dig such deep shafts, easily able to afford a rise in licence fees. They weren't. They were simply desperate, living on a dream until death from a collapsed tunnel or starvation intervened, or a breath of sanity.

But there was unity in poverty. Those who had struck it lucky would 'stake' a new chum (lend him money) for a share of any find, or even a few shillings at least to get them back to Melbourne and a job. A man with a newspaper would attract a crowd, the reader announcing the doings of the world beyond and the increasing resistance to authority.

For the one thing that unified them all was resistance and abhorrence of the troopers who carried out the licence hunts.

Joe's traps

The cry of 'Joe! Joe! Joe!' to warn that the troopers were checking every person had their licence would spread through the diggings. ('Joe' was first used at the time of Governor Charles Joseph La Trobe – his troopers were originally called 'Joe's traps'.) At the cry of 'Joe' the scene of huddled, shovelling men changed in an instant. Crowbars splashed into the water. Men downed tools and began to run. Cradles sat abandoned by the stream. The cry was repeated all along the diggings, like a mob of cockatoos was yelling it overhead. 'Joe! Joe! The Joes are coming!'

The 'Joes' wore the red jackets and long black boots of the British military. But they were colonial troops, deeply corrupt, often violent. That, too, was one of the foundations of the violence that was to erupt. The troopers might take you even if you had your licence, tear it up, grinning. A favourite money-making torture was to tie a man to a bayonet, with his body poised above the point. If he slumped, he died. Meanwhile his friends had to find the money to pay the bribe to free him, running to the bank if they had funds there, or taking up a collection, penny by penny, from other miners. The magistrates were corrupt too, favouring either their friends or whoever paid them the most. The Victorian legislature was comprised of squatters, who made sure that revenue was raised from customs, sale of land and mining licences, not from their own estates, resisting any attempts to widen the franchise.

The miners lived in a state that was the epitome of tyranny, prone to erratic decisions and with no redress. In once incident, described by Carboni:

> One morning, I woke all on a sudden. – What's up? A troop
> of horses galloping exactly towards my tent, and I could hear
> the tramping of a band of traps. I got out of the stretcher, and
> hastened out of my tent. All the neighbours, in night-caps and
> unmentionables, were groping round the tents, to inquire what was

the matter. It was not yet day-light. There was a sly-grog seller at the top of the hill; close to his store he had a small tent, crammed with brandy cases and other grog, newly come up from town. There must have been a spy, who had scented such valuable game.

The Commissioner asked the storekeeper, who by this time was at the door of his store: 'Whose tent is that?' indicating the small one in question.

'I don't know,' was the answer.

'Who lives in it? Who owns it? Is anybody in?' asked the Commissioner.

'An old man owns it, but he is gone to town on business, and left it to the care of his mate who is on the nightshift,' replied the storekeeper.

'I won't peck up that chaff of yours, sir. Halloo! Who is in? Open the tent,' shouted the Commissioner.

No answer.

'I say, cut down this tent, and we'll see who is in,' was the order of the Commissioner to two ruffianly looking troopers.

No sooner said than done; and the little tent was ripped up by their swords. A government cart was, of course, ready in the gully below, and in less than five minutes the whole stock of grog, some two hundred pounds sterling worth, or five hundred pounds worth in nobblers, was carted up to the Camp, before the teeth of some hundreds of diggers, who had now collected round about.'[5]

There was little justice for miners on the Ballarat diggings, and Carboni would document it well.

The rebels of Eureka

Raffaello Carboni was Italian – or, rather, was a member of the Young Italy movement which was dedicated to overthrowing the Austrian and Bourbon rulers and removing the Pope from his estates in order to unify Italy under one reasonably democratic government.

When their 1849 rebellion failed, Carboni travelled to Paris, Berlin, Malta, Frankfurt and, by 1852, Melbourne, and then to the Ballarat goldfields. Until about 1850 most of the new Australian settlers had been either convicts or the respectable poor, and almost exclusively British. But 1848 was the 'Year of Revolution' with popular uprisings in many European countries against their various monarchies. It was a time when Lutherans, Presbyterians, Methodists, Quakers, Congregationalists, Baptists and others demanded freedom of religion from their Roman Catholic monarchies. Revolutionaries in Prussia dreamed of a united Germany; others in Naples or Sicily dreamed that Italy would become one nation.

The immigrants from Britain, too, often had little loyalty to the British monarchy or government. The goldfields – including the Ballarat goldfields where the Eureka gold claim had been made – were still overwhelmingly British. Anecdotally, perhaps half were Irish, and Irish Roman Catholics were demanding and fighting for freedom from their Anglican monarchy. Many English, Welsh and Scots also identified as nonconformists, that is, English subjects who were not members of the established (Anglican) church. English Chartists demanded the rights of workers to form unions.

The revolutions of the 1840s failed. But some of the rebels now came to Australia, dreaming of gold but also of freedom. They had rebelled once, and had the experience and temperament to do it again. Many diggers arrived from California, too, a land where the American colonies had successfully rebelled against England.

The dream of independence

The Eureka rebellion at Ballarat is often portrayed as simply a protest against the cost of a licence to dig for gold. The cost of licences was a trigger for protest, but the rebels would come to call for complete independence from Great Britain, as well as universal male suffrage – the right to vote for every white man in the colony. (They were not so radical as to think that women, Indigenous Australians or those who had come from China should also get the vote.)

On 1 January 1852 Victorian 'mining right' taxes were raised from one pound ten shillings to three pounds a month. Everyone on the goldfields, from cooks to tent keepers, had to buy a licence and have it on them at all times. Thirty-six pounds a year was a massive amount, equivalent to perhaps $100,000 a year now. A head clerk or an engineer would be lucky to make three pounds a week in 1852. A well-qualified governess could be hired for thirty pounds a year, or a good cook for forty-five.

Three thousand miners protested at Castlemaine. At Bendigo, the largest mining community at the time, a miners' protest meeting passed the resolution: 'We therefore pledge ourselves to resist it in every shape and form and we will aid by every means in our power who would do the same elsewhere.' *The Argus* of 10 December reported: '[T]here appears to be an extraordinary demand for guns, pistols, powder and ball, and even cutlasses are inquired for.' Another meeting at Castlemaine drew 12,000 men and declared: '[W]hile deprecating the use of physical force, and pledging itself not to resort to it except in self-defense, at the same time pledges itself to release or relieve any or all diggers on that account of non-payment of the three pound licence fee.'[6]

On 13 December Governor La Trobe rescinded the increase in licence fees, but they were only a small part of a far wider problem. The diggers got little or no government help despite the fees: no roads, little police protection. Even to get to the diggings you had to pass through the 'Black Forest', where 'demons' – ex-convict bushrangers from Van Diemen's Land – failed to follow even the normal courtesy of a highwayman by letting you go free if you offered up your belongings; travellers were killed as well as robbed. Some demons would tie their victims to a tree and leave them to starve or die of thirst.

The roads themselves were mere tracks through bush and paddocks, with so many bullock and horse tracks wandering off on either side that it was easy for a traveller to get lost. And yet still they came, thin men, hungry from a hundred miles of marching, pushing wheelbarrows or lugging swags and shouldering shovels.

A grog-fuelled rebellion

The Ballarat goldfields held an explosive mix: poverty, exploitation, growing anger at the diggers' political powerlessness, and residents who had previously been part of armed rebellions. There is another element that should not be underestimated – grog.

Those were the days when a man would think it a reasonable end to a night's drinking to end up senseless, asleep on the sacks of straw most shanties kept for the purpose. 'Rum' was brewed at a thousand illegal shanties, mostly from potatoes or even turnips. It might send you blind, but at least it gave you oblivion. You could get a cup of 'rum' for a penny.

It was cheaper to get drunk than fill your belly, and drink eased the memory of other pains, too: the aching miner's back, which left most miners hunched over by the time they were forty; the infected fingers from dabbling in sewage-riddled water and mud. But most of all it might erase the whisper that must have come as they gasped for air down their holes: there is nothing here – nothing. You have limped your way to Ballarat and dug into the ground and will get nothing, nothing in return.

Alcohol gives temporary peace, but it also makes men belligerent. Being drunk on an empty stomach lowers inhibitions – enough, perhaps, to make you rebel against the Crown.

Nor could the newly installed Governor Hotham do much to redress the grievances. In June 1854 his government inherited a million-dollar Victorian debt – he was under orders from Britain to resolve the financial situation and had a squatter-dominated parliament unwilling to change the taxation system to reduce it. He was well aware of the brewing rebellions. He also knew that he had little money to hire more men to check them, nor could he call for reinforcements from England or even New Zealand. Hotham cut back all government spending and began rigorous enforcement of all licensing laws, starting with twice-weekly checks of licences.

One small spark could light a riot.

Eureka's spark was James Bentley, who owned the Eureka Hotel. He was a demon, one of the vicious ex-convicts from Van Diemen's Land, where the worst offenders had been sent, those convicted of murder or aggravated rape and assault while they were serving their sentence in New South Wales. Bentley was short-tempered and violent, but he had also made enough from the diggers to pay his bribes to the police and magistrates. Bentley was a man with connections.

On 6 October 1854 two drunken Scottish diggers pounded on Bentley's door, demanding that he give them a drink. Instead he gave them a beating, kicking and clubbing one man to death.

Bentley was arrested. There had, after all, been at least one witness, even if he had been drunk, and other witnesses would come forward. But Bentley was released by Police Magistrate Dawes.

The call of 'Roll-up, roll-up!' was spread through the Ballarat diggings on 17 October. In that time without radios, TVs, or any newspaper that hadn't travelled up from Melbourne, the cry of 'Roll-up', combined with bashing pots, kettles, panning dishes and even blowing a bugle, was the call to a meeting. This meeting resolved to form a committee to get Bentley to stand trial. A larger subcommittee, so to speak, decided to take direct action: a mob of between five and ten thousand miners burned down Bentley's hotel. Governor Hotham tried to be even-handed. He ordered Bentley arrested. He also ordered the arrest of the miners who had burnt the hotel.

But it would take more than a token display of justice to stop the growing rebellion, especially when police, troopers and magistrates were suspected, with reason, of being corrupt themselves. Roll-ups were held almost daily, with the demands becoming steadily more radical.

On 23 October four thousand miners resolved to establish a Digger's Rights (or Right) Society. On 1 November, 3000 miners gathered at Bakery Hill – a high spot where as many as possible could see the speakers, even if they couldn't hear them, and had to reply on the words passed through the crowd.

On 11 November a meeting of about 10,000 diggers formed the Ballarat Reform League under the leadership of the Chartists Henry Holyoake, George Black and J.B. Humffray. They demanded the abolition of the Miner's Licence and Gold Commission and – most importantly by now – the vote for all males.

The illusions of democracy

In these days of universal suffrage, many people recognise that voters often have little sway over those who govern them, and that democracy has limited effect in a party system where there is little choice in who you vote for. But back then the idea of voting for someone who might truly represent you in parliament was heady. Democrats assumed that universal suffrage – for men, at least – would lead to the will of the majority creating just laws. The heartbreak of successful revolutions in Russia and China was yet to come, where, in the words of Henry Lawson, the world would see 'the awful blunders the people made when at last they Woke and Rose'.[7]

The meeting of 11 November passed the resolution 'that it is the inalienable right of every citizen to have a voice in making the laws he is called on to obey, that taxation without representation is tyranny'. This meeting was possibly the first to make it clear that if their demands were not met, they planned open rebellion against Britain. The delegates rode down to Melbourne.

Rumours flew around the diggings: the delegates had been flung in prison. They were huddled there among the rats. No, the delegates had been shot ... no, they'd been hanged and their bodies thrown into prison graves. Notices were pinned on tents and shanty walls:

DOWN WITH LICENSE FEES!
WHO IS SO BASE TO BE A SLAVE?
DOWN WITH NEPOTISM![8]

On 25 November the diggers arrested for burning down the hotel were found guilty of arson, so Governor Hotham decided to send more troops to the diggings to try to keep order. At dusk on 28 November the yells spread across the diggings: troopers of the 40th Regiment were marching along the road to Ballarat.

Men left their camp fires or struggled up the shaky ladders from their mines, a human tide washing across the diggings towards the road. The troopers marched behind their little drummer boy, lifting their feet to his beat: ratty-tat, rattatty-tat ...

Behind the first lot of soldiers were carts pulled by straining horses, their heavy loads hidden by tarpaulins. And then more soldiers and more carts. Again, rumours swept through the crowd: there were cannons on those carts.

Two diggers stepped out into the road, in front of the drummer boy. The child stopped and looked startled, but refused to step backwards. The diggers demanded to know if there were cannons. The drummer boy began to beat his drum again. The soldiers began to march ...

What happened after that is unclear, even to those there at the time. Some claimed the soldiers fired at the crowd, others that men in the crowd had shot at the troops. The mob swarmed onto the road. Horses screamed and reared over the thunder of gunfire. The diggers cut the traces of the horses and pushed the wagons off the road. Diggers and soldiers grappled in the confusion.

As suddenly as it had begun it was over. A captured wagon vanished into the growing darkness of the diggings; another lay overturned, a digger's body lying beneath it. A small body lay on the road, the little drummer boy, his drumstick still in his hand, shot in the leg. He was carried off unconscious but again rumour took over – the troopers believed the boy had died. (A memorial was later erected to him at Ballarat even though he continued in military service, dying in 1860.) This attack on their child mascot enraged the soldiers, and was possibly responsible for some of the savagery to come.

The wagon contained weapons. The soldiers would have carried their muskets and bayonets, but before the advent of repeat-firing firearms a soldier might need several muskets, with one or even two 'loaders' shoving in gunpowder and shot. Presumably the captured muskets were distributed through the diggings. The troopers tried to retrieve the wagon and its contents but were driven back by sticks and stones in the darkness.

The Monster Meeting and the Southern Cross

The next day the roll-up drum sounded, with the thin breathy noise of fifes and the hollow ring of sticks banged against pots or billies. The crowd of about 12,000 stretched for perhaps a kilometre around Bakery Hill in what was to be known as the Monster Meeting. Men jostled, crushed together along the streets and between the tents or up on mullock heaps. Others clambered up on a shanty roof to try to see. Men in mud-stained clothing, men in their Sunday best crumpled from their swags, men with beards that looked like birds had nested in them and men with raw, shiny faces who had shaved in muddy water for the occasion. Children grasped their father's hand or their mother's skirt.

Flags waved from makeshift flagpoles – the English flag, the American Stars and Stripes, and others of many nations. This was also probably the first time the Eureka flag was raised, with blue background and white stars based on the Southern Cross.

It would have been much like a political rally of today, the crowd, the shouting, the music and the cheers. A band played as Raffaello Carboni climbed onto a makeshift stage of pit props and stumps of wood, up on the highest point of the hill.

The bands stopped playing. Even the big drum was silent.

Carboni made a fierce gesture to the sky. 'I hate the oppressor,' he yelled to the multitude, 'let him wear a red, blue, black or white coat.'

The delegates who had ridden to Melbourne reported to the crowd that Hotham refused to compromise. Licences were ceremonially burnt. Once again the miners vowed to use force, if necessary.

Rebellion had come.

The Melbourne road was crammed with diggers leaving before the violence grew worse. But even more were coming to join in, as the word slowly spread among the other diggings that a major confrontation would take place. This was not a small scuffle over mining licences. This was now true rebellion, its aim to create an independent republic, like the one that had been won in the United States.

The next day, 30 November, Gold Commissioner Robert Rede ordered not negotiation but a licence check, and the diggings exploded. When the troops turned out to check the licences the miners threw stones at them. Fights broke out and shots were fired from both sides. Eight diggers were arrested.

A second roll-up was held at Bakery Hill, and this time a new and (temporarily) more radical leader took the stage.

An Irish leader for Irish rebels

Peter Lalor was born in 1827, an Irish engineer who worked on the new Melbourne to Geelong railway before he joined the gold rush. Anecdotally, and from the list of names of the deceased, most of the rebel diggers came from Ireland. Lalor had lived through the Irish Potato Famine of 1846 to 1850, when one million died of starvation while food continued to be exported from Ireland to make money for the absent English owners of much of the country. He'd also seen the failed Irish rebellion against Britain in 1848. His father had been an Irish member of parliament and organised farmers armed with pitchforks to resist landlords who tried to evict poor tenants who couldn't pay their rent. A large number of those on the diggings were Irish, too, possibly a majority of the rebels. They had left their land angry and powerless in the face of the oppression of the English.

At Bakery Hill on 30 November, Lalor leapt onto a tree stump with his pistol in his hand. He demanded that all who were not rebels leave the meeting. Many did. Lalor proclaimed an oath. Men knelt on the ground and recited after him: 'We swear by the Southern Cross to stand truly by each other, and fight to defend our rights and liberties.'[9]

Peter Lalor called for volunteers. His fellow rebels included the Prussian republican Fredrick Vern, who had wanted to overthrow the King of Prussia and have an elected government, Raffaello Carboni, and the Scottish Chartist Tom Kennedy. It seems as if each national group may have chosen their own leader, with Lalor elected as commander in chief.

Several hundred took the oath of allegiance to the Southern Cross. The rebels marched off to an area near the Eureka claim to erect a rough stockade – not a fort, of the sort seen in cowboy movies, but just a collection of timber, old carts and pit props about a metre high and surrounding about half a hectare of land, partly to make a defined area to act as headquarters, and partly to slow down any attack by mounted troops. It wasn't even solely rebel territory: as well as the Eureka mine shaft there were shops, tents, a blacksmith's forge (useful for fashioning weapons), even a washerwoman carrying on her business, scrubbing at filthy clothes, wringing them out and hanging them to dry in return for copper pennies, while the rebellion grew around her.

A barrier, not a fort

The stockade was never meant to be a fortress. When the police and troopers arrived, as the rebels knew they would, Lalor's plan was to fight them down at the Gravel Pits.[10] If the rebels were overpowered there they'd retreat up 'Canadian Gully'[11], where a relatively small number of men could hold the high ground against the attackers, and wait for the reinforcements that would undoubtedly come as the news of the rebellion spread to other goldfields.

All Friday the rebels kept working at the stockade, strengthening it with pit props, gathering as many firearms as possible and forging pike heads (sharp tools that could be used as weapons). More miners started to arrive from other diggings; there were far more discontented miners in the colonies than there were soldiers or police. Many in Australia – respectable people in the towns and cities, like merchants and teachers – already hoped for a republic like the United States, free of English taxes and control. The rebellion was growing swiftly.

The rebel army marched up and down between the tents, practising drilling, marching and firing in line. They weren't just trying to look like soldiers – they needed to learn to stand and fire together to hit the targets. They also needed the organisation and discipline to make sure that there were loaders and shooters to take up shot or weapons and replace men who fell in battle.

So they trained, some men with pickaxes instead of swords or muskets, though a pickaxe can be a formidable tool wielded by a man who has spent years knowing its heft and hold. But there were firearms, too.

So here were 10,000 men of Eureka, plus the volunteers coming, filling the roads to Ballarat as letters and newspapers took the news of open rebellion to diggings far away, and as many bystanders, perhaps, leaving. Miners make good foot soldiers: look at their records in the Crimea, at Waterloo. They're strong and they know how to use their tools. But Eureka had more than that. Eureka had men trained in rebellion – how to foment it, guide it and how to fight it, too. The rebels already had arms. Now they needed horses, to match the British cavalry.

By 2 December about 1500 men were drilling in or near the stockade. In the late afternoon of that day, two hundred Independent Californian Rangers, a newly formed division of former Californian goldminers under the leadership of James McGill, galloped up to the stockade armed with revolvers and Mexican knives. This meant that the rebels now had armed men with horses, not just foot soldiers. The rebels also expected to be joined by what Carboni termed the German Rifle Brigade. There was already a 'Canadian Division' of rebels under Henry Ross, and possibly a Scandinavian one as well.

Thousands of men, including two hundred experienced horsemen, with justice in their hearts and desperation in their bellies, against two hundred police and soldiers? How could they lose?

How darkness won Eureka

They couldn't, except by trickery. Commissoner Rede swore that no attack would come on the Sabbath. But on Saturday, 2 December, the authorities decided to act before the rebellion spread to other colonies and mining centres – and while they still knew exactly what was going on. Governor Hotham and Commissioner Rede had spies in the camp, and they were given their orders: lead as many defenders as possible away from the stockade, into the darkness.

To understand the how the battle for Eureka Stockade failed you need to understand darkness – the deep, impenetrable darkness of twenty square kilometres of diggings, with no torchlight, and few campfires because of the scarcity of trees, already chopped down for fuel or pit props. Few people these days have any experience of trying to find their way in true darkness, with no torch to help them. If you stumbled through the darkness on the Ballarat goldfields you wouldn't just risk bumping into a tent, you were more likely to fall down one of the thousands of mine shafts and either die doing so, or suffocate in the mud.

Darkness was a weapon. Governor Hotham used it well.

The stockade was almost deserted that Saturday afternoon. At about four o'clock the rebels returned to the stockade, and that night there were only 1500 men manning the stockade. According to Carboni:

Thanks to the password, I entered within the stockade. It must
have been not far from midnight. I found everything comparatively
quiet; the majority were either asleep or warming themselves round

the big fire. I spoke in German face to face, for the last time, with Thonen. McGill and two-thirds of the Independent Californian Rangers' Rifle Brigade, in accordance with the avocation expressed in the title, were out 'starring' to intercept reinforcements reported on the road from Melbourne. Nelson and his division were off for the same purpose.[12]

Once again rumour had taken over (probably started by Rede and Hotham's spies) – reinforcements were coming from Melbourne. McGill took most of his Californian Rangers to patrol the road from Melbourne.

Lalor took the chance to have a couple of hours' sleep. So did Carboni. Thirty or forty of the Californian Rangers, with their rifles dug into the base of the stockade, acted as lookouts.

Hotham – a soldier who had wished to serve in the Crimea rather than administer the colony of Victoria – used his next weapon.

Imagine darkness so deep you can't see your hands, your feet. Darkness where the only light is the highway of stars above, and small, almost random flickers of red coals at your front, back, right, left. There is no way of telling what is happening. The landscape you know has vanished till the morning.

Soon after midnight, according to Lalor and Carboni's accounts, the cry came out of the darkness again, and then again: 'The soldiers are attacking!' Each time, more men – armed, angry and protective – ran to help. Soldiers had attacked the camp before; every man there had probably seen innocents suffer. Both red coats and police back then were more often corrupt than law abiding, violent men used to the abuse of power.

Time after time the rebels left the stockade, led into the darkness by the spies. And there they stayed.

Imagine it, that darkness. The spies had torches or lamps to light their way. As soon as their light was extinguished they could slide unseen into the darkness, leaving the men stranded. A well-made dirt road glows faintly in starlight, but I suspect the tracks at Ballarat were more mud than road. Possibly, too, the spies led their parties away even from the roads and tracks, into the heart of the diggings and mine shafts. If the men tried to stumble back to the stockade, the chances were that they would go in the wrong direction. Darkness won that night.

There was no real chance to return to the stockade till dawn. When dawn came it was too late.

The troops assemble

About 267 soldiers and police officers took their positions in the darkness, only three hundred metres from the stockade, at 3.30 a.m. on Sunday, 3 December. Only about 120 men were left in the stockade; the troops outnumbered the stockaders two to one. Thanks to the spies, the troops knew it was now safe to attack.

Captain Thomas had instructed his troops to spare any person who did not show signs of resistance. But by now many of the troops were too angry – or too caught up in the excitement – to care. At about 4.45 a.m. they charged.

According to Carboni:

> I awoke. Sunday morning. It was full dawn, not daylight. A discharge of musketry – then a round from the bugle – the command 'forward' – and another discharge of musketry was sharply kept on by the red-coats (some 300 strong) advancing on the gully west of the stockade, for a couple of minutes.
>
> The shots whizzed by my tent. I jumped out of the stretcher and rushed to my chimney facing the stockade. The forces within could not muster above 150 diggers.[13]

One of the Californian Rangers fired a warning shot to alert the other diggers of the attack. Lalor tried desperately to get his few men into some sort of order. Standing upon a stump, he ordered them to hold fire until the troopers advanced closer towards them, but a couple of bullets struck him in the shoulder.

Lalor yelled at his men to escape. This was not the battle they had been preparing for – this was massacre. He hid among a pile of slabs, the blood from his wound so thick it could be seen flowing down the hill. Carboni was later to write:

There was, however, a brave American officer, who had the command of the rifle-pit men; he fought like a tiger; was shot in his thigh at the very onset, and yet, though hopping all the while, stuck to Captain Ross like a man. Should this notice be the means to ascertain his name, it should be written down in the margin at once … full discharge of musketry from the military, now mowed down all who had their heads above the barricades. Ross was shot in the groin. Another shot struck Thonen exactly in the mouth, and felled him on the spot.[14]

Those who suffered the most were the score of pikemen who stood their ground from the time the whole division had been posted at the top, facing the Melbourne road from Ballarat, in double file under the slabs, to stick the cavalry with their pikes. As Carboni wrote:

The old command, 'Charge!' was distinctly heard, and the red-coats rushed with fixed bayonets to storm the stockade. A few cuts, kicks and pulling down, and the job was done too quickly for their wonted ardour, for they actually thrust their bayonets in the body of the dead and wounded strewed about on the ground. A wild 'Hurrah!' burst out and 'the Southern Cross' was torn down, I should say, among their laughter, such as if it had been a prize from a May-pole.[15]

The 'battle' was over in fifteen to twenty minutes, but the troopers kept bayoneting and shooting wounded diggers, burning tents and slashing at people with their swords. Five troopers and twenty-two diggers were killed or later died of their wounds. Over a hundred diggers were taken prisoner and marched down the hill. At last Captain Pasley, the second-in-command of the British forces, threatened to shoot any police or soldiers who continued the slaughter.

Although officially only twenty-seven died, no one knows how many miners and members of their families were bayoneted after the battle or burnt alive in their tents by the troopers. A count was made at the stockade, but not in the miles of tent cities ripped apart as soldiers burnt and raped and killed. Even the innocent who had been caught up in the savagery had every reason to keep well away from official notice.[16]

Lalor escaped, hiding under the skirt of one of the women in the stockade. His arm was later amputated, on the night of 4 December. Anastasia Hayes, who had helped sew the Eureka flag, took Lalor's amputated arm and threw it down a mine shaft so the troopers wouldn't find it.

The soldiers spread throughout the surrounding camp, burning and slashing at the tents. Again, in Carboni's words, the soldiers:

> deliberately set in a blaze all the tents round about. I did see with both eyes one of those devils, a tall, thick-shouldered, long-legged, fast Vandemonian-looking trooper, purposely striking a bundle of matches, and setting fire at the corner end, north of the very store of Diamond, where we had kept the council for the defence. The howling and yelling was horrible. The wounded are now burnt to death; those who had laid down their arms, and taken refuge within the tents, were kicked like brutes, and made prisoners. The troopers, enjoying the fun within the stockade, now spread it without.[17]

Frank Arthur Hasleham, an ex-soldier and newspaper correspondent, far from a rebel, was shot because he refused to join the troopers.

> After he had lured me within safe distance, namely about four paces, he levelled his holster pistol at my breast and shot me. Previous to this, and while advancing towards each other, he asked me if I wished to join his force; I told him I was unarmed and in a weak state of health, which must have been plain to him at the time, but added that I hoped this madness on the part of the diggers would soon be over; upon that he fired.[18]

Henry Powell was twenty-three and had walked over to the stockade to visit a mate. The police shot him, thinking he was one of the rebels. They then ran their horses back and forth over him and slashed at him with their swords while he screamed for help. Powell died three days later. He identified his killer but the man was let off because Powell hadn't sworn a legal oath before he died.

Several children, like six-year-old Catherine Donnelly, whose father had a store inside the stockade, were separated from their parents and terrified by the violence. Some ran to the distant bush where they were sheltered by the Indigenous people till it was all over.

Freed by a sympathetic official, Carboni ran back to help the wounded at the stockade.

> Old acquaintances crippled with shots, the gore protruding from the bayonet wounds, their clothes and flesh burning all the while. Poor Thonen had his mouth literally choked with bullets; my neighbour and mate Teddy More, stretched on the ground, both his thighs shot, asked me for a drop of water. Peter Lalor, who had been concealed under a heap of slabs, was in the agony of death, a stream of blood from under the slabs, heavily forcing its way down hill.
>
> The tears choke my eyes, I cannot write any further.[19]

It was now between eight and nine in the morning. A patrol of troopers and traps stopped before the London Hotel, as Carboni recalled it:

> Spy Goodenough, entered panting, a cocked pistol in his hand, looking as wild as a raven. He instantly pounced on me as his prey, and poking the pistol at my face, said in his rage, 'I want you.'
>
> 'What for?'
>
> 'None of your d——d nonsense, or I shoot you down like a rat.'
>
> 'My good fellow don't you see? I am assisting Dr. Carr to dress the wounds of my friends!' – I was actually helping to bandage the thigh of an American digger, whose name, if I recollected it, I should now write down with pleasure, because he was a brave fellow. He had on his body at least half-a-dozen shots, all in front, an evident proof, he had stood his ground like a man …
>
> I was instantly dragged out, and hobbled to a dozen more of prisoners outside, and we were marched to the Camp. The main

road was clear, and the diggers crawled among the holes at the simple bidding of any of the troopers who rode at our side.[20]

Atrocities turn defeat into victory

Rede pronounced martial law – the rebellion at Eureka was over. Hotham had won, and the slaughter and severing of the rebel leaders was enough to immediately quieten the diggings. The informants like 'Spy Goodenough' helped round up any remaining ringleaders.

If Hotham had hesitated even a few more days, the rebels would have won. If they had won, other diggings and colonies may well have joined the rebellion. Eureka has been misinterpreted by historians who have never lived in a land of true darkness, couldn't envisage how lost you might be, stumbling without light or torches even half a kilometre from camp.

The darkness won Eureka that night, but it also won the miners' cause. For as the soldiers plunged out into the dawn of the camp they took the flaming torches they had needed with them, setting alight to the tents of innocent and guilty alike.

There was terror in Melbourne when the news of the Eureka rebellion first reached town. Was an army of desperate miners marching under a new flag about to invade Melbourne? But as news of the rampage was published, public opinion swung to support the miners. Public meetings condemning the government were held in Melbourne, Geelong and Bendigo, and Governor Hotham had to post troops to keep order. Hotham and his secretary, Foster, were blamed for the disaster. Foster resigned.

Troopers stopped checking licences. The Victorian jury let off all but one of the miners who had been arrested. Only the editor of the *Ballarat Times*, Henry Seekamp, was convicted and sentenced to six months for seditious libel for publishing an issue of the paper after the rebellion, saying it had been a foul and bloody murder. Luckily friends burnt all but one issue or he might have been hanged for treason instead of spending three months in prison.

A Gold Fields Royal Commission was held and gave the miners almost everything they had asked for – except for independence from

Great Britain. The gold licence was abolished and replaced by a miner's right costing only one pound per year, and giving the digger a right to mine for gold and vote in government elections. In 1855 Lalor and Humffray were elected unopposed to the Legislative Council, and Lalor became speaker of the Legislative Assembly in 1880. On Friday, 24 November 1857, a bill granting universal manhood suffrage was passed in the Victorian Parliament, the first in Australia (ironically, Peter Lalor voted against it).[21]

The Eureka Stockade became a rallying point for freedom of speech and the right of every (white) man (not woman) to have a vote and the right to a fair trial. New South Wales got an elected government in 1855, though Britain could still override any decisions. South Australia, Victoria and Tasmania all got parliaments between 1856 and 1857. The Moreton Bay district separated from New South Wales in 1859 and was renamed Queensland, with its own government, too.

The only rebel aim that had not been achieved was to create a republic for the land beneath the Southern Cross. When the colonies federated to become a single nation, the Commonwealth of Australia, in 1901, the Union Jack still stood on our flag poles, not the blue and white one of Eureka.

And of course, it is still part of our flag today.

The legacy of Eureka

Eureka gave us rudimentary democracy, voters who didn't have to be rich. It is and has been a symbol of many 'fight for justice' campaigns. The United States has Martin Luther King's speech to quote to rally a cause; we have Eureka. The continued importance of Eureka in our national consciousness can be seen in the many attempts to belittle it as an unwinnable, ten-minute scuffle.

The 1850s gold boom also created a national myth that pervades decision-making even today: gold brings wealth. Gold made Melbourne a temporary boom town and contributed to the obsession with mining booms that pervades Australian economic policy. Gold is valuable but mining it is rarely profitable, except in places like Witwatersrand in South Africa, where about twenty-five per cent of the world's gold reserves can still be relatively easily produced. Fortunes were made in the gold rush, but rarely by those who mined or fossicked the gold. Even as I write this in 2013 at a time when gold prices are high, goldmining in Australia is a chancy investment. Australia's great mining fortunes are based on iron ore, aluminium and coal – resources required in large amounts where the demand is relatively steady for a product with major industrial uses.

Goldmining also came at a cost. The gold booms of the 1850s and 1860s depended on an unacknowledged and undervalued corollary: the 1850s rain. Without that rain there would have been no mining boom – a mining puff, perhaps, as miners sought gold in well-watered areas.

Miners need to eat, and food needs rain. Goldmining also requires large amounts of water, both then and now. If the drought hadn't broken – if it had instead bitten deeper – there'd have been no food to feed miners, nor water to work the claims with. Mining was a risky enough financial venture in the 1850s, and Australia was just too far away for cheap food to be imported to feed the far larger population that the gold rushes brought.

But it did rain. And because it rained the mining boom lasted for almost thirty years, destroying the land around the diggings. Newspapers of the time record floods, washing away men and diggings. Even in the 1990s much of the historic gold workings in Australia still bore the scars of mining a hundred years before: denuded topsoil, blackberry-covered mullock heaps, mines that seeped water high in heavy metals when it rained. (Gold is often found in association with metals like cadmium, lead and zinc, all toxic to humans, fish, amphibians and animals and – at higher rates – plant life too.)

Gold brought people, money and economic diversity to Australia, to provide for the new population. But the 'infinite land' myth was in force with the gold boom, too. It still is now.

South Coast of New South Wales, January 2013

The Dargues gold mine opened in March 2013, four kilometres upstream of my home. Within the first two weeks its sediment trap overflowed twice, bringing gushes of mud through the Majors Creek

State Conservation Area next to our property, and polluting our own water system. As I write this, on 27 June 2013, I am looking down on a fourth major spill, with up to half a metre of sand and silt covering what a week ago was a pristine rocky creek bed.

The mine will be five hundred metres deep, with two kilometres of tunnels. It will take a minimum of 66.2 megalitres of water from the Majors Creek–Araluen River catchment every year. Three 25-metre-high tailings dams covering nine hectares will hold a suspension of mining sludge containing the toxic chemical xanthate. If the dam walls give way, everything in the gorge country that I have walked and studied and loved for forty years will die. So, probably, would I.

Actually, despite the inauspicious beginning, I hope that the new conditions that environmental groups fought for and won in the NSW Land and Environment Court, combined with the Environmental Protection Authority's vigilance now that existing and potential problems have been brought to their attention, and the new mine management team, will mean that Dargues may operate with minimal detrimental impact, and some very real good ones: employment and export income for Australia.

But the bush and the peach orchard industry of the Araluen Valley are already balanced on a knife's edge. They are stressed by climate change – less rainfall and progressively higher temperatures since 1973 – but also from increased human pressure as 'tree changers' move to the area and pump out water for houses and gardens. One extra-large water consumer like the mine might create a desert, but only 'might' – we simply do not know.

To say that I love this land is inaccurate: I am part of it. The land is the foundation on which all of my books have been written. Without it, the person I am now, and hope to remain, will cease to exist.

There are scientific reasons to protect this area. It is home to an extraordinary number of critically endangered, threatened and vulnerable species, including the green and golden bell frog. (The fish, frogs and tadpoles in the creek died in the second pollution event. Only one frog species, not endangered, has returned. Hopefully, come spring, the other species will have survived in sufficient numbers to breed up again.) None of these endangered species may be intrinsically significant in themselves, but their presence is an indication of the area's value. The most important reason to preserve the Majors Creek gorge country is because of its contribution to regional environmental resilience. It is deep, almost sunless in winter, but warmth floats up from the wider Araluen Valley, creating a haven in times of cold.

Bushfire jumps across the gorge, or has, up till now. Even in the worst droughts, water seeps from the rock into the deep pools, the only safe water source for at least fifty kilometres around. It is a migration route for at least four species of birds, and a wildlife corridor between the Monga and Deua national parks so that the species there can interbreed. It is so steep that the ecosystems change within metres, providing habitat for an extraordinary profusion of species from dry temperate rainforest through wet to dry sclerophyll forests, including forest types and plant associations not seen elsewhere. Best of all, most of it is so steep and inaccessible it is relatively untouched directly by humans.

It is valuable because species have survived there. It is irreplaceable because species can survive there: if bushfire or human development or climate change wipes out surrounding land, the gorge is one of those places from where species can spread.

But if the groundwater drops even one or two metres because of the mine, the species of the gorge will die. If mining reduces the water that seeps into the rock pools along the Majors Creek fault line (gold seams are usually associated with large or small fault lines), the species that migrate here will still come but find no water to drink, perhaps only the sand that's already washed down the creek. The impacts will be far wider than just on the gorge itself.

But there has been no on-site assessment of the species downstream of the mine, nor was there any cost–benefit analysis that looked at possible impacts on the existing income production in the area. The mine may make between $4 million and $8 million a year; the estimate varies in the press releases. But the industries in the few kilometres downstream already make more than this for the Australian economy. If the peach orchards alone are made unviable by a flood containing heavy metals left from ore processing – and floodwater has covered the valley floor at least three times in the past century – our economy will lose far more than we gain from the mine. Hopefully the mine will be both economically successful and have minimal impact. But there was no requirement for the developers to produce a cost–benefit analysis surveying existing industries or the vulnerability of the land downstream before it was approved.

Australia is still in the grip of the delusions that brought nation after nation to the oceans near our shores to find that mythical land of gold. Our planners and politicians still see the benefits of goldmining, but – perhaps subconsciously afraid of what an analysis might show – do not require a cost–benefit analysis to see if a project will cost the economy more than it will bring in.

As for the consequences for the land, the requirements to show environmental impact are there, as is the duty not to pollute. The New South Wales Environmental Protection Authority acted swiftly and superbly when members of our local community informed them of gold mine pollution. But even as I write this, the devastating pollution in Gladstone Harbour and its effect on fishing and the Great Barrier Reef is being overlooked because of the value of the minerals exported from the port. This may, in fact, be justified, and the environmental and tourism costs worth it. But the cost–benefit analysis has not been done there, nor is it required elsewhere in Australia.

Humans change the land. Australia was recreated by the first settlers of 60,000 years ago, but the 'consensus' decision-making practices that they used was a form of cost-benefit analysis: if we do this, will the land be more or less likely to feed us, and our descendants?

If our land is to remain productive we need to look closely at the land, either by living with it and noting its seasons and changes and vulnerabilities, or using the multitude of scientific tools we have today. We need independent baseline data, both economic and environmental, before decisions are made. Every development comes at a cost. We need those cost–benefit analyses to be able to answer the question: is the development worth it?

Instead, the myth of a fortune, somewhere just beyond the horizon, still makes many deliberately blind to what is actually there.

CHAPTER 11

The history of our nation in a pumpkin scone

You can tell a lot about a society's connection with the land from what they eat, and even more from what they cook, or don't cook. Australians' diet today is much the same as most people in the developed world: packaged cereal that can be simply poured into a bowl, vegetables flown across the world, and the bread of multinationals, spongy and tasting more of dough conditioners than flour. Since about 1900, the introduction of refrigeration and rail transport, and later aeroplanes and diesel trucks, has meant that most of the food Australians eat can be grown far away.

But you can also tell much about a society and its land use by looking at its iconic foods. Iconic foods aren't necessarily the same as the ones we eat every day. Scots prefer curry to haggis these days, but haggis is still carried in with mashed neeps (turnips) and much ceremony on special occasions. Few women in the United States make 'mom's apple pie', and the weekly roast beef of England almost vanished with the arrival of mad cow disease in the late 1980s (which should probably be named 'mad agribusiness' disease, caused by feeding ground-up dead animals to cows).

The food we eat is a product of the land and how we farm it, but we also change the land to fit the foods that we prefer. Just look at damper, pumpkin scones, Anzac biscuits and lamingtons and you have our history in an afternoon tea.

Most nations have iconic foods based on indigenous ingredients, like pumpkin pie, chille (chilli), boiled peanuts, corn on the cob and wild rice in the United States; Mexico's chipotle with lime-softened maize; Southeast Asia's rice; Russia's wild mushrooms; England's mint sauce and crabapple jelly (originally made with honey, not imported sugar); Scotland's kale; Japan's bonito and seaweed dashi. But in Australia, apart from cultivated macadamias (and until recently even those were a variety bred from Australian seedlings taken to Hawaii), indigenous seafood and to a lesser but growing extent indigenous meat like 'kanga bangers', our bush tucker is served mostly as a curiosity.

Colonial settlers brought not just a vision of 'proper farming' but the plants to do it with. Bunya nuts may give a bountiful harvest, but nuts like chestnuts and almonds were already an established part of European cuisine. Why experiment with murrnong daisy roots when you already had potatoes, beetroot, carrots and other root crops? The ground seed of several edible wattles (most are inedible, even toxic) is delicious replacing part of the flour in biscuits, bread, macaroons and cakes, and edible wattle seed can be grown in areas too hot and dry for almonds to thrive. But in these days, when food is routinely shipped vast distances, almond meal is easier to process and buy.

Bush tucker bounty and a land without recipes

Much of northern cuisine has grown from the need to store foods over long, cold winters – jam, fruitcake, fermented fish sauce – or to make cultivated staples less boring with herbs, spices and varied cooking methods. Although many Indigenous nations had developed semi-permanent settlements by 1788, most, if not all, also travelled to take advantage of seasonally available foods.

There are many and varied Indigenous cooking methods: wrapping fish or murrnong roots in seaweed, paperbark or various fragrant leaves like lemon myrtle to roast in coals or underground ovens; smoked fish and eel; bogong moth or bunya nut cakes to take back to those who were too young, old or frail to travel to the feast; delicious crisp or oily bread from grass seeds baked on hot rocks by the fire. But there are no equivalents of combining many flavours and cooking techniques to make a dish, like a complex Thai salad, an Indian korma or an Italian pizza. The most delicious indigenous dishes are the simplest, and the

How to boil a yabby

First, catch your yabby. Get up at dawn and go to a dam or waterhole that is not polluted either by cow or sheep manure, blue-green algae, or seeping sewerage systems and other gifts of the past two hundred years of settlement. (This may involve sending off a water sample to be analysed before you begin to catch your dinner.)

Find a clean pair of old pantyhose. Place a fist-sized rock in each toe, then a piece of stinking meat in one toe and a rotting hunk of lettuce in the other. Hold onto the waist end of the pantyhose, whirl them a couple of times then cast out the heavy toes into the water, keeping a firm hold on the waist end.

Poke a sharp stick into the pantyhose to secure it into the ground. Go and boil the billy or have a snooze.

In the late afternoon, haul up your pantyhose. The yabbies will have hooked their claws into them, unable to get away. Bash them quickly on the head with a rock, then throw them into a pot of boiling water for five minutes. If you don't have a pot, use a small rock pool or even a watertight leather bag or double thickness dried animal bladder filled with water. Add the yabbies, then use a pair of sticks to quickly and carefully drop very hot rocks into the water. The water needs to boil for least two minutes, so you'll need at least six rocks, even for half a dozen yabbies. Eat hot or cold. If you're not going to eat the yabbies straight away, half fill the bath with water and keep them in that for a day or two. Don't fill the bath brimming full or the yabbies will crawl out, under the fridge or into your bed. Don't freeze your yabby. A frozen yabby's flabby.

ones Australians still devour pretty much as they have been for tens of thousands of years: grilled barramundi, Murray cod, flathead, oysters straight from the shell and still sweet with their juices, and boiled yabbies so fresh they need no sauce.

How sheep and damper led to pumpkin scones

The colonists' earliest foods had to survive not only the eight-month voyage from England but also a land without the storage facilities they were used to: cool cellars, wheat silos and stone dairies or icehouses, where straw-covered ice was stored through summer. They also had to be cooked without an oven.

So we have damper. Damper exemplified the early colony's love of wheat bread, and its stubbornness in trying to grow wheat, despite the cost to the land. Round loaves of bread in Australia are still called 'damper loaves' in their memory.

Probably every culture has a grain-based staple, from African teff to South American quinoa and amaranth, the poi (from taro) of Hawaii, or rice, cassava and tapioca from Southeast Asia and Polynesia. Colonial Australia persisted with wheat, even though from the first colonial harvest it was obvious that maize grew better, adapted more easily to climatic extremes and was far easier to store than wheat, which needs parching and dry silos to maintain its quality in storage. Maize can be piled into a barn, still in its protective papery husks, to be used as needed. I have cobs of red and blue corn that I grew nearly twenty years ago sitting in an ornamental bowl by our front door. If I chose to grind them for flour it would still be edible. Millet, too, grows faster and requires less water than wheat, and will grow in far less fertile soil, even orange shale or in the clay banks of dams. Barley, buckwheat and oats are also less demanding cereals in terms of soil and water.

But the British convicts, soldiers and settlers demanded wheat. Maize bread, or 'yellow cake', was the food of poverty. Later, in the Irish potato famines from the late 1840s onwards, even the hungry would reject heavy, gritty yellow cake and demand good, soft, well-risen bread – at least until they were truly starving.

Instead of adapting to the land, colonial Australians adapted the way wheat was grown. The stump-jump plough was invented here to make wheat growing easier in roughly cleared country. William Farrer and other scientists developed rust- and drought-resistant varieties of wheat.

The first century of wheat growing depended on vast areas of unused (virgin) land that could be flogged for wheat growing and then abandoned, or left to cattle or sheep grazing. In the Braidwood district there were six flour mills in the 1870s, with wheat the district's major crop. Now no wheat is grown – the topsoil blew away. The drought of

1877 to 1903 and the wheat rust from subsequent wet years put the nail in the coffin of wheat growing in this district, but the coffin had been crafted by growing an annual crop in land that was ridden hard by gale-force winds, hail, drought and crushing thunderstorms, all of which washes away the soil year after year. Australia had relatively few native annuals for a reason: perennials hold the soil together in a land of 'drought and flooding rain'.

Bread needs yeast to make it rise, but I can find no records of good bread-making yeast being imported on the First Fleet. It is technically possible that it was, even though dried yeast hadn't been invented then – a cook or servant would simply have had to feed the yeast culture every day with a little flour. There are references to all guests being asked to bring their own bread rolls to dinner at Captain Phillip's table on the journey, but even those rolls might have been the yeastless soda bread – and that's where Aussie damper comes in.

Damper's Irish ancestor

Damper is the Aussie version of Irish soda bread. These days soda bread is made with self-raising flour or baking powder, but the first white settlers to Australia arrived before baking powder was patented in 1848.

Irish soda bread was made by dripping water through wood ash to make strongly alkaline lye, or baking soda. Lye can be added to fat to make soap, but when the alkaline lye (or saltash) and flour is mixed with acidic buttermilk the soda bread rises up, rich, light and crusty. Traditional buttermilk was also fermented, unlike the modern supermarket variety, and this helped tighten the loaf in much the same way yeast does. The flour in the first decades of colonial Australia might have been years old, sour and full of weevils, but the sour flour mixed with alkaline saltash, and with water instead of the traditional buttermilk – cows and their milk were a rarity in early colonial times – also produced the air bubbles that would expand when the bread was cooked. This simplified version of soda bread became known as damper in the colony.

Good damper is delicious when warm, steaming and fragrant, though it needs to be eaten fresh. Cold damper becomes heavy and

How to make a great Australian damper

You will need:

a good fire, burnt down to red-hot coals

a spade

a camp oven, billy with lid or a large tin can and with a thin rock to top
it with

3 cups self-raising flour

1 cup water (or buttermilk or coconut milk - either makes the damper
sweeter and moister)

butter, cooking oil or mutton dripping

Optional: *half a cup of currants, and/or half a cup of chopped dates,*
and/or 1 teaspoon cinnamon, and/or 1 teaspoon mixed spice, and/or
quarter cup mixed peel and/or half a cup of sugar

Mix self-raising flour (and spices and fruit if you are using them) and
liquid with a knife till all the flour is incorporated. Do it quickly and lightly
as this is the secret of a light, fluffy damper - knead as little as possible.

With the butter or dripping, grease the bottom of the camp oven,
or the sides and base of the billy or tin can. Make sure the damper
doesn't take up more than a third of the space as it will expand.

dries out faster than yeast-risen bread, even without the additives that
make modern bread stay 'fresh' for days or weeks. The damper of early
colonial Australia was rarely good. The new colony had few cows (and
most of those escaped) to give buttermilk. Goats' milk is naturally
homogenised and can't be used for butter. No butter equals no leftover
buttermilk. So Australian damper became dryer textured than Irish
soda bread, and cooked in the ashes instead of a three-legged pot on the
Irish hearth, which is how it got its name – the fire was 'damped down'
when you raked away the hot coals, threw in the dough, then raked the
coals back over it. Half an hour later you thrust in your spade, shovelled
out the damper, whisked off the ash with the switch from a bullock's tail
(preferably without the bullock attached), threw away the crust if you
were fussy, but otherwise ate it, grit and all. (An English saying, 'We

Put in the damper dough. Put the lid on the oven or find a rock to cover the billy or tin (warning: the rock may explode so cover well with your coals), or use aluminium foil.

Use the spade to scrape the coals from the fire and place the oven, billy or can where the coals were. Now scrape the coals back over the billy or camp oven – all around and on top as well. (Damper cooked on top of the fire gets a hard burnt bottom and a raw middle). Leave your damper to cook for three quarters of an hour, then use a spade to bring it out of the ashes.

Eat your damper straight away – they don't keep well – with butter or just a trickle of golden syrup. Damper is also good with jam and cream. (Even old doormats are better with jam and cream.)

In the oven

Preheat the oven to 200°C – this is important, as damper placed in a cold oven will be heavy. Place the dough on a greased tray, make two deep cuts in the top (to help the dough expand) and bake till the crust is pale brown and it sounds hollow when you tap it. This should take about thirty minutes.

all must eat a peck o' dirt before we die', might possibly have consoled those who dined on damper.)

Gradually the great Australian damper became more refined, especially with the invention of baking powder in 1848 and the camp (or Dutch) oven, a heavy cast-iron pot with a lid that could be shoved into the coals, with more coals loaded on top so the damper browned evenly.

A good cook knew exactly when the coals were right so their damper was neither burnt nor soggy. They knew how much water to add as well: too much made it heavy, too little and you got dry, crumbly damper and insults like, 'Who called the cook a bastard?' 'Who called the bastard a cook?'

The damper evolved with sometimes delicious variations: adding sugar and fruit and spices turned your damper into 'brownie'; frying thin rounds of damper dough in fat in your frying pan made 'Johnnie cakes'; wrapping a thin pancake of dough around green sticks and cooking them over the fire created 'sinkers'.

All could be served with 'cocky's joy' (golden syrup) or sometimes treacle. Sugar dissolved if your bullock wagon rolled into a creek, or became hard lumps in humid weather, but cocky's joy came in tins so could survive flood, upset and cyclone, and lasted for years. The tin could then be used as a 'billy' to brew your tea or cook your stew, or filled with water then placed under your table and bed legs to prevent ants or smaller spiders from climbing up them.

The mutton eaters

A love of roast or boiled mutton and a cuisine based on dripping goes a long way to explaining Australia's love affair with sheep, and its consequences. From the 1820s until the 1970s, when the combined effects of migration, Federation, more efficient transport and the knowledge of what cholesterol was doing to Australian arteries gradually helped olive and other plant oils take over from mutton fat, sheep ruled our meals, whether it be mutton, lamb or hogget (a sheep that isn't a lamb but not an old ewe either). The term hogget has vanished from consumers' lives these days, but in my childhood that was what most cooks wanted: hogget had flavour without toughness.

Why sheep, not goat or cow? Goats are harder to herd in a land without fences, and before refrigeration even a small cattle beast gave too much meat for a farm family to eat before the meat went off. In the days when every meal contained meat if you could afford it, a skinny old ewe or a young fat lamb would be eaten in a week, and the carcass of a sheep hung up in the meat house, away from the flies, would last that long, even in the heat of summer. But mostly, a good fat sheep oozed lots of fat, otherwise known as dripping, the large amounts of liquid that oozed from the meat as it roasted, flavoured with burnt crusty bits of pumpkin or sometimes rosemary, and saved to solidify in the traditional teacup that had lost its handle on the bench by the stove.

Bread and dripping was cheaper than bread and cheese or butter, both when cheese was expensive in the early colony and in subsequent wars and depressions when butter was scarce or cost more than you could afford. Dripping was also the basis for soap, candles, slush lamps, furniture polish, hand cream and liniment for aching backs. It was a remedy for baby's cradle cap or chapped bottom, and kept the damp out of your boots. Dripping went into scones and pastry instead of butter. My Grandma Edwards fried tomatoes in dripping for our breakfast, or lamb's fry (sheep liver) and onions with gravy, or thinly sliced sheep's kidney, or fried bread.

Recipe books from 1890 to 1950 might list butter in recipes for cakes and biscuits, but all thrifty housewives knew that dripping could take its place, and kept better in the heat. Vegetables fried in dripping are crisper than those fried in vegetable oils, and pastry made with dripping is lighter than pastry made with butter or oils. Up until the cholesterol conscious 1970s vegetables, cakes, puddings, pies and even bread were made with a good addition of dripping. I probably will never eat the deliciously moist apple pie pastry of the cake shops of my youth again. Its texture, and its lightness, came from lard.

Early colonial mutton was usually plainly boiled or grilled over an open fire. But to get the best out of a sheep, you need to know how to cook it, slowly roasting that tough bit of meat till the sinews melted and the fat dripped away and it's tender enough to eat with a spoon, the fat poured off to become dripping.

A lack of trained cooks (and women) in the colony led to a badly cooked and monotonous diet, where much of the outback cooking was done by Indigenous women using unfamiliar ingredients, or by men who didn't know much about food preparation in the first place, the classic pre-1950s shearers' cook. (Post-1950s shearers made sure they got good food indeed.)

The general lack of cooking skills slowly changed, especially with the work of reformists like Caroline Chisholm and her 'God's police'. The Scottish brides in particular knew all about tough mutton and how to cook it. Most Scottish chimneys had a niche in the side of them to smoke a leg or two of mutton, or barrels outside to salt them, and a big black pot over the fire for a neck of mutton stew with plenty of potatoes and turnips (the latter was called Irish stew till the 1960s, as it was also popular with Irish cooks).

Mutton wasn't just eaten because it was cheap and easily available but because in the years of large families and wood ovens it fed a lot of people with relatively little work. When we began to run sheep on our farm in 1978, suddenly, after years of student brown rice casseroles and stir-fried veg from the garden, I was back to Grandma's recipes, the ones she learnt from her mother and her own grandmother: great roasts in the wood stove oven (the slow dry heat tenderises and brings out every scrap of flavour, and melts the fat so the meat is moist but never greasy) plus enormous amounts of baked veg from the garden, with a stewed or baked fruit something for dessert from the orchards.

We ate like that because it was cheap or, rather, free – the meat, veg, fruit, eggs and the wood to run the stove were all homegrown. And they were big meals, too, feeding not just us but the wwoofers (volunteer workers who laboured in the orchards or the veg gardens), so suddenly I found myself cooking as my great-grandmothers had done, for a table full of males who'd been digging, fencing, pruning, dipping sheep – and had the appetites that go with it.

It wasn't just the cheapness. It was the ease of cooking, too. Stir-frying is fuel-efficient but time-expensive, all that chopping and slicing before you cook. Like Australian women for 60,000 years, I had no shortage of fuel, not in a land where trees drop branches almost annually. I had more firewood than time. A leg or forequarter or rolled stuffed rib roast of mutton takes a long time to cook but needs less preparation and attention than almost any other meal. It cooks and bastes itself, and the accompanying veg too, with its own melting fat.

And then you pile the meat onto a platter for the most dextrous male to carve. Even better, you still have the leftovers for next day – roast veg to fry up with fresh cabbage and an egg or two to make bubble and squeak for breakfast, cold meat for tomorrow's lunch with salad and fruit chutney.

The glorious Aussie pumpkin

Pumpkin was what you ate with your roast mutton – or instead of if the meat had run out or the goanna had run off with it. To make good gravy you need the little bits of caramelised pumpkin at the bottom of the roasting pan.

Pumpkin eating is as truly Aussie as damper, though it too has evolved with Australian eating habits – we are more likely to have pumpkin gnocchi or Thai pumpkin curry these days than we are to have a squelchy pile of wet mashed pumpkin like my mum used to serve with our grilled mutton chops.

From about 1840 to 1970 pumpkin was pretty much a daily event: roast pumpkin for Sunday lunch, pumpkin with the Christmas chook, pumpkin cake, pumpkin scones or pumpkin fritters. According to the late food writer Richard Beckett, one of the first recipes ever given in Australia for spaghetti bolognaise – from a 'genuine Melbourne' Italian café – included pumpkin in the sauce.

Pumpkin is part of our folklore. 'A pimple on a pumpkin' is an old Australian saying meaning something very small on something very large: a bikini on a fat woman, or a small towelling hat on a very large bald head. According to the *Oxford Concise Australian National Dictionary*, a 'pumpkin squatter' was a small farmer with a swelled head. And of course, many parents refer to their kids affectionately as 'pumpkin'.

I grew up with Steele Rudd's stories of Dad and Dave and Mother in their stringybark hut – how when the wolf was at the door, Mother refused to eat cold meat and just ate pumpkin, because if she'd had any meat someone else would have had to go without; how the pigs were hungry because all the pumpkins were kept for the family; how for Bartholomew's christening party the family picked up all the pumpkins and ripe melons scattered round the yard to try to feed the expected horde and how, when even the pumpkins had given out, they played the accordion instead of eating.[1]

I loved Miles Franklin's images of the squatters' homesteads, with their paddocks for potatoes and corn and pumpkins.[2] Years after I'd read her books I was shown over a now-abandoned homestead by an elderly man who used to live there. 'And that paddock's where we grew the corn,' he said, speaking of the family garden from 1890 to 1969, 'and over there we grew the potatoes, and the flat down by the river was for pumpkins.' If you had spuds and corn and pumpkins you'd manage, and your horses and cows and chooks would eat too.

Pumpkins originated in the Americas. They were grown in Europe from the late 1600s, but primarily as cattle food: big stringy, watery things that didn't keep well. Even now many people from America or Europe really don't get the idea of eating pumpkin, unless it's canned to be made into pumpkin pie.

Understand the history of pumpkin and you go some way towards understanding the history of land settlement in Australia. Pumpkin would grow where no other familiar European vegetables survived, from the arid inland to the tropics (as long as you avoided growing them in the wet season) and down to Tasmania.

Pumpkin was the perfect crop for a land without ovens (you could use a pumpkin instead) and for a land of droughts. The new Australian breeds of pumpkin with hard, thick skins and dry flesh would last not just until the next crop, but often for two years or more, if perfectly cured.

Even better, pumpkin could be grown with virtually no work. Small settlers could plant pumpkin seed in the silt after the creek or river had flooded and then go droving for six months; when they got back they'd have a crop of pumpkins.

When you moved the dunny you planted a pumpkin vine in the smelly but rich ex-hole that remained, and it would cover up to twenty square metres with dozens of giant fruit. Even when the drought bit, pumpkin seed could be planted in bare earth, watered every few days with a dishful of the water you'd used to wash the worst of the grime off yourself or the kids, and it would still give a crop.

Like wool, the Aussie breeds of pumpkin survive long, chancy and harsh transport. But while the wool growers tended to become rich, those with a pumpkin crop to sell managed, at best, a safe life of three meals a day and a roof that didn't leak (or, at least, only when it rained).

Pumpkin seed arrived with the First Fleet, but those pumpkins were probably stringy, wet and somewhat tasteless, like all the European varieties I have come across. It was the Australian varieties of pumpkin, with manly names like Queensland blue, ironbark, iron man – firm, dry-fleshed, hard-skinned (some took a cleaver or a hatchet to cut open), tougher than a bullock wagon – that created pumpkin's niche in our culture.

The ancestor of our Queensland blue and ironbark pumpkins probably came from India, via members of the Indian army or those who had served on the Northwest Frontier and retired to Australia, often with land grants as a reward for service.

According to the *Queanbeyan Age* of 16 June 1870, 'a branded pumpkin of the Ironbark species has been found at Wagga Wagga … the flood having given it a speedy passage there'; even by 1870, 'Ironbark' in relation to pumpkin needed no explanation.

Ironbark is probably the ancestor of the Queensland blue pumpkin, the classic roast pumpkin and backyard grower until it was surpassed by 'jap' pumpkins in the 1990s. Queensland blues were bred at Valentine Plains in the Redcliffe area of southeast Queensland, near Brisbane, in the early 1900s.[3] Redcliffe has few frosts, so pumpkins could be grown year-round and sent to the markets in Brisbane and even Sydney, as they were such superb keepers.

Don't be put off by the often anaemic Queensland blues you buy in supermarkets – they have been picked too young for the early market down south and are insipid. A mature Queensland blue has a good rich flavour – but you may need an axe to peel it.

How to peel an ironbark or Queensland blue

Take the pumpkin out the back and whack it with the axe, then lift the entire pumpkin, with the axe stuck in it, and hurl it down onto the hard-baked ground.

Or just bake it with the skin on, so the tough coat peels off easily.

Even if nothing else grew – the cockies got into the corn, the wallabies were in the orchard, the drought destroyed the lettuces – you'd still have pumpkins. A friend who grew up in Alice Springs in the 1950s and 1960s remembers being regularly served well-boiled pumpkin tendrils by his mum. Traditionally the Aussie dinner plate back then contained meat, potatoes, a yellow veg and a green one, and in the central Australian heat often the only 'green' was pumpkin tendrils.

Pumpkin was the great colonial standby. Mashed pumpkin was added to bread, a habit possibly passed on by American sealers, whalers and gold diggers. (In the United States wild persimmon pulp was added to bread or cake dough so that not as much flour was necessary.) Pumpkin became mock ginger, or candied pumpkin was used instead of candied fruit in Christmas cakes and plum puddings. Boiled pumpkin fruitcake is superb. In the days before refrigeration and air-conditioning, adding pumpkin to cakes and bread meant they kept moist longer, and in the days before comfortable dentures this was probably a blessing also. But it is the pumpkin scone that became an Australian icon.

How damper turned into a pumpkin scone

Break up damper or soda bread dough into rounds and bake them in an oven and you have scones. Add pumpkin and you have not just an Australian icon but a foodstuff that will stay moist even in the worst of summer's heat, when a scone or damper turns into brick five minutes out of the oven.

Scones took over from damper in Australian homes – at least the more affluent ones – by about the 1880s. Scones need an oven while damper does not. You can, if you are a very good cook indeed, make scones in a camp oven, but a damper is far easier. Although ovens have been around for thousands of years, it was only around the 1880s that a middle-class or even working-class housewife would have had her own metal oven – as well as be able to afford the baking powder or self-raising flour to make scones.

Scones migrated to Australia from Scotland, where royalty was crowned on their 'stone of Scone' (Scone being a town, not a small delicious cake, though a badly made or heat-prostrated scone may indeed be a scone of stone). Scones almost certainly evolved from hearth cakes, rounds of dough baked on the hot stones or the 'hearth' by the fire and, later, in a metal frying pan.

They are, in fact, a single serving of Irish soda bread, and one could make a politically incorrect joke here about the thrifty Scots serving a cake for one, as opposed to the spendthrift Irish making one large enough for everyone, and the cow too. Further south, into northern England, similar single-serve soda breads were called 'cutties', probably because they were cut into triangles, though also possibly because the butter is cut into them with a knife, not with hands, as scones made with hot hands can be tough. In the United States, scones turned into 'biscuits', bigger and with more butter or other shortening (fat) added, eaten more often with breakfast sausages, eggs, grits, bacon or red-eye gravy than with jam.

From the 1860s, as more and more Australian homes began to have ovens, scones became one of the basics of Australian domestic life. You served them with butter and jam at afternoon tea (which was a great excuse to show off your different varieties of jam). If unexpected (or even expected) guests came, you could whip up a batch of scones before they'd taken their hats off – one minute mixing, fifteen in the oven, and by the time the cosy was on the teapot and Aunt Delilah had finished explaining about her hernia operation, the scones were steaming on the table.

Scones were also served with stews, to sop up the gravy. Their dough, with some finely chopped parsley added as you mix them, makes excellent dumplings that can be tossed into a goulash or other wet casserole. My grandmother served toasted scones at breakfast that were almost better than when they came fresh out of the oven.

A scone must be fresh if it's to be good (unless of course it's toasted), and I mean steaming fresh. Those nuggety doughy things in cake stores and supermarkets are probably the reason we no longer eat as many scones. And scones are infinitely variable. Grandma usually added chopped dates to hers, or sometimes a few sultanas or currants. A day-old scone, especially a small 'drop scone', made to rise high in a preheated drop scone pan, could also be coated in moist chocolate icing and coconut and turned into a faux lamington.

Yet scones have one major failing: in arid climates (and that's most of Australia) a scone can turn into something resembling a rock. In the 1980s an English friend employed for the first time as a cook in Queensland had shearers playing cricket with her scones. In the harsh dry heat, all the moisture just evaporated – unless she added pumpkin.

A pumpkin scone – like pumpkin bread – used to be an admission of poverty, or at the very least of making do. Certainly they were known by

Bloody good pumpkin scones

1 teaspoon grated orange zest

2 cups self-raising flour

2 tablespoons butter

1 tablespoon icing sugar

half a cup milk or buttermilk

1 well-beaten egg

1 cup mashed pumpkin – as orange and sweet as you can get it, not
     butternut

Optional: an extra egg, beaten, to glaze the tops so they are shiny

Mix the orange zest with the flour, work the butter and icing sugar
in with your fingers. Add the milk and egg and pumpkin – work it as
little as you can at this stage. Roll it quickly on a floured board, using
a rolling pin, tin can or glass. Don't roll too much, or the scones will
be tough. It should just stick together. Now cut into thin rounds about
as thick as the width of your thumb, or do as I do, and don't roll at all,
pinching off nuggets of dough to place in the tin side by side. They are
messier, but lighter. Brush with milk and/or beaten egg and bake in a
hot oven for ten to fifteen minutes.

These scones should be eaten fresh. If there are any left over, toast
them for breakfast, or cut them into slices and bake in the oven till
crisp then crush for very superior 'breadcrumbs'.

the early 1900s, when my grandmother was learning to cook. But although
Grandma taught me how to make pumpkin scones as a standby for mid-
summer in the years I was living without a fridge, she never served one
to her guests. (She also taught me to make an excellent pumpkin fritter,
which is basically a pikelet with mashed pumpkin added, served sprinkled
with white sugar). I suspect pumpkin scones may have become more
acceptable during World War 2, when sugar and butter were rationed;
pumpkin adds sweetness, as well as richness without butter.

Pumpkin scones retained their slightly shameful reputation until
Joh Bjelke-Petersen became premier of Queensland in 1968. His wife,
Florence, known as Flo, contributed her pumpkin scone recipe to

newspapers and magazines and even served them to guests. Her pumpkin scones, she insisted, had to be made with Queensland blue pumpkin as its rival, the butternut, was too fibrous to make a good scone.

Flo Bjelke-Petersen was a member of the Australian Senate from 1981 to 1993, but although she once said she hoped to be remembered for her work as a senator rather than her scones, she did still keep making them.[4] Joh Bjelke-Petersen was knighted in 1984, Flo Bjelke-Petersen became known as Lady Flo, and her recipe became 'Lady's Flo's pumpkin scones'.

The pumpkin scone had arrived.

Pumpkin scones are still made but, in these days of refrigeration and air-conditioning, more for their iconic or even comic value than as a response to the land and its climate. At their simplest they are just self-raising flour and mashed pumpkin, mixed and baked, which results in an edible scone, especially if eaten straight away and you are hungry.

Supporting our boys with Anzac biscuits

Another of our cultural icons, the Anzac biscuit, tells us much of the state of our armed forces in World War 1 and the level of community support for them. Although it is often claimed that these biscuits were named 'Anzacs' after the war, and merely sold to raise money for 'comforts' for fighting men, my grandmother and others of her generation contradicted this firmly, as does the entry in my grandmother's handwritten recipe book dating from about 1916.

Anzac biscuits were sent to men fighting overseas, rich in butter, sugar, and complex carbohydrates from the coconut and rolled oats, then baked in a slow oven so they would last for months, if not years. Perhaps sixty per cent of men at the front had teeth too poor to eat the hard-baked soldier's biscuits that were one of the staple rations, and water in the trenches was too polluted to use to safely soften them.

Men survived on food from home: fruitcakes rich in dried fruit and vitamin C, and Anzac biscuits. If our armed forces had been better fed – or if there had been dentists in the medical services – the Anzac biscuit might not exist, or at least might have been named travellers' biscuits instead, useful for trips to the outback.

Anzac Biscuits

Adapted from the handwritten recipe in the notebook of Mrs Thelma
Edwards, née Sheldon.

Grandma made these in World War 1 to send to relatives and
family friends serving overseas, along with soldiers' 'comforts'
like soap and paper and pencils, or to help fund assistance for
wounded soldiers. She was still making them up two years before
she died.

Quarter of a pound of butter (approx. 125 grams)
Half a cup of sugar
1 tablespoon golden syrup
2 tablespoons boiling water
Half a cup of flour
1 small teaspoon baking soda
2 cups rolled oats
1 small cup coconut

Melt butter, sugar and syrup with the water. Add dry ingredients.
Let stand for 30 minutes, then place small teaspoons of the
mixture on a greased tray and bake in a slow oven for about 30–40
minutes until golden brown, not dark brown. Take the tray from the
oven and leave the biscuits on it till cool. They will turn crisp as they
cool down.

But Anzacs biscuits survived their initial purpose as troop tucker in
World War 1 for the same reason the pumpkin scone evolved – their
longevity. An Anzac biscuit lasts for weeks in the biscuit tin, if the kids
don't find them first. More importantly, they could be made in a hot
kitchen in summer.

Most English cake, pudding and biscuit recipes begin with 'cream
butter and sugar' or 'rub butter into flour'. But in the heat of a drought
summer, without fridges, air-conditioning or sophisticated insulation,
keeping butter in a Coolgardie safe may keep it slightly firm, but as
soon as it is taken out to cook with, it turns semi-liquid. Anzac biscuits

are made with melted butter. They can also be sweetened with golden syrup, not sugar. Sugar dissolves or turns solid in hot humid weather, or the little black ants get into it, especially before rain. But the ants – and humidity – can't attack a can of golden syrup. Desiccated coconut, available from about the 1880s onwards, also stores well.

A harsh land gave us a tough biscuit.

Pack the cart, and don't forget the lamingtons

The harshness of the Queensland climate, and the distance a plate of food needed to travel when its owner went to a dance or a tennis picnic after church, also led to our love of lamingtons, though there are many theories on how the lamington came to be.

One of these says lamingtons were named after the governor of Queensland, Baron Lamington, sometime in the 1890s. The story goes that the Government House cook dropped the sponge cake she was making for dessert into a bowl of chocolate sauce. So she carefully arranged the chocolate-covered cake on a plate and scattered shredded coconut over it, then bore it out proudly, saying: 'Look, Baron Lamington, I have invented a new dessert and named it after you – the lamington!'

There is another claim that lamingtons may have once been leamingtons, named after Leamington Spa in England, but despite much leafing through cookbooks of nineteenth-century England I can't find any reference to a 'leamington', or even a cake covered in moist chocolate icing and desiccated coconut.

Back in the 1980s on radio stations around the country I called for listeners to send in their earliest lamington recipes. Several of my oldest informants declared that a lamington cake was invented by Amy Shauer, who taught cooking at Brisbane Central Technical College from 1895 to 1937, and one claimed to have eaten them at a tennis party after Amy Shauer first made them for a visit to the school by Lady Lamington. Amy Shauer also wrote three very popular cookbooks, developed cookery courses for schools and colleges across Queensland, and was a famous cakemaker and cake judge at shows. Lady Lamington was the college's patroness. My oldest informant told me in most decided terms that Lord Lamington was 'a horrid man' and that no one in their right mind would name a cake after him, but that Lady Lamington was much loved and vigorously encouraged girls' education.

Maurice French (no relation except in our joint fascination with lamingtons), author of the *The Lamington Enigma*, describes the lamington as an 'evolving' recipe.[5] Desiccated coconut – essential for making lamingtons – wasn't readily available until the 1870s. Maurice French found several pre-1900 recipes for iced cakes topped with coconut. But they were not called lamingtons, nor were they cut into cubes or dipped in liquid chocolate icing.

Real lamingtons

125 grams butter
125 grams caster sugar
1 teaspoon vanilla
2 eggs, beaten
150 grams self-raising flour
100 grams plain flour
half a cup of milk

Cream butter, sugar and vanilla till soft; add eggs one by one, mixing well before adding the next one. Then add flour and milk bit by bit, mixing it all gently. Rub a square cake tin with butter, then add a little flour and swirl it around till it covers all the greasy butter. Spoon in the mixture and bake at 220° C for about thirty-five minutes; it should be pale brown on top. Up-end the cake tin onto a wire rack and let it cool.

It is much easier to handle the next stage if you can make the cake a day ahead and allow it to become just a little stale.

Cut it into squares and make the icing.

Icing
4 tablespoons water
2 teaspoons butter
1 teaspoon vanilla essence

The first mention of 'lamington cake' is in the October 1901 *Sydney Mail*, in response to a reader's enquiry. The recipe calls for a cake to be cut into cubes, with chocolate icing covered in coconut. In December the same year a Queensland reader sent a request for lamington cake to a Brisbane newspaper. But once the lamington first appeared, it bred like rabbits, because the lamington was the perfect cake for both Australia's climate and culture of the time.

Cake goes stale fast in an arid climate, but not if dipped in moist chocolate icing then covered in coconut. The outside crust of chocolate

500 grams icing sugar
4 tablespoons cocoa powder
250 grams desiccated coconut

Put the water and butter in a saucepan and heat till it just boils. Take off the heat and add the vanilla essence, then stir in the icing sugar and cocoa. The icing should be just liquid – not too thick, but not too runny either. If it's too thick, add a bit more water about a teaspoon at a time, as it's very easy to add too much!

Put the runny icing onto a wide plate. Put the desiccated coconut onto another wide plate.

Now take a knitting needle or bamboo skewer and thread some squares of cake onto it. Roll the squares on the needle in the icing, leaving them for a few seconds on each side to really soak it all up, then roll them in the coconut.

Now take them off the knitting needle. All but two sides will be chocolate and coconut covered.

Dip each uncovered side in icing then coconut, lick your fingers, wash them and thread another lot onto the needle. Repeat till they're all done.

Store the lamingtons in a sealed container till you want to eat them. And if you have to take your lamingtons on horseback in blistering heat to a dance half a day's ride away, you'll know your lamingtons at least will still be moist and fresh.

icing and coconut also helped preserve the structural integrity of the cakes on long or bumpy journeys. (A slightly squashed lamington will slowly regain its original shape.)

But most of all, lamingtons were perfect 'finger food' for after-church socialising on Sunday afternoons, tennis parties, cricket or Friday night dances. You could eat one without a plate and without ending up with sticky fingers that might need to be licked or wiped on your cricket whites; the coconut keeps your fingers clean, or at least no dirtier than when you began to eat it. Lamingtons didn't need slicing, either, so no servant or put-upon mum was needed to cut and serve them. They were also thrifty: they lasted well, and day – or even week-old butter cake (or, at a pinch, leftover scones or, better still, drop scones) could be turned into makeshift lamingtons.

Look at a lamington, and it will tell you who we were in the first half of the twentieth century: affluent enough to eat cake, and for women to have the time to make fancy cakes, and a gregarious people; most districts, rural and urban, had dances on Friday nights with 'ladies, bring a plate' suppers, cricket on Saturday afternoons with a lavish afternoon tea, and (in rural areas) tennis or picnics after church to make the most of the journey there – all informal affairs where you ate with fingers, not cake forks or often even plates, especially as you might have a cup of tea on its saucer in your other hand.

Lamingtons speak of hot, dry summers, where sponge and even butter cakes dry out fast, but not one coated in moist chocolate icing. But most of all, they come from a land of bumpy tracks and roads, where a layer of cream will slide off your cake before you get to your destination, and iced cakes stick together. But the dry coating of coconut prevents that, even in a humid Queensland summer.

Lamingtons were – and still are – made to sell to raise money for charity, though these days most lamingtons sold at 'lamington drives' are made in commercial bakeries, not at home. They're made of cheap dry sponge cake too, not the traditional moist butter cake.

By the 1970s, with widespread commercial refrigeration and cold storage, you could buy factory-made lamingtons with jam and cream in them. They are not real lamingtons.

The last real lamington I ate was early this year, cooked by a farm woman in the hot Cooma summer and transported over the mountains to the kitchen where I ate it, made for the same reason that a 1915 or 1932 lamington would be: it was extraordinarily moist and delicious, despite the heat and its long bumpy journey. The only thing lacking was the preceding week of heavy farm and domestic work, which would have left me needing to eat at least half a dozen of them.

CHAPTER 12

How a drought made us one nation

For 60,000 years the dryness of much of the Australian continent kept the groups of people separate. But in the late nineteenth century, a drought would draw us together into one nation.

From 1877 to August 1903 Australia experienced its worst drought in recorded history. It became known as the Federation drought, although often only the final, most horrific years are counted. Without that drought there would not have been the bank crashes, nor the hard economic times that led to demands to drop excise duties and tariffs between the states, nor the uniform immigration policies to protect what many unionists saw as the threat from Asian immigrants who might accept lower wages.

It was the lost farm income from the drought that led to the need for farmers to cut the shearers' wages, which led to the shearers' strike, which led to the Australian Labor Party.

And it was the economic problems from drought that made men like Henry Parkes believe so passionately that to survive economically we had to be as one country, with unified immigration and tariff laws, and no tariffs between the states. Without the 1877 to 1903 drought we might still be a collection of unfederated states.

It was also the savage effects of the drought that led to the fervour of the women of the temperance and suffrage movements, who thought that a new federal parliament would bring down fairer laws – not just votes for women but laws that would stop children as young as eight being employed in factories, sleeping on the factory floor, often working for only food, and living short and horrific lives because factory owners too were hard-pressed by drought and the subsequent depression. For every speech given by Henry Parkes there were a hundred given by these women, who collected petition signatures demanding a referendum on the federation question, too, waiting, armed only with their parasols, outside the pubs till the men were too drunk to know what they were signing.

Our nation was founded on desperation and ideals. Most of the ideals of the fathers – and mothers – of our constitution probably aren't ones we'd agree with today, like the passion to keep Australia 'white', and the religious freedom that was only meant for Roman Catholics (like England, the early Australian colonies were officially Anglican). But that drought possibly shaped modern Australia more than any other event in the history of humanity on this continent.

A drought-bred boy

In 1873 a five-year-old boy moved with his parents to a small, marginal selection at Pipeclay (now known as Eurunderee) in New South Wales, a town on the Grenfell goldfields. His father was Norwegian and worked on and off as a building contractor. His much younger mother ran the post office and tried to manage the selection while her husband was away.[1]

There wasn't much to manage. Dust. Sheep. Stale muddy water carried in buckets. Meals where the maggots had to be scraped off the cold mutton and the only vegetable was pumpkin, and when there was no pumpkin, 'bear' – koala, probably caught by the young boy.

When he was eight years old a school finally opened nearby, due to the determined campaigning of his mother. A slab hut with a bark roof and dirt floor – the Eurunderee Public School. He was nine before he actually went to school, and increasing hearing loss made him even more isolated, a boy thrust into the responsibilities of 'the man of the house', watching, always watching, the people and the land around him.

Years later, when the boy had become one of Australia's best-known bush poets, Henry Lawson never wrote much about his early life[2], but the images of his childhood on a dry selection are found throughout his work, in poems like 'Past Carin' ' or short stories like 'Water Them Geraniums'.

In September 1892, with five pounds and a train ticket to Bourke, 25-year-old Lawson set out to tour the inland for *The Bulletin*, urged by its editor, J.F. Archibald, who saw that the young writer might be able to capture the growing desperation of rural people in what was now the second decade of extraordinary drought. (He also possibly wanted to get his protégé out of the pubs where he was steadily becoming an alcoholic.)

Lawson carried his swag and sat in bush shanties, drinking and yarning. But most of all he saw and wrote of the horror of drought and the desperate isolation of bush families, in stories like 'The Drover's Wife' (published in *The Bulletin* in 1892), and poems like 'Past Carin' '.

'Past Carin' ' is the whisper of a woman pushed beyond emotion. She has borne the grief of the death of children and the burden of isolation and poverty, all from the curse of drought, for years or even decades.

> *The crops have withered from the ground,*
> *The tank's clay bed is glarin',*
> *But from my heart no tear nor sound,*
> *For I have gone past carin' –*
> *Past worryin' or carin',*
> *Past feelin' aught or carin';*
> *But from my heart no tear nor sound,*
> *For I have gone past carin'.*[3]

Lawson stayed in the outback for less than a year, carrying his swag from Hungerford to Bourke. He brought back stories that remain classics, published in *The Bulletin* and in a small collection funded by his mother, and then in *While the Billy Boils* (1896).

Was the drought as bad as Lawson described?

It was worse.

How do you measure a drought, especially in a land where postcolonial settlement records are sketchy? In our district, for example, written rainfall records only go back to the 1870s, and all except the last twenty or so years are unreliable. (Even those often can't reliably measure extreme rainfalls when the rain gauges fill with hail and overflow.)

These days the severity of a drought is measured by the soil dryness index, a modern concept not available in the late 1880s. The soil dryness index is more accurate than rainfall measurements as a district can have two hundred millimetres of rain in a year, but if it all falls as one heavy storm most will rush away. The hard-baked soil won't allow moisture to penetrate, tanks and dams will overflow, and topsoil will wash away, even taking manure, sparse grass and bushes with it.

The same rainfall, if it comes as gentle eight-millimetre falls after a four-millimetre fall to soften the soil, may mean green grass, fat cattle and water in the dams and creeks, even if it's not enough to replenish the watertable.

1 January 1983

I had been warned.

'Araluen can get dry,' said Clyde Mundy, as we sat eating our morning tea biscuits in the Bureau of Mineral Resources. 'My word that valley can get dry. Back in the 1890s it never rained at all, not for over ten years. The cattle died, the sheep – even horses were all starving. Then it rained in Araluen – just one thunderstorm, but it was enough to get in a crop of maize. It got the horses through for another three years.'

When I first saw the valley in 1973 the grass was lush, with mist that turned to rain almost every second night. Droplets shone on carpets of maidenhair fern. It stayed that way till June 1978.

Then the rain stopped.

'It did rain sometimes in the 1960s drought, didn't it?' I asked Helen Harrison as we served tea to the parties of fossickers our neighbour Keith hosted (he carefully salted the creek so there'd be a showing of gold to demonstrate gold-panning techniques).

She smiled and shook her head. 'Not much,' she said.

No one can understand a drought who hasn't lived through one, uninsulated by running water from a dam somewhere else, with money to buy food that has been grown elsewhere, too, even air-conditioning so you can forget, for a while, the rage of heat outside.

I was broke, living in a shed. When it was hot – above forty degrees, sometimes reaching up to fifty-six degrees – I was hot too. I worked at dawn and dusk, dozing down at midday by the deep pools that were all that was left of the creek. The vegetable garden died, except for parsley; the kiwifruit died; the orange trees turned yellow, then brown. (They'd come back when it rained. They're tough, those orange trees.)

The worst was 1980. The pools in the creek were almost solid with wild duck droppings, fed by tiny seeps deep in the rock. But they were the only open water for more than twenty kilometres. Animals came, night after night, emaciated, desperate with thirst and hunger.

Every morning my first job was to gather up the bodies of the wombats, wallabies and kangaroos that had died in the night. I couldn't bury them – the ground was baked hard – but I could drag them away. The valley smelled of death.

From 1980 onwards the fences on the way to town were piled almost a metre high with topsoil that had eroded from the paddock uphill or upwind of them (it later washed away in the January 1983 rain). The drought was so widespread that there were few places to agist stock; at market it cost more to sell them than they'd fetch.

By 1981 it was easier. Hotter and drier, but easier. The most susceptible wildlife had died. The animals that were left were the tough ones, wombats that gnawed tree bark, wallabies that tugged at the wire netting around our trees until their paws bled and they finally got inside to have a go at something (almost) green to eat. Most of us had worked out ways to cope by then, too.

In a Canberra café for a brief, luxurious cup of tea, a cloud passed over us with perhaps twenty-four seconds of rain.

'Thank goodness it's rained,' said the well-dressed woman at the table next to me. 'Perhaps the farmers will stop moaning.' Her companion nodded her agreement.

I didn't pour my pot of tea over them. I stood up, left, drove through the Canberra landscape still lush with watered lawns (unlike the Canberra after the 2003 bushfires, when watering was rationed) back through the brown hills, round as skulls and just as dry.

They were still beautiful.

And then, on 1 January 1983, it rained. Clouds like bruised knees were swollen on the horizon, moving as swiftly as a brown snake strikes. An agony of hail first, balls as large as oranges, smashing windows, cars, leaving human injuries that needed stitches. And then the rain.

How much water can the air hold? I can't tell you how much it rained that hour and a half – the rain gauge was clogged with hail and when it melted it was full. A rough estimate, given how fast an empty 44-gallon drum left outside filled, was that we had at least 533 millimetres, with possibly 253 millimetres in an hour. In the first part of that hour the rain was too heavy even to stand up in. No official record will show how much it rained that day – their measuring devices too would have been clogged, then full and overflowing.

I looked outside. The ground moved. At first I thought it was an earthquake and then I saw it was just water, shivering, shaking, covered the detritus of four and half years of wombat droppings, dead leaves, dried grass. The ground was simply too hard for the rain to soak in.

A metre-high tide of water slid down the slope behind the house and joined the water that had just fallen too fast for much to soak into the drought hard ground. The water seeped in under the doors, and then rose higher. It stank. I stood on the bed and held the baby up out of flood reach as the water edged upwards.

And then as fast as it had come, it drained away. The creek crashed boulders in a flash flood down below. But around the house the soil was still dry under less than a millimetre of dampness, too hard baked for any of the sky's largesse to matter.

It rained again after that, several more floods in one year, soaking rain that did sink in and green the valley once again. But if that one thunderstorm had stood alone, on paper it would have looked like a reasonable year – not good, but not disastrous. Half a metre of rain can mean greenery, or disaster.

And that is what it was like, from 1877 till August 1903, year after year of drought and hard-baked soil, with a few destructive storms that didn't even soak into the soil in between.

Our worst drought?

The drought years of 2002 to 2004 were, by measurement of rain alone, worse than the Federation drought, although a lack of accurate rainfall figures and soil moisture index makes this impossible to determine precisely. But the social, ecological and political effects of the 1877 to 1903 drought were far worse.[4]

Don't get me wrong: 2002 to 2004 was hard, even deadly for those who died in bushfires or from the heat. The year 2003 hosted the driest ten months ever measured in our valley, and the summer was the most consistently hot, with maximum temperatures rarely dropping below forty degrees and soaring up to fifty-six degrees on two successive days. Gale-force winds blew regularly over a three-month period fanning a constant series of devastating bushfires around us. There were months when vegetation was coated in red dust blown from the inland, a mountain of eucalypt forest slowly browning, culminating in a day when the air was too thick with ash to see, the sky pulsating flame red as the outskirts of Canberra burned, and the wind blew the ash and smouldering debris over us. But the worst was over in just one year.

There are ecological differences between the 2002–2004 drought and that of 1877–1903, beyond the sheer length of the latter. By 2003 Australia had better water storage and transport solutions, better rabbit control and better pasture management. In many areas groundwater replenishing schemes meant the land did not dry as fast, and farmers were certainly far better educated overall.

In 2003 you could buy water when your water tank was empty, even if it was expensive to cart. Cars and buses could take you for a respite to a city, even a hotel where you could have bath after bath of glorious water. You could watch television, and for a while be part of a world that wasn't hard blue sky and harder ground.

But the main social difference between these two droughts in the area where I live was that most farms were no longer solely dependent on farm income. Sons and daughters routinely left to work elsewhere; two-generation family farms are now rare. Wives (or sometimes husbands) have off-farm jobs. Even the 'primary farmer' of the family is more likely to sell most or all of the stock in a bad year and take work elsewhere, even heading off to Western Australia or South Australia to work in mines, or as a guard in refugee internment camps. This change came in part as a response to the 1980s drought – 'sell stock, take a job and wait it out' is now a recommended strategy for farmers.

But in the 1880s you took your stock droving, to better pasture, leaving your wife in charge of the selection. Or you sold your stock and left your farm to the cockatoos and brown snakes while you went 'on the wallaby', carrying your swag from farm to farm, shed to shed, looking for work, possibly for money but, more usually, simply for enough food to last till the next handout.

Eating bear or soup-kitchen bread

There are no records of mass starvation or whole towns dying of thirst in the 1877 to 1903 droughts, though there are records of death from heat stroke on some of the worst days, when someone thought to keep a count. There was probably enough food in most places, in terms of kilojoules. You'd put down old Bessie the cow when she had stopped giving milk and laid down, her hipbones gaunt, or drag a sheep from the muddy remnant of a dam, slit its throat, and live on the meat for a week or two. There were rabbits and 'bear' (koala) and kangaroo. (If you're going to eat a wombat, one old-timer told me, make sure you hang it for a few days first. It'll be too tough to eat, else.) There might be no cabbages in the vegetable garden, but pumpkins crop even in a drought, if you give them the washing-up water, and pumpkin tendrils were served as the 'green veg' on plates. The growing infestation of prickly pear gave fruit for jam – and vitamin C – as long as you were prepared to laboriously pick out the prickles first. By then many farm families did know some of the edible native fruits to snack on, and even if they could be stewed and served with custard for a 'proper' meal.

But in the cities there was no 'bear' or bunnies to eat. By the mid-1880s charities had set up soup kitchens in Sydney and Adelaide to feed starving workers and their families.

Country town stores back then routinely gave credit for flour, tea and sugar, often waiting months for payment till a crop was in, the cattle sold, or the money order sent from a husband or son out droving. If there were children involved they might keep the debt for years, or even decades. (Some local stores still gave years of credit in the 1978–83 drought – 'we know you'll pay when you can'.)

But mostly there are no records, only descriptions in poems, stories and letters. Even as recently as the 1960s those in isolated areas of the bush might be born or die without official records, or changed identity illegally. Even where there were records, the death toll is hidden: a death recorded as 'heart failure' might be from heat, or prolonged stress and lack of food – or decent food. 'Beef and plenty greens for me,' calls the traveller returned from the bush in one of Lawson's stories. He had eaten nothing but mutton, damper and potatoes in the time he has been away.

Cockies and true merinos

Lawson's stories were of 'cocky' farmers, ones whose small holdings grew more cockatoos than crops. Poet and journalist Banjo Paterson gave a very different view of the bush, but he also mixed with the more affluent. Squatters ('true merinos') often had the wherewithal to move their stock to areas where there was water. They had usually sited their homes on areas of good water, and by the 1880s many also had other investments, from money earned in better times.

I suspect – and hope – that no one in Australia will ever again experience a drought where there is simply no way out, where the ground is bare and food for humans or animal is hundreds of kilometres away, with no means of getting there. As I settle into the second half of my life I hope that it won't be lived in a world of dry. But the 1877 to 1903 drought should be a lesson: Australian droughts can last for decades, even without factoring in global warming.

One of the most crucial factors underlying the severity of the Federation drought is that it covered most of Australia. But that is also why it's difficult to pinpoint its dates.

The Long Drought

The Federation drought is usually described as spanning the years 1895 to 1902, but much of country was already dry in 1877 and didn't receive true replenishing rains until August 1903.[5]

It's probably more accurate to say that what became known as the Great Drought or the Long Drought, depending on where you were, began in 1877 and eventually affected all colonies, with the Federation drought as a particularly horrendous final few years. Queensland and Western Australia possibly fared the worst, with not just vast numbers of dead stock but large areas of bush and swamp dying too.

From 1880 to 1886 most of eastern Australia had little or no rain. The rain that did fall was not enough to replenish watertables, for springs to run again, or even to soften the ground so that rain could penetrate – you need three good years in our climate for the soil structure to change back so that rain penetrates easily. By 1888 it was extremely dry in Victoria, especially in the northern areas and Gippsland, Tasmania was dry and New South Wales had the driest year since records began. Queensland, South Australia and Western Australia in the central agricultural areas lost many sheep.

The years 1890 to 1895 were not even the driest of the drought years, but it was in 1892 that a young Henry Lawson was sent out to record the impact of what had already been more than a decade of dry. If what he saw – the dying children, the hopeless women, the dust, the near starvation – was so bad in the relatively good years of the early 1890s, it must have been close to hell as conditions grew worse.

One statistic we do have is sheep. In 1891 Australia had an estimated 106 million sheep, despite the poor conditions since 1877. By 1902 there were only 54 million.[6]

From 1895 onwards some areas saw almost no rain for years; other parts of the country had reasonable rain in 1900 and early 1901, but with the coming of spring in 1901 very dry weather set in across the whole of eastern Australia. By 1902 Sydney was about to run out of water. The New South Wales government declared 26 February a day of 'humiliation and prayer', with services held in churches and halls across the state praying for rain. There was virtually no wheat harvest. The

Darling River dried up near Bourke, New South Wales for over a year from April 1902 to May 1903.[7]

Even more than in the 1840s, the severity of this drought was exacerbated by human mismanagement. A drought is not just a lack of rain and water.

The land blows away

There was the dust. In good years, large parts of Australia had been cleared to create grasslands for sheep and cattle, or for wheat, maize and other crops. Even the saltbush country had been destabilised by overgrazing, especially by the introduced rabbits that were now in plague numbers. The hard, cloven feet of the sheep and cattle were much more unforgiving on the soil than the feet of roos and wombats. The soil became compacted, so hard that water ran off it instead of sinking in, especially on the tracks that the sheep and cattle made as they trailed across the landscape.

During the 1860s and 1870s many of the large 'squatter' holdings had been broken up into smaller 'selector' holdings, and in so doing they became more vulnerable to drought. On a large property stock can be moved to lessen the impact of hooves compacting the soil, and to take advantage of the slow seep into waterholes that might give a mob water for a few days, then must be left alone to fill again. Selectors needed to crop part of their land to make a living – dead pumpkin or tomato vines don't give fruit. But stock can survive eating dead grass, and if you have enough of it to last until it rains, you will still have all your stock.

The land blew away. Up to a metre of topsoil in some places disappeared with the wind, and when it rained the subsoil washed away too, beginning the network of deep erosion gullies that became etched like wrinkles into rural Australia until various government and community projects from the 1980s began to stabilise and correct them.

Red dust from the inland covered the land to the coast – even gardens and houses in Sydney, Brisbane and Melbourne were red with dust. At times the dust storms were so thick that a horseman couldn't see his way clear in the main city streets.

Facing the fire

Bushfires were a constant fear each time the wind blew hot and fierce, and during a drought, as hot air rises, winds are usually stronger too. Bushfires today are often deliberately started by people. Back when fire was the only way to cook your food, the fires of selectors or swaggies could easily and accidentally spark a bushfire, especially in those gale-force days.

Lightning from thunderstorms also often sparks a fire then is quickly put out as rain flows, but in a drought you may get lightning but no rain. A wind of eighty or ninety kilometres per hour can spread a bushfire more than a hundred kilometres in a day. The stronger the wind, the more flaming debris is caught up, whirling high but still burning, to light spot fires tens of kilometres away. Each time the wind direction changes, the flame front grows wider.

Once again, there are no reliable records of bushfires, except for those near large towns or cities, or exceptionally large ones. Until the 1990s, in our area as with many in Australia, most fires were tackled by the local bushfire brigades – or just by locals if the fire brigade was already busy. Of the several I helped fight in this district in the 1978 to 1983 drought, none was officially recorded or responded to as the fire truck was already busy elsewhere. If you hadn't lived here at the time you could look at the records and assume there had been no fires. We fought the fires with green wattle branches, bashing at the flames, and, just once, a ranger had a single official McCloud tool (a combined rake/hoe) that was useful for hauling down burning bark and debris to be stamped out on the ground.

We do know that in early 1898 most of eastern Victoria, the Gippsland district, was burnt. Melbourne endured a 'bushfire night', a day when the air turned black. Ships at sea had to slow in the darkness as no light can shine through ash. The fires were so bad and the winds so strong that even Sydney was dimmed by the smoke.[8]

Ruin by rabbit

Then there were the bunnies.

By 1850 a few people in Australia bred rabbits for their meat, but rabbit meat was still a luxury. Rabbits had been difficult to farm in

England; people called warreners were employed to try to keep rabbit colonies healthy and productive.

In 1859 a Victorian squatter named Thomas Austin brought twenty-four rabbits, five hares and seventy-two partridges from England and released them on his sheep run near Geelong. Within ten years the rabbits has escaped from his property and spread all over the neighbourhood. Rabbits thrived in the warm climate. They also liked all that grassland cropped close to the ground by sheep ... By the 1860s, farmers were routinely shooting the eagles, goshawks and predator birds that might have helped control them, assuming – incorrectly – that those birds killed healthy lambs, not the dead or dying ones they really hunted.

By 1879[9] rabbits were a plague across New South Wales, destroying thousands of acres of grazing land and starving out many native animals as well as causing massive soil loss and erosion. Native animals like roos, wallabies and wombats graze grass, but rabbits and sheep eat it so close to the ground that the roots die, and they kill the hundreds or thousands of other ground species too. Rabbit meat was suddenly cheap; even in the 1860s hawkers were taking freshly killed rabbits from door to door, calling, 'Rabbit-oh!' Now in the 1880s and 1890s the rabbits gathered at the last remaining dams or waterholes. They died in their thousands of heat as well as starvation and thirst.

Biting the bunnies

In 1973 our farm was a paradise for rabbits, their warrens thick on the bare hillsides or under blackberry clumps. A minute's shooting on the kilometre walk down to my neighbour's for supper was enough to get three to six. (They died instantly and were eaten by my neighbour or my family, a humane way to control the feral animals causing erosion and outcompeting native species like bandicoots and bettong.) There were no large predator birds to eat them as all birds bigger than a wren had been routinely shot by previous owners. By 1990, with the bush regenerating, we had no rabbits or droppings, nor had I shot a rabbit since 1983. The white goshawks and powerful owls ate them instead.

The rabbits probably (there are again no official records) ate far more than the stock. The drought also probably reduced rabbit numbers, but as dying rabbits tended to gather near the water they desperately needed, they were likely to die around settlers' huts and townships, too. The dead rabbits stank. The precious remaining water, already polluted by human faeces, grew even more dangerously toxic.

Barcoo rot and furnace heat

Outbreaks of typhoid and cholera grew more frequent, as did Barcoo rot, a skin infection characterised by pus-filled sores and ulcers that came from a bad diet and poor hygiene. Named after the Barcoo River region, it was present throughout rural Australia.

The first heatwave occurred in January 1896[10], furnace-like winds from central Australia pushing temperatures well into the forties across much of eastern Australia. Bourke in northwest New South Wales had an average maximum temperature over three weeks of forty-four degrees Celsius, with four days in a row reaching forty-eight. Many fled by train but about 160 people still died of heat and disease.

The summer of 1897–98 was even hotter and windier[11]; in New South Wales alone the death rate rose by about twenty per cent. Water supplies dwindled ever lower in towns, and death rates from heatstroke and typhoid grew. On 1 January 1900, the first day of the new century, Western Australia, Tasmania and Victoria were recovering from savage bushfires, there was a cyclone off Townsville and the temperature was forty-four degrees in the shade in parts of New South Wales and South Australia. Riverboats on the Murray ran aground, and on some properties in Queensland even the kangaroos were too weak from thirst and hunger to move.

These days Australia's population can retreat to air-conditioned homes, offices or even malls on hot days. Imagine summer after summer with no retreat: no creek, foul water, sick children, the stench of dead rabbits, the white bones of the last of your stock, husband and sons old enough to work – twelve, or even younger – off droving, or shearing, on the wallaby.

Then the bushfire smoke would come.

The power of hope

Hardship is not a reason to federate. My year eleven history teacher, Dr Martin Sullivan, once bounded into class and declared: 'Revolutions don't happen when things are at their worst. They happen when people begin to hope.'

The shared experience of drought, heat and smoke did perhaps draw Australians into mutual sympathy. But starving, hopeless women and thirsty men droving far from towns do not lead or even join a movement advocating Federation. The lack of water even hindered the slowly stirring movement to join the states into one nation, with arguments between New South Wales, Victoria, South Australia and Queensland over the use of water in the Murray–Darling system (arguments that are still going on in much the same terms today, but with a fifth interested party, environmentalists).

Ideas cost nothing. The dream of Federation gave people who were better off hope that a solution – many solutions – to social problems might be solved at the ballot box. Even in a drought you can dream. In a drought, dreams are probably more necessary: something good to work towards, even if the sky is too dry to weep. And this is even more essential when drought leads to economic depression.

A drought-fuelled depression

The drought – and the poor land management that created tragedy instead of the mere 'lack of abundance' it might have been two hundred years before – caused major long-term depression, in the cities as well as the bush. That 1880 to 1903 depression brought conditions so horrendous that it would spark passionate dreams of reform, dreams that could most easily be achieved by creating a national parliament that would pass new laws to encompass the entire country.

By the 1880s, starving women, children and a few men (most had headed out 'on the road' to look for work) lined up for hours at city soup kitchens. By the 1890s, prices for both wool and wheat fell in Britain. State governments had borrowed heavily for large building projects, expecting that the prosperity of continuing high wheat and wool prices and the revenue from goldmining would keep their states prosperous.

It didn't. Land prices in both cities and rural areas had mushroomed beyond the land's real worth. They crashed too.

By the early 1890s crowds were gathering outside banks, desperate to withdraw their money so they could pay the rent or feed their families. Governments stopped public works. Even more people lost their jobs.

Visionaries like Henry Parkes could see that it made economic sense to drop the tariffs on trade between the states and to standardise the width of state railway lines so that one train could carry goods and people into different states (without having to stop at state borders and move people and freight onto a different train). Uniform immigration laws would also stop what many regarded simply as cheap labour – the 'blackbirding' or kidnapping of Pacific Islanders to work on Queensland sugar farms, and the growing number of Chinese immigrants. The latter were unpopular as they seemed all too successful, even in the drought times, creating market gardens, working in furniture factories, and expanding into hardware stores and tanneries. When times are bad it is good to have a physically identifiable enemy to blame.

Federation was something to hope for – you could harness dreams to the idea of national Federation. Federation might bring Australia back to prosperity. It might also alleviate the appalling poverty and squalor of the cities.

Grinder Brothers' Alley

Sydney's slums dated from the first arrival of Europeans and the ramshackle huts put up by the sailors of the First Fleet for their doxies, the female convicts, before the ships sailed back to England. Most harbours of the time had slums near the waterfront, where sailors could get pickled with cheap gin and women hired themselves out for five minutes in an alley. Slums also housed factory workers and the factories they worked in, as well as crooks and brothels. But recession meant hard times for factories too.

I haven't been able to find reliable figures for child labour in Australia during the 1877 to 1903 drought, but certainly child labour predated the Great Drought. In 1890s England, children as young as ten would 'go into service' as servants, be taken on as apprentices,

Exploiting the desperate

The poverty and desperation of the 1880s and 1890s did not affect everyone. For the first time in the continent's history, humans could be insulated from two of the country's most persistent threats: heat and lack of water.

Houses built in the 1880s and 1890s had solid, high ceilings, thick brick walls that helped keep out the heat, and decorative touches like leadlight windows, carved bannisters and decorative plaster ceilings. They could be kept snug in winter by wood fires. City water systems meant large green gardens. Those late Victorian houses are often far better built, insulated and soundproofed than the McMansions of today. Wages were low because of high unemployment, so a good house was relatively cheap to build.

By the 1890s, the house of a middle-class city family where the male income earner still had a job (women were only supposed to work from absolute necessity, and even then their wages were difficult to survive on) would probably have a wood-burning stove instead of or as well as a kitchen fireplace and hearth, far easier to keep alight and to keep the kitchen free from dusty grease around the walls. A Coolgardie safe, using evaporating water to cool the contents, would act as a fridge. In larger towns and cities the 'iceman' in his sacking apron and with his giant tongs would bring blocks of ice once or twice a week. Middle-class houses also had running water, sewerage (or a dunny man to collect the pans), neat gardens with roses out the front and a vegetable garden out the back.

Cheap servants made home life even more comfortable. Even households where the husband held only a labourer's job could afford a woman to come in once or twice a week to 'do the rough' – stove blacking, floor scrubbing, carpet beating and laundry. Middle-class homes employed at least one servant as well as the 'slavie', who washed up, scrubbed the vegetables and the floor, someone to do the laundry, and a full- or part-time gardener. Smaller homes had a 'couple', husband and wife. But these neat houses were in suburbs carefully distant from the factories and the people that worked in them, the slums of Sydney, Melbourne and Brisbane.

work in woollen mills, and pull carts underground in Welsh coalmines because they were cheaper than pit ponies. Adults are stronger and have more endurance than children. They make better workers – if you can afford to pay them.

Even if we don't have reliable statistics for child labour in Australia in the 1890s, we do have the tragic images created by Henry Lawson and other writers of life in squalid alleys where children worked from dawn till dusk, sometimes sleeping on the factory floor, paid in pennies or even not paid at all. Henry Lawson is now remembered for his bush stories and poetry, but from the time Lawson moved to Sydney to be with his mother when he was sixteen, three years after his parents' marriage had broken up for the last time in its crumbly history, Lawson was mostly a city dweller. His work also detailed the horrors of slum life but these stories and poems are, perhaps, too harsh and realistic to be as popular as his bush poetry today. Unlike Charles Dickens's novels of English poverty, stories like 'Arvie Aspinall's Alarm Clock' don't have happy endings. Arvie dies sleeping in the Grinder Brothers' factory doorway, so that he doesn't oversleep and lose the job that – not quite – feeds his family.[12]

It was the horrors of slum life – not just the child labour, endemic alcoholism and violence but also the casual prostitution (faced with a choice between a slow death in a factory or a life as a prostitute, it was no wonder that so many chose the latter) – that led to the formation of groups like the Women's Christian Temperance Union.

The demon drink

The temperance movement began as a drive to stop the drinking of alcohol; 'lips that have touched alcohol shall not touch mine' is one of its more enduring slogans. It is easy now to portray the women of the 1890s temperance movement as wowsers – anti-sex, anti-grog and anti-fun – especially as in 1898 one of the Tasmanian branches urged that a bell be rung at 9 p.m. to send all young people, especially girls, off the streets.

But there was a full and awful truth in their phrase 'the demon drink'. Ever since spirits became cheap in Britain and Europe, thanks to the availability of slave-grown sugar in the seventeenth century and potatoes in Europe, much of society was drunk for at least part of each day. A male aristocrat's worth was measured in how well he could hold his drink, measured by bottles, not glasses, of brandy, wine and port a night. Alcohol was the great solace of the poor, and gin was cheaper than bread. Bush songs like 'Click Go the Shears' extolled the place of the pub or shanty:

> *The first pub we come to it's there we'll have a spree*
> *And everyone that comes along it's, 'Come and drink with me!'*

Shearers and drovers routinely cashed their cheques at the first pub they came to, and little if anything might make it back to their families. The 'working man' was paid in cash and, again, Friday night at the pub might see a large part or even all of the money gone in one glorious night of oblivion, as well as paying the 'tab' for the previous six nights' drinking.

Women were forced to take in washing, lodgers or mending to feed their families, even when their husbands were adequately paid, but spent most of their wages on grog. A drunk man was more likely to bash or rape his wife, an alcoholic more likely to abandon his family – or to be abandoned as they fled to safety.

It was this true 'demon' that was the prime focus of the Women's Christian Temperance Union (later the National Women's Christian Temperance Union), but they also had another cause: child labour, the curse of the alley where Lawson's Grinder Brothers had their factory. Falling profits meant that factory owners needed to keep costs down and children were cheap, even expendable. They could be paid in food and sleep on the dirt of the factory floor. While the women of the union campaigned in streets and outside pubs, trying to get men to 'sign the pledge' to give up alcohol, they also saw that only legislative change could bring major relief in matters like child labour. But the women of the Temperance Union, like all women, did not have the right to vote.

A new parliament – a national one – might see new labour laws brought in, and female suffrage across the continent.

The mothers of Federation

Henry Parkes, a constitutional lawyer, is called the father of Federation. Few Australians, perhaps, would be as comfortable acknowledging that our nation is as much, or even more, the child of the Women's Christian Temperance Union (WCTU). They were indomitable.[13]

The first local Temperance Union was set up in Sydney in 1882 and the first branch of the WCTU founded in Sydney in 1885, prompted by a visit by Mary Leavitt from the American union. Branches in Queensland, rural New South Wales, South Australia and Tasmania quickly followed. The Women's Christian Temperance Union of Australasia (later renamed the National Women's Christian Temperance Union of Australia) was formed in May 1891, Australia's first national women's organisation in the country. By 1894 they had 7400 members.

By 1900 the constitution of the national union outlined their aims: 'We believe in total abstinence for the individual, prohibition for the state and nation, equal standard of purity for men and women, equal wages for equal work without regard to sex, the ballot in the hands of women, arbitration between nations.'[14]

They were not alone. By the 1890s there were many groups of women, often associated with literary societies[15], gathering signatures for petitions and lobbying both for female suffrage and laws to give women equal rights and to protect children. (Henry Lawson's mother, Louisa Lawson, was prominent both as a political radical, writer and publisher.) The Australian Women's Suffrage Society had been formed in 1889 to win the right to vote as well as equal rights in marriage and divorce, equal rights to own property and the right for women to be given custody of children in the event of divorce.

The fight for female suffrage was inextricably linked with both the move to Federation and the battle to improve the lot of women and children. British women wouldn't get the vote on the same terms as men till the 1920s, despite what might arguably be a larger class of articulate, educated women with strong political connections. Even the major contribution of women to the war effort from 1914 to 1918 didn't earn all women a place at the ballot box.

Why did Australian (and New Zealander) women win the vote so early? It may be partly because while the role of an English woman of a certain class in Victorian times was still to arrange tennis parties and the church flowers, Australian women had had more experience of managing properties and businesses while the men of the family were off looking for gold, droving, shearing or working at other jobs due to the drought. Many of the prominent women in the Temperance and Suffrage movements came from rural backgrounds, where women worked, even if their management role was never acknowledged. Once again the land played an active role in our history, forging women such as Louisa Lawson who'd had to simultaneously run a business, a farm and a household, giving them both confidence in their own ability as well as the experience of the suffering of women unprotected by just laws.

But there were many other factors, including a radical, often Irish Roman Catholic anti-authoritarianism simmering in the community that may also have contributed to a broader sense of social justice. But the groups who campaigned for female suffrage weren't arguing just to have a basic human right to share in public decisions. They were also fighting for the laws that a new federal parliament might pass, ones that restricted child labour and protected and gave educational opportunities to women and children. Once again, the horrors of the drought fuelled the passion of the campaigners.

Large petitions urging female suffrage were gathered in the various states. South Australia collected 11,600 signatures in 1894, Queensland collected 11,366 signatures in 1894 and 4000 more in 1897, and Tasmania collected 2278 signatures in 1896. In New South Wales petitions were gathered from 1891, and from 1899 in Western Australia. But none were as large as the 1891 Victorian one that had 30,000 signatures and became known as the 'Monster Petition'.[16]

The dreams that came out of the drought were never entirely fulfilled. South Australian women were granted the right to vote in 1895, followed by Western Australia in 1899, New South Wales in 1902, Tasmania in 1903, Queensland in 1905 and finally Victoria in 1908. Australian women (except Aboriginal women) were enfranchised for the new Commonwealth Parliament in 1902 and first voted in its second election of 1903. And yes, some new federal laws did help women and children, but politicians would mostly be male for the next seventy years. It wouldn't be until the late 1960s (and a far less socially relevant drought) that the votes of women were even partially harnessed to fight for reform.

How drought created the Labor Party

Australia, like Britain, would almost certainly have eventually developed a party to represent the working class, but in Australia the Great Drought provided the trigger and much of the passion.

Worsening economic conditions due to the drought and its consequences led to lower wages and harsher working conditions. Strikes spread across the country in the late 1880s, from ship's officers to seamen, waterside workers, shearers, miners and many others. The colonial governments and their police forces supported the employers. Bitterness grew between workers and employers. Worsening conditions increased the sense of solidarity among workers – and solidarity increased militancy.

Australia's first workers' organisation was the Shipwrights' Union, formed in 1830. Others followed, even though in Britain unions were illegal until 1871. But by the 1880s, drought-fuelled desperation from appalling – and worsening – working conditions made the Shearers' Union the most militant of all Australian unions of the time.

The Shearers' Union was formed in July 1886 when squatters wanted to lower the rate of pay, and refuse payment for any sheep not 'properly shorn'. Its militancy may also have been partly due to the comradeship of the outback, men willing to work together for a common cause. Its stroppiness might equally have been partly due to grog and hangovers.

In 1891 around the Barcaldine area in central western Queensland members refused to work at stations unless the Squatters' Association met their demands for better conditions. Eventually 50,000 miners, transport workers, shearers and other farm workers were on strike along the east coast, some for up to three months. The army, police and special police were called in to break up mobs of protesting workers. The strike lasted till 7 August, when the last of the shearers went back to work after the leaders of the strike had been arrested for conspiracy and

Labor not Labour

'Labor' was not a spelling mistake. It is American English spelling, and the US 'labor' movement was influential in Australia. It also differentiated the federal party from the many local labour movements.

sentenced to three years' jail. But strikes broke out on other properties for many years, either for better wages and conditions or to protest against property owners' employing non-union labour.

In June 1894 Queensland pastoralists decided to offer shearers less money. On 2 July unionists fought with strikebreakers at Oondooroo Station. When the river steamer *Rodney* arrived laden with strikebreakers on the Darling River on 6 August, it was met by a furious mob and burnt. Dagworth Station's shearing shed was burnt down. On 9 September the Queensland parliament passed the *Peace Preservation Act*, giving itself exceptional powers to deal with the strike – and the strike was called off.

But the anger on both sides remained.

A new federal government might be the way to bring in industrial laws covering the whole of Australia. The first meeting of the Australian Labour Federation General Council was held in Brisbane on 31 August 1890. The trade union movements sponsored new labour parties in all the states, though before Federation they only contested elections in Queensland, New South Wales and South Australia, winning major reforms like 'one man, one vote' in New South Wales. These state parties would be the basis for the Federal Labor Party, formed after labour representatives met together in May 1901 following the first federal election.

The dreams come true (and still it didn't rain)

On 1 January 1901, when the Constitution of Australia came into force, Australia did finally become one nation. The new nation had been created by both idealism and self-interest. But its major shaping force had been the drought.

Federation, however, was not enough to make it rain. Australia wasn't entirely free of drought until the good rains of August 1903 came.

That long drought had changed Australia physically and socially. It created erosion gullies, dust storms and land too depleted to grow crops. But it also gave us the anger and idealism to fight injustice. Other droughts had and would shape both Australian government policy and the Australian character.

That drought gave us a nation.

How to predict a drought

You can smell a drought, just before it begins to bite. The wind here comes hot from the northwest, strong enough to bring new scents. When rain falls in the first few months it is always less than you'd imagined or the weather bureau predicts. There are other scents, too, a sharp clear smell of eucalyptus oil evaporating in the heat, the slightly cooked scent of hot flowers. But if you know your land, you can tell what the next year, or even decades, will bring.

The spring last year told us what the summer weather of 2012-13 would be. The clematis bloomed prolifically, but not the wonga vine. Clematis grows in dryer soil; wonga vine likes damp gullies. The goannas were out early – light, not heat, seems to determine their hibernation patterns. Gully gum (*Eucalyptus smithii*) had had the longest, strongest flowering I've ever seen, a vast strip across the valley. No other gum trees bloomed. The gully gum likes dry, hot conditions.

But along the coast, about thirty kilometres from us as the crow flies, although an hour and a half away by road, the spotted gum had the best flowering in years. Put that information together and you get a long-range weather forecast: weak lows coming from the southeast would release their rain onto the coast, even flooding it at times, but little of that rain would reach this far inland.

But the vegetation last spring also indicated that it wouldn't be a bad bushfire year – at least here. The three acacia species didn't set much seed, nor did the *Bursaria* or *Indigofera*. So it was unlikely we'd have the weeks-long hot bushfire north westerlies, nor dry thunderstorms with lightning strikes.

This summer of 2013-14 should be much the same for this small part of Australia. There'll be rain, most possibly as violent thunderstorms. They will be interspersed with long weeks of dryness and above-average heat. It will be much like last summer: a few extremely bad weeks, with fires around that may possibly reach us too; not a lush year, but enough rain to get by. If we get a flood it will be a sudden gusher, not many days of relentless rain.

We've had no long, loud wombat mating games, which would indicate in extremely lush green year to come, but there are more young wombats than usual in the pouches. Nor have we had signs of a truly bad year, although as I revise this in June 2013 it is too early for me to really tell, until the spring buds begin to swell in a month or so, and I can see how much seed has set from the winter blooming plants. 'Pretty much like last year' isn't much of a prediction, but I'm relieved that all indicators put a really bad drought at least a year or two away. I am all too aware how limited my knowledge and experience is, compared to men and women now long gone, who could predict years in advance. I can only predict a year in advance, with a 'maybe' for a few years after that. Nor does the year here – as in most of Australia – fit into the conventional four European seasons. Instead we have six or eight that include two 'springs', one of which is windy, and with cold nights, but full of growing abundance. The other 'spring' has blue and gold days that can linger till December, or vanish in November. Nor do the seasons start and end on a particular date each year.

But the predictors and seasons above only work for this end of this valley. Each area and its different species will respond to a coming drought in different ways. The land's signs (here, at any rate) have been more accurate than weather bureau forecasts, although this may change: the science of weather patterns is rapidly advancing, and should continue to do so unless dingbat politicians cut the funding.

Hopefully within the next few years the conventional science of weather prediction will be as good or better than predictions based on watching a piece of land one knows well. It takes decades of watching, combined with lessons from those who have known this part of Australia for many generations, to do the kind of weather forecasting I've described. A science degree takes only three or four years, as long as the climate and weather patterns have been accurately worked out for the students to study. Scientists are only beginning to understand the many influences on Australian weather. These include an El Niño pattern, when waters along the western coast of South America are warmer than usual and cause a tendency to drought in northern and eastern Australia, and La Niña, with abnormally low air pressure over Australia, and a tendency to more rain and floods. But the influence of the temperatures in the Indian Ocean to our west, as well as the strength of weather systems to our far south, are only just beginning to be understood, as is the influence of the strength of the jet stream that circles the earth.

A land of drought and flooding rain needs accurate predictive models. To get that, we need adequate resources directed to research. They may not appear to bring in immediate financial reward, but in the long term Australia's economic and ecological survival may depend on them. We also need planning decisions based on worse-case scenarios, assuming that some time in the next decade fresh water will be critically short.

But there is one sure weather prediction for Australia: drought will come. We need better predictive science and local insight based on millennia of observation to know when.

CHAPTER 13

Truth or propaganda? The bronzed Anzacs of Gallipoli and Kokoda

Sunbronzed, forged by the land that bore them, the bravest of the brave, our soldiers saved Australia at Gallipoli and Kokoda …

Or did they? How much of what we think we know about those campaigns and the men who fought in them is myth? And how much did the land contribute to the quality of our soldiers in the iconic campaigns of Gallipoli and Kokoda?

Gallipoli, 25 April 1915, 1.30 a.m.

The moon sank into darkness that could be either land or sea.

On the decks of each of the three battleships the men waited, the first wave of 4000 soldiers (the 3rd Infantry Brigade of the 1st Australian Division) crammed together. They came from what Charles Bean[1], Australia's first official military historian, called the 'outer states' – Western Australia, South Australia, Tasmania and Queensland.

Every second man had a pick or a shovel to dig trenches to shelter them from enemy fire – if the enemy left them alive long enough to dig. Each also carried the massive bulk of their equipment on their backs: overcoats, 250 rounds of ammunition, two to three days' food – mostly army biscuit – and as much water as they could carry, as well as rifle and bayonet.[2] They had spent the day at the grindstones, sharpening the latter. Now the tops gleamed in the starlight. From the three battleships they were organised into groups to be towed ashore.

The enemy waited on the shore. The Turks were not just defending their land from this invading force: they had been told that if they lost, their country would be under the rule of Russia. They would become serfs, Russians slaves; a gift from Britain, Russia's ally.

Each Australian Imperial Force man had volunteered, unlike many of their allies and their enemies. Many had been given two gold sovereigns to spend when they reached Constantinople, the Turkish capital. Turkey was an ally of Germany. When England had refused to agree to let Germany pass through its ally Belgium to invade France, England and Germany were at war. The men on the big grey ships were fighting for 'the Motherland', England, the place where perhaps a fifth of the Australian forces had been born, and most still called home.

The men had already been told it would be bad. They would face enemy fire when they landed – the Turks were in trenches behind the beach, halfway up the hill and on top of the cliffs. The Australian troops had been told that an estimated one in five of them would die.

Twenty kilometres south, the main British force was to land at Cape Helles. The untried and, in the British eyes, only semi-trained Australian and New Zealander soldiers had been given the subordinate but still critical role of heading inland to capture high ground, the promontory of Gaba Tepe and what would be known as Hill Number 971. Reinforcements would then push even further inland.

Originally the campaign was supposed to be a primarily naval operation, or at least be supported by fire from the big ships. But the fear of mines meant that the men had only darkness, not naval guns, to protect them. They needed to take the enemy by surprise – or as much of a surprise as three battleships and seven destroyers could pose. The Turks knew they were there. But at least, in the darkness, any shots fired into the night would not have a visible target.

The rope ladders swayed as one by one the men clambered down to the landing boats, so crowded that they sat low in the water. There was no room to duck. The barges began to tow the boats towards the darker line that was the shore. The only light was the red flashes of Turkish gunfire.

Or was there? Some men who were there described the enemy gunfire as they rowed ashore, and even of bodies dragged off from the deck before they disembarked. But the official accounts say that there was no answering fire from the shore till 4 a.m., when the first boats were about thirty metres from the shore.

Once they reached the shallows all the boats had to be rowed as the barges headed back for reinforcements. The boats went slowly through the waves, the men so crowded in that it was impossible to pull the oars far back.

More shots, or possibly the first shots; at least one machine gun. Blood, brains and bone-splattered uniforms, bodies slumped into the water.

The rowers kept on going. As a rower was shot and slumped to the bottom of the boat he was replaced by another man at the oars. The stars on the eastern horizon were just beginning to dim into predawn grey. Bursts of red and green and yellow slashed across the black. Shells screamed above them. More bullets slashed across the sea. Young officers stood to give the orders – and died in that instant, with a bullet to the head. The snipers targeted the officers, thinking that would cause chaos and panic.

The first of the boats hit the beach. It was narrow, cut by a shallow trench with about seventy Turkish soldiers, waiting. Further down, the more open beaches were lined with barbed wire fences.

The Anzacs staggered out, each man wading through the water, trying to keep his footing on the slippery and uneven pebbles and rocks. Some were lucky enough to be only knee deep. Others found themselves up to their necks in water. Many drowned, unbalanced by the weight of their packs.

Even before the first Anzac boot hit the beach the sea was red with blood. Above the men were steep cliffs, cut with narrow fissured gullies and dappled with thornbush. On the cliff more Turkish soldiers waited, firing down. Orders were yelled into the darkness: drop the packs, take only rifle, ammunition, bayonet and haversack.

The first to land at least had the cover of darkness. They overran the first Turkish trench and started upwards, digging those sharpened bayonet points into the cliff to haul themselves up or bushwhacking up the gullies. The sheer strength of numbers overwhelmed the Turks in the trench halfway up the cliff, too. But still above them the larger Turkish force fired down.

The dawn light shone around them. Each man was a target now, but still they kept on scrambling up the gullies. About a kilometre from shore the Allied ship *Bacchante* accidentally fired a volley of shot, bursting in front of and splintering one of the boats. Most of the men drowned but some survived, to be taken back to the ship and then placed once more into a rowboat for shore.

The second wave followed.

By 9 a.m. on that first day about 8000 Anzacs made it up the cliffs, thrusting their bayonets into the dirt to haul themselves upwards. The sun danced across a thin line of cloud, well above the horizon. The beach seemed to melt in a great hot wave of light, but there were shadows on it now as well from boxes of stores and ammunition brought ashore, though at times it was hard to tell which were shadows and which were pools of blood.

Many of the officers had been picked off by snipers; the officers' habit of standing up in the boat to give orders made them easy to target. The units had become mixed up – there was no time to look for the identification patches on your comrade's sleeve to see what unit they belonged to. Captains Lalor and Tulloch led two parties of Australian troops that fought their way inland.

Other men – alone, or in twos or threes – fought what was almost their own war[3], shooting, stabbing with bayonets, fighting hand to hand with the enemy, crossing rocky ravines and hillocks that hadn't appeared on their maps. (Although the area had been well surveyed by army intelligence in the weeks before, the maps had not been passed to the troops who would be landing there.) It was heroism. It was also, in both senses, a bloody mess, as men or groups headed off on their own without the strategy that might have made their position defensible. At last they reached the high ground they had been told to take.

Then lost it. Turkish reinforcements arrived and enough Allied reinforcements did not. By the next morning, the surviving Anzacs were huddled under the cliffs at what was to be known as Anzac Cove, waiting to retreat back to the ships.

They didn't. New orders came from England. Even though the high ground was occupied by the enemy, they were to try again, again and again. In four days, seventy per cent of the men from the 25 April landing would be dead.

But the rest kept fighting, and when the reinforcements arrived they did too, for seven months, until – again – the orders came to retreat.

By then legends had been born: of courage, mateship, men who died with a last joke on their lips, who refused to salute officers but who would give their lives for a friend. The legends were simplified, often inaccurate. It is fashionable now to claim that the legends of bravery were created as propaganda, and some of it certainly was, or at least embellished.

How much of the Anzac legend is true?

Who were the first Anzacs?

Gallipoli: you can't say the name without evoking images of young tanned men charging at the enemy, like we see in movies. It was said at the time, and still even now, to be the true birth of our nation, as the world – or at least the British Empire and its enemies – learnt that the Australian colonials could fight.

Who were the Australians at Gallipoli? Were they really a superb fighting force, superior to others? Were they larrikins, who refused to salute an officer? Did their irreverent senses of humour stay with them to the end? Would they give their last crust of bread to a friend? Had the land they came from somehow created a soldier who was different from the British soldiers they fought with, with whom they otherwise shared most of their recent ancestry?

Probably to some extent at least. They are men that I knew, my grandfather and his generation, and my father-in-law's. You can't understand Gallipoli – or Kokoda, the World War 2 campaign that furthered the legends – without knowing the land that shaped the men who fought there. There are aspects of the Gallipoli legend that certainly aren't true: they weren't fighting to save their country, and most weren't the boys or young adults shown in movies. Nor were they necessarily good soldiers at the start of the campaign – that first tenacious assault up the cliffs and gullies to high ground was heroic, but it was also disorganised, with possibly far greater loss of life because of it.

But the rest? Let's examine them, point by point.

The make of the man

Were the Anzacs fitter and better able to endure the conditions at Gallipoli than those from England, despite the fact that about a fifth of them had been born in Britain?

Possibly, even probably. Those first Australian troops were carefully selected. So many enlisted at the beginning of the war that the army authorities couldn't even process them all. That meant they could be picky, and only about one in three volunteers were taken. Later, as the need for more cannon fodder grew desperate, the requirements were dramatically lowered, and then lowered again.

In August 1914 when the first men destined for Gallipoli enlisted, the requirements were that they be between eighteen and thirty-five years old, a minimum height of five feet six inches, and chest measurement of thirty-four inches, although a skilled driver could have chest that was only thirty-two inches (a chest measurement is a rough but reasonable test of fitness).[4]

The men had to pass a medical examination, and it is probable that, as in the Boer War, preference was given to those who could shoot. Back then, men who could shoot wouldn't have been members of gun clubs, shooting only at targets. They'd have potted rabbits in the dusk, dark and dawn (rabbits aren't out feeding during the day). Potting rabbits wasn't just a good day out – it added meat to the pot (hence 'potting') and you got a good price for the skins. Rabbits were in plague numbers, and farmers were eager for anyone to shoot them. Many or even most suburban lads made enough to buy their bicycle, tools for their apprenticeship or just to help mum put bread on the table by selling rabbit skins.

A rabbit moves fast, and relatively unpredictably, so if you can shoot rabbits you are a good shot. It is also more difficult to shoot a living target. (The ex-soldier who taught me to shoot the rabbits I swapped with a neighbour for chickens warned me of that – at first your hand instinctively moves away from taking life.) My grandfather, Colonel A.T. Edwards, who supervised Australian psychiatric services in World War 2, estimated that only one in four soldiers was capable of killing an enemy in battle, and that that one had probably been 'blooded' by shooting living targets like rabbits, wild pigs, or sheep before he went to war.

Preference was also given to single men, or married men who agreed to sign over two-thirds of their wages of six shillings a day (far higher than the English soldiers' one shilling a day) to their families, with a shilling a day kept as deferred pay to be given as a lump sum at the end of the war.

When each man enlisted, little information was taken: their age, which they didn't have to prove with a birth certificate; their height and chest measurements; medical fitness; name of mother and father; place of enlistment; and trade. We don't even know how many had grown up in the bush as the records only give us where the men enlisted. Many came from rural areas to country towns or Melbourne to enlist, especially in the first wild enthusiasm.[5]

But back then many townsmen would spend weekends or holidays on a relative's farm, or the farm of a mate's relatives, taking the train out on Friday night and being picked up by horse and cart at the station. It is not unreasonable to expect that the majority of Anzacs were able to pot a running rabbit in the dusk at two hundred yards, spend three days and nights with no sleep fighting a bushfire or rescuing stock or neighbours from floods, and were used to hauling sacks of wheat or bales of hay or sugar cane. The bush was not 'out there' in 1914 and 1915. It was still very much part of our cities, and of the lives of all but inner-city slum dwellers who, due to poverty, disease, alcohol and deprivation, were unlikely to reach that five feet six inches in height or have a thirty-four-inch chest. Unlike a man from London, the Anzacs would have grown up on a meat and milk-rich diet, with plenty of sun-given vitamin D. They were strong, fit, and experienced in relying on each other rather than authority.

Tradesmen formed the largest proportion of those who enlisted (about 112,000 men), followed by labourers (99,000), 'country callings' (57,000), clerical (24,000), professional (15,000) and seafaring (6000).

Possibly a high proportion of those 'labourers' had come from country areas. In 1914 most of Australia was in the grip of a severe drought. Farm labourers – and younger sons – could easily have been spared when stock numbers were reduced, and there was less need to shepherd stock in areas which still were unlikely to be fenced; in droughts stock gather by waterholes at least twice a day, and usually camp there at night. This meant that in 1914 much bush labour was redundant, and many people were also short of cash.

There was also another form of tribalism that bound the battalions at Gallipoli together. Many of the Anzacs were from suburban Melbourne, and a common grounding in Australian Rules football helped shape their allegiances to each other – they came from the same suburbs and played for and supported the same footy teams. Even into the 1960s every suburb and country town had its own cricket team. While sports were a major part of British life, too, the portraits given of city and rural life in England in the 1900 to 1915 period do not show sport to be as ubiquitous as it was in Australia in the same period.

But if the men recruited had replied honestly when asked what their hobbies were they might also have added 'having a stoush Friday and Saturday nights'. Boys fought in schoolyards, with lookouts to yell if a teacher approached, not just in anger or argument but serious competition; 'pushes', or gangs, fought on the street. C.J. Dennis's verse novel *The Songs of a Sentimental Bloke*, set in prewar Melbourne and published in 1915, deals with just such regular stoushes, and features Ginger Mick, stoush expert and AIF volunteer, and casualty.[6] At the annual local agricultural shows – held in both cities and country towns – young lads would be called up to the boxing tent to see if they could beat the champion and win a purse. There was no shortage of volunteers.

From a land of extremes

Australian men were used to rough terrain. This meant little in the mud and slog of the Somme, but it mattered in the gullies and crags of Gallipoli. They also knew about working with only a nominal leader in bushfire brigades. And most importantly, perhaps, they were extremely familiar with climatic extremes.

The invasion at Gallipoli started in the relatively mild weather of spring. It would continue through a hell of a summer, and then the frost of winter. It has often been said that the Anzacs had the advantage of long experience of fierce heat at Gallipoli but were at a disadvantage in winter. But in most of Australia except the far north, the winters are bloody cold, especially in those southern states where the majority of early recruits came from. (Even those from Western Australia mostly came from the southeast of that state.)[7] My father once showed me how to make 'Anzac trousers' – you line your trousers and shirt with newspaper. 'We all did that,' said Dad. 'Doing sentry duty, sleeping on a train platform in mid-winter. It'll keep you warm even if it's snowing.' Years later, stuck on an icy mountain while backpacking, I did what Dad suggested. It worked.

Pa Jack

Often we think of soldiers as either heroes or cowards. Usually they are neither.

'Pa Jack' (John) Sullivan was number 1338 of those who had enlisted at Brighton in Victoria to fight overseas in the AIF. He was twenty-three when he reached Gallipoli (most of the Anzacs at Gallipoli were in their twenties), a mechanical fitter. He was my father-in-law, but I never met him. Pa Jack was a city boy, but his sister, listed as next of kin, was a nurse at Sunbury, then rural. He could pot a rabbit, fight a bushfire, and help find a kid who had wandered off into the bush.

He could also lead men – on his return he'd be a foreman at Cockatoo Island dockyard in Sydney – but his records show that when he was promoted to lance corporal he insisted on returning to the rank of private. Like others of the time, he couldn't bring himself to be the one to enforce what seemed ludicrous and heartless orders coming from England. Between 1915 and March 1918 his pay was docked twice for refusing to carry out orders. In August 1915 he was evacuated to the Greek island of Lemnos from Gallipoli with shell shock. He was hospitalised again a year later, once more with shell shock from the trenches of France. By March 1918 doctors were no

Australia is a land of climatic extremes: heat, freezing, flooding and drought. The soldiers at Gallipoli would experience all four. Unlike the English, French, Indians and Newfoundlanders, the Australians were used to them all. And perhaps the worst was lack of water.

The Gallipoli peninsula had no steams or springs of fresh water, merely gullies that might run briefly after rain. The army would sink a few wells, but they quickly ran dry. It was rock, brush, pine trees, and Mediterranean wildflowers that bloomed in spring after rain: anemones, ranunculi, oregano, poppies.

A sedentary man needs about eight litres of water a day, although much of this can be taken in food like fruit or vegetables. The men were rationed to one quart of water (just over a litre) a day. They mostly

longer allowed to diagnose 'shell shock' in case of future invalid pension claims. A compassionate doctor instead diagnosed 'high blood pressure' – which Pa Jack never suffered from – and sent him home after three years of almost continuous service.

Postwar he became a functioning alcoholic, able to carry out his work admirably as dockyard foreman and generous to his mates, helping them build their caravans or children's swings or scooters. At home he was bitter, violent and drunk. He married late in life but was most at home, perhaps, in the comradeship of the Anzac Memorial Club. It was seventy years after Gallipoli that his son learned what his father had faced: airless trenches, sometimes with blackened, rotting bodies piled three deep about him, guts spilling out of wounds, flies and maggots crawling everywhere, the smell of death, the smoke from explosions, the roar of mortar fire and the screams of the dying.

Pa Jack's military career is probably as typical of the Australians at Gallipoli as is his background, a tradesman in his twenties. He was neither especially heroic nor a coward, not mentioned in dispatches at any point except when he was made lance corporal after the death of the man who'd held that position. He volunteered, did his best, and stuck it out. Unlike one in three of his comrades, he managed to survive.

drank this as tea, even sometimes shaving in the leftovers. The troops up on the Gallipoli heights ate army biscuit, dry and hard, and tinned bully beef, heated into stews to soften the biscuit in if they were lucky.

Who orders an army to fight on slopes that don't have water? Someone who assumes that their army will succeed, and advance quickly enough to either reach a water source or establish enough of a hold for water to be transferred safely to the men on high ground.

This never happened. For the entire Gallipoli campaign water had either to be carried from the big ships by barge or boat to the shore, then carried by man, mule or, for short distances, water tankers, up a gully where the enemy occupied the high ground. The early morning was the most dangerous time as the Turks could stand with the sun at their backs, the Anzacs below virtually blinded if they tried to spot the enemy.

The Turks had the easiest access to supplies, including water. As they held the high ground and the land behind the Gallipoli peninsula, their supplies could be brought in relatively easily. If the Anzacs did achieve more than their English and French counterparts, perhaps one of the reasons was their ability to survive – and fight – on little water. It is also possible that they suffered more from dysentery because they were far more likely to bathe in the heavily polluted sea; the 'Poms', the Aussies said, 'kept their towels dry'. Australia's dry and dust led to a nation that would be among the first in the world to popularise showers from the 1890s onwards.

The best and the bravest?

Endurance, fitness, strength and tenacity do not necessarily add up to a superb soldier. The landing at Anzac Cove demonstrates courage. It was also, strategically, a mess, as the men on the ground fought what were almost their own private battles instead of creating a defendable line.

Nor was the Gallipoli campaign a victory for Australia and Great Britain – it was a defeat. But the campaign was also made up of a series of battles, and some of those would be won. The two greatest, the only ones that did capture high ground, were won by the Australians at Lone Pine and the New Zealanders at Chunuk Bair, showing extraordinary tenacity. Lone Pine was meant to be a diversion for an attack elsewhere, but the Australians just kept going till they'd achieved their aim.

Anecdotally, Australians seem to have believed they could outshoot the English troops but not necessarily the Turks. It's hard to think what data could substantiate or disprove the claim of 'best and bravest', but it probably didn't involve showing unearned respect to their British 'betters'. The mateship and mutual reliance needed to fight a bushfire does not necessarily translate into a soldier who will do exactly what he is told no matter how ill-conceived the order. And this was what was expected in World War 1. Australians would be repeatedly lauded for their courage, endurance and ingenuity at Gallipoli. It may speak of their unwillingness to bow to authority that they weren't referred to as the best soldiers of the Empire.

But were the tributes to their bravery simply the propaganda of the time?

'The Bravest of the Brave' was the (translated) name given by Sikh soldiers to Private John Simpson Kirkpatrick, the 'man with the donkey' who was an Anzac stretcher-bearer.[8] Kirkpatrick was an Englishman who had jumped ship in Australia and enlisted there under his mother's maiden name in case his desertion caught up with him. In the last letter Kirkpatrick's mother wrote to him – tragically, not knowing he had died – she referred to the newspapers lauding the bravery of the Australians, and her pride that her son was serving with them. Was she a victim of propaganda?

There is an obvious reason why that heroism should be exaggerated, or even fabricated at the time. The war that was expected to be over by Christmas 1914 was obviously going to last for years. Warfare in 1915 depended upon having large numbers of troops. Firepower – like the few machine guns on the peninsula and the naval 'big guns' – made a vital difference, but manpower was literally the foundation on which tactics were built. Further – and larger – enlistments were vital. Talk up the heroism and more men would enlist in Australia; families that had been reluctant to lose a breadwinner would urge husbands and sons to glory.

But to achieve that you needed to publish only rousing stories of heroism in the Australian papers. Praising another country's troops

– even when they were also fighting for the motherland, as England was known – would be counterproductive. Yet the same stories of extraordinary courage were in English newspapers. The Australians' extreme determination and bravery was mentioned in the British parliament. Some stories of heroism certainly were concocted for the public back home. But I can't see eyewitness war correspondent and military historian Charles Bean constructing falsehoods, or even embellishing reality, though he presumably chose not to mention incidents of cowardice or confusion, as well as the large medical list of syphilis and gonorrhoea cases too, contracted perhaps from visiting Egyptian brothels. Nor did Bean dwell on the fact that three out of four men hospitalised at Gallipoli were treated not for wounds sustained in battle but for the Gallipoli trots, a form of acute dysentery spread by flies, rats and infected drinking water and probably from bathing in a sea full of blood and faeces. Bean was a man of dedication and integrity who undoubtedly chose which parts of the story he wanted to tell. But the bits he did put in his reports or histories, by all accounts, would be true.

Time and again, Bean recounts incidents where he claims the Anzacs in particular showed exceptional gallantry, as with his description of the stretcher-bearers. According to Bean, it was an unvarying point of honour with the Australian stretcher-bearers to always answer the call for assistance if a man was wounded. As Bean stated, the spot where a man had just been wounded by an exploding shell was the most dangerous position of all to go to as a second shell would usually follow within seconds before the gun was moved again. But Bean reported that the call was always immediately answered by two men.

The statistics perhaps best support the claims of courage.[9] World War 1 cost Australia more men than any other war. There were fewer than five million people in Australia at the declaration of war but 416,809 Australians enlisted for service, representing 38.7 per cent of the total male population aged between eighteen and forty-four.[10]

Sixty thousand Australian men were killed, 150,000 to 200,000 more were wounded, gassed or suffered 'shell shock' and other mental problems. At almost sixty-five per cent, the Australian casualty rate (proportionate to total embarkations) was the highest of any nation involved in the war.

Diaries, too, rarely lie. For decades most of what we knew about Gallipoli came from war historians like Bean and propagandists like E.C. Buley, who did indeed pick and mix his accounts to produce something less than the truth. Even the officers' accounts were often written weeks or months later as the men lay wounded in England, with women volunteers taking down their words so a picture of the campaign could be strung together. For security reasons it was illegal to keep a diary, and letters were censored.

Yet some men did keep diaries on thin paper hidden in their boots or folded into pockets. Now these extraordinary stories are being published or made available to researchers by their descendants, so that for the first time we can hear the whispers of the past from the men who were there.

They were not written for propaganda or publication purposes. They show that the essentials of the Gallipoli Anzac legend are true: the extraordinary courage that led to headlines across the world wondering at the Anzac bravery; the lack of respect for officers and their often stupid orders; the comradeship, the compassion and, especially, the jokes in the face of death.

Stop laughing, this is serious

It is a defining Australian characteristic, and one admired in our culture: when things are bad, we laugh about it. The worse they are, the better the joke. It is perhaps a product of a land where unexpected disasters happen often and, in 1915, where your friends and community rather than government or religious authority help out. In a disaster it helps to be respectful to the government or other authority who might assist you. If you only have your mates, it helps much more to laugh. A classic 1933 Australian cartoon by Stan Cross shows two men dangling from a tall building site, about to fall; one is clinging to the other's trousers, which are falling off. The other says: 'For gorsake, stop laughing: this is serious!'[11]

Black humour and lack of reverence for officers is part of the Anzac legend. It is likely accurate. Written evidence both of the gallows humour and irreverence comes from the various trench newspapers produced by the men in the Gallipoli campaign. *The Bran Mash* of the 4th Light Horse had only one issue handwritten in pencil and copied on two sheets of typing paper using carbon paper, but it included such gems as a piece of art captioned 'A black oblong titled "Night" by O'Keapit-Darke', and the poem 'The Trooper's Lament'. This is the first verse. You need to add the word 'bloody' into the gaps to make sense of it, and even then you may find the vernacular hard to understand. It's about a bloke who takes his horse to war, but is only paid half of what it's worth, and just as he is about to go off and get drunk with the money, his commanding officer puts him in detention.

> I come from good old Woop Woop and me monicker's Gus
> Headers
>> An' I joined the _)/4th Light … 'orse out at Broad … Meadows,
>> I brings along me own old prad, and shoves the claim in 'ot,
>> But the … vet 'e crools me pitch, an 'arf was all I got.
>> I gathers in the … cash and gets off on the spree,
>> And th' CO ups and passes me a week's C … B
> GORSTRUTH!!![12]

Funny? No, not to us, now, even if we still used slang like 'prad' or 'crools me pitch'. It's black humour, only funny if you've suffered the same.

Another trench paper, *The Dinkum Oil*, grew out of a shipboard magazine called *Snipers' Shots*. Major Thomas Blamey, the 1st Division's intelligence officer, was concerned about false rumours (known as 'furphies' after the brand on the army water carts that soldiers used to gather around to swap stories and rumours) in the trenches. He asked Bean early in June 1915 to 'get out a "furfies [sic] gazette", with these furfies so exaggerated as to laugh them out of court'. The result was *The Dinkum Oil*[13], handwritten, hand-drawn and stencilled on one side of a foolscap sheet, and lasting for fifteen issues. It may or may not have stopped inaccurate rumours, but it was full of black humour. It included ads like, 'To Let – Nice dugout on the skyline. Owner leaving for field hospital.' Other newspapers would follow in France, while copies of still others may never have made it home from Gallipoli.

One of the most telling examples of the mix of gallows humour and larrikinism is the slang that grew up in the short Gallipoli campaign. They included:

Anzac soup: a shell hole filled with water and bits of dead body.

Anzac button: a nail to hold up your trousers.

Auntie: a Turkish broomstick bomb, as in, 'Look out! Auntie's coming callin'!'

Axle grease: butter, usually rancid.

Banjo: a shovel. Playing or swinging the banjo meant digging a hole.

Bellyache: a major body wound, usually fatal: 'He got a bellyache and ended up in the stiffs' paddock.'

Body-snatcher: stretcher-bearer.

Bumbrusher: any officer's servant, from batman to those who served in the officers' mess.

Doing the Gallipoli gallop: diarrhoea

Luna Park: Cairo Hospital, named after the fun park in Melbourne.

Outed: dead, killed.

Stiffs' paddock: soldiers' graveyard.

To throw a seven: to be killed. When you play with two dice, seven is supposed to be the most frequent number called.[14]

Read any diary or collection of letters from those days and you'll find more humour: mostly laconic statement of fact (though sometimes poetic), with no self-pity, a great deal of irreverence and extraordinary and matter-of-fact courage.

The legendary lack of respect for officers is also likely to be accurate, a function of the land the men came from. Australia did, and still does (to a limited extent), have a class system, but nowhere near as integral a part of everyday life as in Britain, where a cap had to be doffed to those of a superior station, and marriage between two people of different classes was if not unthinkable then at best unlikely. Class mattered in 1915, but it mattered far less to the Australians. Nor had they had as much formal training as their English counterparts by May 1915, which included showing respect for an officer, even – or especially – when you didn't feel it. While the wealthy in Australia expected respect, many were also uncomfortably aware their parents or grandparents had been convicts, squatters or members of the notorious New South Wales Rum Corps – or even all three – with a fortune based on good luck or shady dealing, not on illustrious ancestors. Even today Australians enjoy scything down tall poppies.

The most common offence committed by Australian troops was the charge of impudence to an officer or refusal to salute. Nor did they have the spit and polish of British troops. On leave in London from the Somme in northern France, Brigadier 'Pompey' Elliott would be arrested by military police for impersonating an officer – they couldn't conceive that any officer, much less a brigadier, would look so shabby. English troops polished their boots; Australians held mock horse races and bet on rats. Both mirrored life back home: the boot blacking of a servant in a large house or farm labourer on an estate, and the bush races held wherever you could get three horsemen, or women, together.

Six-shilling tourists and the great adventure

So if they cared so little for their English superiors, why were the Anzacs there? The obvious answer is 'for their country'. But the nearest German territory to Australia was in New Guinea, and that was taken under control by the Australian forces before Gallipoli. The speeches of the time emphasise saving the motherland – England, not Australia. Even 'true dinkum' Australians spoke of England as 'home', even if neither they nor their grandparents had been born there, and they never expected to actually go there.

Politicians' speeches do not necessarily reflect the mood of those who enlisted, yet there is no doubt that Australia was electrified with patriotism, and the often-spoken desire to show the world what this new nation of Australia could do. But there was also adventure. In the first year war was even spoken of as the 'Great Adventure' until, perhaps, uncensored letters began to arrive home. European Australians were descended from adventurers – or criminals – who had crossed the world to get to the furthest habitable point from their own homes. The land itself was an adventure, its floods, droughts, fires, snow and lonely wildernesses.

From Australia it was expensive and time-consuming to travel anywhere other than New Zealand, so this was probably the only chance most volunteers had to see the world. Australian was a land of born travellers, trapped on an island nation. In many case the vast distances meant that labouring men or farmers would never even get to the nearest large town, much less the capital city.

Now they could – and they would be paid six shillings a day to do so. They even had a phrase for it in 1915: the six-shilling tourists.

And then they faced the enemy.

The verdict of hindsight

The Gallipoli campaign failed. The British Royal Commissions reporting in 1917 and 1918 described the operations as ill-conceived and ineptly executed, with thousands of lives needlessly squandered.[15]

Were the British authorities who had engineered it more incompetent than was usual for the time? Might the campaign have been won if the Turks had a leader less determined than Mustafa Kemal? Was calling Russia into the war with the promise of hunks of the Ottoman Empire victory enough?

If the Gallipoli campaign had been successful it might have been seen as a triumph of strategy. And, yes, mistakes led to the death of thousands, but this was nothing unusual in the wars of that time: troops were known as cannon fodder. How much was true ineptitude and how much the accepted tactics of the time on both sides is still a matter of intense debate.

Gallipoli still matters. The images of the soldiers at Gallipoli reflected the way Australians thought about themselves then: tough, determined, loyal. Just as you might talk of 'the spirit of the bushman' you'd also talk of 'the spirit of Gallipoli', and your listener would know what you meant: determination, self-sacrifice, larrikin humour and courage. The images of Gallipoli are used by politicians, filmmakers, songwriters and novelists (of whom I'm one).

No, it's not the whole truth. Nor is it 'nothing but the truth'. Filmmakers and novelists have added much to the image that is now taken as history. But truth is there. Australia gave Gallipoli strong, fit

The battle of Lone Pine

The battlefield of Lone Pine was called after the lone Turkish pine tree that stood there at the start of the fighting. The battle plan was only to divert the Turks away from the real aim being undertaken by a separate unit: to capture the ridge of Sari Bair and Chunuk Bair, one of the higher points along that ridge.

The Turkish position was so strong at Lone Pine that none of the Turks expected an attack there. It seemed an insane place to attack – there would be incredible loss of life. The commander of the Australian 1st Division, General Walker, tried to argue against it, but General Sir Ian Hamilton, the British commander, insisted that the attack go ahead.

Walker did his best. There were ninety-one metres between the Allied trenches and the Turkish trenches, the latter about 200 metres wide. Walker ordered the men to dig tunnels till they were only about thirty-five metres from the Turkish positions. Then for three days the Turkish trenches were bombarded with rockets and gunfire to give cover to soldiers who ran through the smoke and confusion to cut much of the barbed wire between the trenches.

Near dusk on 6 August the Australian 1st Infantry Brigade attacked, half of the men coming up through the underground tunnels and half forcing their way through the barbed wire. But the Turkish

men, used to working and fighting together under tough conditions, who did their best, and stuck it out. Gallipoli gave us back an enduring legend.

Our second Anzac legend: The Kokoda koalas who tried to save Australia

In World War 2 Australia's geography made us a target: a thinly populated land with the resources Japan desperately needed to win against the United States and control the Pacific region. Geography may also have saved us: the jungles and mountains of New Guinea to our north, making lines of supply and command almost impossible for the Japanese army.

trenches had thick pine logs on top of them. Some of the logs were set alight, some bombed, some bayoneted into fragments.

The Australians managed to take part of the Turkish line in the first couple of hours. But for six days after that there was a furious battle, mostly hand-to-hand fighting in the trenches or with grenades, as the Turks tried to take the few metres back. The Australians even used walls of dead bodies as barricades.

Once the Allied commanders saw that Turkish territory had been taken instead of the fighting just being a diversion, reinforcements were sent to keep it. It was a victory – of sorts. About a hundred metres of land had been taken from the Turks, but only for a short while as Lone Pine, too, was deserted by the Allied evacuation. But the determination of the Anzac forces created a legend from disaster.

That lone tree was the only remaining pine of a group that were cut down by the Turks, the timber and branches used to reinforce their trenches. After the battle a couple of Australian soldiers retrieved a few pine cones from the shattered branches and brought them back to Australia. Seedlings were grown from these cones and distributed to be planted as memorials. Lone Pine trees have been planted in parks, schools and people's private gardens in Australia, New Zealand and at Gallipoli itself to commemorate those who died in the battle and the campaign in general.[16]

Australia's landscape, and the social conditions it had created, certainly influenced the capabilities of its soldiers at Gallipoli. But was this still the case in World War 2, and in the iconic struggles that have become known as 'Kokoda'?

The taxi driver and the tree on the wall

I met him on one of those choking Sydney days, when the exhaust fumes mingle with the smell of melted bitumen and it seems as though cars have taken over the world. As the taxi lurched to a stop at another red light, he said, 'Where you from?'

'Araluen,' I said, and waited for the inevitable next question.

Instead he said, 'Yeah, I know Araluen.'

I turned to look at him. He was small, one of those shrunk-monkey men, with a big chin and bigger nose.

'I went there after the war,' he said and I knew from his grey hair he meant World War 2. 'I reckon that valley saved my life.'

Then he told me his story.

He enlisted in the militia on his eighteenth birthday in 1942. The militia was not supposed to serve outside this country, but the Japanese were heading down to Australia and New Guinea was designated 'Australian territory'. It is often claimed that the average age of the militia boys was eighteen and a half, but many were older. They had been in reserved occupations or simply hadn't enlisted before. The militia had little training, and were desperately badly equipped. But they stood between Australia and invasion: or that, at least, is what they believed.

The enemy they faced, the Japanese army, had not had a major defeat since invading China in 1936. They had even brought down the seemingly impregnable British stronghold of Singapore and destroyed most of the United States Pacific navy in a surprise attack on Pearl Harbor. They were experienced jungle fighters, ruthless and disciplined, with expert tactics.

'I knew I was going to die,' he said. 'It wasn't just the bullets ...' The taxi swerved to avoid a semitrailer. 'It was the suddenness,' he continued. 'The enemy came out of nowhere. All you saw was green leaves and then the bloke beside you died. It was the mud and the rain and heat. It was the smell, too; of things rotting, leaves and trees and flesh, so you knew it would be you next ...'

The world narrowed till that was all that was left: death and the fear of death and the smells of things decaying, and there seemed no room in the world for anything more. 'I knew I was going to die,' he repeated. 'I knew it from the first week there.'

He didn't say, 'I was fighting for my country.' He didn't say, 'But you can't let your mates down.' He didn't say, 'If the Japs had conquered us they'd have made us slaves, as they did in other nations they had conquered.' He didn't say that his sister might have been a comfort woman, his mum working in a factory for a ration of rice.

He just said, 'We kept on going because we had to.'

Finally he was wounded, as he knew he would be. He remembered nothing about it – not the shot, not even pain, just the rifle in his hand one minute and then the next there was white light, not green shadows, and someone whispering, 'Sh, not so loud. There's a boy dying in there.'

He was in hospital. How many days had the Indigenous men they'd later call the fuzzy wuzzy angels carried him on a stretcher, unconscious, bleeding, to get to a small landing strip? How had one of those small planes that seemed to be made of cardboard and duct tape flown between the misty mountain crags into a small stretch of green and, somehow, miraculously, taken off again, and brought him and the other wounded down to Port Moresby?

He said: 'I thought, that's me they're talking about. I'm the one that's dying. And then I thought, that means I'll never go home again.

'But, you know, it didn't worry me. I thought, I'll just open my eyes once and then I'll go back to sleep again. So I opened them, and that's when I saw it.'

It was a painting on the wall beyond his bed, of a smooth green hill with a single tree, and smoky blue hills behind.

'I thought, that's home. All I have to do is live and I'll get back there. Home hadn't been real before that; it was like the jungle and the mud had killed it too. But now I knew that it was there, and I wanted to go home.'

It took three weeks before he was able to ask a nurse where the scene in the painting was.

She said, 'I don't know.' Then she said, 'I'll have a look for you but.' She turned the painting over and there was writing on the back. She said, 'It says "Araluen Valley, New South Wales".'

'That was the first thing I did when the war ended – well, one of the first things, any road. I looked up Araluen Valley and said, I'm going there. I'm going to find that bloody tree.'

'Did you find it?' I asked.

'Sure,' he said. 'It was easy. It was the tree on the hill in front of the pub. I reckon the bloke that painted it just sat on the veranda and painted away. I took my wife back there just after we were married. I took my kids back there too. It's still there, isn't it, the tree?'

'Yes,' I said. 'It's still there.'

'Haven't thought about that place in years,' he said. 'Mostly go up to the beach for holidays. You ever been to Surfers?'

'Years ago,' I said.

'I retire in three weeks,' he said. 'I reckon I'll take my grandkids to see that tree. Has it changed much, the valley?'

'No,' I said. 'A few more houses. More peach trees. It doesn't change much.'

The taxi pulled up at the airport and I got out.

Don't get me wrong about that story. He wasn't a hero, even if he had been heroic. Or was he? You need to know someone for a lot longer than a twenty-minute taxi ride to know them. He wasn't a bushie, either. He was possibly the most city person I've ever met, weaving his taxi in and out of the traffic, the radio snickering away about the pet hate topic of the week. But that tree was a symbol. He did believe that if it had never been there, he wouldn't have survived.

It was, in a way, what he'd been fighting for.

The chocolate soldiers

The 'koalas' were the young militia men who fought in New Guinea in 1942 on what is now known popularly as the Kokoda Track, most often in the news when a middle-aged man trying to walk it has a heart attack. Back then there were many such tracks through the jungle, as the Japanese headed south towards Australia, with only the koalas and a few regular soldiers, to save us.

The militia boys were also known as chocolate soldiers, or chockos. Chocolate soldiers melt in the heat of battle, although the name perhaps first came from George Bernard Shaw's play *Arms and the Man*, all glittering uniform but no courage beneath.

Koalas (the furry kind) weren't meant to be exported or shot, and nor were these young men. They were for defence at home, until things grew so desperate that they were sent to New Guinea. You had to be twenty-one to enlist in the AIF[17]; the koalas could enlist or be conscripted at eighteen and a half. The Citizen Military Force (CMF) had begun as a volunteer organisation but now young men were being conscripted into it, although many, like my father, enlisted in the militia on their eighteenth birthday rather than wait another three years before they could serve overseas.

Like Gallipoli, Kokoda has become a national legend, the young, untrained troops who delivered us from the enemy when the British army had failed. The implication is that being Australian – the rabbit potting, surfing and general bush skills – somehow created fighting men able to defeat men of far greater experience. No one doubts the young and untrained bit, but were those young men the outstanding soldiers we like to think them?

Was Australia even really at risk?

The testimony of maps

As far as Australia being at risk goes, the answer has to be an unequivocal yes, despite the opinion of the British, United States and Australian intelligence services of the time that the Japanese only wanted to capture Port Moresby to harass US supply lines. Their opinions were based on a small amount of evidence, and in the triumph of decryption of local enemy communications they may have given what they'd decoded too much weight, and taken it out of context. They also did not have access to the strategic plans of those in command in Tokyo. These are the same intelligence services that so firmly believed that Singapore would not be attacked and did not pick up on the several reports that a large Japanese air attack was heading to Pearl Harbor, where they would destroy most of the United States Pacific Fleet.

The most reliable sources of Japanese intent in 1942 are those of the Japanese commanders themselves. In an interview on 20 February 1946, Admiral Nobutake Kondo, commander of the Naval Southern Expedition Forces, stated that his primary aim was the overthrow of the British Empire. To do this the Japanese needed to do two things. The first was to conquer India, only possible if Germany could cut off British oil supplies from Iraq and Iran. Admiral Kondo unequivocally stated that the second main Japanese target was Australia.[18]

Japan lacked the United States' natural resources. Submarines and planes had a far shorter range in 1942 that they do now. Both Japan and the United States needed a safe base for the large number of troops needed in the Pacific campaigns. Australian resources, supplies and bases were vital if Japan, rather than the United States, was to control the Pacific.[19]

Not only was the Japanese invasion planned but a propaganda movie had been made showing the invasion: Japanese bombers flying over Canberra while politicians fled from Parliament House. The newsreel was even shown in Tokyo, the distributors presumably unaware that the invasion hadn't happened on schedule. The dates had been set back, then further back, as their troops faced an unexpected quality of opposition.

If the Japanese documents are so clear, why has the misapprehension arisen? Partly this is because Japanese army commanders on the ground whose communications had been captured by the Allied intelligence services were far less optimistic than the naval commanders and generals back in Japan. The military officials back in Japan believed their own propaganda: invincible forces that would keep going no matter what. It was a crime punishable by death to even hint that victory was not inevitable, and battles being won. The commanders on the ground in New Guinea knew how badly equipped and supplied their forces were. Japan had conquered several countries already with relatively poor supply lines, relying on food, ammunition, weapons and slave labour from the country they occupied. Here in the New Guinea jungle, the men were starving, reduced to three-quarters of a pint of rice a day, eating sticks and leaves and even resorting to cannibalism, eating the limbs of dead enemies.[20]

Even when the generals back in Japan decided not to pursue the campaign to Port Moresby, much less Australia, the communications lines in New Guinea were so poor that many Japanese troops weren't informed of it.

Even reading the public government documents of the time can give a misleading impression. The immensity of the danger was carefully downplayed. The government wanted to keep the population alert and working for the war effort, but they didn't want to spread panic. My uncle, Ron Edwards, for example, was serving in the AMF in Darwin during the bombings, but it wasn't until fifty years later that my mother learnt of the true devastation from the bombings. And it was also fifty years until I was able to read the newly released papers that told the true degree of the submarine threat and damage to shipping along the east coast of Australia.

But the most vital evidence can be obtained simply by looking at a map of the Pacific showing the Japanese advance down towards Australia: a small nation with few national resources run by a military elite heads to large, lightly populated country, with major reserves of coal and iron ore, dockyards, factories, and the skilled workers to run them. New Guinea was simply a pathway to Australia. Port Moresby alone was not worth the massive Japanese commitment in New Guinea.

Yes, in early 1942 Australia was the target of the Japanese southern advance. But by the time the militia boys met the Japanese forces in battle, the Japanese lines were overstretched, the men weak and demoralised. The real enemy for both sides was the terrain. With better (though not good) supply lines, and eventually greater numbers, the Allies, including the Australians, were better able to survive the jungle.

To some extent, the balance between real and perceived danger is irrelevant. The koala boys believed they were fighting to save their country from the threat of immediate invasion. Despite the government censorship, which meant that most Australians never knew the extent of Japanese air raids on Australian soil and the toll that Japanese and German submarines and ships were taking on our own shipping, Australians of the time believed it, too.

Desperation

Things looked bad for Australia in 1942. British Prime Minister Winston Churchill had told Australian Prime Minister John Curtin that Singapore would stop the Japanese advance to Australia.[21]

He lied. Churchill had already written off the defence of Singapore, knowing that it lacked tanks, artillery, adequate air defences and modern fighter planes. Churchill was really only concerned with defending British-controlled Burma and India in the Asia–Pacific region. He wanted the Australian troops serving in the Middle East to deploy to Burma.

Curtin insisted the AIF return to defend Australia against the Japanese.[22] Until they returned the militia had to fill the gap, as Japanese submarines patrolled the Australian coastline, large subs that could launch midget submarines, and spotter planes flew across coastal towns and even Sydney.

The outlook was grim. Far more colliers and other ships had been sunk by the Japanese than the Australian government admitted to the general population. Where possible everything had to be sent by land. There was no modern network of highways: to get from Sydney to Brisbane in 1942 you travelled along narrow gravel roads, and waited for a ferry to cross rivers. The sea surrounding us was no longer ours. Even in a land of abundant food and firewood, there were massive shortages because of the lack of efficient ways to transport them, especially with so many men in the armed forces. Children collected spare saucepans or any spare metal for the war effort. The Prime Minister exhorted school children to grow their own vegetables, even giving helpful hints about growing tomatoes, a crop that could survive heat and lack of watering. Women volunteered their spare hours to make camouflage nets.

And then the bombs began to drop. On 19 February 1942, fifty-four land-based bombers and approximately 188 attack aircraft were launched from four Japanese aircraft carriers in the Timor Sea heading for Darwin. The first attack began just before 10 a.m. and lasted forty minutes. Bombs fell across the town and harbour; dive-bombers attacked ships, the aerodromes and the hospital. The second attack began an hour later. For twenty-five minutes the Royal Australian Air Force base at Parap was bombed.

The two attacks killed at least 243 people and between three and four hundred were wounded, although the government insisted that only seventeen had been killed to try to stem the panic.[23] About half of Darwin's population fled south towards the Adelaide River and the train station, desperate to go further south to safety. Many servicemen deserted, too, racing south in what would be later known as 'The Adelaide River Stakes'. The empty houses and buildings were looted by some who remained.

The government planned mass evacuations of civilians from northern Australia down to Charters Towers inland of Townsville if the Japanese landed, accompanied by a 'scorched earth' policy – everything that might be useful to the Japanese was to be destroyed as people left. Townsville was only to be defended by its local brigade, but Brisbane was to be defended against all attacks.

The bombings continued, Darwin being hit sixty-four times.[24] On 3 March, two weeks after the first attack on Darwin, seventy people were killed and twenty-four aircraft destroyed at Broome in Western Australia, with Wyndham bombed too. On 20 March, the bombers returned to Broome and Derby. Horn Island in the Torres Strait was first bombed on 14 March 1942, with more raids after that.

In May, midget submarines launched from a larger 'mother' submarine outside the Heads attacked Sydney Harbour. Japanese spotter planes had been seen over Sydney and along the east coast, launched from the Japanese submarines that patrolled the coast and targeted Australian shipping vessels. Townsville, the site of Australia's most important air base, was bombed three times in late July 1942. On 30 July a single bomb was dropped near a house in Cairns.

There had been thirty-three bomb attacks altogether, killing about nine hundred people. Australia lost seventy-seven desperately needed aircraft and ships, too.[25]

Australia expects invasion

Australia – and Australians – were seriously preparing for invasion, even while the government tried to downplay the actual attacks.

Road signs had been taken down. From 1940 to 1942, petrol, sugar, butter and meat were rationed.[26] Buildings were sandbagged and air-raid shelters dug, not just on the coast of Queensland, Western Australia and the Northern Territory but in Sydney and along the New South Wales south coast too. Maps and signposts vanished. Many beaches were fenced off with barbed wire and roads leading inland from the coast were defended with mines, with army and unofficial and semi-official and volunteer observers day and night, watching for invasion.

We wouldn't give in. Children were to be evacuated from areas in imminent danger of enemy occupation to Alice Springs, where vast amounts of food were transported and stored. The rest of the population was expected to become resistance fighters. Local unofficial 'people's army' militias were formed, with old weapons usually used for rabbit shooting. Pamphlets and books explained how to make homemade bombs. Even Mum could make a stand, with a bayonet made from a broom and a carving knife.

Girl Guides and Brownies as young as seven studied semaphore, so that messages could be passed on if the phone lines were down or radio stations taken, and practised hiding behind hedges to eavesdrop on the enemy.[27]

Land prices plummeted in Sydney, especially for harbourfront properties. Many fled to the Blue Mountains, and children were sent to stay with relatives inland. The Australian public of the time were in no doubt that an invasion was imminent.

'Oh, how ridiculous,' said my mother, Val French, reading a revised history claiming that Australia had been in no immediate danger. She had sheltered her younger brother under the stairs as the midget submarine shelled near their home in Sydney. 'We all drilled for invasion. Every schoolchild had to wear a box on a cord around our necks, holding everything we needed for an air raid. We weren't allowed to take that blooming cord off. All windows had to be taped in case of bombing. The school I went to was closed, because it was too near the harbour, and vulnerable to bombing from submarines or planes launched from the bigger subs. We had air-raid practice at school, at the hospital and when the sirens went the public had to find shelter, too. We knew the invasion was near.'

The Japanese advance

In March 1942, Japanese forces landed at Lae and Salamaua. In July 1942 more troops landed at Buna and Gona on the northeast coast of Papua New Guinea, only three hundred kilometres as the crow flies from Port Moresby on the southeast coast, the last port before the Australian mainland. In between Port Moresby and Buna and Gona was the Owen Stanley Range, steep, wet jungle mountains, with only a few foot tracks across them, far too steep for vehicles. The Kokoda Track was one of these.

In August more Japanese reinforcements landed at Milne Bay on the southeastern tip. Australia had only two militia brigades stationed in Port Moresby, to defend both the port and prevent the Japanese from continuing their sweep down into Australia.

Australian General Blamey and American General MacArthur assumed (incorrectly at the time) there was no immediate intention of invading Australia. Military intelligence led the commanders to once again leave a vital area (temporarily) poorly defended. The young Australian militia boys and a few trained servicemen were on their own.

Could a young, untrained and poorly armed militia – conscripts mostly, not volunteers – stop experienced jungle fighters in the hell that would become the New Guinea battlefields?

A complex victory

The Japanese were certainly stopped. How much of that was due to the militia boys will remain a matter of debate, depending on which sources the history is taken from. A large part of the Allied victory was due to the Japanese lack of supply lines and reinforcements. The militia's main achievement was probably in slowing down the advance till reinforcements arrived, and the Japanese strategy was revised as they realised that the expected swift victory over the United States was not going to happen.

Even though US and British intelligence reports suggesting that Japan did not intend to invade Australia were initially incorrect, they ended up being right. In an emergency session, the Japanese authorities in Tokyo decided that they could not support fronts in both New Guinea and at Guadalcanal. They had seriously underestimated the United States' ability to mobilise after Japan had destroyed most of their navy in the surprise attack on Pearl Harbor.

The Japanese forces in New Guinea would get no more reinforcements. General Horii, the commander on the ground in New Guinea, was ordered to withdraw his troops along the Kokoda Track until the issue at Guadalcanal was decided, even though the Japanese were close enough to see the lights of Port Moresby. The invasion of Australia was off the agenda.

The achievements of Australia's 39th Battalion, in particular, given the terrain, the overwhelming odds and their lack of formal training, were extraordinary, but they had at least some supplies and reinforcements. By the time they began their retreat the Japanese had none.

In terms of the whole PNG campaign, the Allies committed about 30,000 men, although at any one stage fewer than 3500 were probably fighting and the Australians were at many stages outnumbered. By comparison, a total of 13,500 Japanese were ultimately landed in Papua for the duration of the campaign, of whom only 5000 made it back to Buna on the north coast. The Japanese troops had a saying: 'Java is heaven, Burma is hell, but you never come back alive from New Guinea.'[28]

Invincible koalas?

The legend of the invincible 'koala boys' implies that you could take good, tough Aussies and expect them to become instant soldiers. But this wasn't what happened.

In March 2007 General Peter Cosgrove, former chief of the Australian Defence Forces, addressed a Sydney fundraising dinner for the Kokoda Track Foundation, a not-for-profit organisation seeking to repay the help given to Australian soldiers by Papua New Guineans in World War 2. He stated that despite the work of revisionist historians, the nation knew that Kokoda was the stuff of survival. Those young men, he said, untrained, should have fragmented in their first few days of action. He spoke of the innate guts of the young soldiers, and the leadership of Lieutenant Colonel Ralph Honner in particular, who took untrained, untested men and led them not to victory but to 'stubborn and ceaseless resistance, tenaciously holding on to successive crags and ridges until finally reinforced'.[29]

But there are also accounts of confusion and cowardice among other units, as well as extraordinary heroism and achievement. There were major discipline problems where men spread out in panic instead of

The Kokoda Track

Most Australians have only heard of the Kokoda Track in Papua New Guinea, but there were many tracks used and fought over in 1942.

It was goldminers in the 1890s who originally walked the Kokoda Track as they travelled north from Port Moresby to the goldfields of Yodda and Kokoda. Then it became the mail route over the Owen Stanley Range, starting from McDonald's Corner, up to the Myola Swamp and on to Kokoda.

After walking the track for an hour or so the soldiers were faced with the Golden Stairs, two thousand timber steps cut by engineers into the mountainside. From the Uberi section of track they rise four hundred metres in two kilometres before dropping five hundred metres, then climbing another seven hundred metres in the last two and a half kilometres.

Men slid and fell, breaking ankles, knees, collarbones; they reached the top of one mountain to see another, and then another or, even worse, a bank of cloud and fog that could hide anything – including Japanese planes. Climbing down the slopes was even more dangerous than climbing up.

Even today, with no enemy shooting at you, dropping bombs or grenades, climbing down a muddy slope is hard and dangerous for anyone who isn't fit and experienced. There is a skill to walking down muddy slopes: depending on terrain, you splay your feet and body from side to side, a bit like penguins on the ice, or go sideways, changing sides to use different sets of muscles. You learn the art of the 'controlled slide'. You can use sticks to help keep your balance, but if you fall the stick can be lethal, poking out your eye or piercing your body. Presumably the men worked this out, eventually. Injuries in mud – especially mud mixed with faeces and blood – are soon infected. All who used the tracks – Japanese, Papuan and Australian – would be bruised, battered and exhausted at the end of each day.

staying with their unit. In some cases, poor leadership led to continued resentment. The koalas arguably had excellent military potential, but you need superb leadership to turn raw recruits into effective soldiers. The leadership was often far from superb.

This does not diminish the heroism or achievements of the men who volunteered to serve in New Guinea. In 1942 no army had managed to hold back Japan's inexorable advance, and it seemed impossible that any should. Even though at first the Australian and Papuan forces too were beaten back, it was in relatively planned stages, not a rout like the campaigns in Crete, Singapore and Malaysia.

It was not like any warfare Australian soldiers had seen, or trained for. Infantry – foot soldiers – were used to being supported by tanks, aircraft and heavy artillery. One group would move forward while the one behind covered them, firing at the enemy with artillery, submachine guns and grenades. In World War 1 – and in other theatres of war in World War 2 – long sweeps of solders advanced, taking new territory. Not in New Guinea.

Apart from the major battles, much of the fighting and plain survival in New Guinea was undertaken without generals or commanding officers, small groups of young men fighting hand-to-hand with the enemy, whether it be Japanese or jungle.

In the thick New Guinea bush, on slopes you had to scramble up, hauling on vegetation so you didn't fall back into the mud, the enemy could be two metres away in the green and you wouldn't see them. An army might be half a kilometre away, hidden in the cloud, fog or rain. The best visibility was only twenty to fifty metres, and often far less, so conventional tactics of the time were useless. Reconnaissance was almost, though not quite, impossible (some men would perform miracles, hunting out the enemy). But communication and leadership was almost impossible too. Company and platoon commanders often could not even see their own men, much less communicate with each other or with headquarters.[30]

The soldiers adapted, fast. Groups of four to six men crept through the jungle. A scout might locate a Japanese trench. Part of the group would fire on them while the others went in fast and low to try to lob grenades into the trench, either killing the occupants or forcing them out to die in rifle fire or to surrender. It was a series of tiny battles, fought by small, close-knit groups.

Conditions were appalling. As at Gallipoli, bullets were only one of the hazards: add to them typhus, malaria, hookworm, dysentery, vomiting, diarrhoea, pneumonia from the cold of the high mountains ... The men were dressed in camouflage for the desert, sandy khaki colours that were all too obvious in the jungle, with thin shirts and shorts that allowed leeches to cluster on their legs and creep up their body, eventually dropping to the ground satiated and swollen with blood.[31]

They were offered no protection from the cold of the mountains, nor the tropical rain. The entire force of 553 at Deniki had seventy blankets between them and no waterproof ground sheets. Their uniforms rotted; so did their boots and feet. Ulcers swelled on arms and legs, or where cloth chafed at their knees. Each man had to carry at least eighteen kilograms plus their rifles, but most carried far more. Their boots were not made for mud and moss – the Papuans' bare feet served them far better.

The rations of biscuits, bully beef, chocolate, tea and sugar were spoiled by heat, rain and rodents. Later, tinned fruit, dried potatoes, sausages, vegetables, jam, butter, beans and dehydrated mutton both survived better and provided better nutrition. The lack of planes and airstrips, and tracks that were only barely passable at best, made supplying the troops a nightmare. Nor were the Papuan carriers able to bring in stores: it would take them eight days to reach the troops, and one man in that country could only really carry enough food to feed himself for eight days. Most rations were dropped by what were known as the 'biscuit bombers' – small planes flying through clouds and crags to drop a hundred kilograms of ration packs.[32]

Reading the despatches, memoirs and letters of these men you are struck by two overwhelming themes: you do not let your mates down, even if it means your death; and you do not let your country down, even though you know your death may be inevitable.[33]

The New Guinea campaign could be seen as a collection of stories of heroism: Private Charlie McCallum, with a Bren gun in one hand and a Tommy gun in the other, covered the withdrawal of 12th Platoon.

When his commanding officer was killed and his sergeant badly wounded, Corporal Lindsay Bear took command as the Japanese began to break through the Australian lines, potentially taking the whole battalion. Corporal Bear manned a Bren gun and held them off until he was too weak from loss of blood. Fainting, he passed the gun to the man next to him, Private Bruce Kingsbury. Kingsbury stood, the Bren gun on his hip, then charged the Japanese, firing from the hip, as the enemy machine-gun fire rained around him – and through him. He cleared a path of a hundred metres before he died, creating enough time and space for the battalion to retrieve their position and beat the Japanese back. Kingsbury was posthumously awarded the Victoria Cross.[34]

John French (no relation, although an uncle with the same name did serve in New Guinea) was also to win the Victoria Cross when with the 2/9th Battalion in August 1942 their company came across three Japanese machine-gun posts. John French ordered his men to take cover. He lost his life while single-handedly taking the first two Japanese posts with hand grenades.

Medical officer Tom Fletcher volunteered to stay with seven wounded while another forty-two men stranded behind enemy lines tried to get back to their own forces. When rescue finally arrived, all eight were dead. Tom Fletcher could have fled, saving himself. He didn't.[35]

From city boys to fighters

As with the Anzacs at Gallipoli, there is some truth to the long-held popular belief that the Australian lifestyle made these boys not necessarily good soldiers but good military potential. Unlike the Australian Anzacs at Gallipoli, the militia boys of World War 2 had already been cadets at school, spending at least one afternoon a week and usually one weekend a month learning how to drill, fire and clean weapons, put up tents, follow orders and understand the basics of army discipline.[36]

These militia had also grown up in the Great Depression, when in some areas one in four men were unemployed. (There are no statistics on the percentage of women breadwinners unemployed.) There were no unemployment benefits, only 'susso' rations. In Australia, the Depression was survivable if you worked together, building shanties or at least a closed-in veranda at a relative's, and sharing vegetable plots. As Depression boys, many had gone on the road from as young as twelve looking for work. Like the Gallipoli veterans, these men had also potted rabbits to feed their families.

Even city boys from Sydney and Melbourne spent their high-school holidays lugging bales of hay, dossing down each night in the farmer's shed. They fought bushfires together, especially from 1939 to 1942 when the older bushfire brigade men were serving overseas, and boys as young as twelve were expected to cycle to the fire shed at the first sign of smoke. They were competitive in their sports and intensely physical in a way that any post-1950s generation can't understand.

The men of the militia were used to hardship in a land of long distances and bad roads, few phones or fridges, and where local communities created makeshift hospitals during polio or diphtheria epidemics. When I remember the men of my early childhood – every one of them a veteran – they seemed to exist in groups, whether it was for sport or some community project. In the days before social services, TV and computers, Australian society functioned more in larger units.

And they were still larrikins. When you read the letters from the men in New Guinea, like 39th Battalion member Alan Sullivan, they tell of pranks, not valour: hiking up the Laloki River with his mates, swimming nude near a Catholic girl's mission school, then hiking over to what turned out to be a nunnery dressed only in his shorts and getting a thorough ticking off by the priest. It is telling that despite serving with eight units in World War 2 and experiencing many battles, Alan Sullivan wrote of skylarking, not heroism and battles. He also stated that of all the units he was attached to, none could possibly compare with the 39th, especially in comradeship.[37]

I knew several of the New Guinea pilots, too. They were mostly from a wealthier middle- or upper-class background; you had to be reasonably well off to afford lessons and access to a plane, plus be able to afford the leisure time to fly. To understand their achievement in New Guinea you need to know the combination of larrikinism, skill and offhand courage with which these men flew in the 1920s and 1930s, gaining the experience that would enable them to do almost impossible flights through the mountains of the New Guinea highlands, landing in clearings rather than on well-prepared strips and dropping supplies even with wild headwinds.

Most pilots came from rural areas, or lived near an airport and were fascinated with all things technical. Flying was both a young man's sport and a way of getting supplies to remote areas. Passengers told hair-raising tales of taking off from wheatfields, eventually carrying what seemed like half the crop with them. The airmen landed in stock-filled paddocks, assuming that the noise would scare the cows, sheep or roos away. They flew without air-traffic controllers, reckoning via landmarks below, or compass bearings, or by moon and stars.

They dropped supplies at mountainous places like Binnabura in southeast Queensland, or Ben Lomond in Tasmania. One pilot told me how they would choose a windy day, fly into the headwind, then slow down to just above stalling speed and open the back to shove out supplies or building materials. The headwind was essential as it allowed the plane to be almost stationary, an awe-inspiring flying for the time. The land created superb pilots, and the air force relied upon their expertise.

If you have a mate, you might survive

Mateship is perhaps the strongest of Australian clichés. Other cultures play sport together and hunt together, but they don't put the same weight on the word 'mate'. Mate is something more, and less, than 'brother' or 'comrade'.

In World War 2, in the horrors of the Japanese prison camps, the Australians boasted that no Australian ever died alone. With a few exceptions – including one officer who returned fatter and with his uniform intact – officers shared the privations of their men. In the 1990s, collecting oral history from the men who had survived these camps and trying to find a common link between who survived and who did not, I was told time after time, 'If you had a mate, you lived.' If you had a mate, they'd bring you food and water when you had dysentery. A mate would talk to you when you were down, when you thought that you'd die here in the alien jungle. A mate would get you through. Next day, perhaps, you'd get them through instead.[38]

Over 60,000 years the land of Australia forged a culture of cooperation. If you didn't cooperate – if you didn't live with a fierce concept of consensus – you died. European Australians had been on the continent for less than two hundred years at the times of Gallipoli and Kokoda, but it is that same force that would create the concept of 'mate'.

The men on the tracks near Kokoda were ostensibly fighting for their country. I suspect, in the day-to-day operations, they were mostly fighting for their mates. If you did less than you were capable of, your mates would die.

So they kept going.

CHAPTER 14

A land of flooding rain

The rain came, soft as a whisper, in the late afternoon of 2 June 1852.[1] By evening it fell, heavy and impenetrable, on the town of Gundagai, the wattle and daub houses, the more substantial two-storey homes, the blacksmiths' forges, the harness repair shop, the grog shanties and the hotels that catered for the travellers on their way to Melbourne or Adelaide, waiting for the ferryman to take them across the river. Mud ran down to the river, carrying the droppings of the horses and the mobs of sheep and cattle that had passed along the main street.

It kept on raining.

By the second week of rain Morleys Creek, an anabranch of the Murrumbidgee, had risen, a wide rush of water and debris too high to get across. The river was rising too.

The old black women had warned that a big flood was coming. The river and the creek were mother and daughter. Now their arms were going to close, sweeping away the town. But what did darkies know? Most in the town had been there fifteen years, or more. The river often rose, slipping up a foot or two towards the houses, nibbling at doorways. There had been a bigger flood, back in '44. There was nothing to be worried about now.

Still the rain fell, hard and cold. The river rose, its water rushing now, down to the Murray, but the rise was slow and steady. The rain must stop soon. And if it didn't, there'd be time to get away.

The rain eased, just a little, yet it was as though the river didn't know about it. When dawn broke on the morning of Wednesday, 23 June, filled with a grey cold wind, the river's flood on one side and Morleys Creek on the other had cut off Gundagai. But the rain had stopped.

The ferryman was wary, despite the blue sky that now peered through the grey. He offered everyone a free ride on his punt to the higher ground to the south of town. Most refused. The wind blew the clouds away. The people of Gundagai went to bed without the sound of rain for the first time in weeks.

The townsfolk woke on Thursday to another sound. The river had risen again, lapping through the streets, nodding at low doorways, swollen and yellow, tree trunks twisting and rolling in its tide. The ferryman still poled his punt up to the south, but the force of the water made it hard to control now. The townsfolk moved to the highest homes and to the hotel, dragging their belongings with them.

The flood kept rising the next night, black and cold. The river's roar was a constant now, the ground vibrating with the force of water. The air smelled of death and debris. All night the inhabitants of Gundagai retreated, up to second storeys and, finally, onto the roofs, hauling children on their backs, shoving dogs through windows, bringing blankets if they could, a loaf of bread, cold meat, some cheese. They waited for daylight while under them the buildings shuddered.

Dawn came as though it had never known clouds. Trees crashed and tumbled in the water, which was now two metres high. Dead animals floated by, stiff and swollen. Gundagai was a few specks in a flood lake more than a kilometre wide.

The ferryman had valiantly tried to keep up his rescue work but his punt had crashed into a tree, killing all but one passenger. The force of water was too strong for rowing boats now.

The survivors sat helplessly on rooftops, watching the swirl as a hut wall floated by and an edge of foam rose to meet them.

A lone figure appeared in a small canoe. His name was Yarri, of the Wiradjuri people. According to the *Sydney Morning Herald* report he was 'belonging to Mr Andrews'.

He belonged to no man now.

Yarri manoeuvred the tiny canoe between the clumps of debris, managing to paddle it exactly where he wanted despite the force of water, edging it against the roof so that someone could scramble down. The canoe was only big enough for one other passenger. Even then it dipped, almost below the water. But Yarri kept on paddling, weaving between the logs and bucking tables, up to the safety of the high land to the south, pausing only long enough to let his passenger scrabble up the mud to safety, digging his paddle into the flood again, heading back to town.

All day he paddled, back and forth and back and forth, rescuing children, women, men, forcing his fragile craft through flotsam, twisting in the currents of the flood.

When darkness fell on Friday night the water was still rising fast, over a metre an hour. By now the survivors had swum to the few remaining rooftops as theirs were swept away, or clung desperately onto the tree tops. But even in the darkness Yarri kept on going, one wet and shivering passenger after another.

By Saturday morning the river had peaked at six metres and was over one and a half kilometres wide. The town had vanished. All of Gundagai had been swept away except for the flour mill, and few survivors left were still clinging to the trees, battling hypothermia, exhaustion and terror as the yellow water raced around them.

Yarri still paddled, one person against the flood. This was a man with not just the skill and power to manoeuvre a bark canoe through the debris and torrent of a flood but to keep at it in darkness too. This was a man of compassion. Yarri would have been raised on tales of a dispossessed people, but he still risked his life to save the dispossessors.

On Saturday morning, Yarri was joined by another Wiradjuri man known as Jacky Jacky (almost certainly not his real name but a nickname or contraction of his name assigned to him by Europeans). Jacky Jacky wielded a slightly larger canoe that could hold more people. At least two other Wiradjuri men, one called Long Jimmy and the other unnamed, now also manoeuvred their canoes through the flood, rescuing as many as they could carry.

The four men kept paddling that day, all Saturday night and well into Sunday. By then Yarri had paddled his flimsy bark canoe for three days and two nights. It was a superhuman effort of heroism and stamina.

These men knew how to match their bodies and their strength to the flood.

Yarri rescued forty-nine people in those three days and two nights. Jacky Jacky rescued about another twenty. There seem to be no figures for those rescued by the other two men. At least eighty-three people died – it was possible to count the number of townspeople dead or missing, and the bodies recovered, but it is suspected there were many more travellers who went uncounted.

The Murrumbidgee floods every few years. You don't need much land lore to understand evidence of regular flooding – it's as easy as tracking an elephant over a bowling green. Grass and sticks lodge high in trees, tidemarks of wreckage lace around high points. Then there is the rich alluvial soil itself, laid down by flood after flood. So why build a town on land that had almost certainly been recently flooded? How had the disaster happened?

If Gundagai had been built in the last thirty years the answer would probably have been 'profit'. Fifty years ago, when I was growing up in Brisbane, no one built on creek edges, or on the sweep of land between the bends of the Brisbane River. No one built on the swamps behind Surfers Paradise either. This was land that had flooded before, and would again. But land in cities is scarce and valuable, especially river frontage. Even sandy swamp areas are drained and built on – and then they flood after the developers have moved on. Somehow, within a decade, it seemed that the flood maps had been lost. Councils no longer refused to give building permission for flood-prone land.

But back in 1840 there was a choice of land around the river ford where Gundagai was built, including the high ground of what is now Mount Parnassus. Why risk a flood?

The answer is water, and a degree of European arrogance and ignorance.

Water's blessing and water's curse

Gundagai's town plan was laid out in between 1831 and 1838. It was gazetted as a town in 1840, fertile land on the rich Murrumbidgee River flats, good for growing the grass that would be sold as hay to travellers, or for vegetables and gardens.

These days, cheap and flexible plastic and PVC piping as well as reliable pumps mean that it's relatively easy to get water from a river or creek to a house, hotel or farm. Yet as recently as the 1960s I remember the labour of hefting great metal pipes and the challenge of screwing or welding them together.

But back in 1840 the only cheap (though labour-intensive) method of getting water was to dig a water race, a channel dug into the ground that directed water from a high point on a creek or river to a lower point. Gullies would be crossed with pipes of hollowed logs, or even bark. (One of these built in the 1850s begins on our property and its remnants wind more than three kilometres around the hills down the valley.)

But that means that the end point of the water must be both downhill and downstream. Other landowners would fetch water in buckets, tempting them to be as close to the river as possible. And, of course, there was that good alluvial soil. Even if the hotel owners didn't grow crops, they needed areas of good grass for travellers' horses and bullocks.

And floods cleared the land, too. Those lovely river flats were relatively free of large trees, ready to clear to build or farm. It's likely the track towards Melbourne from Gundagai followed the course of the river not just as an easy way of navigating across unknown land (for tens of thousands of years humans have used rivers as easily identified routes) but also because those flood-swept river banks may have been easier to make a track along for bullock trains than in the more heavily timbered country above.

Flood warnings to the strangers on the river

There are references to white settlers being warned by the local Wiradjuri people back in the 1830s that they were building on a dangerous place. But new settlers hadn't grown up with a tradition of understanding this land.

Some, perhaps, might know land lore from Britain – how thistles could indicate a fertile paddock; red sky at night, shepherd's delight – but they didn't know this land. If they had noticed the evidence of past floods they'd probably have assumed that they'd have warning, as rain fell day after day and the river began to rise. They might lose their buildings, but the shanties of that time were easily and quickly rebuilt from local materials, stringybark roof and wattle and daub walls. The buildings near the river had lofts or a second storey, where people could easily scramble out of the reach of the water with some of their goods. There would be plenty of time for families and even horses and stock to get to high ground. It was worth the inconvenience of rebuilding or repairing flood damage to have fresh water close by.

But the Murrumbidgee doesn't flood like one of the relatively short English rivers. The Murrumbidgee river system is 1500 kilometres long, with a large hilly to mountainous catchment upstream. The floodwaters of the Murray and Darling systems can take months for the water to come down the channels. Heavy rain upstream of Gundagai can create a wall of water, or, if the rain eases and then returns, several walls of water.

In Gundagai's early days the Murrumbidgee flooded every few years. Travellers were stranded for a week or so till the water went down, but the floods never rose more than about half a metre. A larger flood hit in 1844, rising to a metre and forcing people up onto the roofs. Some voices urged moving the town to higher ground.

But in those days when travel was by horse, bullock or feet, the town had to stay clustered around the school, store, saddler, dentist, wheelwright, carpenters' workshops and hotels. Their owners stayed – and so did the rest of the town.

In the years after the 1852 flood Gundagai was moved to a safer spot. Yarri and Jacky Jacky were given bronze medallions to wear about their necks and were entitled, it was said, to demand sixpences from everyone in Gundagai. There is also a fine gravestone in the Gundagai cemetery that honours Yarri and one of the local reserves is called Yarri Park in his honour.

If this seems a trifling reward for such efforts, it's worth remembering that many foot soldier veterans of the Battle of Waterloo in 1814 and in Crimea a little more than a decade later ended up begging on the street. Officers, on the other hand, were granted land, pensions and their descendants even given military scholarships in perpetuity. The

British Empire was not a place of social equality. Nor was it a place where Indigenous expertise was respected.

Predicting a flood in that particular month didn't need much skill, not if you had experience of rain depressions like that. But predicting the severity of that particular flood, and that it would come in a few weeks' time and be high enough to sweep the town away, required a deeper knowledge.

Indigenous predictive ability

It is likely that the elders did know exactly when and how and why the flood would happen. They knew their land well.

Almost from the first European settlements in Australia there are records of Indigenous people giving colonists accurate warning that devastating floods were coming. In late February and early March 1799, settlers along the Hawkesbury were puzzled by yells and gestures from the Bidjigal people. The settlers and the Bidjigal were almost in a state of war – any Bidjigal coming near a farmhouse was in danger of being shot. Yet they still appeared, desperately trying to get their message across.

On 3 March the flood arrived, turning the farmland along the river into an inland sea, with only a few roofs and hills visible above the swirling water. Men clinging to rooftops fired their muskets to tell the rowboats where they were.

In 1806, according to the *Sydney Gazette and Advertiser* of 27 March, the Hawkesbury flooding was even worse, rising over twelve feet (roughly four metres). Nor had the settlers changed where they lived or how they farmed to accommodate the threat. They lived with 'a false sense of security which many had imbibed, from the supposed confidence that there would never be another heavy flood in the main river, though without assigning any cause for such an idea'.

Australia is a land of climatic extremes. Our valley has an average of a thousand millimetres of rainfall per annum, but the actual rainfall has usually been far above or far below that 'average'. In 2003 we had a ten-month period with only 10.5 millimetres of rain, as well as bushfire winds and temperatures above forty degrees for most of three months, even reaching fifty-six degrees one day. We have had 584 millimetres of rain fall in a single day, more than 250 millimetres in an hour. Years like the one in which I write this with neither drought nor flood (at our end of the valley, at least) are the welcome exception.

Our society has inhabited this land for more than two hundred years, yet the arrival of a flood – in the same places that have had floods irregularly but frequently – still takes both planners and bureaucracy by surprise.

Queensland, 1974

The radio had talked of the river rising in Brisbane all day. At last, about 6 p.m., I called to check that my family was okay. In those days you still needed to go through an operator for an interstate call.

The operator put me through to my mother's house. My younger brothers and sister were fine, the house well above flood level. The operator called my father's house, but there was no answer.

I was about to hang up when she whispered, 'Would you mind keeping talking? The water is rising all around our feet and I'm scared.' She hesitated, then added, 'I'm new, and the other women are just going on as though nothing is happening. They say we need to keep the phones working as long as we can. I don't want them to see me cry.'

We kept on talking as the water rose at the telephone exchange. When it reached her knees she climbed up onto the bench – I suppose it was a bench, for I only heard what she described that night.

'It's black,' she said 'I didn't know water could be so black. It's swirling in through the door.'

She lived with her mum and dad. No, she hadn't rung them. She didn't want them to worry.

At last she said, 'There's a rowing boat. They're taking the women near the door first.' And then, 'It's nearly up to the bench now.'

Half an hour later she said, 'They're taking me. Thank you. Goodbye.' The phone went dead.

I checked the newspaper the next day. All the telephone operators had survived.

I suspect the telephonist remembers that flood. The planners chose not to.

Queensland, January 2011

The phone call came mid-afternoon. 'It's Ben's mum here. I just want to let him know I'm all right.'

We didn't know what she was talking about till we turned on the radio and heard about the Townsville flood. We gave our friend the message when he came in.

He called his mother back then told us her story. She was driving down to the supermarket when she saw a wall of water sweeping down the street. She did a swift U-turn, outrunning the flash flood and accelerating up the slope to home, beeping the horn and flashing her lights to try to warn others to turn back too.

They didn't. 'They kept on going into the water,' she said. 'All those cars just kept going.' She had grown up with floods. They hadn't. They didn't know the savagery of water.

How had the Townsville tragedy happened?[2]

Rain had fallen for most of the past month.[3] The ground was sodden. The water from one particularly heavy fall could no longer soak into the ground and instead rolled down the slopes, funnelling into a flash flood.

Three people died that day, including thirteen-year-old Jordan Lucas Rice. As the water rose around their stranded car, he insisted that rescuers take his little brother first. His heroic mother, Donna Maree Rice, died too.

Within the next few days, floods inundated other communities in the Lockyer Valley, Ipswich and Brisbane, and along most major river systems in Queensland, parts of New South Wales and Victoria, and then in Western Australia. The initial damage bill was about $1 billion, with total losses of perhaps $30 billion. More than forty people were killed.

Why?

It had been a wet year in 2010, a La Niña year, when the cooler water of the Pacific current usually (but not reliably) brings rains to eastern Australia. A monsoonal low had crossed from the Coral Sea on 26 December and Cyclone Tasha had brought rain as well.

Yet Queensland is hit every year by cyclones, tropical lows and storm cells bringing heavy rains. Every few years they coincide with a La Niña year, too. Why was this worse?

It wasn't. The Brisbane flood peaked at 4.46 metres in Brisbane City.[4] It was only about the tenth highest in the city's history, several metres below the 1890 flood and the two major floods in 1893, and probably lower than the 1974 flood too.

The 1974 Brisbane flood was recent enough to mean flood-prone areas could be easily identified[5], but the houses that had been flooded then were reoccupied. Worse, land that was even more flood-prone was built upon, as the demand for land and real estate prices in inner Brisbane increased. The 'vacant blocks' of my childhood along the creeks or on swampy land had been built on, and 20,000 houses in Brisbane were inundated.

I grew up in Queensland. I grew up with floods, too. Two or three times a year the street we lived on became a short-lived river. We loved it, when we were kids. We dangled our feet over the veranda as the brown water lapped round the stilts of the house. Once we formed a human chain to stop my mum's small car floating down the street. We tied it to the peach tree. The car was fine, once it dried out.

It never occurred to us to be scared of floods; every house we knew was built above flood reach, the stilts allowing the water to pass instead of banking up. We all knew which streets turned into rivers when the tail of a cyclone whipped past, flinging corrugated iron and garbage bins against the fences. 'Under the house' was a great place to play on wet days, too, or hot ones, and the air gap meant the house cooled fast at night.

Don't ever camp by a creek bed, our teachers told us, in case a flood comes down in the night; if you hear a roar, get to high ground. Never play near the creek after rain, or explore stormwater drains. (We did, but not when it was raining.)

Don't go swimming after rain, Mum said, as we kids swam on unpatrolled beaches. Don't swim at dawn or dusk – that's when the sharks are feeding. They come close to shore after storms or when it is cloudy. Don't swim in a thunderstorm in case lightning hits the water. Don't feed those dingoes or try to pat them – just ignore them, and they'll ignore you. These were just the elementary safety precautions Australians grew up with. Don't live in a house on land that floods – or if you do, make sure it's flood-proof.

The flood-prone suburbs were only part of the problem in 2011 though.[6] The water moved faster, and in different ways, than the 1974 flood. That was a preventable planning disaster, too.

As land is cleared, water runs down the slope faster with nothing to impede its progress, and the faster it flows, the less soaks in, even when the ground isn't already sodden. The more land that is covered in roads, footpaths, houses or even compacted ground in parks or paddocks, the more water will run off, too.

By 2011 there was much more cleared land than in 1974. Houses had been built on flood plains that were labelled 'never to be built on' in my childhood, but were covered by homes and gardens now. Rainfall that the land might once have soaked into the land now flowed deeper, faster. Deadly.

Dad's last story

My father was frail and living next to the river in January 2011, cut off by floodwater that wrenched half a kilometre of wood and wire and concrete boardwalk out into the river. If it had been left in the floodwaters it could have hit and knocked down the Gateway Bridge that spans the river. It may also have mown down riverside apartment houses like Dad's. Dad watched from his balcony as a tiny tugboat pushed and shoved the concrete walkway out to sea. All I could do was stay on the phone as he sat on his balcony and watched the river rise.

Dad was always a storyteller, and I can still hear his voice showing me the dramas as he watched the river, hour by hour: the police rescue boat racing after a family stranded on an out-of-control houseboat, the café that floated past, still with the tables set for lunch. It was his last story. 'I feel guilty enjoying it,' he said. 'It's better than watching TV.' Dad died not long after.

My brother provided shelter to other families whose homes were underwater. The power might have been off but the barbecue gas bottles were full, and when they rang to say they were safe I could hear laughter in the background.

My nieces cooked and cooked. Another niece, a nurse, helped care for the residents in a dementia ward, as well as those who came to the nursing home for shelter. They were cut off for about thirty-six hours, and no other nurses could get in to relieve them. They kept on going: 'It's just what you have to do.'

As the water receded, my brother and nephew joined thousands of others with mops, spades and hoses. My nieces kept cooking for the clean-up, linking via the internet with others to keep all the volunteers fed.

More than 60,000 volunteers registered that first day; probably double that number just turned up.[7] But the most extraordinary thing was that none thought of themselves as heroes. They just did what was needed – and did it with jokes and laughter, too. It was so very, very Australian, from the women in hijabs who gave out boxes of apples, to those of so many religious and ethnic heritages working side by side. Disaster can create community – as long as the survivors are in a country affluent enough for them not to have to compete for their or their family's survival. September 11 made New York a village again.

Australians respond well after natural disasters. We're used to them. We volunteer money, time, skills and even our lives, too. Australia's major disaster agencies are made up of volunteers: SES and the local bushfire brigades, supported by other volunteer organisations like the CWA, Lions, Apex and Rotary clubs. When times are tough, any Australian club – be it a football, book, RSL, writers' or office social club – may raise funds, prepare food or take in those who need shelter.

I had thought in the 1980s and 1990s that what's usually referred to as 'just doing your bit' was confined to country towns and the bush. But after the January 2003 fires, Canberra, too, behaved like a giant country town. When the Emergency Services Bureau lost power and was threatened by nearby fire by mid-morning on 18 January, Julie Derrett of ABC Radio 666 in Canberra, with her producer and the receptionist, took over coordinating the disaster, with a map spread out on the studio floor and reports phoned in from all around Canberra.

My husband and I sat in the darkness that day. Torches can't shine through air filled with ash. Above us the sky pulsed red and orange and yellow, a flame sky, as though the air itself burnt. Birds dropped, grey with ash, their wingtips burning.

How to read if it will rain

The following indications work in this valley; perhaps they work elsewhere, perhaps not.

Watch the termites. From late winter to late summer they will fly twenty-four hours before rain, dropping their wings and crawling to light – and down clothes and into your underwear too. We call them ooglies. If the ooglies fly for two or three nights in a row, there'll be more rain coming after the initial shower. (If the sap-sucking bugs fly instead, you are due for days or weeks of dry heatwave.)

Ooglies only tell you that rain is coming, not how much; a low pressure that brings a small drizzle is enough to get the ooglies flying. Ants, too, are not always accurate. They'll build tall edging to their nests to help keep out water before rain, but they can be fooled by a big low coming, too, one that brings cool weather but no rain. In a drought we get low after low, and no rain with it. The ants are fooled even more often than the weather bureau.

Reptiles are better forecasters than the termites. Snake-necked turtles head uphill ten days before a flood. I see them mostly as they cross the road from the wetlands called Jembaicumbene, but sometimes I see them here, too, leaving the creek to head upwards. I mark it in my diary: day ten, there'll be a flood. In forty years they haven't been wrong.

Look at the level of creeks and springs if you want to forecast the breaking of a drought. The level falls and falls; then overnight – it seems to happen at night – the water level rises, only a few millimetres perhaps, but at a time when it should drop. The timing isn't as precise as the snake-necked turtles' evacuation; the water can rise anywhere from forty-eight hours to three weeks before the drought breaker. Usually (not always), the longer the period of rise before the drought-breaking rain, the more rain there will be.

Want to predict a thunderstorm? Long before the bruised knees gather on the horizon the golden skinks will know. They dart across the paving, not hunting insects but running at each other till one of them retreats.

The most extraordinary reptile warning was back in 1977. The day had been hot, that breathless heat that leaves you gasping. By mid-afternoon I headed down to the creek for a swim. Then stopped. Every few metres small rolls of twigs twisted across the ground. But they weren't twigs, they were lizards, biting, gouging lizards, six to ten in each ball, chewing chunks off each other. Over on the track I saw two black snakes lunge at each other. I ran back to the shed. We have eight species of snakes here and giant goannas - I didn't want to see what they were doing too. Just over two hours later the storm hit, the wildest I have ever known. The creek rose in a wall more than two metres high, tossing boulders on its crest. It thundered down, bringing logs and more rocks with it. The reptiles were quiet.

I might have doubted what I had seen that day if I hadn't met a zoologist years later. He had been about twenty kilometres downstream on a similar day. He saw snakes, not lizards, giant coils of them, the dry riverbed wriggling as they savaged each other. He said he ran, terrified, away from the riverbed and the maddened reptiles. He had just got to his car when the thunder crashed and lightning parted the sky.

Birds know a storm is coming. When they vanish, it's best if you vanish too.

Australia was peopled by more than three hundred separate nations, each with their own traditions and language and knowledge. Now we try to apply one method of forecasting to a vast and varied land.

Don't get me wrong: I listen and watch the scientific forecasting, too. We need more of it, not less.

But we need observation too.

Julie's voice was the only link to the world, in between the hooting of the ABC emergency siren. In the ashy darkness, the gale winds howling across the valley, the fire could have been twenty kilometres away or two hundred metres.

The land shapes those who live on it. It's not the only factor, or even the most important factor, especially in these days when TV shows from the United States or Britain inculcate much of our culture and values.

But from earliest settlement – black or white – Australians made do.

Disasters like the Canberra bushfires, when our national capital showed a country town's generosity, or the 2011 Queensland floods make you realise that mateship isn't just a politician's cliché trying to weld us into a jingoistic voting majority, but something that is far beyond politics. We respond to clichés of mateship because we have felt it.

The disasters that shape both our landscapes and our culture can, to a large extent, be predicted, and even are predicted. These days there are enough experts who understand the land, not from 60,000 years of observation and handing down lore, but using scientific instruments and techniques, and catching glimpses of those 60,000 years in the process.

But as happened at Gundagai in 1852, on the Hawkesbury more than two hundred years ago and in Queensland on 31 January 1974, as floods covered about three quarters of Queensland, the disasters happened because planners ignored evidence, or because political decisions were taken ignoring their advice. Disaster planning takes money – best shut your eyes and hope you'll have moved on before the disaster comes.

Accepting that disasters happen

It is not difficult to predict most natural disasters. The hardest step in predicting them is to accept, both emotionally and intellectually, that they can happen, and that today may not always be like tomorrow. If there is one thing that history teaches you it is that things change. Sometimes slowly – tectonic-plate slowly – sometimes fast as a flash flood or a gale-driven bushfire or an earthquake. But the irreversible truth is that the land, and the climate, changes.

A possible major Christchurch earthquake had been predicted for at least a decade. There were even warnings on the Australian Foreign Affairs website of a high magnitude earthquake in the South Island of New Zealand. Christchurch was built on swampy land that was vulnerable in an earthquake. Much of that disaster was a man-made one, just like the floods.

When – not if – the sand dunes that line much of the land south of Gosford are washed away in a 'once in a hundred year' storm, and land that is below sea level reverts to the sea, most of that disaster will be man-made, too, by all of those complicit in the decision to allow people to build there. Australia is not short of land to build on (though we should not build on good farmland, either). The decisions to build houses and infrastructure on land known to have a major flood risk are made for profit, not necessity. The islanders of Tuvalu may have no choice but to build their homes where floods and rising sea levels will eat them. This is not the case here.

The front page of the *Gold Coast Bulletin* of 16 October 2012 announced that the Gold Coast Council is facing debts of more than $20 million in ratepayers' money to stop millionaires' homes being washed into the ocean. A council report stated that Palm Beach foreshores are so eroded that a major storm could damage or even destroy the beachfront homes. Storms combined with king tides have already swept away parts of some backyards.

Some recent studies show that the rate of air temperature warming may be slowing, but the global air temperature is still rising.[8] Ocean temperatures are rising even faster. The sea is rising between two and three millimetres each year as the world's ice melts, though this figure will vary across the word. Water levels in the Pacific rise in an El Niño year and fall in a La Niña, but this now slow, inexorable creep upwards will mean that in what is probably one great roar of a storm, and not in a quiet nibbling, the houses will go.

Or will they? For centuries the Netherlands has successfully used dykes to keep out the water. Now the nation is using about thirty per cent of its gross national product to survive climate change in a variety of ways. Ironically, many of the dykes are being demolished and the country is preparing itself to live with salt water instead of only barricading it out. Their innovations include houses designed to float in flood, with deep-rooted chains to keep them in place and floating boardwalks so residents are not stranded, and new public buildings with deep underground car parks that will act as reservoirs for floodwater that can be pumped out when the flood retreats. Even more importantly, new strains of crops are being trialled that will grow in salty water or saline swamps. Wind generators will float on platforms out at sea, instead of taking up land, and even towns may float on man-made islands.[9]

It is possible to create a flood-proof house or commercial building. The houses of my childhood, high on their stilts, were reasonably flood-proof in the 'gully washers' of violent summer storms, as long as they weren't in the way of logs and other debris being swept downstream. The water ran too fast to stand up in but, like the outer edges of most floods, the debris was only grass and twigs and the odd bicycle, not the giant logs or entire houses that are swept away in a river.

It wasn't till Cyclone Tracy destroyed most of Darwin and led to the evacuation of most of the city – white-faced women with hollow-eyed children waiting for the evacuation planes, seen on national TV – that an official standard for cyclone-proof housing was developed in the 1970s and, by and large, kept to.[10]

It is possible to build a fireproof house, too. CSIRO has created one prototype made of hardwood and corrugated iron that withstood all known extremes of bushfire. As I write this they are about to test another, with strawbale insulation.[11] Japanese engineers are designing villages that may be tsunami-proof.[12]

In 2012 the *Canberra Times* reported that there had finally been a decision in the case against the New South Wales Rural Fire Service, alleging that in the fires that raged through Canberra on 18 January 2003, killing four people and destroying almost five hundred homes as well as burning many properties and tens of thousands of hectares of parkland and grazing land, they had negligently failed to control the blazes when they were small enough to manage. Chief Justice Terence Higgins, however, ruled that because of protective legislation, neither the New South Wales government nor the Rural Fire Service and their employees and volunteers were liable for negligence payments. There would be no redress for what he described as an 'inadequate and defective strategy'. Chief Justice Higgins identified failures in 'strategic planning' but he did not level any blame at individuals.

In late 2002 various friends in Canberra thought I was panicking as I tried to find a safe place to leave irreplaceable documents. 'It's going to be a nightmare fire year,' I told them. And in our valley, by the time things get bad the routes away from both the valley and even the district can be more dangerous to use than staying. Two households on the edge of Canberra offered to take my documents. They were surprised when I refused. It seemed impossible to them that their own houses could be vulnerable to bushfire.

Our house didn't burn that year, though fires ringed us for much of three months. Both those who had offered to store my things evacuated as fire burned around their houses. In the event, their houses survived, although possessions were lost or smoke damaged.

The first step in surviving disaster is to accept that it can happen.

How to predict a flood

It doesn't take enormous skill or experience to predict if a flood will come within the next ten, twenty or fifty years. Look for tidelines from previous floods, where the lightest debris has left a lace-like pattern on the ground. Look for debris caught in trees or shrubs. Wind knocks debris down; flood twists it into branches and twigs. If there's debris above ground level, water has flowed there, fast, and probably higher than the debris.

Look at the ground. Good soil in Australia is most often a sign of a flood plain; our continent had few glaciers to gives us fertile grasslands like those of Europe and North America. Sand is carried by water, but it's often covered with a layer of silt, too. Layers of silt and sand are a warning. Dig down half a metre, and look for layers of sand or debris.

A flash flood can cover grassland. Look for boulders dropped where the water has carried them. Water rises from low land; it also cascades down from the heights. Even if you are above a valley floor a tide of water may roll onto you down the slope. Mostly, look at the records. Ask those who remember the land ten, twenty and fifty years ago.

CHAPTER 15

A short history of great big farming misunderstandings

Araluen, 1978

Our sheep were Tukidales, carpet wool sheep. At the time, their fleece was worth about five times that of a merino. We planned to keep a small flock for their wool, sell most of the lambs each year as 'fat lambs' and, in the meantime, they'd keep the grass and weeds down in the orchards.

We'd also have as much mutton as we wanted to eat.

When my first marriage ended, the sheep went too. I miss them, now and then, especially in spring, when the lambs' tails are wriggling up on the tableland above us as I drive into town.

But it was only when they'd left that I saw how the sheep had changed the land. We only had forty ewes, two rams, and their offspring, on 106 hectares over about two and a half years. But even that had caused local exterminations.

The yam daisies had vanished. The bettongs – small hopping marsupials – had gone too, and the shaggy nests they made in the tussocks. The sheep ate the tussocks and the bettongs moved on. (They may be returning: I've recently tripped over what might be new nests.) A few grass orchids survived, and slowly over the past two decades they are building up again. But countless other grassland species – literally, for I knew too little to even catalogue them before they were gone – vanished in those few years of sheep. Even lightly stocked and for so few years, the land lost far too many of its species.

And yet Australians are learning – relatively quickly – how to measure their impact on the land and repair much of the damage of the past two hundred years.

By the 1990s farmers and rural landowners were cooperating in small groups to repair the land, as well.

Landcare

In the early 1980s things looked grim for much of Australia beyond the capital cities, with widespread drought and fences half-covered with drifting soil. In large parts of Australia – anecdotally, for there was no official measurement – many native animals became regionally extinct. Erosion gullies spread through paddocks, becoming deeper with every rainfall. And thousands of hectares were still being cleared each day.

Then came the revolution: Landcare.

Landcare Australia Limited was formed by the Commonwealth Government on 10 October 1989 as a private non-profit company. It receives funds from governments, corporate organisations and private donations.

In the past twenty years much of the farmed land in our area has changed dramatically. Erosion gullies have been stabilised. Trees along waterways are no longer chopped down to 'stop them taking all the water' (unless they are weed species). Instead the water is slowed down with fallen logs or dams to help replenish the watertable. Vast areas of weeds have been successfully cleared (even if some have grown worse from overuse of herbicide without resowing other species before the weed seeds sprout again). Eroded streambeds have been stabilised, and millions of trees planted in shelter belts and as 'wildlife corridors' to help isolated populations to interbreed with surrounding but discrete populations.

In the 1970s here the average farmer wanted to cut down as many trees as possible. These days the average farmer – still, in many cases, the same farmers – is planting trees, accepting that not only does it raise the value of their land but also increases productivity. The Landcare movement didn't just provide money to repair damage. It encouraged farmers to look at the land, identify its problems and work out solutions, and to develop new methods to make their farming sustainable.

Never call farmers conservative. As I write this, our car industry follows much the same game plan as they did twenty years ago. But farming has been revolutionised. The narrow colonial vision of Peter Ffrench has almost vanished.

Modern farmers don't just look at their land themselves. They increasingly rely on integrated pest-control monitoring, use consultants who help them recontour their land with swales to divert water to the new tree plantations, and utilise electric fencing to micromanage their stock, reducing the impact on the fallow and allowing it time to recover. It is a long way from ideal yet, and not all farmers do this. But the change is large enough to call it a revolution – and the revolution grows.

Yesterday was 'eco farming' day in our local town park, dozens of sustainable businesses and land management experts in marquees offering everything from testing of soil moisture and humus levels to biological pest control and kangaroo or feral goat sausages. We've come a long way.

The Landcare success shows how little is needed to create a revolution in our approach to the land.[1] But then, it was aimed at those who already loved it: the farming families of Australia.

The 'land crimes' of the past two hundred years, though, have been so vast that repairing them is beyond the ability solely of farmers. Many have also been misunderstood.

So what crimes have sheep or, rather, those of us who stocked them, committed, all with good intentions but with neither the experience nor the patience to wait, look and understand? And other farmers, too?

A dozen crimes against the land

1   Clearing

Clearing seemed so obviously a Good Thing, a priority on the list of necessary improvements to gain title of a leased block. Trees were ringbarked and then burnt, the stumps dug out or left to rot while you used a stump jump plough. (Those rotting stumps would lead to the proliferation of phytophthora and other fungi that would contribute to the massive dieback of eucalypts in the 1970s and 1980s.)

A three-volume book could be written on the impact of clearing. But, briefly, in dry sclerophyll forest types, soil is held together by a multitude of thin-leafed plants that minimise their exposure to sunlight by their small leaf size. Remove these native ground covers and the rain falls heavily, washing away the soil till only rock and shale is left. The gentle drainage lines where the water flows grow deeper and deeper till they are erosion gullies.

Remove the trees and you let in sunlight. Many wallabies, including the black-tailed or swamp wallaby, *Wallabia bicolor*, slowly go blind with excess light. They stumble, starve and die. Koalas, possums and hundreds of species of birds are left homeless. Other species, like fruit bats, starve without eucalypt blossoms, so they invade orchards and gardens looking for food, and roost in places like the Sydney Botanic Gardens.

2 The curse of the bush fly

Australia has various native dung beetles. They evolved to cope with the smallish dung pellets of native marsupials or even the larger but softer wombat dung, not the giant pats of cattle or the massive gut production of sheep. Back in the 1970s any area where there were sheep or cattle had so many bush flies that you were constantly swishing them from your face, or wore a fly net or swaggies' corks on your hat – that fly-dispersing wave was the great Aussie salute. Yet you could go to national parks, just ten kilometres from stock, and there'd be no bush flies – or not enough to annoy you. Flies made farm life a minor purgatory, even when you were used to them. Now, thanks to introduced South African dung beetles, the salute is rarely needed. But I still wonder what Australian insects – or dung beetles – have been displaced with such a major change in the environment.

3 Vanishing bettongs, wallabies and wombats

Bettongs nest in long grass – they tie it into nest shapes, perfect for tripping over and wrecking your knees. Sheep eat the grass down to the roots or even pull up the roots in drought. No long grass means no bettongs.

Theoretically, rock wallabies, which live, naturally, among rocks, should have been relatively safe. But even without feral dogs and cats their habitat has been fragmented, so that clans become inbred. A generation, or two or six, and they gradually die out.

Wallabies and wombats were (and are) also shot by farmers as pest species, who thought they ate the grass that should belong to their stock. The myth is perpetuated even now, but only by those who know nothing about what wallabies and wombats eat.

Wallabies and wombats are browsers. Wallabies, especially the most common species, *Wallabia bicolor*, the swamp wallaby, prefer a varied diet. They eat regrowth trees, young thorny shrubs, even the tendrils from blackberry and lantana. Wallabies help keep pasture as pasture, and the land cleared under a tree canopy.[2] They can keep grassland free of weeds as effectively as fire. Ironically, if you clear the bush you may kill the wallabies, which need it for daytime shelter. No forest = no wallabies = regrowth shrubs in pastures. Wombats eat tussocks and their seeds. A population of wallabies and wombats helps pasture health – it doesn't reduce the number of sheep or cattle you can stock.

Swamp wallabies need to shelter in shade during the day or they go blind. Wombats are dependent on the structural integrity of the soil for burrows. They need tree roots, boulders or the perfect soil structure, otherwise the entrances of their burrows collapse.

4 Deeply misunderstood kangaroos

We do at least know a little about the role of the kangaroo, and their numbers, partly because of research targeted at seeing if it can be not just a viable human food source (we know it can) but if it can be an economically viable one in the long term and, if so, exactly how profitable. But most of the frequently heard assertions that kangaroos can quickly breed to plague numbers are still unsubstantiated.[3]

'There are now more roos in Australia than ever before' is one of the oft-repeated claims by farmers who shoot them.[4] (Usually illegally – I have yet to come across any farmer in this district asking permission to shoot the 'vermin', nor, when such illegal shooting is reported, of police or National Parks taking action against the perpetrator, unless illegal firearms, drunken behaviour or trespass is also involved.) How do we know what the pre-colonial population of kangaroos was?[5] There has never been an accurate census of kangaroos, nor was there the means to do so before the 1960s at the earliest, with aerial surveying. The claim is based on local observation, but the presence of a larger than usual number of kangaroos in an area can be because mobs of roos have recently moved there, and not necessarily because of the rapid build-up that happens in a good season when roos breed every year. Roos usually live in mobs of twenty to thirty at most, though two or three mobs may join together. Claims of 'mobs of hundreds' need to be substantiated. Claims of 'mobs of starving roos that must be culled for their own good' also need to be substantiated, by measuring the circumference of the animal's tails to check how much flesh and fat they have. (This does not necessarily involve catching the roos – it can be done visually.) This rarely happens.

Roos can travel hundreds or even thousands of kilometres in a drought to reach better water or grazing. (They are possibly the most expert travellers in the mammal world, both in the efficiency of their bounding gait and their ability to cool themselves and survive long periods with little water.) It is also true that more land has been cleared for pasture, and roos, unlike wallabies, wombats and most other bush animals, flourish on grasslands. There are more dams, too, enabling roos to survive in dry areas or to travel even longer distances to new land to survive. But the supposition that Australia now has more roos and therefore we need to cull them misses the point.

Kangaroos are one of the species most capable of regulating their own numbers. If there is a drought or lack of food, roos don't breed – the foetus is either reabsorbed or doesn't develop until conditions are better. They will never be in plague proportions. When farmers see mobs of roos they often don't realise that this same mob may be grazing a twenty or even hundred square kilometre area, depending on the degree to which high fences and roads limit their movement. They are also mostly seen around houses, where grass may be watered or where there are stock troughs, or along the road verges.

Road verges have green growth even when the paddocks are bare, a fact known to the many farmers who take their stock out onto the 'long paddock' in dry times, spending years on the road. Roads rise in the middle – or they do if the grader driver or engineer knows their job – so that rain washes off down into the gutters. On bitumen roads this means that no moisture sinks into the road, but washes down onto the verges, keeping them green. Even gravel roads are usually so hard-packed that water runs off them, giving the verges far more water than they'd get in rainfall alone. Even a heavy dew or mist may give enough run-off to allow green pick on the verges.

In winter, the road absorbs heat and radiates it back to the verges, thus allowing more grass (and weed) growth than in the paddocks beyond. And despite the 'long paddock' use by drovers, road verges aren't as heavily grazed as paddocks. Their soil is less compacted, it retains more moisture and can be a haven for species that have been ploughed or sprayed or grazed into extinction in paddocks. Verges tend to have many more ground cover species (including introduced weeds) than paddocks.

All of which means they are excellent grazing for roos, wallabies and wombats. But road verges are also the place where these animals will be most visible.

Every dry year I meet the aggressively ignorant, those who don't even know the breeding rate of wombats or wallabies, like the local landowner who shot more than sixty wombats in a month last year, who told me that wombats give birth to litters of young like rabbits and breed up in their hundreds during a drought. Every drought there are claims in newspapers and around cups of tea that the roos and wombats have 'bred up' and must be culled. Roos do not 'breed up' in a drought – they simply become far more visible as they seek out grass and water.

Our grasslands' health also needs kangaroos. The grass seeds that are found inside roo droppings survive drought, drying up and then germinating when it rains one, ten or even twenty years later. This also happens to a lesser extent with sheep and even cattle droppings, but these sour the soil below them and the seeds that survive are more likely to be weed seeds. Look at a paddock of cattle sometime; lift an old dry pat and see the bare ground below. Then go to a roo camp and see the green grass, except under the trees where the roos lie in the shade and that wouldn't have been grassed anyway because of the shade from the canopy and competition from the tree roots.

Roo droppings also appear to contain microflora that may survive and help the uptake of phosphorus and other minerals in low phosphorus Australian soils. This is only a 'likely possible' – the research that indicated this might be happening was never followed up in the research cutbacks that have taken place from the 1990s until the present day, just as research on the nodules caused by certain bacteria on casuarina roots that help in the uptake of phosphorus was never followed up either. (Inoculating pasture with those bacteria may have led to a lower dependence on fast-shrinking supplies of superphosphate. Superphosphate may also contain the toxic heavy metal cadmium that can build up in the soil.)

Kangaroos only consume a third of the food a sheep does (referred to as the dry sheep equivalent, or DSE, a dry sheep being one that isn't feeding a lamb). A dry cow or steer has a DSE of around twelve, that is, they eat twelve times as much as a non-lactating sheep.[6] The *Australian State of the Environment 2006* report found that across all low-intensity grazing land (sixty per cent of Australia), kangaroos eat 0.08 per cent of pasture. Research by the CSIRO and the University of New South Wales indicates that kangaroos rarely compete with sheep for pasture, and competition only occurs during extreme drought – which is when the sheep and cattle should either be removed from pastures to stop compacting and wind erosion, or hand-fed in a small area (a sacrificial paddock) that can be rehabilitated once the rains return.[7]

Our land survives a combination of kangaroos and drought well – and has done so for millennia. It does not cope with sheep, cattle, goats and drought, except with extremely good management.

Roo meat has fewer kilojoules and less saturated fat per gram than protein from even fish or chicken, and is far cheaper both in terms of money, fencing and ecological impact than any other species in Australia. This is not to say that current roo harvesting is either sustainable or desirable. I don't have the data to assess such a claim – sufficient long-term data has never been gathered or collated. Licences for roo shooting are based on hearsay, wishful thinking or political pressure that makes it difficult for national park rangers and bureaucrats to refuse landholders' applications. It sounds more acceptable to say 'the roos are in plague numbers' than to admit 'the roos are in the way'.

Even if roo numbers have increased in Australia as a whole – and, remember, that is still an unsubstantiated *if* – they have become locally extinct or possibly inbred in many rural areas. When I came here forty years ago, there were 158 red-necked wallabies (*Macropus rufogriseus*) and about fifty roos (more mobile so harder to get accurate numbers) in the twenty square kilometres around our house. There have been no red-necked wallabies in a ten-kilometre radius – which is as far as I survey, so it may be much further – since 1987. I have seen only four kangaroos – two females with young at heel and, possibly, two more in the pouch – in the past twelve months.

Admittedly, the last year gave lush grass, and roos avoid our shady valley in good years, using it as a refuge in times of drought or bushfire. But even in 2003, during the last serious drought, only seven roos were sighted, and possibly three of those were counted twice, at different stages of growth. In other words, I never saw more than four roos at any one time. But I did see the bones of dead roos at farmhouses – dog tucker – and the corpses of shot roos placed along the roads, as though they had been draped there as hunting triumphs. (They had not been shot where they lay.) The myth of kangaroo plagues is a convenient one for recreational shooters, farmers wanting dog tucker, or for local authorities who want to cut down on kangaroo–car collisions, and so use 'plague' numbers as an excuse to cull them.

5   Mange and toxoplasmosis in wombats

I don't know how many wombats there are in Australia. I don't know how many there once were or how fast their populations are declining. No one does. Research into native species is primarily privately funded and, as a director of one of those funding bodies, I know how little research is done. But I have surveyed the wombat population in the roughly five square kilometres where I live for nearly forty years. This is an area with almost no stock pressure, apart from the relatively small flock of sheep that was here for less than five years, on a very small portion of that land. But there are approximately only one-sixth the number of wombats here today.

Why? Drought, and less water from both closer settlement upstream but also greater water use for gardens and bores put in for domestic water, to create city gardens in rural areas even during droughts. Though there has been enough water to drink, the quality has diminished. Repeated pollution with herbicides upstream may also have had a major effect – it has killed both aquatic and amphibious species as well as a good deal of flora, both in the creek and where it was used for watering. There has been vibration and noise from test drilling for a local mine, at one point so loud that the wombats came out at 1.30 p.m. and screamed for over half an hour. There has been increased traffic on the roads and shooters who see wombats as vermin, or at least as a slow-moving target. There was even one young man who hunted them in his car, to run them over for sport.

There has been mange, exacerbated by drought. Wombats can tolerate a certain level of infestation by the mange parasite, but once it gets above that level the itchiness becomes unbearable. They scratch the lesions that then become infected, and their eyes crust over and then their ears, so they become blind and deaf. Maggots infest the wounds. They can be literally driven insane by pain and itch, till they bash their heads repeatedly against a rock to try to gain unconsciousness.

Mange is spread by foxes but is now so endemic that even if foxes vanished the mange would remain. It is curable – a topical application of pesticide will cure them, administered either in a small dose from a bottle suspended on a gate over their hole or, as I do, by using a water pistol from a distance with a measured dose.[8] But mange control requires money and manpower, and no National Parks and Wildlife Service has either to spare.

Wombats are all more prone to worse mange infection when their skin is irritated, and large amounts of direct sunlight from tree clearing or competition for grassland with stock can do that.[9]

Plus, of course, there's the national death toll on the roads. One estimate is calculated at two thousand a day by extrapolation from the observed fatalities on the Canberra to Braidwood roadside, but this is unlikely to be anywhere near accurate. The real figure may be far more, or far less, and would change from season to season, with more fatalities in droughts as more animals are attracted to the verges or need to cross roads to find water and food. Wombats are attracted to the road verges because they are less grazed and because run-off from the tarmac provides green grass even in a drought. But wombats 'see' the world by smell – they take about forty-six seconds to process sound. If they hear a car they stop to process the sound, and at a hundred kilometres an hour the car reaches them just as the wombat dashes across the road to cover and safety.

Dead wombat.

Toxoplasmosis is perhaps an even greater but less obvious threat than staggering, blind, mange-infected wombats. Toxoplasmosis is spread by feral cats and, to a lesser extent, by domestic ones.[10] It appears to lessen the intelligence of many species that are infected with it but its effects are rarely noticeable in wombats. It was only detected recently, after orphaned wombats failed to thrive in the care of humans. But it explains a growing phenomenon: brain-damaged wombats in our valley.

Wombats are not muddle-headed. They are extremely intelligent – if they are interested. I have known a wombat to use a lever, and another to move a box to a chair to climb up both to escape confinement. Another learnt to count to six, too long an experiment to detail here. But starting about 2000, I began to see wombats that were mentally incapable of surviving: one, from a house where she had learnt to eat cat food, would drop asleep wherever she was, even during the day. We had to rescue her from heat prostration. She even once tried to walk towards us through the creek – not swimming, just unable to realise that wombats cannot walk underwater. She died at about two years old.

Other wild wombats have shown similar symptoms. One, who we named Totally Confused, would turn in circles for minutes, unable to work out which way to dash across our track out of the way of the car. The first time was funny, but as more wombats showed the same brain-damaged behaviour it became tragedy instead.

Once wombats are eradicated from an area it is difficult to re-establish them. Contrary to myth, wombats are lousy engineers – good diggers, good renovators of any old hole, but most new holes they dig collapse. What appear to be 'new' wombat holes are often re-openings of old ones, centuries or perhaps even millennia old. A wombat dies in them and they are abandoned for years until a new wombat digs out the entrance, clears soil falls, spring-cleans the bones and moves in. (I have only known one successful new hole near our house and that was under our bedroom. The first attempt – before that wing of the house was built to give it a weatherproof roof – collapsed or filled with water whenever it rained.) Wombat burrows also need either exactly the right combination of soil and position, or a tree root or rock to act as a lintel to stop the entrance collapsing. Heavy-footed stock both collapse holes and compact the soil, especially around the sandier creek banks and slopes that are favoured for easy hole engineering but lack the required structural integrity for a good, sound burrow.

It is possible to create new holes for wombats by reinforcing the first few metres with corrugated iron or drainage pipe. Once those crucial entrances are safe the wombat can extend the burrow down into the more stable subsoil.

Does the loss of so many wombats matter? Locally extinct in many areas, they may soon become endangered, so it certainly matters to those who love wombats or wish to protect Australian icons. But does it matter to the health of the land? I don't know. There have simply been too few studies on wombats and their place in bush ecology.

6   Deliberate extermination of Tasmanian tigers, eastern quolls and spotted quolls

The Tasmanian tiger is dead, extinct, no more. Even if it were to be resurrected by cloning, it would only survive in refuges. Reintroduce Tasmanian tigers into the wild and they could become extinct again because of lack of bush to feed in, wild dog attacks, or possibly infections like mange.

Eastern quolls only exist in Tasmania now, mostly in the high country populated by skiers, not farmers. Spotted quolls are deemed to be 'vulnerable' in some areas, 'endangered' in others – and extinct in many more. In the 1970s in my own area, I used to see fresh spotted quoll scats at least twice a week around our henhouse (netted on the top to stop the quolls climbing up and over to eat the chooks). Quoll chook raids were at least a monthly occurrence up at the village of Majors Creek. There have been only two quoll raids in a fifty-kilometre radius in the past decade. One of those quolls was caught in Majors Creek and taken tens of kilometres away last month, to save the chooks – or rather, to save the chooks whose owners have not provided them with a quoll- and feral cat-proof wire-covered run. That quoll will try to go 'home' and may well be shot or run over as it does so. I haven't seen any fresh quoll scats in the past decade and have had only one sighting of another and her young last year – they were feeding on wombat roadkill by the side of the mountain track.

Quolls have been killed by farmers with shotguns or dogs, or trapped and poisoned. These are what killed the Tasmanian tiger, too. But quolls face an even worse threat: toxoplasmosis spread by feral cats.

It appears that there is considerable individual difference in reaction to toxoplasmosis. For now, far too little is known about it and the research that is being done is privately funded, not governmental. It may be that the animals most susceptible to behaviour modification will die, leaving a stronger residual population. It may also be possible that, like the Tasmanian tiger, our native predator animals may all become extinct.

Why does this matter, except to sentimentalists? (Of whom I'm one: I want these animals to survive because they are beautiful and because they add to the diversity not just of the ecology but of my life.)

The more simplified an ecosystem the more vulnerable it is. One grass species can die in a drought or a wet year. Forty ground cover species mean stability: if one dies out there are others to take its place. Yet other predators like foxes, feral cats and wild dogs have taken at least part of the quoll and tiger's places in our ecology, cleaning up dead meat and taking the weakest of their target species so that the survivors breed strong young.

But not entirely. Feral cats feed mostly on birds and lizards. Foxes, in our area, eat roadkill carrion, and fruit like avocadoes, blackberries and apples (at times they are almost entirely vegetarian). When they do hunt in our area, it is mostly frogs. Wild dogs are large enough to haunt the edges of paddocks to take lambs, a lot more meat and easier hunting than rabbit or hare.

Quolls and Tasmanian tigers had different prey. Quolls in our area feed mostly on animals that are already dead, although they eagerly raid hen houses and, in our valley at least, also eat frogs. Tasmanian tigers probably scavenged much of their food from dead animals too. They were more scavenger than predator. But quolls – and probably Tasmanian tigers – also kill and eat sick, elderly and weak animals. It may seem illogical to encourage a predator which might eat other endangered animals, but to think this is to misunderstand the role of a predator, to fail to listen to the land. A certain degree of predation makes a species genetically stronger, so that the weak do not breed, and the fastest, fittest and most intelligent survive.

Quolls – and tigers – were part of the balance of the ecology where they once fed. This is even more clearly seen in the loss of predator birds.

7 Predator birds and plague cockatoos

Farmers believed eagles, goshawks and other predator birds ate lambs. They do – dead or dying ones.[11] But they were shot and poisoned in their tens of thousands, and some still are despite their protected status. The birds were also forced to hunt in the open paddocks where they were vulnerable because their favourite prey – young possums, wonga pigeons, even frogs – had vanished with the forests.

These days cockatoos are seen as the most destructive of bird pests. They consume entire crops and will even destroy verandas and red cedar garden furniture. For sixteen years I tried to keep the sulphur-crested cockatoos off our walnut crop. I failed. Finally, I left the nuts to the cockatoos. About five years later they noticed the newly fruiting apple trees by our house. Disaster, I thought. Then I noticed one white cockatoo sitting slightly apart from the others. A hunchbacked cockatoo.

It wasn't. It was a white goshawk. White goshawks eat sulphur-crested cockatoos, but only if they haven't been shot or their eggs made fragile by DDT or other poisons, including surfactants from herbicide spraying or from eating prey that themselves have eaten poisoned bait.

If you watch a mob of white cockatoos feeding – the long drives near Canberra's Parliament House are a good place to spy on cockatoos – you'll see that they always have lookouts posted high in the trees while the others feed on grass seeds. Once, before white farmers and their guns and poisons, a mob of cockatoos would be followed by predators, like white goshawks, who have evolved to be able to sneak into a flock, grab one and be off.

That year the cockatoos moved off a few hours after the white goshawk arrived – slightly fewer cockatoos than there had been before.

Australian orchardists and crop farmers and back yard gardeners do not have a sulphur-crested cockatoo problem: they have a white goshawk deficiency – and a powerful owl, wedge-tailed eagle and little eagle deficiency too, and of the many other large birds that eat cockatoos. But any meat-eating bird is vulnerable, at the top of the food chain where pesticides and other toxins like heavy metals bioaccumulate. And as our waterways become more polluted, the predator birds dwindle in numbers.

By how much? Good question. It is a pity that the funding has been cut to the institutions that might be evaluating just that, and its implications.

8   The decline of snakes and lizards

How much have snake and lizard populations declined? Don't know. What are the implications? Don't know that either, and from extensive trawling through research papers for the past forty-five years, I strongly suspect that no one else knows or is even working on a viable way to find out. Australia has some of the deadliest snakes in the world and had an extraordinary diversity of lizards. They have had some significant role in the ecology, but what it was and its ramification will probably never be known.

I do, however, have one anecdote. Every autumn, for forty years, we have had a build-up of roof rats: not bush rats, which may run across the rafters of our shed and hop onto the benches, but the introduced brown rat, *Rattus norvegicus*. Sometimes we have rats nesting in our ceilings all year round, but not in the past twelve months. No scuffles, no squeaks, no arguments with the ringtail possum who lives above the dining room.

What is different this year? It's been the third year in a row of reasonable rainfall, so there should have been more rats, not fewer. But early this spring I met a large, pure black python in our vegetable garden, asleep on the bed where we grow our early zucchini. It heard me, then sped off towards the house.

I don't know what species of python it is – there are diamond pythons nearby so it may be a different-coloured variant. It may also be a species that has never been identified, and possibly won't be before it becomes extinct. Black pythons have, however, been sighted as far away as Monga, thirty kilometres to our northeast, and twelve kilometres downstream in Araluen, though that specimen was dead and may have been washed down by floodwater. The snake is known locally as a 'marsh snake'.

Pythons eat rats. Pythons also like ceiling spaces, especially above rooms heated in winter, so they have no need for such a long winter hibernation. This was a big, well-fed python. And perhaps, just perhaps, it has kept the rats under control over about four hectares.

Mice and bush rats breed up into plagues that devastate wheat and other crops. Perhaps if we had left more snake and lizard habitat – boulders, rocks, swampy bits at the bottom of the paddock, shrubby undergrowth along streams – and not turned the land into one vast grassland (wheat, too, is a grass) we might have more reptiles and fewer, or far smaller, rat and mouse plagues.

9   Christmas beetle plagues

Plagues of Christmas beetles are almost certainly a postcolonial event. Like many pests, Christmas beetles recognise their food supply by its silhouette. The park-like paddocks created by the colonials – a few trees left in each – were perfect Christmas beetle territory, allowing them to pass from one food supply to another.

Every Christmas for sixteen years, the stringybark sapling outside our front gate would be totally defoliated by the beetles. The same species, roughly the same age and two metres away, was untouched and grew to a twenty-metre tree in that time, while the stringybark by the gate stayed stunted.

The difference? The one two metres away was in bush – real bush, with over forty species of shrubs and sub-shrubs around it. The other stood sentinel-like by itself. Eventually that sapling did grow into a tree, but only after the other bush species grew around it.

There were other factors, of course: one of those shrubs is a *Bursaria spinosa*, host for various parasites that eat Christmas beetle larvae. But mostly it was simply that the beetles could easily find the tree. Australia is not naturally like European parks or farms. Our trees grow with other species, in clusters by waterholes, along watercourses, in bush or in gullies. They don't stand alone like specimen trees in your front garden. And, if they are made to do so, they'll get eaten, or develop root rot (*Phytophthora cinnamomi*) from lack of microfauna to control it. (*Phytophthora cinnamomi* is inhibited by wattle bark and wattle slash mulch and, I suspect, by the decaying wattles of natural bushland too. Wattles are short lived and many species regularly shed their bark or a large numbers of seedpods.)

In Europe, sheep and cattle like sunlight, often a rare commodity. In Australia they seek shade, and the ground under mature gum trees is often their camp during the day, leading to soil compaction. No new seedlings emerge from the hard ground as the tree begins to shed copious viable seed before it dies or, if they do, they are eaten or sat on.

The European farm vision of men like Peter Ffrench could have been perfectly designed to create agricultural disaster.

10   Introducing weeds and helping them flourish

I am not going to attempt to find figures for the amount of pastureland lost to weeds; the cost of weed removal each year in Australia; the impact of herbicides on amphibian and other non-target species (I doubt if substantiated figures exist). Shall we just say that the answers to these questions would be 'lots'.

But I will tell you about the broom and blackberry up in Majors Creek. Almost annually for forty years these weeds have been sprayed with herbicide. Each time they die back, and more seedlings grow in the bare ground and take their place. Each year the herbicide spreads a little further than the weeds – spraying tends to do that. Without the ground covers, broom seeds and blackberry runners take the place of grass. Forty years of spraying has led to roughly four times the area under broom and blackberry than there was forty years ago.

This is not a difficult pattern to see. But every few years, someone takes up the dream of controlling the weeds with a good spray, hoping that, by some miracle, the easy solution will work this year. The weeds will stay there until they are managed by someone who accepts that it isn't enough just to kill the weeds. You need something to colonise and stabilise the soil where the weeds have been.[12]

Weeds colonise ground left bare by erosion and overstocking. Weeds are natural colonisers: they need disturbed ground to take over. (This can happen naturally, after storm and flood, but it's rare. The bush here that has neither been grazed nor burnt in bushfire is pretty much weed free, despite the heavy weed burden metres away.)

Introduced farming and grazing techniques creates opportunities for weeds. They also introduced most of the weeds. Look at the declared weed list for your area: it is unlikely that there will be many – or even any – that are native to your area, though there may be a few native to another state or even a different area of your own state. (Native plants, like Cootamunda wattles and *Pittosporum undulatum* can become weeds outside their native territory.)

These weeds are a product of a vision of our land as 'one nation'. Australia was once hundreds of nations and is still a land of thousands of eco-types. Yet a red flowering gum from Western Australia is regarded as a 'native plant' in New South Wales, comparable to calling Italian lavender native to Scotland. Cootamundra wattle is not a weed in Cootamundra, nor are pittosporums weeds here, but in places like the Dandenongs in Victoria they are invasive and to be avoided.

11 Pollution of waterways

Polluting of waterways with superphosphate and nitrogenous fertilisers leads to algal blooms, dead fish, sterile water systems, loss of frogs, illness in humans and plagues of mosquitoes, whose larvae would otherwise have been eaten by those frogs.

We have lots of frogs; at least we did and I hope will have again. Apart from times of eco-catastrophe, the tadpoles and frogs here control the mozzie larvae. Frogs also eat mosquitoes. Lots of frogs equals few mozzies. Lots of frogs also equals lots of snakes, who eat the frogs (and the bush rats). I try to remember that each time I have to hop away to avoid a snake.

12 Loss of paper wasps and other predator species

Thirty years ago I washed nappies by hand in two tubs under a giant paper wasp nest. Every day part of the insect haul they had paralysed and brought back to feed their larvae fell into the water where I soaked the nappies: nine days of cabbage butterfly larvae from my crop of cauliflowers, then five days of pear and cherry slug, a few red-back spiders (I hoped they were well and truly paralysed), then other caterpillars I couldn't recognise.

I took notes over a year of nappy washing. Each time, when I could identify the species, I tracked down their source. The polistes wasps seemed to totally clean up a pest before they moved on to the next – in that location, anyway. That year I was growing over an acre of cauliflowers, but the wasps were enough to do the entire pest control.[13]

Most market gardeners are not so lucky – or, more likely, they have unknowingly destroyed their native wasps and other predators with pesticides that kill both predator and their food supply. Paper wasp nests can grow to at least twenty square metres, enough to clear up huge numbers of pests. But they are very vulnerable to any pollution from pesticides. One spray of Mortein has been enough to stop them breeding above the sink or the entire window that they tried to colonise one summer.

All pest problems are really lack of predator problems. Locust plagues are a severe ibis deficiency: a mob of ibis can eat two tonnes of grasshoppers a week, and there are native wasps that eat juvenile grasshoppers, too.

When I first came here our orange trees were dying from scale infestation. Three weeks later – after we had saved up enough money to buy spraying equipment and (organic) white oil spray, but had yet to spray it – there were no scale left to spray, but a heck of a lot of ladybird larvae.

And so on

Itemising the many ways our land has been misinterpreted by the vision of colonial farmers could make twelve volumes: feral animals, from camels to cane toads, feral cats, rabbits and goats; myrtle rust devastating remnant bush areas; disruption of aquifers from mining; wild dogs – each deserves at least one chapter on its own (and each is well covered in other books, too). It is easy to see the individual problems, but the overarching effects and root causes are often too broad to be easily grasped.

Our country was once a generous land. In all but the most arid regions it was impossible to walk more than a few steps without passing food. Decades ago – before motherhood, deadlines, email and boxes of mail – I walked this land for much of every day and night. I didn't carry water, or food. I ate as I walked: berries, leaf tips, oozing sap, nectar from blossoms. It didn't replace dinner and breakfast (though much of that was gathered from the land too) but it was enough to travel on, to keep up energy. Even without the creek there were sources of water, in tree hollows or spring seeps. But this was in land that was relatively untouched by humans. The lower parts of the valley had been grazed, mined, burnt and cleared, but not the steeper land. It remained – and still does as I write this, though I do not know for how much longer – relatively pristine.

When my son first became a weekly high-school boarder he rang me to say, 'There's no food here.'

'Don't they feed you?' I asked in horror, remembering *Tom Brown's School Days* and other boarding school nightmares.

'Only in the dining room,' he said.

Until then I hadn't realised that he took a generous land for granted, surroundings where there was food always in reach.

We have lost so much. It is impossible to measure the number of species lost, as most had not been identified before they became extinct. (I am roughly extrapolating from the species I know here: at least three appear to be extinct without ever having been formally identified.)

It requires enormous lobbying to even get a species declared as endangered or critically endangered either in the state or federal systems and, even then, few are monitored or so much as given a recovery plan – and when they are, often no one even monitors the recovery plan, much less implements it or prosecutes those who destroy declared species.

Our greatest crime of all, however, was to simplify the bush. For most urban and even rural Australians, 'the bush' is tree canopy and ground cover, or shale and tussocks. Repeated burning has created forests where there is almost no understorey, just burrawangs and thin bush, perhaps, where once there were thousands of species.

There may be no such thing as true wilderness in Australia; all our landscape has been modified by humans over millennia. But there is bushland that still has at least a large part of the pre-colonial diversity: pastures with 10,000 ground cover species and over a hundred shrubs and sub-shrubs; grass or terrestrial orchids that have not even been catalogued yet, like the ones I noticed just before Christmas that smell more intensely of roses than any perfume counter but are so high above my head I can't reach them; lichens; thousands of fungi, again, not even identified; the varied mistletoes; ants that mutate into differing species within three metres.

Even on our place I have catalogued the death of species: the giant ants with high, gold abdomens that looked like they'd been wrapped in gold thread – it has been over a decade since I have seen any – and the green ants with a savage bite that couldn't be identified. I have never tried to study or catalogue the ants here, but those two were unmistakable.

And they are gone, like the blue bees, the black native bees, the giant striped ground wasp, and the tiny blue-winged butterflies. I don't even know why they have vanished. Species do become extinct, and not necessarily because of humans. Perhaps they may even reappear from remnant populations. I do not know. I have watched and studied my impact on my land – and that of others – and yet, I do not know.

CHAPTER 16

This generous land: Terrapaths, moral omnivores and how to survive the next millennia

When a wombat 'sees' the land, they smell it. The scents tell them not just what is happening now, but what happened days or even months or years before. Looking at land 'like a wombat' means seeing today's land as a continuum, a small blip in a long line of past and present. The greater your knowledge of the land today and yesterday, the more accurately you can predict what will happen tomorrow.

Listening to the land does not just tell you whether there will be rain, drought, fire or locust plague or when and what to plant. It is – or should be – the basis for our economic and defence strategies, our health and population and migration policies. Humans are an integral part of Australia's ecology. That ecology, in turn, influences outbreaks of new and old diseases, economic booms and busts, even how we relate to each other on a day-to-day basis, or in an emergency.

You need good baseline data to make good political and planning decisions.

Even though much traditional knowledge has been lost, our power to 'read' the land is now far greater than it's ever been. With tools that range from satellite mapping to the examination of ice cores, we can watch storms gather force thousand of kilometres away and read the fossil records to tell us the story of evolution and the changing environment over millions of years.[1]

Yet much of this data is never used in land management or political decision-making – political decisions are even made to deliberately *not* get the knowledge, so that no action need be taken. Australia's previous chief scientist resigned because in the three years of her tenure she had never once been consulted. CSIRO has been more than decimated, its research – and that of most university departments – turned to short-term economic gain, not the long-term pursuit of knowledge that can lead to far greater financial gains from new technologies.

Most political and planning decisions are *re*-active: produced with little forethought because of opinion polls or political necessity. Too few are *pro*-active: produced from a long-term study of trends and necessities. Our nation was created and shaped by the land. It is time we paid more attention to its voice.

Sixteen suggestions for survival in a changing world

1   Learn your land

One lifetime isn't enough to know a valley, nor even ten lifetimes. I have been lucky to have teachers, who had teachers too. In a small way – I am all too aware of how much I do not know – I've been given the knowledge of hundreds of generations, mostly women's knowledge, but some from men, too.

'Drought's good for the land,' said Bernie Ffrench at eighty as I looked at the ridge of gum trees, browning in the heat and dry. 'You look how it grows again after.'

He was right. Trees died, wattles crumbled, vines withered, but after two years of almost average rainfall the accumulated fertility meant a lushness I'd never seen before, the eucalypts that seemed dead sprouting thicker leaves than before, losing branches but providing more new leaves and blossom for the animals and birds to feed on.

'Kurrajong will give you all you ever need,' said old Neeta Davis.[2] 'I spent years bringing kurrajong seedlings up to the house paddocks. Chop them up for the stock when it's dry; bake the roots if you've got nothing left. You can make a rope from kurrajong, or a light. It's a woman's tree,' she said. 'It'll give you everything you need.' A dozen uses later, I was convinced.

Jean, in her seventies, knew the magic of getting raspberries to grow in forty-degree summers. She could kill, gut and pluck a chook in under three minutes. Ned had been watching floods and fires for sixty years and knew pretty much what any of them would do. There was Bill, too, whose memory I'd probe in his rare visits back to the place where he'd lived most of his life.

'When will it rain?' I asked Bill, the third summer I was here, when what had been a reliable twice-weekly rain shower suddenly turned into month after month of dry. He shook his head. 'If the gully dries up in spring it won't rain till after Christmas. But I reckon we're in for a few dry years.'

'Why?' I asked.

He shrugged. 'It's feeling like it did back in the sixties.'

He was right. It didn't rain properly for another five years.

I'd almost forgotten Bill's answer when someone asked me during the 2003 drought when we'd have good rain and, without thinking, I said March next year.

'Why?' they asked, and when I thought about it, there were answers I could give: the various shrubs had set seed, as though their roots knew that later in the season there'd be solid rain to make the seedlings grow, the smell of mating wombats and their shrieks in the night.

Before my son was born, I walked this valley most nights for years, watching and tracking the animals, seeing how plants really do grow, not how books said they must. Why did the wild fruit trees – even the seedling apples and peaches – bear year after year without pruning or fertilising, while my trees had to be fed and watered, pruned and sprayed? But, of course, those wild trees *were* being fed, with the droppings of those that the tree fed in its turn.

If we are going to adapt to the changing world – and the world always does change, even if not at the speed with which it is changing now due to human impact – we need not just to listen to the land, to learn it, to study it, but also to use that knowledge to make political and planning decisions. Good decisions need good data. Each major planning and political decision should require substantiation, independently aquired and then verified, with publicly available data to support it.

2 Leave areas of biodiversity, even if large areas must be developed

The present vast areas of Queensland rainforest were once reduced to small pockets. Then the climate changed, and the species spread. Our creek has been polluted five times in the six months since a mine project began upstream. Fish and frogs vanished. Yet there have been fish and frogs again as the water cleared and I hope that they will return once more, if there's no long-term soil contamination or changes to the creek bed, and be here in the future, too.

I'm not saying it is safe to devastate land as long as a small area is left with species to recolonise it. But if that devastation is going to happen, it is even more important to preserve the areas of biodiversity, with as many species surviving in them as possible, and areas that have shown themselves to be resilient, or havens in drought, fire, heatwaves, storm or flood. Endangered species may not be significant in themselves, but they may be an indication of resilient land that needs to be preserved The very fact that they are endangered may also be a red light indicating poor or non-existent land and resource management. To paraphrase John Donne, ask not for whom the bell tolls. Today the hairy-nosed wombats. Tomorrow, the world's fish reserves, or us.

3 Be part of the society around you

Humans survived as a species by cooperation. Individuals survive best by cooperating too. But generosity between people isn't enough. We need to be generous to the world as well, to rejoice in it and extend to it the duties and rights that we offer each other. This isn't because of any religious or pantheistic imperative. It's because humans operate most efficiently when we are generous.

In the last decades we have begun to learn that other hominids survived right up until the last Ice Age, almost beyond it: the Neanderthals, the Denisovans, *Homo floresiensis* (the 'hobbit' people of Flores). I suspect we will find more.[3]

But only *Homo sapiens* survived. Was it the 'sapiens' bit, our cleverness, that let us outlast the most recent Ice Age and the rising waters after it, not just the cold but the unexpected disasters that fast climate change brings, like the floods that broke open the Straits of Gibraltar and turned the Mediterranean into a sea, or isolated the islands off the Great Barrier Reef or Kangaroo Island? Fifteen thousand years ago Tasmania was part of the mainland and we were joined to present-day New Guinea. The changes to our coastline in the next hundred years may be as dramatic as that – and faster.

So how did we survive?

We walked. We talked. We cooperated. We had the intelligence to be able to communicate with strangers: we bring no threat, just hunger and desperation. We had the empathy to understand the needs of strangers. A community doesn't have to be geographical. It can be a stamp club or an amateur dramatic society or the place where you work; it can even be a community threaded throughout the world via the World Wide Web.

Many longitudinal studies conducted by different, mainly American universities have shown that churchgoers had longer lives, even though theoretically the more social contacts you had – especially in a crowded church – should have meant more infections. Prayer? Possibly not, for the studies also showed that the more of any kind of social encounters you have, the better your health, and the slower your deterioration from Alzheimer's disease is too.

Of course, if you're in poor health you probably don't manage to go to church often, and you'll probably miss out on many other social encounters too. I'd rather believe that even though the methodology might have been slightly shonky, the results are true: the more you involve yourself in a community, even if it's the Woop Woop Embroiderers' Guild, the healthier you'll be, and the longer you'll retain your sanity for good years to come. If you sponsor a local netball club for teenagers, you may just find that one of the kids on drugs who goes along but also mugs people for money will 'sort of know you' – or even someone in your family – and say, 'No, don't hurt him. He's okay.' The more we are linked by good things, the safer we are.

How to tell if you're a local

1. Do you know the names of the main native and introduced trees in your area and the main native flowers? Not necessarily the Latin names. They can be the names your gran or kids gave to them – billy eyes or dainty sues or butter berries. If you've given them your own names because you love them (or hate them, just as I call vetch 'sticky weed' because the stuff sticks over everything), all the better. Pet names denote knowledge and intimacy.

2. Do you have pet/family names for any local features: road, sharp corner, big hollow tree, locally owned shop?

3. Which direction do the worst bushfire/cyclone/heatwave winds come from?

4. How do the local bird/lizard/insect/frog populations change in winter?

5. Who looks after your [insert name of rec ground, local hall, cemetery or church garden here]?

6. When was the last local flood/frost/cyclone/tornado/earthquake (insert favourite local disaster)? How often do they occur, and when you might next expect one? What is the likely damage, where would you go for refuge, and how could damage be reduced?

7. Do your neighbours know you well enough to accurately (if good-humouredly) insult you, to rescue you if you call them at 2 a.m, or work with you to survive an epidemic/tsunami/terrorist attack or months-long power failure?

8. Name or describe three likely sources of local graffiti and whether they indicate a social danger or just that Bill got drunk last Tuesday.

9. Compare and contrast the recipes from two local church, preschool, community group or school cookbooks.

10. Does it take you at least five minutes of chat when you dash in to the bakery/coffee shop and grab a loaf of bread/coffee on a Saturday?

4 Evaluate what experts say rather than stick with your preconceptions and ideology

Which part of the economy employs the most people?

If you said 'mining', disqualify yourself from public office and any planning role. In 2011 (the latest year's data available as I write this) mining employed 1.9 per cent of the Australian workforce, less than the number employed by the arts and recreation industries (2.9 per cent).[4] Mining contributed only ten per cent of our gross national product (GNP) at the height of the last mining boom. (The figure may be lower now the boom is bust) Sixty per cent of GNP was contributed by the service sector of the economy, including tourism, education and financial services.

The mining industry, however, contributed more than half of the export income earned by Australia in 2011. The profits go to far more than the 1.9 per cent employed in the industry. Part goes to government revenue; a larger part goes to shareholders, of which I (or at least my superannuation fund) am one. It's often claimed that about eighty per cent of profits go overseas. I haven't been able to verify the claim, nor find a different estimate. I am (in an extremely small way) enriched by the mining boom. But the associated costs must also be evaluated.

The mining boom has pushed up the price of the Australian dollar, vastly reducing the opportunities for other industries as they are less competitive globally. Factories close as mines open.

In 2012 the OECD economic survey recommended dropping the subsidy to extractive industries. Subsidies? To what are supposed to be the most lucrative industries in Australia? Yet the diesel subsidies alone are $2 billion a year. Ditching that one subsidy would pay for a heck of a lot of education and technological research, increasing employment, productivity and long-term economic prosperity.

Why subsidise the supposedly most lucrative industry in Australia, and one where a large chunk, at least, of profits go overseas? Lack of imagination? The power of lobbyists? I suspect the real answer is that just as England, France, the Netherlands, Spain and Portugal kept hunting for the land of gold they knew was somewhere around here, our leaders – political, industrial, media and others – are locked into a world view that says extractive industries are the foundation on which our prosperity rests, and we niggle at them at our peril.

This mindset is equally bad for the mining industry. It may get the diesel subsidy, but much that is vital to maximise development and regional benefits and new projects – or even make them possible – is also ignored. Our mining industry is usually boom or bust, instead of steady, productive development – better for communities, as well as profits.[5] Give northern and regional Australia better infrastructure – roads, rail and, especially, northern port facilities that are nearer to the mines. If the port of Darwin was expanded, and roads to it improved, there'd be less need for ports and shipping near the vulnerable and economically valuable Barrier Reef. Encourage technical apprenticeships instead of closing down tech colleges. The approval process requires an overhaul: it needs to rigorously look at the cost–benefit analysis before any project is even given encouragement to work towards approval but it also needs to be far faster, so that major projects aren't kept dangling for years while their prospective market vanishes to competitors. Don't subsidise major industries – facilitate them.

The cliché syndrome doesn't just relate to mining. What proportion of the Tasmanian workforce is involved in forestry – or was, in 2011, before the cutbacks? Half of one per cent.[6]

From 2001 to 2013, General Motors Holden received $2.2 billion in subsidies from the federal government to keep their factories operating in Australia. In the same time it spent $5.9 billion on wages.[7] This too appears to be a decision based on a mindset – large car factories are major employers – instead of based on cost-benefit analysis. Subsidising smaller, innovative companies may well create more reliable long-term employment than can be provided by an industry that must be massively subsidised to keep operating. If you are a politician, bureaucrat or voter, demand substantiated data. Do the cost–benefit analysis. Listen to what the scientists say.

All humans are ignorant. Some exist in a state of 'aggressive ignorance', where they reflexively and forcefully reject any information that makes them rethink the way they prefer the world to be. 'I don't know' is a courageous and necessary statement, and should be treated with respect, not derision.

5 Develop sensibly

We need to evaluate all criteria of a development to be able to say that we have weighed the losses and the gains. If the gains outweigh the losses the project will go ahead. If the reverse is true, it won't. All development proposals need a cost–benefit analysis, as is now done in China, looking at health and quality of life impacts as well as financial. At the moment too much emphasis is put on too few environmental criteria.

Those assessments need to be independent: paid for by the developer, but carried out by an independent public service, who will not be swayed by what their employer wants. At present the terms of environmental impact assessments (EIAs) are set out by the developer and carried out by contractors paid by that company. Conditions may be imposed to limit environmental damage, but I have not been able to find an example where a single mining development has been ruled out at EIA stage. (Developments however have been halted by public appeals against the approvals, involving extraordinary amounts of research and fund-raising.) Except in rare instances of major pollution – and again, usually only after public objection or whistleblowing – the company is responsible for policing their own conditions of approval.

Philosopher Val Plumwood wrote of 'captured bureaucracies', where public servants are either drawn from industry or eventually go to an industry position, effectively working as industry representatives in public service jobs.[8] Public servants should have no personal or financial links to the industry they may be assessing.

Any decision by a minister or senior public servant that goes against advice from the experts in their department or working in the field needs to be scrutinised, and substantiated. (This should apply in health, defence, education and other portfolios, as well as planning and all other areas.) Overwhelmingly, political and planning decisions are made based on inadequate data, or data that contradicts experts' assessments. Adequate on-ground, baseline data must be collected *before* decisions are made. Without baseline data you can't assess what effects there may be, or assess what effects are happening. Instead developments are approved with self-monitoring to determine if there will be health or environmental damage. If that damage occurs there are often few, if any, repercussions, except a 'try to do better'.

Development approvals should include a 'polluter pays' principle. For a development to be cost-effective, it must be able to clean up after itself, and compensate those adversely affected by it. Environmental protection legislation is an empty shell unless conditions are independently monitored, and breaches are both policed and reparation enforced.

6 Eat good food

All food choices are ultimately political decisions. English sweet biscuits needed colonies and slaves to provide the sugar. Tomatoes airfreighted from Israel, garlic from Mexico and snow peas from China means our strategic policies are dominated by the need to ensure the oil that lubricates it all.[9]

Good food connects you to the world. Refusing to eat bad food is one way to make change happen.

Good food isn't frozen, or at least not for long. Place skull and crossbone symbols on all packs of frozen carrots – I have never met a frozen carrot that I've liked. Feeding kids frozen vegetables should be a minor crime against humanity – you're training the kids' palates to accept crap.

Good food isn't refrigerated, either, or again not for long. (Widespread refrigeration is a blessing on one hand, but it's also meant that many humans now eat food that has had most of its flavour sucked away by prolonged cold.)

Good food is fresh. Good food is seasonal. But most of all, good food is idiosyncratic. It's just what the eater feels like at that moment. Good food either means growing stuff yourself or knowing how and where to buy, be given or swap reasonably local, mostly organic tucker – all of which needs a time-rich life and lots of social contacts, unless you happen to be a hermit with a really good garden. It means learning how to cook a basket of tomatoes oozing juice, a choko invasion or a dozen mushrooms from the back paddock that sprang up overnight and the yabbies the kids caught before breakfast, rather than following recipes.

But also: eat anything made for you with love. (Or – in the case of possibly fatal consequences – at least make a show of doing so).

7 Become a moral omnivore

A moral omnivore eats whatever are the most ecologically sustainable foods – and that may include meat. Vegetarianism isn't necessarily an ecological virtue, though eating much less, and different, meat certainly is. (Vegetarianism may be a spiritual or even a social virtue, but that's different.) Large-scale fruit and vegetable production fences out wildlife, killing them as surely as a bullet, but more nastily.

Most animals raised for meat in Western societies contribute to an ecological blight, especially anything lot-fed, like beef, industrialised hens or pigs, fish farms that need four tonnes of wild fish to produce one tonne of farmed fish, or even crocodiles farmed on chicken carcasses. But meat can also come from free-range hens that scratch around the yard one minute and are in the pot the next (if you are a very, very good chook dispatcher and plucker, anyhow) without even a second of fear. It often makes more sense ecologically to imitate peasant cultures and raise small animals like hens, pigs, guinea pigs, rabbits, guinea fowl, goats and fish to dispose of weeds and kitchen scraps, and to provide small amounts of meat to be eaten as flavouring or on rare feast days.

It makes even more ecological sense to eat feral animals, because large hunks of our country are vanishing into feral gullets and under feral feet. Twenty-five years ago our entire gorge was 'dry rainforest', a canopy of *Backhousia* trees, maidenhair ferns, sandpaper figs and tree ferns. And then a hobby farmer released his goats into the gorge – the price for goat meat had plummeted and he didn't want to pay to take them to the market.

Once-green gullies became orange desert as the plague of goats grew, changing the bush to parkland with only tall trees, the young ones nibbled to death and then to bare eroded earth. As the big trees died there were none to replace them, just as the shrubs, orchids and hundreds of other species were lost to the goats' browsing teeth.

It is taking a significant effort just to keep the goats relatively under control. (Eradicating goats completely from this area would require more resources than we can mobilise.) The most motivated hunters are those who plan to eat the meat, or serve it to friends. But similar plagues are happening right across Australia. Feral goats, pigs, rabbits, carp, cane toads – okay, maybe I'm not advocating we eat cane toads, but they do make interesting leather.

I don't like killing things. I would much rather the government put all the research dollars slashed from biological control programs into sterilisation (instead of a lethal disease) for feral goats, rabbits and the others. But at the moment the ferals are munching away the world I love. And the most humane way of controlling them isn't to trap them and truck them – crammed and terrified – to a distant market, where they may well be sold for meat anyhow, but to get an able shooter to kill them with one swift bullet. (If a shooter needs more than one bullet to kill an animal instantly they shouldn't be hunting.)

Nor am I advocating game hunting in national parks. At the moment, no one in Australia is tested for their ability to hit a target before they get a gun licence, or even on their ability to handle an actual firearm, much less be an effective and humane hunter. The written exams are ludicrously simple, and almost impossible to fail, even with no study or knowledge of laws and regulations.

Humans are omnivores – look at our teeth. We have tearing, chewing and grinding ones. We can chomp, rip, nibble, suck, lap, sip and guzzle – the least specialised mouths on the planet. Now look at what our culture *doesn't* eat. Aztecs pressed together mozzie eggs to make a sort of caviar. Is this really more repulsive than eating fish eggs? Grilled locust abdomens (another pest that needs controlling, due to over-clearing and over-spraying) are tastier than most factory-made snack foods. How many of our pests – from silverfish to termites – would no longer be problems if we ate them, as other cultures do? (Make sure the silverfish or termites haven't eaten anything toxic in the past three weeks, and try them fried light brown and crisp, to fit a little more closely to our culture's food preferences.)

If drivers were legally obliged to eat what they run over (other humans excepted) there might be less roadkill.

8 Learn to love the shabby and give up the addiction to the new

The average age of the furniture at our place is about seventy years, with nothing younger than a decade. And while Buckingham Palace might boast that their furniture is centuries-old antiques, ours isn't, although all of it was built to last. Even the washing machine has passed its twenty-ninth birthday.

Once upon a time things were made to last. Grandma used the iron and vacuum cleaner she was given as wedding presents till she was eighty-six and moved into a nursing home, and I used that vacuum cleaner for decades after that. Good 1920s construction.

Most modern machinery is obsolete within three years these days, often less. People don't want their consumer 'durables' to last longer. They want a new model kitchen every seven years, a remodelled bathroom, cars with the latest gadgets. (My truck is even older than the washing machine. A few bits melted off in a bushfire twenty-seven years ago, but it still hauls in the wood.) Even gardens are instant – annual flowers that give a rush of brilliance, annual vegie gardens that must be tended to give food.

Short-lived things mean you have to keep on hurrying to replace them: shop for a new TV, compare new cars, plant the lettuces to replace the ones eaten or gone to seed. All this newness takes time. It takes mental energy, too, that could be spent finding our place in the universe (in my case, just next to the wombat hole). Even the way most people understand home and community these days is short-lived – you upgrade to a better house or a nicer spot by the sea. There is little compulsion to say, 'I've put down my roots. They're going nowhere, except further down.'

Too much money leads you to silly choices, like the holiday on a Thai beach, and a long exhausting journey to get there, instead of a quiet mooch across the local sandhills or along the river to the swimming hole.

9   Accept that 'natural' or 'native' does not necessarily mean 'best' or 'harmless'
A species that is native to one part of Australia may become a weed or pest in different conditions, like Cootamundra wattle or the flying foxes that killed trees in the Sydney Botanic Gardens. Natural pyrethrin insecticides, which cause allergic reactions in perhaps two per cent of those exposed to them, may harm human health more than artificial permethrins. Genetically engineered does not necessarily mean bad, though it may well be bad if the only reason for the design has been profit, not public good.

10   Get it in writing
Be wary of anyone in authority who refuses to, or doesn't get around to it.

11   'Critically endangered' may not necessarily be the best criteria for preserving an area or species
I fight to preserve critically endangered species because they are an index of the complexity of the land. The simpler an ecosystem, the more vulnerable it is. In our valley certain species thrive in dry times, others in wet years; a multiplicity of species make the whole more resilient, able to withstand extremes.

Endangered species may be an index of ecological health, but not – necessarily – valuable in themselves. A development may be held up or be excessively modified because of the presence of a single endangered species, like the green and golden bell frog. I am fond of the endangered green and golden bell frog – they visit our bedroom, catching insects attracted by my reading light – but their extinction may not matter in the long-term ecological health of the valley. Other species may take their place. (I say 'may' here. I do not know.)

12   Be deeply suspicious of anyone who says, 'That's impossible!' unless they can substantiate it with a minimum three-year study of the proposition
There are two great myths about living a sustainable lifestyle. The first is that our standard of living is going to have to fall. Our lives will become

grey and meaningless while we squat in the dark in a mud hut. And the second is that it's impossible.

There's magic in the word impossible. It means we don't have to try. I've lost count of the number of ecologically positive things that are supposed to be impossible:

It's impossible to grow as much food without pesticides or fungicides. Then why does productivity go up – not down – in countries that reduce pesticide use? Answer: Pesticides kill the predators that control the pests. A reliance on pesticides and fungicides *increases* pest problems.

It's impossible to grow fruit and veg without shooting/trapping/poisoning wildlife. No it's not. Grow decoy fruits.

It's impossible to produce meat, dairy products and eggs in an ecologically sustainable and humane manner. Tell that to our pampered grasshopper- and fallen fruit-eating chooks, and Jackie the Cow (deceased). Much meat, dairy and egg production *is* unsustainable and inhumane, but it doesn't necessarily have to be so.

It's impossible to run a community on wind or solar power. Of course it's possible. It's happening. Solar power is currently the cheapest form of *new* Australian power, as opposed to power from existing power plants. (This is partly because of current subsidies and taxes.) It is not, however, the easiest to get access to, nor are our electricity grids usually designed for a large amount of locally generated power from roof top solar or wind systems. The answer is to redesign new grid systems but also to link communities to local power sources, only accessing the grid in peak load times, or using one of many ways to store surplus power, such as using solar power to pump water to a high point, where its fall will generate hydro power at a peak load period.

It's impossible to build houses that survive bushfires, floods, cyclones and even tidal surges. CSIRO has successfully trialled bushfire-safe houses. The Netherlands is pioneering flood- and tidal surge-proof houses. Japan is pioneering towns that may survive major tsunamis.[10]

It is possible to live a fulfilled, rich life while doing all of the above.

13 Be cautious. Be kind. Be wary of anyone who tries to make you angry. Expect war, too

Caution allowed humans to survive on this continent for 60,000 years. Unless there is immediate danger, a slow decision deliberated upon by many for years is likely to be better than a fast one. Lady Macbeth's 'If it were done when 'tis done, 'twere well it were done quickly', as she prepared to stab her king, is a superb illustration of someone subconsciously knowing that they are about to embark on something they would not do if they waited and evaluated. If you find yourself uttering similar phrases, or hear leaders saying them, assume the decision is likely to be, at best, unsubstantiated, and at worst, disastrous. Be even more wary of those who try to make you share anger. Think of those leaders in the past or present that you abhor: have they all at some stage used anger against a common enemy to gain power over their followers? Hatred is contagious. So is kindness. There is a quote frequently attributed to the Dalai Lama: 'Be kind if possible. It is always possible.'

Kindness can be an effective weapon, but it does not mean you won't have to make grim and hard decisions. If the land can only support so many people or animals, who and how do you choose will live there, or is it kinder to wait for desert to take over so they may all die? If one person or racial or religious group attacks another, what is the kindest way to proceed?

This is not a rhetorical question, implying that force is the best or the worst solution. Foreign aid ('we will bribe you to act the way we think you ought to'), biological warfare with one of the many blights poppies are prone to, thus wiping out the opium money behind various dangerous groups, or tranquillisers in the water supply allowing the easy and fast occupation by a peacekeeping force are possible, though not necessarily desirable, nor are the last two acceptable under the strangely antiquated – but probably needful – protocols of modern warfare. Allowing a stranger, enemy or potential enemy, to be kind to you is arguably even more effective than helping them. Humans resent those with the power and resources being kind to us. We are more likely to feel warmly to those we have helped or protected. An

Institute of Effective Aggressive Kindness might offer interesting insights.

Beware of anyone who tries to make you angry: that anger will give them power over you, and probably not for good. When times are hard – drought, heatwave, crop failure, recession – the solidarity of hating a common enemy can make you temporarily feel better. Expect more droughts, heatwaves, crop failures and recessions. Expect more hatred. Expect more war. In World War 2, Germany fought for *Lebensraum* (room to live) and Japan fought to gain access to the resources they had been denied. Battles for desirable land or resources or even the best bunch of fruit predate humanity. Future wars will be fought for the same millennia-old reasons, but with new methods and technology.

14 Beware of the terrapath

We call humans who don't feel empathy with other humans sociopaths or psychopaths, so little empathy that they can hurt or kill and feel no guilt. Maybe we should begin to call those who have no feeling for the planet terrapaths.

How do you recognise a terrapath? Terrapaths are the ones who know that what they are doing, whether it be mining or logging a forest, will hurt the other species of the earth and simply don't care, as long they make a profit from the activity. Others even take a joy in destruction – the pyromaniacs, or those who find the disorder of untamed nature so frightening that they long to concrete it all over.

I suspect true terrapaths are rare. Often those who hurt the earth aren't aware of how much harm they are causing, or don't have the confidence or the habits of mind to look for different ways to do things. Most humans have just never learnt how sapient *Homo sapiens* can be. If humans can't outwit cockroaches, pear and cherry slugs, fruit fly and possums, and work out how to gather timber, grow food and utilise minerals without irreparable harm to other beings, we don't deserve our name. But maybe we also need to recognise terrapath as a severe mental disorder that needs treatment, fast, just as we would respond to a psychopath or sociopath. Psychopaths may kill tens of humans. Terrapaths are a danger to us all.

15 Be optimistic

Optimism invented the wheel, processed the first olive, and, okay, created the atom bomb, too. Pessimism stayed glum till dinnertime, and then complained.

Humans are tougher than cockroaches. Cockroaches die at forty-six degrees Celsius; humans don't (mostly). Humans really are one of the toughest and certainly the most widely ingenious species on the planet.

It's worth remembering though that we gave ourselves the name 'sapiens' (meaning intelligent, wise) like a king of three paddocks and a dunny calling himself 'Emperor of the Universe'. But that's humans for you. We see other species as the humbler creations and feel we have the right to fence them out or take their homes and food supply, which amounts to the same thing. But we also should be (moderately) confident in the abilities of our species, too.

Think of what humans can do with the most unpromising places to live or grow food. No water? It rains everywhere, even if not often or much. Your water supply depends on the size of your storage area: tank, cistern, dam, plus recycling and water retention methods. Water can be recycled indefinitely, even in greenhouse agricultural systems where you need only bring in as much water as you take out in the form of crops, instead of losing perhaps ninety per cent to evaporation.[11] Mountains? Terrace, and fit your house to the land. No land? Grow ten hectares of vegetables up the wall of a skyscraper. It's called vertical gardening and turns a city into roughly ten times the amount of productive land than it was when it was mostly horizontal. A city of green walls and rooftop forest, connected by animal-sized crossings, could intensively host more wildlife than a national park. Not every endeavour will succeed. But it's more fun trying than watching 'someone else's reality' TV.

16 Love your country

Perhaps the first step in learning how to live well on the land is to love it. The European sailors saw a land with no easily visible safe harbour, with tough ground covers instead of the lush grass to cut for the hay needed for their voyages.

The mutton eaters saw a land to be transformed into the fields of home, with grass, not tussocks, and fat sheep and cows. Who was the first colonial, I wonder, to actually see the land as it is? How long did it take the first emigrants, 60,000 years ago, to say, 'This land is who I am.'

What is it to love a country?

I love the creek here, smooth deep holes in granite bedrock, worn by a hundred thousand floods; I love the sunlight turning the casuarina dew to diamonds, the frozen spider webs on barbed wire fences. I love the land I know.

My knowledge is deepest here, but if this valley is my partner, then Uluru is a sister, Western Australia a brother. They are familiar, known, though not as closely.

Where does the love stop? At the Pacific Islands? Malaysia, which I've never seen? The United States on 9/11, or Indonesia and Japan after their most recent tsunamis? I wept for them then, and for the first time realised those lands were my brothers too.

Maybe the love of country eventually stretches to the whole planet, because finally – as humans, as creatures of this planet – the breeze from the butterfly wings that sweep across the African plains does eventually reach us here.

Love the planet and you will work for it. Love your neighbours and you will fight for their survival, or at least offer them a casserole when they are crook. Remember that a frog may be your neighbour, too. Love this life, its richness and diversity, and it will (mostly, or at least quite often) be good.

How to make stringybark twine in the Araluen Valley in the twenty-first century

Follow the path of the white clematis in mid-spring, as it twines about the tops of trees and bushes, creating a highway of white to show your way. The clematis blooms at just the right time to harvest the stringybark for twine, while it's still soft and new.

The path will take you through damp gullies, where you can stop to drink. Two hundred years ago they'd have been rich in frogs to eat, but these days the green and golden bell frogs and the giant burrowing frog are critically endangered and all native animals are protected. Don't take the bird eggs, either, and ignore the ground orchids, even though their tubers are sweet and good when baked. Bring sandwiches instead and, as you eat them, dream of the days when this valley would have been rich in waterlilies. You might have made cakes of their pollen or eaten the stems or roasted the seeds. You might still find some late kangaroo berries on the vines, but don't pick the similar bright oranges berries from bushes – they're toxic. You need to know your berries in the bush.

Three hundred years ago you'd have found plenty of bush honey, too, from the solitary blue bees or dark native bees, both stingless. But don't risk tracking the wild hives of what are probably feral European bees now or you may get badly stung. Don't eat the watercress and other wild greens either, unless they are well cooked, because of introduced liver fluke carried in tiny native snails.

You'll find the stringybark trees on the downside of small ridges, above the gullies. Take the small stone from your pocket that will cut, grind seeds, crush sinew for sewing and a hundred other tasks. Cut long thin strips off the bark, right down to the smooth shiny inner layer. Each strip should be no wider than your hand. Don't take too much – if you ringbark the tree it will die, and if you over-strip it the tree may rot before the scar heals. Each strip should be as long as you can make it.

Take your strips of bark to a cool spot by the creek. Use the dry, short-fibred, outer bark as tinder to help light your campfire. (Even after heavy rain much of it will be dry).

Now use your fingernails to take a tiny strip of the innermost fibres - they are very thin indeed. Pull slowly and steadily - you should get strips at least thirty centimetres long and, with practice, much longer. When you have a goodly pile of fibres, take four to six of them (six is better, but I can only manage four). Hold the fibres together and tie a knot in the top. Now begin to plait them, moving the one at the right over the next one to the left, till the one on the far right is now the one on the far left. Now begin again with the new 'far right' one. Don't worry - this sounds much more complicated than it really is.

About ten centimetres before you come to the end of one of the fibres, thread in another to replace it. Keep going until your string is a metre long, or ten metres long, or however long you'd like it to be.

Your fire should be flickering well now. Take your plaited string and run it slowly through the tip of a flame. It will start to sizzle and you'll think it'll catch on fire. It won't - or, at least, don't hold it there so long that it does. Instead the tip of the flame will melt the separate fibres together, causing the sap to bubble out and seal the string into a single waterproof strand. If you don't have a campfire, a lighter will do the job as well.

It will last for years. It is also far stronger than any similar string you'll find in a hardware store. Use it for fishing line (it's waterproof and won't rot) or to make a belt to carry baskets to leave your hands free. If you want an even stronger rope, plait this string with four to six other lengths of string.

A few words of caution: if this string or rope is made from the correct fibres, at the right time, in the correct way, it will be very strong indeed. But just in case it isn't, do test it for strength before you risk life or limb with it.

Then follow the clematis road back home.

CHAPTER 17

The next hundred years: Twenty-four predictions

We don't need the spectre of human-triggered climate change to know that disasters like flood, fire, plague, pollution or badly planned human activity will visit us again and again. History doesn't end yesterday. It is woven into the fabric of the present. History is part of the future, too. History's best lesson is to teach us – emotionally as well as intellectually – that things change.

The Indigenous people of this land created cultures around the worst scenarios. Their populations stayed at what the land could support in bad times; they cherished food resources, and moved on before they could be depleted. The Indigenous nations were built on the concept of climatic extremes.

Our culture instead works on assumptions that industrial population growth can continue indefinitely; that there won't be a pandemic this winter, a fire this summer, a flood in the next decade, or not at least till the planner who approved the new development has moved jobs.

We are aggressively blind to the lessons of both the past and the land.

The land is going to continue to shape our future, just as we, too, shape the land. If we are to survive the next few thousand years, we need to learn to see where we are going.

Prediction 1: Humanity can survive climate change. We might even survive fast climate change.

Humans have survived massive climate change before. The weather changes in the northern hemisphere's 'little ice age' (not a true ice age as it wasn't a global event, with large local variations) between 1550 and 1850 may have been greater than those even our great-grandchildren will probably face.[1] Humans are *good* at climate change. Each of us is descended, after all, from those who survived the last Ice Age and the catastrophic sea-level rises that followed it when so many of our near-human cousins died out.

A greater danger comes from pollution: humans have not yet survived a world where change is coupled with the loss of so much of the planet to pollution. An even greater danger are the myths that shape our culture: that development is always good, instead of looking at its cost-effectiveness; that a three-minute shower helps to save the planet. (You don't use up water when you shower. You borrow it.)

Knowing history doesn't make us less likely to repeat it – knowing about Boer War concentration camps just made it easier to envisage more effective ones. But looking at the past does show us that tomorrow, eventually, won't be like yesterday, that our fate is decided by how we can adapt to the planet and how it shapes us or how we shape it.

We can survive climate change, but only if we accept it *always* happens, whether it had been sped up by human release of carbon dioxide and methane or not, and only if we adapt to it. (I would be more worried by an impending ice age, and certainly of a nuclear winter where dust obscures the sun for years to decades, caused by either large-scale war, massive eruptions from super-volcanoes or the debris thrown up by the impact of a meteor on our planet.)

To survive we need to change the way we do things: how we assess development, how we farm and what we eat, and ensuring we preserve islands of biodiversity so that when change happens there are more likely to be species that can adapt, or play a greater role in the ecosystem.

Mostly, we need to learn to look at the land again – or take notice of those who do.

Prediction 2: The 'boat people' will keep on coming.
The phrase 'boat people' originated in the early 1970s, when refugees from the Vietnam War, that Australia had fought in then abandoned, came in small, fragile boats to our shores.

Refugees from war, persecution, poverty or ecological catastrophe will keep coming. People have sailed across the dangerous ocean to Australia for perhaps the last 60,000 years. Probably they always will, as long as there are humans and boats to sail in.

Look at a map and you will see why: we are at the end of the world's migrations. Follow the coasts till you get to Southeast Asia, island-hop down, or surge across the Indian Ocean on the trade winds. This has long been the final refuge. Some years there will be fewer boats. Other years there will be more.

Australia cannot support, either physically or culturally, all the world's refugees, or even all of those who wish to come here. The land itself has constraints about what population it can support, not just for this century but considering the centuries to come, too. We are a land with relatively little fertile soil and fresh water. Australia already faces severe depletion of its aquifers as more artesian water is pumped out than is replaced.

There are social and cultural constraints, too. Trying to merge too many strangers into a culture has rarely, if ever, worked. Instead of offering a place of safety we would create a culture of anger, racism and even possibly the repression in a search for order – or worse, the social devolution where trivial cultural or religious differences mean attacking your neighbour with firearms or poison gas, instead of proceeding through the courts.

But we do need well-considered strategies to deal with the desperate, the hopeful or even the manipulative, who will always try to land here. The past decade's strategies have been costly, both in money and psychological harm to those in the camps, and possibly in a small way to Australians too. They have often been created on the hop, to manipulate opinion polls rather than create workable policy.

In *Pennies for Hitler* (a novel for young people) I wrote that hatred is contagious, but so is kindness. Sometimes being good to others – as a nation or as individuals – can be as powerful as guns. My grandmother was proud that she greeted visitors with a cup of tea and fresh scones or apple teacake. No matter who the new arrivals are, or what they have done – or for how long we decide they should stay – we owe them the equivalent of Grandma's welcome – a cup of tea, a scone (and decent education and medical help while they are here) and some compassion.

Yes, we should plan and examine carefully who, how and how many people come to Australia. But we should always remember that our families were once in those boats, too. And every year, in varying numbers, they will come.

Prediction 3: Australia will continue to be a target for our resources, both as the subject of equitable trade, but also possibly using economic sanction or other force.

Look at the map, then look at the history of Southeast Asia for the past four hundred years. This is the region where others come for the natural resources that will make them rich, from spices to rubber. Steel and coal were why the Japanese swung south to Australia in World War 2, diverting resources from their attack on India. Australia's population, while possibly too high for the land to continue to support at our present level of consumption and way of life, is still stationed well away from our richest resource areas, especially the oil and gas of the North West Shelf.

We need to show that we can defend the North West Shelf and other resource-rich areas with more than a resolution from the UN Security Council saying 'naughty, naughty' if one of the nations that depends on our resources decides to secure them by force, rather than accepting the taxation and development conditions prescribed by the Australian agencies.

I am a pragmatic pacifist. Almost invariably aggressors lose the war, although it may take decades for this to happen. Physical force only has a lasting effect if it is used to change the mindset, as in Japan and Germany after World War 2 when the Allied victory and occupation helped dismantle the social system that had the military at the top. Peace is not easily made or kept. Military force is just one of the elements necessary to the role of peacekeeper or defender of your country. Its greatest use is possibly as a deterrent – but to be a deterrent it must demonstrably exist.

Prediction 4: Our centralisation leaves us vulnerable to natural disaster, human error, or attack.

If you look at a detailed map that shows where our power plants or phone and water systems are, you will see just how few terrorist attacks – or long-range drones – would be needed to cripple our society. Knock out a communications satellite or two, cut a few major telephone cables, cripple eight power plants, bomb eight airports, blow up two bridges in each capital city, and you have – what? Our cities have food for perhaps three days. Back-up generators have diesel for a few days, not weeks or months. Many are in the basement of buildings, which means they are useless in a flood. Our hospitals have central air-conditioning systems and few, if any, facilities to isolate patients in a pandemic.

Australia also shares the massive worldwide reliance on satellite-based communications, from navigation to banking and data storage. On 1 September 1859, the earth was hit with a sudden and massive cloud of magnetically charged plasma from a solar flare. It took only seventeen hours and forty minutes to reach the earth – too short a time to do much to mitigate the damage. Telegraph wires shorted out across the planet and remained inoperable for days; some telegraph equipment burst into flames. The next night even the equator flamed red with auroras usually only seen at the poles. No flare of that magnitude has affected earth as much since, although a far smaller one on 13 March 1989 knocked out power to the whole of Quebec, Canada, causing tens of millions of dollars damage. If – or when – a similar solar event occurs, or a meteor passes too close to our satellites, crippling the communication, transport and power systems we now rely on, the whole planet will be affected. Bank accounts, tax, health and vital research records will vanish with their data cloud, with little or no paper backup. We are terrifyingly centralised.

So here is the prediction: in the next two decades we will see at least one major disaster caused because our large country's supplies of fuel, power, water, transport, communications, navigation, banking and food are disastrously centralised. There will be more.

Prediction 5: Within the next ten years there will be at least two major natural disasters.
Or, rather, two that are precipitated by bushfire, cyclone, flood or pandemic, but really caused by a lack of political willingness to recognise the threat.

(A note here: as I revise this, in January 2013, six months after writing those words, we are in the middle of a natural disaster, with fires in Tasmania, Victoria and New South Wales. We have just had a recorded message on the phone telling us to evacuate to a safe area, but no authority has nominated what a safe area might be. As the fires have cut the highways between here and the neighbouring cities, there appears to be no safe, or even possible, evacuation route. The Victorian Fire Service's web system has crashed, so no one can log in to see where they're in danger.)

Prediction 6: Within fifty years the low-lying land between Gosford and Sydney will be a disaster area.
So will the canal developments of coastal Queensland, large parts of South Australia and anywhere else the land is below sea level, or is surrounded by land below sea level, or is less than a metre above sea level, or is on a tidal flood plain.

The sea level is rising at an average rate of about two to three millimetres a year, and that rate may increase as feedback mechanisms warm the world even faster, meaning that ice melts at a faster rate. Sea levels also rise in Australia during an El Niño year. The last strong El Niño year was 1997, with a moderate one in 2009. The years 2010 to 2013 have been La Niña periods, or neutral. Expect higher seas when El Niño returns.

Even without a sea level rise, our land is subject to storms of extreme violence. Many of our rivers, like the Murray, naturally flow out to the sea in some years, or bank up with dunes for decades and it takes a major flood or storm to wash them away. The mouth of the Murray has been kept open to the sea by a combination of weirs along its length, barrages to separate the saltwater from fresh, and, since 2002, dredging to maintain a channel supplying fresh seawater to the Coorong. The mouth has silted up repeatedly in its history and also shifted its position along that stretch of coast. Whether it is open to the sea or not is the result of a complex combination of conditions comprising inland rainfall or floods and wave action, and storms along the coast.

Bodies of water like Lake George near Canberra can be dry for more than a hundred years then fill up in months. Our land has many dry lakes. They may have been dry for decades, or even centuries. But they will not always be dry. This can be a land of long, long seasons.

Even a hill that is above sea level may not be safe for long. Islands exist either because their rocky shores protect them from waves and storm or because storms deposit even more sand as dunes, which protect the land behind. A hill may survive the night's deluge but not the next few storms.

Prediction 7: Pacific Islands like Vanuatu will vanish within a few decades.

Not because of global warming but because they are sinking, part of the cycle of plate tectonics of our planet[2], whereby some territories rise and others are subducted into the sea, and because sand islands have always been relatively temporary, washed up by storms, held together as birds drop seeds while different pieces of land washed up and eventually eroded away again. Other areas, like the land under Greater Jakarta, are dropping by up to ten centimetres a year due to the pumping out of groundwater. Large parts of the city, including the airport, will be sea, not land, by 2030. The head of water resources at Indonesia's Energy and Mineral Resources Ministry, Dodid Murdohardono, has stated that groundwater has dropped by thirty metres since the 1960s. Indonesia has the financial and technical resources to combat this, with a giant dam around the bay and other measures. As I write this there are several plans around the world to create man-made islands, both residential ones off major cities where land prices are high or local violence is prevalent, and to be used as cropland. But small and impoverished nations don't have that option. Sixty thousand years ago our land was settled because of local natural disaster. Where should islanders go for refuge now?

Prediction 8: Expect earthquakes.

Earthquakes happen; usually we don't notice them because most of them happen in unpopulated areas. But as populated areas expand, expect more devastation. It is likely that humans sometimes trigger earthquakes, too, as well as the more common land subsidence, by pumping too much water from aquifers.

To a limited extent, earthquakes in some areas can be predicted, at least with a known level of risk even if not with the precision to say, 'On the fifth of June at 5 p.m.' Stress levels on some known major fault lines are routinely measured, and information like this has led scientists to predict an even worse earthquake for the South Island of New Zealand than the one that caused so much damage in Christchurch. There are predictions for massive quakes near Indonesia, Tokyo and California. With all of these it is 'when', not 'if'.

But most fault lines in Australia are not adequately mapped, including one that runs through our property and is adjacent to the mining project that will dig half a kilometre into the earth, nor have stress readings been taken along it. There is insufficient data to assign any level of risk; and this is the case with nearly all of Australia's fault lines.[3]

Prediction 9: Expect a major east coast tsunami.

Sand deposits inland along the east coast of Australia indicate that tsunamis occur roughly every two hundred years, as the detritus on the continental shelf builds up and then collapses down into the depths. Today? Tomorrow? A hundred years hence? Just don't think our east coast is immune. (Nor is it alone: New York exists under threat of a major landslip in Madeira, a large part of the USA will be made uninhabitable when the super-volcano under Yellowstone National Park erupts, and California will be unrecognisable when the San Andreas Fault rips again.) Our north and northwest coasts are even more vulnerable to the effects of frequent underwater earthquakes in the 'rim of fire' regions nearby.[4]

Prediction 10: Expect a new pandemic within the next twenty years.

This will probably be caused by a zoonosis, a mutated virus or prion passed on by mosquitoes, droplets, blood, mucus, or faecal or food contamination from other species that are the normal reservoir for that disease, such as poultry, pigs, fruit bats (via horses infected by flying fox droppings in their feed in the case of hendra virus), waterbirds or even from wildlife such as chimpanzees.

Plagues of pests are eventually attacked by predators. The plague build-up of human numbers will host a new virus, or many viruses. Pandemics are worst when humans move large distances to major population centres, as happened at the end of World War 1 when there were more deaths due to influenza than the war. These days we move more than ever: twenty mutated smallpox carriers in twenty planes each infecting twenty people, who infect another twenty – you do the maths. How many are infected in eight weeks' time?

But a pandemic can be predicted just by looking at a map of human settlement. There are a lot of us. If we were grasshoppers or rabbits we'd be called a plague. Plague numbers crash due to a rise in predators or disease or starvation and a host of other controls. The more crowded a species is, the easier it is to transmit disease or parasites; the more a species travels, the wider the infection area. What is the most common cause of death for women? Hands up if you said heart disease, childbirth, cancer or starvation.

It's none of these – it's AIDS. In 2012, 14.4 per cent of global female deaths were from AIDS. The most common cause of male deaths is heart disease (12.8 per cent), with AIDS and road traffic accidents in second place (10.7 per cent each).[5]

Plague proportion populations are not viable indefinitely. Humans are not immune.

Prediction 11: There is a brown snake slithering unseen in the salvias outside my study window.

The red-browed finches are trilling 'snake alarm' calls. (I never promised you all the predictions would be profound.)

Prediction 12: Expect fire from the sky. Also locust plagues. And boils.
At 10.49 p.m., fifteen years ago, I looked up at the night sky to see
the burning wreckage of a giant plane silently hurtling down on us.
I blinked, and then it wasn't a plane, but a spinning ball of burning
green and pink that split in two, then three, then vanished behind the
mountain. After several calls to astronomers at Stromlo, Parkes and
Coonabarabran, that giant fireball was identified as a large meteor,
mostly nickel, quite common. As there'd been no sound, despite its size,
and given its trajectory, it probably landed in the sea between Sydney
and Lord Howe Island. No one else reported seeing it; relatively little
of our skies are surveyed. If it had landed a few seconds earlier, on
Sydney, the office of HarperCollins Australia may not have survived in
its present form to publish this.

Asteroids that explode before they hit the ground and are large
enough to damage areas wider then a kilometre probably land on
earth about every 1.3 years. Asteroids large enough to form a crater
1.2 kilometres wide, with far greater surrounding devastation from the
impact blast, occur about every 5200 years. About five hundred much
smaller meteors make it to the ground each year. Asteroids usually
land in the sea, because seventy-one per cent of the earth's surface
is ocean (these may cause tsunamis if the asteroid is large enough),
or where there are no people to see them. Australia has about thirty
known and ancient asteroid craters. One of the most recent is about
5000 years old at Boxhole in the Northern Territory and about 170
metres wide. The 20,000-year-old crater at Veevers in Western
Australia is about twenty metres wide. Both are well within the time
of human settlement.[6]

As the world grows more populous and people remote from cities
now have phones with cameras to record such events, expect to hear
about more them. It won't necessarily mean that there are more, just
that they are now being seen and causing damage that affects us.

Locust plagues? We've already caused them, and with increased
water use that drains the swamps where their predator ibis live, there
are increasingly fewer natural controls. As rain is one of the best ways to
prevent swarms growing to plague size, expect more in future droughts.

Boils? Antibiotic-resistant bacteria are a growing threat, but one that ingenuity, combined with relatively immediate financial gain for the company that produces them, might counter.

Prediction 13: The weather will change.

It has always changed. Do not expect the last decade to be a guide to the next. For at least the past 60,000 years Australia has been a land where dry times can last centuries, or decades as did one from 1877 to 1903, and flood seasons last for years. But what we face now is more rapid change. According to the Australian Climate Commission, Australia is already experiencing a pattern of increased weather extremes, drought in southeast and southwest Australia, heavy rain and cyclones in northern Australia, bushfire in southeast Australia, as well as unprecedented flooding. The commission also stated that the climate has already changed in parts of Australia, since the 1970s for southwest Australia and the 1990s for the southeast. The commission's report has been backed by climate scientists in Australia as well as the CSIRO, the Bureau of Meteorology, and the UN's chief science body on the subject, the Intergovernmental Panel on Climate Change.

As well as rising temperatures there also seems to be a rise in extreme events, as weather patterns move more slowly, globally. This means that their effects intensify: hotter periods get hotter, colder ones get colder, dryer ones even more dry, and wet ones more rain. A cold front that lingers means metres of snow, instead of centimetres or at least a longer period of more severe cold; a rain depression that stays steady for weeks, not days, means increased flood. In our area of Australia we are experiencing longer periods of hot, dry bushfire winds before a cool change arrives. Forty years ago most hot days ended with 'Araluen Billy', the cool southeasterly mist which arrived at about 4 p.m. The weather fronts are weaker, too, so that many cool southeasterlies no longer reach our valley, thirty kilometres inland.

Even without the variable of global warming, expect the unexpected – and promote both traditional as well as new technological ways to reduce the unexpectedness.[7]

Prediction 14: Heatwaves will continue to kill more people and animals in Australia than floods or fire.

Flood and fire are dramatically televised; death from heat-precipitated heart failure mostly isn't. A prolonged heatwave here has long-ranging and complex effects on animals: several species of frog stop breeding; bees may not forage for as long and so not have the pollen to feed young bees; wombats may go hungry as it's too hot to feed till late at night, and so become more prone to mange; our hens stop laying; and native birds that may normally raise two broods a year only raise one, or none successfully. But nectar-eating birds may also starve during long wet springs, when the nectar is too dilute to feed them. On the other hand, in tests here and elsewhere, many or even most indigenous food species have shown the ability to survive in climates far hotter and colder than where they originally grew, and after the January heatwave of 2013, seven introduced species of spring-blooming fruit tree flowered again, with a second crop ripe by autumn. We still know very little about the species we share this continent with.[8]

Prediction 15: Expect famine.

For the first time since global measurements began, obesity is a greater global problem than malnutrition.[9] But, as always, there are and will be areas that because of war, natural disaster or crop failure can't rely on their normal food sources or delivery systems.

Much of the world eats globally now, which means there is an enormous reliance on transportation systems – and the fuel that runs them. An eruption of a super-volcano, a war that disrupts oil supplies, or a problem with the satellites that are necessary for most transportation systems (a large solar flare would be enough to cause this) and areas may not get enough food. But climate change brings another threat.

As I write this, wheat rust has decreased the Middle East's harvest of wheat over the past three years by about forty per cent. It is possible that part of what we call the Arab Spring of 2010 to 2011 and the subsequent political unrest was triggered as much by the rising costs of food as the direct desire for political change. (The mobs of the French revolution called for bread before they called for the death of the aristocrats.)

A warming world means rusts and other diseases in farming areas that used not to be susceptible to them. Much of the world's food is grown in river deltas that may be flooded or affected by increasing salinity as sea levels rise.

Countering this, vast areas of the now frozen or semi-frozen tundra beneath the Arctic may be opened up for cropping, and extraordinary achievements are being made in breeding crops that will grow in brackish or even salt water, or in solar-powered greenhouses or floating man-made islands that turn seawater into fresh water for growing vegetables. But here the more affluent nations have the advantage, with both the educational resources and the capital needed to experiment and establish new growing systems.

This prediction should probably specify 'expect famine in poorer nations and expect food prices to rise in affluent ones'. This is not, I admit, a prediction that should startle anyone, although the reasons for it may not be what they'd have assumed.

Prediction 16: Australian agriculture will adapt to climate changes.
All Australian farming is an adaptation to this land. We're a wealthy, educated nation. Farmers will keep adapting.[10]

Prediction 17: Storm surges will worsen.
There is no consensus and probably far too little data to predict what effect global warming has had or will have on cyclones, tornadoes and other major weather events. They may increase in numbers and intensity in some areas; decrease in others. But storm surges of four to eight metres or higher appear to be increasing. According to the Australian Climate Commission, March 2013, Australian sea levels have risen by twenty centimetres since 1880, and the rate of increase is rising.[11] Suggestion: do not buy beachfront land, or any land near the coast that has been reclaimed from a swamp. Or, for that matter, any land that can only be reached by beachfront road or rail, unless you are happy to get home by rowing boat. In Bangladesh it is the poor who

are most affected by flood. In Australia it will be the rich. This may make taxpayer-funded compensation or mitigation more or less likely: the rich have more political clout but are the focus of a lot less public sympathy.

Prediction 18: Invest in unreality.

When times are bad, humans like escapism: movies and sport in the Depression, computer games, online communities and the virtual world supplying a lot of our escapist fantasies now. I prefer a life of flood and drought to air-conditioning, and an orchard to a supermarket. On the other hand I am tempted by the idea of 'eating' a calorie-free box of chocolates, or having my mind spliced into the speed, data and breadth of a hard drive.

Prediction 19: Invest in (well-managed and innovative) health care companies.

My grandfather said that if you wanted to understand human health, you only had to look at our bodies, the long legs that make us walkers. Walking makes us healthier. Sitting makes us crook.

Look at our broad shoulders and pelvises – weight-bearing exercise makes and keeps our bones strong. Look at our mobile faces – we evolved as communicators, happiest with our clan. Now we sit. Machines do our lifting. We communicate through machines and not our faces.

Our life span is also increasing dramatically globally. Since 1970 the average age of death in Australia has risen by nine years; 7.5 years in the USA; 14.3 years in Central and South America; 24.1 years in Bangladesh; 13.2 years in Africa, 12.9 years in Asia, with the Maldives leading with 28.4 years following improvements in health programs. But that also means that the problems associated with old age, from dementia to arthritis to bone loss, are increasing.

Expect more crook humans. Also expect more ingenious humans to come up with solutions and others to form companies to market them. The good ones will make money.

Prediction 20: Nuclear power costs per kilowatt hour will go up; solar and wind power costs per kilowatt hour will go down.
According to the *World Nuclear Industry Status Report* from July 2012, of the fifty-nine current nuclear reactor construction projects around the world, eighteen are behind schedule by more than a year and, of the remainder, none have yet reached projected start-up dates. Nuclear projects are failing to attract the capital to build or complete them.[12]

The arguments about the dangers of radioactivity or nuclear waste may be irrelevent. Nuclear power plants generate vast amounts of power, but also have enormous construction and maintenance costs, as well as the costs of containing their waste products.

Wind, wave, thermal and solar power stations can be small – small enough to fit on three million rooftops or the walls of ten million buildings. The cost of doing that may be higher than a nuclear power station for the same or even less power (though that is now debatable). But these decentralised power stations can be built up piece by piece, rooftop by rooftop. And if disaster comes, as it did with the tsunami at Fukushima, we would not see a third of the country lose its power. Decentralisation equals resilience.

Decentralised power provision is also more cost-effective. Few Australians – and also possibly planners – know that between thirty and forty per cent of power generated is lost in its transmission. Small regional or even suburban power plants are far more efficient than centralised ones. But our power infrastructure is not set up to allow enough feed in from stand-alone systems to the grid. Changing the way we get our power will require the ability and the courage to imagine and implement a different world.

Prediction 21: Expect extinction and to watch parts of the bush die.
This is hard to write; it is emotionally difficult to accept. But the continent of Australia is no longer isolated geographically; our quarantine services have been so drastically cut back that new parasites – pests like the Argentine fire ants, the varroa mite that devastates bee colonies, the myrtle rust that may kill vast forests of eucalypts – are a continual threat, nor is there anything resembling adequate resources to

control these when they are still only isolated outbreaks. The research of state departments of agriculture and the CSIRO have been so dramatically extinguished or redirected that we simply do not have the studies to know what threatens us most, nor what to do about it. What if Barmah Forest virus and Ross River virus become major problems rather than rare? Will we see Lyme disease established in Australia? What unknown zoonoses may be spread by flying foxes that migrate into urban areas when their forest habitat is destroyed by drought, fire, disease or clearing?[13]

As I write this, southern hairy-nosed wombats are facing critical decline due to poisoning from introduced weeds, and some bare-nosed wombats suffer such mental confusion after catching toxoplasmosis from feral cats that they are unable to survive long in the wild. In dry years, when they are forced into sunlight more to get their food, introduced mange becomes so severe it leads to local extinctions. But we simply do not know enough to evaluate the severity of any of these.

I do not want to face the bush with no wombats. But can Melbourne or Sydney survive a world where the bush around their catchment dams die and the land turns to desert, silting up the dams or making the water undrinkable? Will global warming lead to the increase of toxic blue-green algae, or cryptosporidium or other deadly agents in our water systems that present filtration and treatments cannot clean out? In this, too, we need to follow the example of those who survived here for 60,000 years: prepare for the worst and, above all, keep your water clean.

Prediction 22: An unexpected invention will change the way we live within the next decade.
No, this one is not gleaned from watching the land, but it belongs in a list of predictions. I love old sci-fi stories, but neither those sci-fi writers nor the scientists writing at the same time (in some cases the writers were both) accurately predicted either the technologies that would alter our lives nor major social changes, such as the way contraception, TV, mobile phones, the internet and personal computers have transformed

our society. The sci-fi writers from the 1890s to the 1950s also assumed that women would always and only be wives and secretaries.

(Arthur C. Clarke and Robert Heinlein did predict some of today's technology, or possibly their imagining it inspired others to create it. But sci-fi is better at examining its own culture through extrapolating and exaggerating existing features than predicting what comes next.)

Prediction 23: We may actually become the lucky country.

Wealthy countries may survive climate change better than poor ones: they have the money for disaster care, and the resources – both financial and technical – to change strategies. Australia is wealthy and relatively well educated. We are also generous. This matters.

But we have one other major advantage too. Most of our land is desert, impossible to survive in without experience and knowledge. Refugees to Australia – both in the past decades and the past two hundred years – mostly wanted to come to cities, where life might approximate what they had known. With few exceptions, like the German farming communities of South Australia, they did not set up small settlements of their own. Our cities and developed areas are inviting. Our land – by and large – is not.

Australia may yet be a place where we care for each other as times get worse, where we have the education, ingenuity and resilience to cope with a changing world.

Australia, too, tends to be a land of generalists – with a small and far-flung population we have had to be. My husband describes working at Honeysuckle Creek Tracking Station, near Canberra, during the Apollo moon project. The visiting NASA representatives tended to specialise in one small area. The Australians wanted to know how everything worked, and exactly what new things they could do with it. (And when the oxygen tank on Apollo 13 ruptured, the Australians' tendency to play with every scenario meant they had already come up with the procedures, and tested them in a simulated disaster, to track both the spacecraft and the following rocket.)[14]

Forty years ago we were a land of tinkerers, of blokes in sheds. We are still a land where kids experiment with strapping Mum's mobile phone onto their remote-control toy truck to see what's happening in their sister's bedroom, where high-school projects are valued for their innovation, and of stroppy women (which effectively gives us fifty per cent more ingenuity than countries where women are suppressed). If the central water supplies fail we'll rig up water tanks; if the power fails each street may have wind generators, bodged out of bits that fell off the back of a truck … and the very word 'bodged' says much about Australia too. A land of bodgers is likely to survive.[15]

So will our best farmland, but then we have experience of repairing poor land too, despite the closing of the agricultural research stations, the slashing of CSIRO's budget, and the fact that much of that experimentation and development is now being done by private companies and individuals.

As a nation we have made some extraordinary blunders, blighting large parts of our continent. But when we put our minds to it we are reasonably good at if not solving the problem, then at least mitigating it.

Prediction 24: Tomorrow will be pretty much like today.
But one day it won't be.

Notes

Like most knowledge packrats, I tend to cut out articles of interest without noting their proper references. Even more data is consigned to the 'this is relevant' portion of my memory without attribution. I apologise for the lack of page and other references in some endnotes; apologies, too, for having too many endnotes for easy reference, and perhaps too few to adequately substantiate each assertion. Many points would need their own book to do so.

INTRODUCTION: THE GOAT DROPPINGS THAT CHANGED HISTORY

1. Beaglehole, John Cawte (1901–1971) & Cook, James, 1728–1779. *Voyage of the Endeavour, 1768–1771* & Hakluyt Society, *The journals of Captain James Cook: addenda and corrigenda to volume 1, The voyage of the Endeavour, 1768-1771*. Published for the Hakluyt Society at the University Press, Cambridge, 1968.
2. Hasluck, Alexandra. *Portrait with Background: a Life of Georgiana Molloy*. Oxford University Press. Melbourne 1955.
3. *Australian Rainfall Patterns*. Climate Information. Bureau of Meteorology. www.bom.gov.au/climate. Accessed 13.7.2013.
4. Carboni, Raffaello. (1855), *The Eureka Stockade*, first published 1855. Retrieved 28 June 2013, from Project Gutenberg Australia (e00015.txt).
5. Ibid.
6. List of Indigenous Australian Group names. Wikipedia.en.wikipedia. org/wiki/Indigenous_peoples_of_Australia. Accessed 12.7.2013; Maps. AIATSIS. Australian Institute of Aboriginal and Torres Strait Islander Studies. (www.aiatsis.gov.au/research/language.html)

CHAPTER 1: THE REAL FIRST FLEET

1. O'Connor, Sue. 'Out of Asia', *Australasian Science*, May 2012.
2. Young, Emma. 'New arrival date for earliest Australians', *New Scientist*, 18 February 2006.
3. Marshall, Michael. 'Humans colonised Asia in two waves', *New Scientist*, 22 September 2010. Breaking News. Issue no. 2902.
4. Hooper, Rowan. 'Humans took the scenic route out of Africa', *New Scientist*, 21 May 2005. Issue No 2500.

5. Sara, S. (Presenter), MacDonald, A. (Reporter) & Cooper, A. (Guest 'Evidence of gene flow between India and Australia 4000 years ago', radio broadcast, in M. Colvin (Producer). *PM*, 15 January 2013, Australia: ABC Radio National. Sydney.

6. Ibid.

7. Dr Jonica Newby. *Catalyst*, ABC TV, 20 September 2012.

8. Nichols, R. J., & Cazenave, A. (2010). 'Sea-Level Rise and Its Impact on Coastal Zones', *Science, 328* (5985), 1517-1520.

9. E. Hagelberg, M. Kayser, M. Nagy, L. Roewer, H. Zimdahl, M. Krawczak, P. Lió and W. Schiefenhöve, *Molecular genetic evidence for the human settlement of the Pacific: analysis of mitochondrial DNA, Y chromosome and HLA markers,* Published 29 January 1999. Retrieved at doi: 10.1098/rstb.1999.0367Phil. Trans. R. Soc. Lond. B 29 January 1999 vol. 354 no. 1379 141-152. Accessed 12 July 2013.

10. Wroe, S., Field, J. H., Archer, M., Grayson, D. K., Price, G., Louys, J., et al. *Climate change frames debate over the extinction of megafauna in Sahul Pleistocene Society*, University Press, Cambridge, 2013.

CHAPTER 2: THE ICE AGE THAT MADE THREE HUNDRED NATIONS

1. Kearins. Judith. M. 'Visual spatial memory in Australian Aboriginal children of desert regions', University of Western Australia, *Australian Cognitive Psychology,* Volume 13, Issue 3, July 1981, Pages 434–460.

2. Curr, E. M. *Continental Australia: showing the routes by which the Aboriginal race spread itself throughout the continent.* Australian Institute of Aboriginal and Torres Strait Islander Studies: www.aiatsis.gov.au/research/language.html

3. Nichols, R. J., & Cazenave, A, op. cit.

4. Sara, S. (Presenter), MacDonald, A. (Reporter) & Cooper, A. (Guest), op. cit.

5. Wroe, S., Field, J. H., Archer, M., Grayson, D. K., Price, G., Louys, J., et al., op. cit.

6. Nicholls, N., 'Historical El Niño/Southern Oscillation variability in the Australian region', in H. F. Diaz & V. Markgraf (eds), *El Niño: Historical and Paleoclimatic Aspects of the Southern Oscillation*, Cambridge University press, Cambridge, 1992.

7. List of Indigenous Australian Group names, Wikipedia, op. cit.; Maps. AIATSIS, op. cit.

8. *Ancient aquaculture site is now a heritage treasure.* ECOS. (Not attributed). CSIRO Publishing. 1.8.2004.

CHAPTER 3: COOPERATE OR DIE

1. Sherwood, Steven, Kjellstrom, Tord & Green, Donna, 'Heat Stress in a Warming World', *Australasian Science*. December 2010.
2. Sara, S. (Presenter), MacDonald, A. (Reporter) & Cooper, A. (Guest), op. cit.; Curnoe, Darren, Cooper, Alan & Roberts, Richard, commenting on 'Aboriginal Genome Reveals New Insights into Early Human', *Australasian Science*, November 2011; List of Indigenous Australian Group names, Wikipedia, op. cit.; Maps. AIATSIS, op. cit.; O'Shannessy, Carmel. 'New Australian Language Discovered', *Language*. Linguistic Society of America. June 2013.
3. Luntz, Stephen. 'Butterfly Behaviour Link to Warming', *Australasian Science*. May 2010.
4. Beaglehole, John Cawte, Cook, James & Hakluyt Society, op. cit.

CHAPTER 4: THE WOMEN WHO MADE THE LAND

1. Donaldson, Susan Dale, Ellis, Patricia, Feary, Sue, NSW Southern Rivers Catchment Management Authority: Djuuwin Women's Perspective on the Moruya Deua River Catchment, August 2012. Draft Final Report. NSW Southern Rivers Catchment Management Authority. 2013.
2. Luntz, Stephen. 'Indigenous Migraine Treatment', *Australasian Science*. May 2010; 'Research Confirms Aboriginal Medicine "kinos" Promising Antibacterial Treatment', ScienceNetwork Western Australia. *Australasian Science*, December 2012.
3. *Australian Rainfall Patterns*. Climate Information. Bureau of Meteorology, op. cit.
4. 'Shaking more from bush trees' *ECOS*. (Not attributed). CSIRO Publishing. 1.9.1996.
5. Yeang, Lily & Woodward, Emma. 'When the Ghost Gum Peels, Bull Sharks Are fat in the river', *Australasian Science*, May 2013.
6. Tester, R. *Wombat or wallaby: reminiscences of a trip overland to Melbourne and the goldfields*. Mss. B1652. New South Wales: Mitchell Library, n.d.
7. Meredith, Louisa Anne. *Notes and sketches of New South Wales during a residence in the colony from 1839 to 1844*. John Murray, London, 1844.
8. Young, Emma. 'Controlled bushfires damage – not protect – wildlife', *New Scientist*, 6 October 2003.
9. Inglis, Tim. 'Dangerous Ground', *Australasian Science*, December 2010.
10. Gerritsen, Rupert. 'Evidence for Indigenous Australian Agriculture', *Australasian Science*. July/August 2010.

CHAPTER 5: TERRA INCOGNITA: DREAMS OF GOLD AND A LAND WITHOUT GRASS

1. Hasluck, Alexandra, op. cit.
2. Beaglehole, J. C. (John Cawte, Cook, James & Hakluyt Society, op. cit.
3. Marco Polo and Rustichello of Pisa, *The Travels of Marco Polo*, Volume 1. Project Gutenberg. Retrieved 1 June 2013.
4. Ibid.
5. Tasman, A. J., *Abel Janszoon Tasman's Journal of his discovery of Van Diemen's Land and New Zealand in 1642: with documents relating to his exploration of Australia in 1644: being photo-lithographic facsimiles of the original manuscript … with an English translation … to which are added Life and labours of Abel … by J.E. Heeres … and Observations made with the compass … by W. van Bemmelen.* Frederik Muller, Amsterdam, 1898; Heeres, J. E. (n.d.). *Abel Janszoon Tasman's Journal.* Project Gutenberg Australia. Retrieved 27 June 2013, from (0600571h.html).
6. Heeres, ibid.
7. Dampier, William, *A New Voyage Around the World.* 1703. www.archive.org/details/anewvoyageround00dampgoog. Accessed 1 June 2013.

CHAPTER 6: THE GOAT, THE GROCER'S ASSISTANT, AND THE MISTAKE THAT LED TO A NATION

1. Dalrymple, Alexander. *An historical collection of the several voyages and discoveries in the South Pacific Ocean.* Printed for the author; and sold by J. Nourse, T. Payne, and P. Elmsley, London, 1770.
2. Cook, James, Beaglehole, John Cawte, Skelton, Raleigh Ashlin & Hakluyt Society, op. cit.
3. Cook, James. *Captain Cook's Journal During His First Voyage Round the World Made in H. M. Bark Endeavour 1768–71* (1893). A Literal Transcription of the Original MSS. with notes and introduction edited by Captain W. J. L. Wharton, R.N., F.R.S. Hydrographer of the Admiralty. Illustrated by Maps and Facsimiles. Project Gutenberg Australia. Retrieved 27 June 2013, from (e00043.html).
4. Ibid.
5. Boswell, James. *The Life of Samuel Johnson*, 1791. Page 457.
6. Burney, James, 1750–1821 (2010-10-03). *James Burney – Journal on HMS Discovery, 10 Feb. 1776–24 Aug. 1779.*

CHAPTER 7: THE COLONY THAT DIDN'T STARVE

1. Frost, Alan. *Sir Joseph Banks and the transfer of plants to and from the South Pacific, 1786–1798.* Colony Press. Melbourne. 1993.

2. Collins, David. & King, Philip Gidley. *An account of the English colony in New South Wales: with remarks on the dispositions, customs, manners, &c. of the native inhabitants of that country*. Printed for T. Cadell Jun. and W. Davies, London, 1798.

3. Phillip, Arthur. *The voyage of Governor Phillip to Botany Bay; with an account of the establishment of the colonies of Port Jackson & Norfolk Island; compiled from authentic papers ... embellished with fifty five copper plates ...* London: printed for John Stockdale, 1789.

4. Collins, David. & King, Philip Gidley, op. cit.

5. Phillip, Athur, op. cit.

6. White, John. *Journal of a voyage to New South Wales with sixty-five plates of non descript animals, birds ... and other natural productions*, 1790. In Project Gutenberg Australia. Retrieved 28 June 2013, from (0301531h.html).

7. Ibid.

8. Cribb, A. B., Cribb, J. W. & McCubbin, Charles. *Wild Food in Australia*. Fontana, Sydney, 1987; Gammage, Bill. *The Biggest Estate on Earth: How Aborigines Made Australia*. Allen & Unwin, Crows Nest, NSW, 2011; Hardwick, Richard. *Nature's Larder: a Field Guide to the Native Food Plants of the NSW South Coast*. Homosapien Books Jerrabomberra, NSW, 2001; Maiden, J. H. *The Useful Native Plants of Australia (Including Tasmania)*. Compendium, Melbourne: 1975; Smith, Keith, Smith, Irene. & Norling, Beth. *Grow Your Own Bushfoods*. New Holland, Frenchs Forest, NSW 1999; Waverley (NSW Municipality) Council & Australian Archaeological Survey Consultants Pty Ltd. *The Waverley Council area: an Aboriginal perspective: a report to the Waverley Council*. 1995.

9. White, John, op. cit.

10. Collins, David. & King, Philip Gidley, op. cit.

11. Crittenden, Victor. *William Dawes: The Unknown Man of the First Fleet*. E book version available from Amazon UK.

12. White, John, op. cit.

13. Phillip, Arthur, op. cit.

14. Tench, Watkin. *A Narrative of the Expedition to Botany Bay: With an Account of New South Wales, Its Productions, Inhabitants, &c.: To Which Is Subjoined, a List of the Civil and Military Establishments at Port Jackson* (Second edition). London: J. Debrett, 1789; also Tench, W. *A Complete Account of the Settlement at Port Jackson in New South Wales, including an Accurate Description of the Situation of the Colony; of the Natives; and of Its Natural Productions: Taken on the Spot*. London: G. Nicol and J. Sewell, 1793.

15. White, John, op. cit.

16. Tench, Watkin & Flannery, Tim. *1788: Comprising a narrative of the expedition to Botany Bay and a complete account of the settlement at Port Jackson.* Text Publishing, Melbourne, 2009.

17. Collins, David. & King, Philip Gidley, op. cit.

18. Ibid.

19. Ibid.

20. Ibid.

21. Ibid.

22. Ibid.

23. Ibid.

24. Ibid.

25. Mackaness, G. *Some Letters of Rev. Richard Johnson*, Sydney, 1954. Quoted by various authors. Original text not consulted.

26. Tench, Watkin, *A narrative of the Expedition to Botany Bay,*op. cit.

27. Collins, David. & King, Philip Gidley, op. cit.

28. White, John, op. cit.

CHAPTER 8: THE SECOND, THIRD AND FOURTH AUSTRALIANS

1. Historical Census and Colonial Data Archive. hccda.anu.edu.au/. Accessed 12.6.2013.

2. Early Australian Census Records. guides.slv.vic.gov.au. Research Guides. Accessed 12.7.2013; Australian Census Records. search.ancestry.com.au/search/grouplist.aspx?group=AUSCENSUS. Accessed 12.7.2013.

3. Objects Through Time 1830–1840: Australian History Migration Timeline. www.migrationheritage.nsw.gov.au/exhibition/objectsthroughtime. Accessed 1 June 2013; Early Australian Census Records, op. cit.

4. Ibid.

5. Johnson, Samuel. *A journey to the Western Islands of Scotland.* Printed for W. Strahan and T. Cadell, London, 1775.

6. Historical Census and Colonial Data Archive, op. cit.

7. Ibid.

CHAPTER 9: THE LOST TIGERS AND THE SHEEP THAT ATE AUSTRALIA

1. Lawson, Henry. 'How the Land was Won', *Humorous and Other Verses*, 1900.

2. Anderson, Ian. 'Australia's growing disaster', *New Scientist*, Issue 1998. 29 July 1995.

3. Historical Census and Colonial Data Archive, op. cit.

4. Nicholls, N, op. cit.; Hendon, H. H., Thompson, D.W.J. & Wheeler, M.C., 'Australian rainfall and surface temperature variations associated with the Southern Hemisphere annular mode', *Journal of Climate* 20: 2452–67, 2007.

5. Cribb, Julian. 'Solutions to the Global Food Crisis', *Australasian Science*, April 2013, based on a paper presented to the Australian Academy of Science's 2nd Earth System Outlook Conference.

CHAPTER 10: HOW WE ALMOST WON EUREKA

1. Hargraves, Edward Hammond. *Australia and Its Goldfields: a historical sketch of the progress of the Australian colonies from the earliest times to the present day with a particular account of the recent gold discoveries and observations n the present aspect of the land question to which are added notices on the use and working of gold in ancient and modern times and an examination of the theories of the sources of gold, with a map and portrait of the author.* H. Ingram and Co; London, England, 1855.

2. Clarke, William Branwhite. Papers and notebooks, 1827–1934. ML Mss. 454. State Library of New South Wales.

3. Ibid.

4. O'Brien, Bob, Huyghue, S. D. S. & Sovereign Hill Goldmining Township. *Massacre at Eureka: the untold story.* Sovereign Hill Museums Association, Ballarat, Victoria, 1998.

5. Carboni, Raffaello. *The Eureka Stockade*, 1855. In Project Gutenberg Australia. Retrieved 28 June 2013, from (e00015.txt).

6. Australian Government Cultural portal: www.culture.gov.au/articles/eurekastockade/index.htma. Accessed February 2008.

7. Lawson, Henry. 'A Song of General Sick and Tiredness', Written 1908. From *Henry Lawson's Poetical Works.* Angus & Robertson. Sydney. Reprinted 1951.

8. Turner, Ian & Lalor, Peter. *Australian Dictionary of Biography*, Volume 5, Melbourne University Press, 1975, pp 50-54.

9. Carboni, Raffaello, op. cit.

10. Turner, Ian & Lalor, Peter, op. cit.

11. Carboni, Raffaello, op. cit.

12. Ibid.

13. Ibid.

14. Ibid.

15. Ibid.

16. Ibid.

17. Ibid.

18. 'Ballarat: The statement of Frank Arthur Hasleham', *Geelong Advertiser and Intelligencer*, 28 December 1854. Accessed 11.08.13 at Trove: trove.nla.gov.au/ndp/del/article/91861589

19. Carboni, op. cit.

20. Ibid.

21. An Act to Further Alter 'The Victoria Electoral Act of 1851', assented to 22 May 1855. www.austlii.edu.au/au/legis/vic/hist_act/aatfaveao1851atitnomotlcov1084.pdf Accessed 1 June 2013

CHAPTER 11: THE HISTORY OF OUR NATION IN A PUMPKIN SCONE

1. Rudd, Steele & Fischer, A. J. 'On Our Selection', *The Bulletin*, Sydney, 1899; and Rudd, S., 'Our New Selection', *The Bulletin*, Sydney, 1903.

2. Franklin, Miles. *Childhood at Brindabella: My first ten years*. Angus & Robertson, Sydney. 1963.

3. Smith, Michelle, Gee, Patricia & Redcliffe Council. *Redcliffe remembers: the war years 1939–1949*. Redcliffe City Council, Redcliffe, Qld, 2004.

4. Bjelke-Petersen, Flo & Cameron, Helen. (1998). *Lady Flo: politics and pumpkin scones*. [Helen Cameron] Kingaroy, Qld, 1988.

5. French, Maurice. *The Lamington enigma: a survey of the evidence*. Tabletop Publishing, Toowoomba, Qld, 2013.

CHAPTER 12: HOW A DROUGHT MADE US ONE NATION

1. Matthews, Brian. 'Lawson, Henry (1867–1922)', *Australian Dictionary of Biography*, Volume 10. Melbourne University Press, 1986, Melbourne.

2. Lawson, Henry. *In the Days When the World Was Wide*, 1896. In Project Gutenberg Australia. Retrieved June 28, 2013, from Lawson.html.

3. Lawson, Henry. 'Past Carin', first published in *The Australian Magazine*, Sydney, 30 May 1899.

4. Garden, Donald. *Droughts, floods & cyclones: El Niños that shaped our colonial past*. Australian Scholarly Publishing, North Melbourne, Vic, 2009.

5. Ibid.

6. *Official Year Book of the Commonwealth of Australia*. No 4. Commonwealth Bureau of Census and Statistics. 1911, page 335.

7. Department of Lands, NSW. *Annual Report*. Government Printer, Sydney. 1900–1912.

8. 1898 'Bushfires in Victoria', Research Guides at State Library of Victoria. guides.slv.vic.gov.au. Research Guides. Accessed 1 June 2013.

9. 'The Rabbit Plague', *The Maitland Mercury*, 16 January 1870. Trove. trove.nla.gov.au/ndp/del/article/18823632. Accessed 1 June 2013.

10. 'Heat waves in New South Wales', Papers Past, National Library of New Zealand. paperspast.natlib.govt.nz/cgi-bin/paperspast?a=d&d=WDT18981020. Accessed 1 June 2013

11. Issues between Monday 1 January 1900 & Friday December 1909 from *The Australian Town and Country Journal*, NSW. National Library of Australia, Canberra: trove.nla.gov.au/ndp/del/issues?title=52&yyyymmdd=1900-01. Accessed 1 June 2013.

12. Lawson, Henry & Mahony, Frank. *While the Billy Boils*. Angus & Robertson, Sydney, 1896.

13. The National Women's Christian Temperance Union of Australia. In Trove. Retrieved 1 July 2013, from nla.gov.au/nla.party-762051

14. Ibid.

15. 1891 women's suffrage petition. Parliament of Victoria, Melbourne, 2005.

16. Ibid.

CHAPTER 13: TRUTH OR PROPAGANDA? THE BRONZED ANZACS OF GALLIPOLI AND KOKODA

1. Bean, C.E.W. *The official history of Australia in the war of 1914–1918*. Angus & Robertson, Sydney, 1921.

2. 'Reports by War Correspondents at the Landing including the Commonwealth of Australia *Gazette*', No 39, Monday 17 May 1915. www.anzacsite.gov.au. Accessed 1 June 2013.

3. Marshall, Robert. *Journal, Scribblings and Letters 1915*. Transcribed by Angela Marshall. Unpublished.

4. 'Enlistment Statistics and Standards, First World War', Australian War Memorial, Canberra. www.awm.gov.au/encyclopedia/enlistment/ww1/. Accessed 1 June 2013.

5. 'Enlistment for the First World War in Rural Australia', Australian War memorial. Canberra. www.awm.gov.au/journal/j33/mcquilton.asp. Accessed 1 June 2013.

6. Dennis, C. J. *The Songs of a Sentimental Bloke*. Angus & Robertson. Sydney, 1915.

7. 'Enlistment for the First World War in Rural Australia', op. cit.

8. Francis, C. 'Testament of Courage', *Reveille*. Accessed at wwwl.aiatsis.gov.au/dawn/docs/vii/so4/10 pdf. Accessed May 2008; Bean, C.E.W, op. cit.

9. Great Britain War Office. *Statistics of the military effort of the British Empire during the Great War. 1914–1920*. H. M. Stationery off, London, 1922.

10. Scott, Ernest. *Australia during the war*. Angus & Robertson, Sydney, 1936.

11. Cross, Stan. Cartoon: 'For gorsake, stop laughing: this is serious', *Smith's Weekly*, 29 July 1933. Accessed State Library of Victoria. www.slv.vic.gov.au

12. *The Bran Mash*. 4th L.H, Anzac Cove, [Turkey] (*Bran Mash, no.1, 15 June 1915 AWM SI14*).

13. Schmidt, N. *The Dinkum Oil*. [Gallipoli], 2010. Nos 1–7 1915. Australian War Memorial. Access number AWM 419/46/30/Acc 21435. Retrieved from www.awm.gov.au/blog/2010/09/30/the-dinkum-oil/

14. 'Soldiers' Slang', Australian War Memorial. Canberra. www.awm.gov.au/education/resources/slang/Accessed May 2010.

15. Fisher, Mackensie, Cawley, Clyde, Gwynn, May, Nicholson, Lord, Pickford, Roch. British Official Publications Collaborative Reader Information Service, February 1917. Accessed 12 July 2013.

16. Bean, C.E.W, op. cit.

17. Johnstone, Mark. *The Journal of the Australian War Memorial*. Issue 29. November 1996.

18. Goldstein, Donald M & Dillon, Katherine V. *The Pacific War papers: Japanese documents of World War II (1st ed)*. Interview with Admiral Nobutake Kondo Potomac Books, Washington, D.C., 2004.

19. Cook, Taya Haruko, and Cook, Theodore. *Japan at war. An Oral History*. The New Press. 1992.

20. Ibid.

21. 'Crisis at Home and Abroad', john.curtin.edu.au/manofpeace/crisis.html. Accessed 1 June 2013.

22. Cablegram from Curtin to Churchill. 17 January 1942. vrroom.naa.gov.au/print/?ID=24242. Accessed 1 June 2013.

23. Australia Attacked – Air Raids – Australia's War 1939–1945. www.ww2australia.gov.au/underattack/airraid.html. Accessed 12 July 2013.

24. The Bombing of Darwin. National Archives of Australia. www.naa.gov.au/collection/fact-sheets/fs195.aspx. Accessed July 2013.

25. 'Air Raids on Australian Mainland – Second World War', Australian War Memorial. www.awm.gov.au/encyclopedia/air_raids/ Accessed 12 July 2013.

26. 'All In. Living with War', *Australia's War 1939–1945*. www.ww2australia.gov.au/allin/livingwar.html. Accessed 12 July 2013.

27. 'Girl Guides Association of Australia', Australian War Memorial. ID number: MSS1484. www.awm.gov.au/collection/MSS1484/. Accessed 12 July 2013, as well as personal experience by the author.

28. Cook, Taya Haruko, and Cook, Theodore, op. cit.

29. Cosgrove, Peter (General). 'Ralph Honner Address', Kokoda Track Foundation. March 2007. www.39battalion.org/GG146-APR-07.pdf. Accessed June 2013.
30. 'Australia's War 1935–45'. Text, documents, graphics and video. www.ww2australia.gov.au. Accessed June 2012.
31. Ibid.
32. Ibid.
33. Ibid.
34. Ibid.
35. Ibid.
36. 'History of the ACC – Australian Defence Force cadets'. www.cadetnet.gov.au/AAC/WHOWEARE/Pages/History.aspx. Accessed 1 June 2013.
37. Alan Sullivan. *Newsletter 39th Battalion*, April 2007. www.39battalion.org/GG146-APR-07.pdf. Accessed 1 June 2013.
38. Edwards, Theophilous Alfred (Colonel Dr). Personal communication circa 1960–69.

CHAPTER 14: A LAND OF FLOODING RAIN

1. 'Gundagai 1852 Flood lists', *The Sydney Morning Herald*, 5 July 1852, page 2. Trove. trove.nla.gov.au/list?id=4440. Accessed 12 July 2013.
2. *Townsville Bulletin*, 15 January 2011. www.townsvillebulletin.com.au/article/2011/01/15/200131_news.html. Accessed 12 July 2013.
3. Flood Flag maps 12 January 2011. qldfloods.org/maps/floodflagmaps. Accessed 12 July 2013.
4. Zukerman, Wendy. 'La Niña and monsoonal winds flood northern Australia', *New Scientist*, 4 January 2011; '1974 Brisbane Floods', *The Australian*. www.theaustralian.com.au/news/nation/gallery-e6frg6nf-1225985694831?. Accessed 12 July 2013.
5. Abrahams, M.J. 'The Brisbane Floods January 1974: their impact on health', 1976. www.ncbi.nlm.nih.gov/pubmed/1018676. Accessed 12 July 2013.
6. Flood Flag maps 12 January 2011, op. cit.
7. Personal conversations with volunteer organisers and Premier Anna Bligh, January–July 2011.
8. CSIRO Marine and Atmospheric Research. *Sea-level Rise: Understanding the past – Improving projections for the future*, 2013. Retrieved from www.cmar.csiro.au/sealevel/
9. *Netherlands National Climate Change Response Programme*. National Climate Research, the Netherlands. www.climateresearchnetherlands.nl. Projects and Methods. Accessed 12 July 2013.

10. 'Coming to terms with cyclones', *ECOS* magazine, CSIRO. ecosmagazine. com/?act=view_file&file_id=EC05p13.pdf. Accessed 12 July 2013.

11. 'Burning Down the House', *Catalyst*. ABC TV, 10 June 2010. www.abc. net.au/catalyst/stories/2922902.htm. Accessed 12 July 2013; Phillips, Nicky. 'CSIRO Bushfire Proof Houses', *Sydney Morning Herald*. 17 April 2010; 'Balancing fire risk at the urban fringe.' *ECOS*. CSIRO. 21 November 2011. www.ecosmagazine.com/view/journals/ECOS_Print_Fulltext.cfm?f; Bushfires. CSIRO. 23 Nov 2011. www.csiro.au. Home. Environment. Accessed 12 July 2013.

12. 'Islands on land could make towns tsunami proof', *New Scientist*, 15 February 2012. www.newscientist.com/.../mg21328525.800-islands-on-land-could-make. Accessed 12 July 2013.

CHAPTER 15: A SHORT HISTORY OF GREAT BIG FARMING MISUNDERSTANDINGS

1. Lowe, Ian. 'Landcare Evolves But Bean Counters Haven't', *Australasian Science*. November 2012.

2. Munn, A.J., Dawson, T.J., McLeod, S.R., Croft, D.B., Thompson, M.B., & Dickman, C.R. 'Field metabolic rate and water turnover of red kangaroos and sheep in an arid rangeland: an empirically derived dry-sheep-equivalent for kangaroos', *Australian Journal of Zoology* 57, 23–28. 2009. dx.doi. org/10.1071/ZO08063

3. Beeton, R.J.S., Buckley, K.I., Jones, G.J., Morgan, D., Reichelt, R.E. & Trewin, D. (2006 Australian State of the Environment Committee). Australia State of the Environment 2006 Independent report to the Australian Government Minister for the Environment and Heritage, Department of the Environment and Heritage, Canberra, 2006.

4. Olsen, P. & Low, T. *Situation Analysis Report: Current state of scientific knowledge on kangaroos in the environment, including ecological and economic impact and effect of culling.* Prepared for the Kangaroo Management Advisory Panel, March 2006. dx.doi.org/10.1071/ZO08063

5. Beckmann, Roger. 'Kangaroos on the farm', *ECOS*. CSIRO Publishing.1.12.1990.

6. Munn, A.J., Dawson, T.J., McLeod, S.R., Croft, D.B., Thompson, M.B., and Dickman, C.R., op. cit.

7. 'Living with wildlife on the farm', CSIRO Division of Wildlife Research. *ECOS*, CSIRO Publishing. No 8. PP 28.

8. Vasquez, Sonia. 'Mange in Wombats, New trial to assist wombats with sarcoptic mange'. Autumn 2002. www.marsupialsociety.org/02au03. html. Accessed 12 July 2013; Skerratt L.F., Phelan J., McFarlane, R.

& Speare, R. 'Serodiagnosis of toxoplasmosis in a common wombat', Department of Public Health and Tropical Medicine, James Cook University, Townsville, Queensland, Australia. April 1997. www.ncbi. nlm.nih.gov/pubmed/9131574. Accessed 12 July 2013; Barnes, Michelle. *Husbandry Manual: Common Wombat.* Fourth Crossing Wildlife. www. fourthcrossingwildlife.com/CommonWombatHusbandryManual. Accessed 12 July 2013.

9. Living with Wildlife. www.jackiefrench.com
10. Anderson, Ian. 'Should the cat take the rap?' *New Scientist.* Issue 1926. 21 May 1994.
11. Ridpath, M.G. 'The wedge-tailed eagle', *Australian Natural History* 16, 209–12, 1969.
12. French, Jackie. *Organic Control of Common Weeds.* Aird Books, 1993, rev. 1997.
13. French, Jackie. *Natural Control of Garden Pests.* Aird Books, 2007.

CHAPTER 16: THIS GENEROUS LAND: TERRAPATHS, MORAL OMNIVORES AND HOW TO SURVIVE THE NEXT MILLENNIA

1. Garnaut, Ross. *The Garnaut Climate Change Review. Final Report. Projecting Australian Climate Change.* Cambridge University Press. 2008 www. garnautreview.org.au/pdf/Garnaut_Chapter5.pdf. Accessed 13.7.2013.
2. Donaldson, Susan, Dale, Ellis, Patricia & Feary, Sue, op. cit.
3. Morwood, Mike & Van Oosterzee, Penny. *A New Human: the Startling Discovery and Strange Story of the Hobbits of Flores, Indonesia.* Smithsonian Books/HarperCollins, USA, 2007.
4. Australian Bureau of Statistics. www.abs.gov.au. ABS Home. Accessed 12 July 2013.
5. Young, Emma. 'Hunting for Australia's rich natural resources', *New Scientist.* Issue 2564. 12 August 2006.
6. MacIntosh, A. & Denniss, R. 'Tasmania's forestry sector akin to "work for the dole"', *Crikey,* 2012. Retrieved from www.crikey.com.au/2012/08/21/ tasmanias-forestry-sector-akin-to-work-for-the-dole/
7. Robin, M. 'Car subsidy sums: should Australia just keep Holden on?', *Crikey,* 2013. Retrieved from www.crikey.com.au/2013/04/04/car-subsidy-sums-should-australia-just-keep-holden-on/
8. Personal conversations 1973–1981, but the term is also used in several of her books and papers.
9. Hamzelou, J. 'Overeating now bigger global problem than lack of food', *New Scientist,* 2896/97. 7. 2012.

10. 'Balancing fire risk at the urban fringe', *ECOS*. CSIRO. 21 November 2011; www.ecosmagazine.com/view/journals/ECOS_Print_Fulltext.cfm?f; Bushfires. CSIRO, op. cit.; Barbard, Jeff. 'Tsunami Resistant Port to be Built in Crescent City', *Huffington Post*. San Francisco. 22 November 2012; 'Islands on land could make towns tsunami proof', *New Scientist*, op. cit.

11. Water Services Association of Australia, 'The WSAA Report Card 2006/07: performance of the Australian urban water industry and projections for the future', WSAA, Melbourne, 2007.

CHAPTER 17: THE NEXT HUNDRED YEARS

1. World Meteorological Organization. *The Global Climate 2001–2010: a decade of climate extremes – Summary Report*, 2013. Retrieved from library. wmo.int/pmb_ged/wmo_1119_en.pdf; CSIRO Marine and Atmospheric Research. *Sea-level Rise: Understanding the past – Improving projections for the future*, 2013. Retrieved from www.cmar.csiro.au/sealevel/; Garnaut, Ross, op. cit.; Anderson, Ian. 'Australia prepares to measure the rise and rise of the Pacific', *New Scientist*. 22 July 1989.

2. CSIRO Marine and Atmospheric Research, 2013, op. cit.; Yu, wen-che. 'Shallow Focus repeating earthquakes in the Tonga-kermadec Vanuatu Subduction Zones', *Bulletin of the Seismological Society America*. February 2013, pages 463–486. bssa.geoscienceworld.org/content/103/1/463.abstract. Accessed 12 July 2013.

3. Nowak, Rachel. 'Australia's quake-ridden past is uncovered', *New Scientist*, Issue 2398, 7 June 2003; 'Volcanic eruption "overdue" in Australia', quoting Bernie Joyce from the University of Melbourne, *New Scientist*, Issue 28206, July 2011; Peterson, Christian. 'The quake Australia thought could never happen', *New Scientist*, Issue 169806, January 1990; Zuckerman, Wendy. 'Volcanic eruption "overdue" in Australia', *New Scientist*, Issue 282006, July 2011; Gibson, Gary, Rosenbaum, Gideon & Pascale, Adam. 'Christchurch Earthquake: Experts Respond', *Australasian Science*, February 2011;

4. Jones, Nicola. 'Meteorite impacts frequently trigger tsunamis', *New Scientist*. Issue 2360. 14 September 2002.

5. Mackenzie, Deborah, 'Bird flu may soon land in Europe and Australia' (in News), *New Scientist*. Issue 2507. 6 July 2005; Anderson, Ian. 'A real headache', *New Scientist*, 4 April 1998; Anderson, Ian. 'Plague's progress: A deadly mosquito-borne disease is poised to enter Australia', *New Scientist*, 28 February 1998; 'Horseshoe bats in the frame as source of SARS' (in News), *New Scientist*, Issue 2520, 8 October 2005; *New Scientist*, p 7, 22–29

December 2012, quoting the Global Burden of Disease Report of nearly 500 scientists from five countries.

6. Probability of Asteroid Impact. www.risk-ed.org/pages/risk/asteroid_prob. htm. Accessed 12 July 2013; R. Marcus, H. J. Melosh, & G. Collins. *Earth Impact Effects Program, an online calculator for qualitative estimation of impact effects.* Purdue University, Imperial College London.

7. Garnaut, Ross, op. cit.; *Australian Climate Commission Report* 2013. Climate Commission. Accessed 12 July 2013; Anderson, Ian. 'Australia prepares to measure the rise and rise of the Pacific', *New Scientist*. 22 July 1989; Coghlan, Andy and Slezak, Michael. 'Australia faces another week of "catastrophic" heat.' *New Scientist* 14:42 08 January 2013; 'Changing wave heights projected as the atmosphere warms', *Australasian Science*, April 2013: quoting Dr Mark Hemer, CSIRO, Canberra. Australia, in the journal *Nature Climate Change* on April 25; 'Climate tug of war disrupting Australian atmospheric circulation patterns', *Australasian Science*, June 2013: quoting co-authors Mr Guojian Wang and Dr Wenju Cai in the *Nature Journal Scientific Reports*; CSIRO, 'projections of days over 35°C to 2100 for all capital cities under a no-mitigation case', data prepared for the Garnaut Climate Change Review, CSIRO, Aspendale, Victoria, 2008; CSIRO & BoM 2007, Climate Change in Australia: Technical report 2007, CSIRO, Melbourne.

8. Hendon, H.H., Thompson, D.W.J. & Wheeler, M.C., op. cit.; Nicholls, N., op. cit.

9. Hamzelou, J., op. cit.

10. Sabto, Michelle. 'Can urban farms feed city and soul?' *ECOS* 27.5.2013. No. 183, CSIRO Publishing; 'Saltgrass part of innovative farm-system for saline land' (not attributed), *ECOS*, CSIRO Publishing, 18 March 2013; 'Model may help farmers better deal with seasonal variability' (not attributed), *ECOS*, CSIRO Publishing, 21 January 2013; 'Salt-tolerant wheat hybrid and saltbush for farming salinised land' (not attributed), *ECOS*, CSIRO Publishing, 12.08.2012; 'Farming a climate change solution' (not attributed). *ECOS*, CSIRO Publishing, 22.2.2008; 'The farmers' tree program that's growing potential' (not attributed), *ECOS*, CSIRO Publishing, 21.11.2005; 'Bacteria help wattles "re-green" Australia' (not attributed), *ECOS*, CSIRO Publishing, 1.2.2004; 'Rising salt: a test of tactics and techniques' (not attributed), *ECOS*, CSIRO Publishing, 1.9.1998; Deeker, Wayne & Bennet, Bryony. 'Winning back the Wheatbelt', *ECOS* No. 78, CSIRO Publishing, 1.12.1993, Pages 30–33; Lowe, Ian. 'Antipodes: Becoming clever in the country: Ian Lowe hears about high tech farming', *New Scientist*, Issue 2039, 20 July 1996; 'Landholders gravitate to carbon farming', CSIRO Publishing.

August 2011. Thwaites, Tim. 'Down under on the up and up', *New Scientist*, Issue 2527, 26 November 2005.

11. *Australian Climate Commission Report* 2013. Climate Commission. Accessed 12 July 2013; 'Changing wave heights projected as the atmosphere warms', *Australasian Science*, April 2013, op. cit.

12. Schneider, M., Froggatt, A. & Hazemann, J. *World Nuclear Industry Status Report 2012*. Retrieved from www.worldnuclearreport.org/

13. Zukerman, Wendy. 'Fungus out! The frog resistance is here', *New Scientist*. Issue 2790. 10 December 2010.

14. Sullivan, Bryan and French, Jackie. *To the Moon and Back*. Angus & Robertson, Sydney, 2004.

15. 'New stars of innovative sustainable design' (in News), *New Scientist*, 8 August 2011; 'Wind farm to meet regional city's domestic power needs' (not attributed), *ECOS*, CSIRO Publishing, 10 September 2012.

Bibliography

Australian Dictionary of Biography (1993). Carlton, Vic: Melbourne University Press.

Beaglehole, J.C. (ed.) and Cook, James (1968). *The Journals of Captain James Cook: Addenda and Corrigenda to Volume 1, The Voyage of the Endeavour, 1768–1771.* Cambridge: Cambridge University Press.

Bean, C.E.W. (1938). *The Story of Anzac: From 4 May 1915 to the Evacuation of the Gallipoli Peninsula.* Sydney: Angus and Robertson.

Bean, C.E.W. (1948). *Gallipoli Mission.* Canberra: Australian War Memorial.

Bean, C.E.W. and Fewster, Kevin (1983). *Gallipoli Correspondent: The Frontline Diary of C.E.W. Bean.* Sydney: George Allen and Unwin.

Blainey, Geoffrey (1963). *The Rush that Never Ended: A History of Australian Mining.* Parkville, Vic: Melbourne University Press.

Blainey, Geoffrey (1966). *The Tyranny of Distance: How Distance Shaped Australia's History.* Melbourne: Sun Books.

Blainey, Geoffrey (1975). *Triumph of the Nomads: A History of Ancient Australia.* South Melbourne, Vic: Macmillan.

Blainey, Geoffrey (1990). *A Game of Our Own: The Origins of Australian Football.* Melbourne: Information Australia.

Blainey, Geoffrey (2000). *A Short History of the World.* Ringwood, Vic: Viking Books.

Blainey, Geoffrey (2004). *Black Kettle and Full Moon: Daily Life in a Vanished Australia.* Camberwell, Vic: Penguin Books.

Brennan, Frank (2003). *Tampering with Asylum: A Universal Humanitarian Problem.* St Lucia, Queensland: University of Queensland Press.

Brune, Peter (2003). *A Bastard of a Place: The Australians in Papua, Kokoda, Milne Bay, Gona, Buna, Sanananda.* Crows Nest, NSW: Allen and Unwin.

Butler, A.G. (1938). *The Official History of the Australian Army Medical Service in the War of 1914–18.* Melbourne: Australian War Memorial.

Clark, Manning (1993). *History of Australia,* abridged by Michael Cathcart. Carlton, Vic: Melbourne University Press.

Clendinnen, Inga (2003). *Dancing with Strangers.* Melbourne: Text Publishing.

Collins, David and Fletcher, Brian H. (1975). *An Account of the English Colony in New South Wales, with Remarks on the Dispositions, Customs, Manners, etc. of the Native Inhabitants of That Country.* Sydney: Reed, in association with the Royal Historical Society, London.

Cook, Haruko Taya and Cook, Theodore Failor (1992). *Japan at War: An Oral History*. New York, NY: New Press.

Corfield, Justin J., Gervasoni, Clare and Wickham, Dorothy (2004). *The Eureka Encyclopaedia*. Ballarat, Vic: Ballarat Heritage Services.

Cribb, A.B., Cribb, J.W. and McCubbin, Charles (1987). *Wild Food in Australia*. Sydney: Fontana.

Dalrymple, Alexander (1770). *An Historical Collection of the Several Voyages and Discoveries in the South Pacific Ocean*. London: Printed for the author and sold by J. Nourse, T. Payne and P. Elmsley.

Donaldson, Susan Dale, Ellis, Patricia and Feary, Su (2012). *NSW Southern Rivers Catchment Management Authority Djuuwin Women's Perspective on the Moruya Deua River Catchment*. Draft Final Report. NSW Southern Rivers Catchment Management Authority.

Eyre, Edward John (2010). *Manners and Customs of the Aborigines and the State of Their Relations with European, from Volume II of Journals of Expeditions of Discovery into Central Australia*. Adelaide: Friends of the State Library of South Australia.

Flinders, Matthew, Westall, William and Brown, Robert (1814). *A Voyage to Terra Australis: Undertaken for the Purpose of Completing the Discovery of That Vast Country, and Prosecuted in the Years 1801, 1802 and 1803, in His Majesty's Ship The Investigator*. London: G. and W. Nicol.

Flood, Josephine (1980). *The Moth Hunters: Aboriginal Prehistory of the Australian Alps*. Canberra: Australian Institute of Aboriginal Studies.

Flood, Josephine (1990). *The Riches of Ancient Australia: A Journey into Prehistory*. St Lucia, Qld: University of Queensland Press.

Flood, Josephine (1995*). Archaeology of the Dreamtime: The Story of Prehistoric Australia and Its People*. Pymble, NSW: Angus and Robertson.

Flood, Josephine (1996). *Moth Hunters of the Australian Capital Territory: Aboriginal Traditional Life in the Canberra Region*. Downer, ACT: J.M. Flood.

Flood, Josephine (1997). *Rock Art of the Dreamtime: Images of Ancient Australia*. Pymble, NSW: Angus and Robertson.

Flood, Josephine (2006). *The Original Australians: Story of the Aboriginal People*. Crows Nest, NSW: Allen and Unwin.

Frost, Alan (1993). *Sir Joseph Banks and the Transfer of Plants to and from the South Pacific, 1786–1798*. Melbourne: Colony Press.

Frost, Alan (1994). *Botany Bay Mirages: Illusions of Australia's Convict Beginnings*. Carlton, Vic: Melbourne University Press.

Gammage, Bill (1974). *The Broken Years: Australian Soldiers in the Great War*. Canberra: Australian National University Press.

Gammage, Bill (2011). *The Biggest Estate on Earth: How Aborigines Made Australia*. Crows Nest, NSW: Allen and Unwin.

Goodall, Heather (1996). *Invasion to Embassy: Land in Aboriginal Politics in New South Wales, 1770–1972*. St Leonards, NSW: Allen and Unwin in association with Black Books.

Groves, Colin P. (1989). *A Theory of Human and Primate Evolution*. Oxford and New York, NY: Oxford University Press and Clarendon Press.

Ham, Paul (2004). *Kokoda*. Pymble, NSW: HarperCollins Publishers.

Hardwick, Richard (2001*). Nature's Larder: A Field Guide to the Native Food Plants of the NSW South Coast*. Jerrabomberra, NSW: Homosapien Books.

Harris, Alexander (1964). *Settlers and Convicts, or, Recollections of Sixteen Years' Labour in the Australian Backwoods*. Parkville, Vic: Melbourne University Press.

Hasluck, Alexandra (1966). *Portrait with Background: A Life of Georgiana Molloy*. Melbourne: Oxford University Press.

Hegarty, M.P., Hegarty, E.E., and Wills, R.B.H. (2001). *Food Safety of Australian Plant Bushfoods*. Kingston, ACT: Rural Industries Research and Development Corporation.

Holden, Robert (2000). *Orphans of History: The Forgotten Children of the First Fleet*. Melbourne: Text Publishing.

Horton, David (1994). *The Encyclopaedia of Aboriginal Australia: Aboriginal and Torres Strait Islander History, Society and Culture*. Canberra: Aboriginal Studies Press for the Australian Institute of Aboriginal and Torres Strait Islander Studies.

Isaacs, Jennifer (1987). *Bush Food: Aboriginal Food and Herbal Medicine*. McMahons Point, NSW: Weldons.

Johnson, Samuel (1775). *A Journey to the Western Islands of Scotland*. London: W. Strahan and T. Cadell.

Johnston, Mark (1996). *At the Front Line: Experiences of Australian Soldiers in World War II*. Cambridge and Melbourne: Cambridge University Press.

Korzelinski, Seweryn and Robe, Stanley (1994). *Life on the Goldfields: Memoirs of a Polish Migrant: 1850s in Victoria*. Carnegie, Vic: Mentone Educational Centre.

Lawson, Henry and Barnes, John (1986). *The Penguin Henry Lawson Short Stories*. Ringwood, Vic. and New York, NY: Penguin Books.

Lawson, Henry, Kiernan, Brian and Cronin, Leonard (1984). *A Camp-fire Yarn: Henry Lawson Complete Works, 1885–1900*. Sydney: Lansdowne Press.

Lawson, Henry and Wright, David McKee (1951). *Poetical Works of Henry Lawson*. Sydney: Angus and Robertson.

Low, Tim (1989). *Bush Tucker: Australia's Wild Food Harvest*. North Ryde, NSW: Angus and Robertson.

Maiden, J.H. (1975). *The Useful Native Plants of Australia (including Tasmania)*. Melbourne: Compendium.

Meredith, Louisa Anne (1844). *Notes and Sketches of New South Wales During a Residence in the Colony from 1839 to 1844*. London: John Murray.

Molony, John N. (2001). *Eureka*. Carlton South, Vic.: Melbourne University Press.

Moorehead, Alan (1959). *Gallipoli*. London: Arrow Books.

O'Brien, Bob and Huyghue, S.D.S. (1998). *Massacre at Eureka: The Untold Story*. Ballarat, Vic: Sovereign Hill Museums Association.

Phillip, Arthur (1789). *The Voyage of Governor Phillip to Botany Bay; with an Account of the Establishment of the Colonies of Port Jackson & Norfolk Island; Compiled from Authentic Papers* ... London: John Stockdale.

Plomley, N.J.B., Tassell, C.B. and Cameron, Mary (1993). *Plant Foods of the Tasmanian Aborigines*. Launceston, Tas: Queen Victoria Museum.

Plumwood, Valerie and Sylvan, Richard (1975). *The Fight for the Forests: The Takeover of Australian Forests for Pines, Wood Chips and Intensive Forestry*. Canberra: Australian National University, Research School of Social Sciences.

Renwick, Cath and the Wreck Bay community (2000). *Geebungs and Snake Whistles: Koori People and Plants of Wreck Bay*. Australian Heritage Commission for the Wreck Bay Community.

Serle, G., Ritchie, J., Nairn, B., Pike, D., Cunneen, C., Langmore, D., Bennet, D., and Nolan, M. (1966). *Australian Dictionary of Biography*. Melbourne and London: Melbourne University Press and Cambridge University Press.

Smith, Keith (1995). *Keith Smith's Classic Vegetable Catalogue*. Port Melbourne, Vic.: Lothian Books,

Smith, Keith, Smith, Irene and Norling, Beth (1999). *Grow Your Own Bushfoods*. Frenchs Forest, NSW: New Holland.

Tasman, A.J. (1898). *Abel Janszoon Tasman's Journal of His Discovery of Van Diemen's Land and New Zealand in 1642: With Documents Relating to His Exploration of Australia in 1644 ... with an English Translation ... to which Are Added Life and Labours of Abel ... by J.E. Heeres... and Observations Made with the Compass ... by W. van Bemmelen*. Amsterdam: Frederik Muller.

Tench, Watkin (1789). *A Narrative of the Expedition to Botany Bay: With an Account of New South Wales, Its Productions, Inhabitants, &c.: To Which Is Subjoined, a List of the Civil and Military Establishments at Port Jackson* (Second edition). London: J. Debrett.

Tench, Watkin & Flannery, Tim (2009). *1788: Comprising a Narrative of the Expedition to Botany Bay and a Complete Account of the Settlement at Port Jackson*. Melbourne: Text Publishing.

Tench, Watkin (1793). *A Complete Account of the Settlement at Port Jackson in New South Wales, including an Accurate Description of the Situation of the Colony; of the Natives; and of Its Natural Productions: Taken on the Spot.* London: G. Nicol and J. Sewell.

Tindale, Norman B. and Jones, Rhys (1974). *Aboriginal Tribes of Australia: Their Terrain, Environmental Controls, Distribution, Limits and Proper Names.* Canberra: Australian National University Press.

Waverley Council and Australian Archaeological Survey Consultants Pty Ltd (1995). *The Waverley Council Area: An Aboriginal Perspective.* Sydney: Waverly Council.

White, John (1790). *Journal of a Voyage to New South Wales.* Republished electronically by Project Gutenburg Australia. Retrieved 28 June, 2013.

Zola, Nelly and Gott, Beth (1992). *Koorie Plants, Koorie People: Traditional Aboriginal Food, Fibre and Healing Plants of Victoria.* Melbourne: Koorie Heritage Trust.

Maps

Aboriginal Australia (2000), wall map, compiled by David Horton, third edition. Canberra: Aboriginal Studies Press for the Australian Institute of Aboriginal and Torres Strait Islander Studies.

Journals

Australasian Science

ECOS (CSIRO Publishing)

New Scientist

Rural Research

The Journal of the Australian War Memorial, Canberra.

For children

The Dinkum History Series, published by Scholastic Books, illustrated by Peter Sheehan:

Shipwreck, Sailors and 60,000 Years: Before 1788 (2006)

Grim Crims and Convicts: 1788–1820 (2005)

Rotters and Squatters: 1820–1850 (2007)

Gold, Graves and Glory: 1850–1880 (2007)

A Nation of Swaggies and Diggers: 1880–1920 (2008)

Weevils, War and Wallabies: 1920–1945 (2009)

Rockin', Rollin', Hair and Hippies: 1945–1972 (2010)

Booms, Busts and Bushfires: Australia 1973–2011 (2011)

Selected historical novels with backgrounds that feature in this book, all published
by Angus and Robertson, Sydney, Australia:

The Goat Who Sailed the World (the story of the goat on the *Endeavour*)

The Camel Who Crossed Australia (the story of Dost Mohamet and the only camel
to survive the Burke and Wills expedition)

The Donkey Who Saved the Wounded (Gallipoli)

The Night They Stormed Eureka

A Rose for the Anzac Boys (World War I)

Nanberry: Black Brother White (the story of the early Port Jackson colony)

A Waltz for Matilda (set 1892–1915; Federation, women's suffrage, the
temperance movement, Indigenous knowledge)

The Girl from Snowy River (1915–1919)

The Road to Gundagai (1932; the depression in Australia)

Pennies for Hitler (World War II)

Refuge (60,000 years of migration to Australia)

Acknowledgements

This book is the product of a lifetime of gifts: knowledge, stories, research. It is impossible to even begin to acknowledge all the contributions made to it. Each statement should have at last six footnotes, making the footnotes far longer than the book.

To start chronologically: to my grandfather, Dr Theophilous Edwards, who found a seven-year-old child grasping an observation of photosynthesis and provided her with the University of Sydney science courses; my grandmothers, Thelma Edwards, and Jean McPherson Ffrench, two of the indomitable ladies who changed our nation and its history; to my parents, Barrie Ffrench and Val French, whose stories, wisdom and analysis of their long lives and their times, as well as access to history books, have so enriched my life; to Dr Martin Sullivan, the history teacher who galloped into our high-school classroom and explained the French Revolution with such passion and insight that I saw history as patterns for the first time, not just names and dates; and to Professor Geoffrey Blainey and author Thomas Keneally, whose books sealed the passion; to Oodgeroo of the Noonuncle, who I knew as Kath Walker, Pastor Don Brady, Sam Watson senior, Maureen Watson (Auntie Mug) and so many of their communities, who ignored the colour of my skin and saw only the need for knowledge and belonging; to Neeta Davis, Bill Mather, Ellie, Jean Hobbins, Jack, Ned Wisbey, 'Old Dusty', my dear friend Val Plumwood and the many others, human and four-legged, who taught me how to see this land; to Angela Marshall, Noel Pratt, Fabia Pryor, without whose broad knowledge, research expertise and ever-generous friendship this and most of my historical fiction could never have been written; to Lisa Berryman (if an author was given a single wish, Lisa is the editor they would wish for), who made possible the writing of the many historical novels and the research that led me to this book; to Anne Edwards, who turned scrawled footnotes and queries like 'date published? Who?' into footnotes and bibliography; to my husband, Bryan Sullivan, who tolerates long declamations about forgotten niches of our history and even, sometimes, listens; to my son, and to my grandchildren and great nieces and nephews to come, the inheritors of our families' past and the builders of its future; to the many I can no longer ask if they would allow their names to be mentioned: this book is as much yours as mine, with love and gratitude.

This book would not have been written without the enthusiasm and guidance of Catherine Milne of HarperCollins and editor Simone Ford, nor hauled to publication date without the wonderful Katie Stackhouse of HarperCollins, who laboured beyond the call of duty.

To say 'thank you' is inadequate. But, still: thank you.

Index